A-HA

DOWN TO THE TRACKS

By Barry Page

A catalogue record for this book is available from the British Library.

This edition © This Day In Music Books 2020. Text ©This Day In Music Books 2020

ISBN: 978-1-9162582-4-2

Cover artwork and layout by Tom Korsvold www.coverart.no Interior page layout and design by Gary Bishop
Printed in the UK by Sound Performance

This Day In Music Books Bishopswood Road, Prestatyn, LL19 9PL

www.thisdayinmusic.com

Email: editor@thisdayinmusic.com

Exclusive Distributors: Music Sales Limited 14/15 Berners St London W1T 3JL

For Sara and Julianne

CONTENTS

INTRODUCTION

My introduction to a-ha came in the autumn of 1985 when 'Take On Me' was beginning its rapid ascent into the UK Top 10. Like many other teenagers from the 80s I was mesmerised by the song's eye-catching video, but I also remember being really impressed when the Norwegian trio followed it up with 'The Sun Always Shines on TV', a powerful song that in many ways eclipsed their extraordinary debut single. It marked the beginning of a lifelong affection for the band's music, a deal that was sealed when I discovered I shared a birthday with the band's singer, Morten.

In the years since I was enchanted by *Hunting High and Low* and its attendant singles, I have written several articles about a-ha and their members' various side projects. In 2018 I was commissioned to write the liner notes for a special edition of *Våkenatt*, the aborted follow-up album to *Fakkeltog* by Bridges, a band that included both Pål and Magne in its line-up. A dream assignment in many respects, and one that has led to the writing of this book.

During my research, I was particularly drawn to a comment from Morten in an interview with *Aftenposten* in October 2009, which read: 'We're creating music that has many layers and aspects to it, music that's challenging to perform and compose, challenging to analyse. A-ha's music has always had a complexity to it, as well as an ability to reach a larger audience.'

There is much truth in what Morten said, but therein lies much of the band's appeal. Given their progressive rock origins, it's perhaps unsurprising that the music is often of a complex nature, while the band's lyrics – which draw from a multitude of literary and cultural sources – are often tricky to decipher.

In this book I have looked at the majority of a-ha's back catalogue in track by track detail, pulling together the stories behind their albums using archived resources and recent reminiscences from within and outside of the band. For added perspective, I have also included some period reviews. Additionally, I have taken a detailed look at both the band's pre-fame years and the three members' side projects, work which I have treated with as much reverence and importance as a-ha's.

Barry Page
February 2020

PART ONE

THE EARLY YEARS

One must fight to get to the top, especially if one starts at the bottom.

– Franz Kafka, *The Castle*, 1926

CHAPTER ONE

BRIDGES

Pull down walls and chains
And closed doors
In your mind
Free your body
And regain the lost
Cos now the bridges
Are free to be crossed

– The Bridges, 'Prisoners of Hope', 1979

Prior to a-ha's official formation in September 1982, Pål Waaktaar-Savoy and Magne Furuholmen had both been members of an Oslo-based band named Bridges who'd performed several shows in Norway's capital and released an ambitious self-financed album titled *Fakkeltog* [Torchlight Procession] in 1980.

Far from being the prototype a-ha recordings that many a-ha fans expected, the tracks owed more to the psychedelia of the Doors than the synth-pop sounds that would characterise much of the Norwegian trio's earliest songs. Furthermore, the roots of many of their hit singles stemmed from Bridges sessions and recordings, including 'Take On Me', 'I've Been Losing You' and 'You Are the One'.

VINYL DAYS

The story of Bridges begins in Norway and the relatively new borough of Manglerud, which lies in the Østensjø district of Oslo. Manglerud and other satellite towns such as Lambertseter and Ammerud – which was notable for its distinctive high-rise architecture – had arisen following an urgent need for housing development following Nazi Germany's occupation of the country during World War II. (Until Norway's North Sea oil prospecting in the 1960s, reconstruction had given the country one of its hugest spurts in economic growth.) However, these building developments didn't arrive without some teething problems: For instance, Oslo's T-Bane subway system wasn't completed until 1966, so there were some obvious commuter issues for some residents.

In terms of the local music scene, both Marius Müller and Trond Granlund had grown up in Manglerud and went on to enjoy some commercial success. (Granlund was also notable for being one of the few Norwegian artists who sang in English.) But, by the end of the 1970s, the area was more notable for its successful hockey team, Manglerud Star, than its local music scene.

Havreveien [Oats Road] was then one of Manglerud's newest suburban developments, dating back to circa 1960. Two of its residents included Pål Waaktaar Gamst (born 6 September 1961) and Magne Furuholmen (born 1 November 1962), who became acquainted in the mid-70s, largely due to a shared love of music.

Prior to the eventual formation of Bridges, both Magne and Pål had played in different school bands. 'The first-ever band I tried to form was a motley mix of not-so-highly motivated instrumentalists from the school band,' said Magne, 'so it had the exciting line-up of flute, trumpet, a snare drum, a guitar and tuba . . . I played flute and guitar, but not at the same time, sadly! We rehearsed once or twice and I then quickly realised this was not going to be my future.'

Magne also remembered an early performance of Pål's: 'Walking home from school, I saw a group of five or six random people looking up at a second floor balcony and heard some rather quiet noises coming out of an open door. It was only when two scraggy young boys came out and raised their hands in the air to the imaginary audience that I realised there was a kind of musical performance going on. The music was an eclectic mix of whatever the organ player knew how to play I think, and the line-up was simply organ and drums. I decided I had to meet these guys.'

As it turned out, both Magne and Pål had similar tastes in music. 'In early youth it's all about not sticking out from the rest of your schoolmates,' recalled Magne. 'That's why I listened to Deep Purple, Nazareth and those bands that were big in the early 70s. But it so happened that Pål had an older sister who was a lot hipper and cooler than us, and thanks to her we were introduced to 60s rock. Even though we were in the mid-70s by then, we started listening to the great heroes from the 60s. I remember well that we listened to Janis Joplin a lot, and the summer when we were 13–14 years old we got a big kick on Hendrix.'[1]

Pål's elder sibling, Tonje, was certainly an influence, and the pair listened to each other's musical discoveries on a shared turntable at their family home. 'At 13 to 15, I listened to Deep Purple, Uriah Heep, Shocking Blue, Steppenwolf and *Hair* [the musical],' she said. 'Discovering Janis Joplin blew me away! Both Pål and I dived into the 60s: the Beatles, Jimi Hendrix, Cream, Joni Mitchell, Jefferson Airplane and the *Woodstock* album.'

According to Magne, it was he who introduced the pair to the Doors. 'I accidentally stumbled across the Doors and the album *Waiting for the Sun*,' he said. 'I was totally blown away and went over to Pål's to show it to him. Neither he nor Tonje were aware of them at the time, and Pål resisted the band for a little while – as we generally would for any ideas not our own – but eventually they became the most influential band on us growing up.'

According to Pål, some of the music he brought home didn't exactly meet with his parents' approval: 'Whether it was Hendrix and the Doors in the 60s, Bowie and punk in the 70s or Joy Division in the 80s, much of the music – the melodies, the lyrics and the artists' lifestyles – were far from the norm in society; in the eyes of the parents' generation at least,' he said. 'But the self-destructiveness and the rebellious nature of these artists attracted me. Much of the music I brought home really tested my parents' values.'[2]

MAKESHIFT

Pål and Magne had both grown up with music coursing through their veins, and their parents were particularly influential during their formative years. Pål's father, Olav, was a classical music enthusiast who regularly took the family to concerts. 'We had these tickets where we went to a concert or ballet or opera every week,' said Pål. 'I guess I was bored sometimes, but things like *Carmen* or *Romeo and Juliet* by Prokofiev or *Peer Gynt* by Grieg really stuck in my mind. They're dramatic works. I think that's why I like bands like the Doors, where the music always seems to come in pretty soft and then ends up with a scream.'[3]

There were some early attempts at songwriting, too, as Pål recalled: 'I still remember the first song I wrote. It was a piece of nothing written on a recorder when I was 10 or 11, and I loved the feeling it left me with . . . carrying it around in my head, adding the words, working it over, imagining what it could sound like.'[4]

According to Magne, it was the rock band Deep Purple and their drummer, Ian Paice, that influenced Pål's initial choice of instrument. Much to his neighbours' annoyance he practised at home, using a makeshift cardboard set. However, his instrument of choice soon became the guitar as his interest in songwriting gained pace. He was a quick learner, too, copying licks from old blues records played at half-speed, as well as practising folk songs such as 'Tom Dooley' at an after-school club.

Magne's father, Kåre Furuholmen, was a well-travelled musician, playing trumpet for the Bent Sølves Orkester, a six-piece jazz band which had been named after his son's favourite teddy bear. He also released a single in 1968: a cover of James Last's 'Laguna'. Tragically, in the year that the popular band also released a single – 'Casatschok', backed with 'Toi Toi Toi' – on the Nor-Disc label, Kåre and the rest of his entourage died in an airplane crash on the way to a show in Linköping, Sweden, on 1 May 1969.

Magne played the flute as a child and took some piano lessons but wasn't interested in the application and discipline required to master the instrument. He was, however, drawn to songwriting from an early age. 'Picking up an instrument at four or five years old, I think the only pleasure for me then was discovering and making up combinations of notes that would form some kind of unique atmosphere,' he said. 'So, in a sense, writing music was always the attraction and, in truth, the only reason to play an instrument. Then, after my father passed away, I remember the piano being a place to come to lose oneself in a landscape of sound. To begin with, the extent of my writing was simple hooks and little short melodies which I could remember and return to the next time I sat down to play. These discoveries were often

followed by impromptu performances to very patient family members. Sharing my discoveries and the feeling that this produced was the first realisation that writing and performing music was a form of communication.'

BUILDING BRIDGES

Later in Magne's childhood, the present of an electric guitar from his grandfather would awaken a passion for learning, and he impressed Pål with a run-through of Nazareth's 'Sunshine'. With their shared love of music, it was almost inevitable that the pair would form a band, and there were some interesting early conversations about their musical direction. 'Musically, we went through a bunch of phases,' recalled Pål. 'For a while, it was rock opera. We were going to compose some grandiose stuff about earthquakes in Guatemala – our ambitions had no limits!'[5] (A catastrophic earthquake in Guatemala on 4 February 1976 resulted in the loss of over 23,000 lives.)

One of the pair's earliest bands was Spider Empire. 'This was a name Pål toyed with later in our conversations, as I recall,' said Magne. 'He loved that name and had a drawing design for his bass drum mapped out. Thinking up band names was a big hobby in the early days, and our imaginary bands could change names daily.'

On Norway's Constitution Day (17 May) in 1977, the pair reportedly performed a version of Deep Purple's rock classic, 'Smoke on the Water'. 'That was on the lawn outside Magne's home,' said Tonje. 'It sounded unpolished, but I was excited and proud.'

Magne and Pål's first serious band was the short-lived Thala and the Layas Blues Band. Joining them was Viggo Bondi, a former tuba player. 'I started playing bass in 1975,' he said. 'It was a guy in my neighbourhood in Asker who knew Magne and Pål from Oslo who told me that he knew two very good guitar players who were looking for a bass player. This must have been in the spring or early autumn of 1978.'

Completing the line-up was drummer Jan Erik Ødegård, and the new band performed a short set at Askerfestivalen [Asker Festival] on 9 November 1978. (There was a brief mention of the set in the local paper, *Asker og Bærums Budstikke*, although the band's name was misspelt as Tala and Delaya's Blues Band.) I asked Magne what he remembered about the performance. 'Thankfully not so much,' he said. 'A recurring problem at this time was instruments going out of tune and singing being really difficult, what with bad acoustics, unbalanced sound systems and hyper-cranked amplifiers as well as bandmates – or myself – out of control in the situation. Drums and guitars were always too loud, and vocals felt like losing a screaming match with other noises. I do think, however, that this was the occasion where, after our set, an American friend of a friend of ours – Bill Leadham – sat down on the drums and played a drum solo, and we were just floored! Floored by how good he was in comparison to our drummer. It was like a bolt of lightning and quite depressing to return to our rehearsal space together after that, knowing there were people out there – our age – who were so much further along than us, technically. I think this experience actually prompted changes in the line-up later.'

One such line-up change occurred in the new year (1979), with Viggo's friend Erik Hagelien replacing Ødegård on the drum stool. The pair had previously played in a band called Essens [Essence], along with guitarist Audun Jøsang and keyboardist Jostein Nygard, and they played covers of songs by the likes of Deep Purple and Pink Floyd, as well as an original song by Viggo titled 'Bond-up'.

'I had played with another Asker band for a short period where we tried out playing with two drummers,' Erik explained. 'Viggo contacted me to ask if I would join his new band with two young enthusiasts – Magne and Pål – which I accepted. The band name Bridges was created and adopted by the four of us. Later, we introduced another old friend, Jostein Nygard, on keyboards. He brought his organ, Fender electric piano and his old Minimoog, which required quite some time to warm up and stabilise the oscillators.' (Nygard later contributed to the *Three Fates* project in 2012, featuring symphonic versions of various Keith Emerson works.)

As for the band name, 'It was a direct reference to the Doors and to Jim Morrison's inspiration taken from Aldous Huxley's *The Doors of Perception*,' confirmed Magne. 'The sales pitch was, "The doors have been opened, now we need to build bridges". Gotta love the attitude!'

Because of musical differences, Nygard left after a few rehearsals and the band eventually reverted to a four-piece with Pål in a dual guitar and vocal role, while Magne was persuaded by Pål to switch to keyboards. 'I had played on my grandfather's piano my entire life so, even at the outset, I had some rudimentary knowledge of the instrument and how to play chords, etc,' he said. 'With the music of the Doors becoming the major influence in my life, I had a role model and inspiration in Ray Manzarek. Originally, I did not switch happily from guitar to keys, but it did add a richer palette to work from, which then developed the sound of the band into something new, so it all worked out. I took all of four piano lessons. This was a little later – in order to try to learn a better technique – but it was completely soul-destroying to go back to reading sheet music, which I had used to do back in the day when I took classical lessons on the flute. I decided I would learn by doing and find my personal style on my own and with the band.'

While Magne was heavily influenced by Ray Manzarek's technique of playing bass melodies and riffs, Pål coincidentally possessed a baritone voice akin to that of the Doors' singer, Jim Morrison. He was also attracted to Morrison's abstract wordplay and Robby Krieger's inventive guitar work, which would both prove to be highly influential.

'I always said that the songs composed by Magne and Pål at that time were heavily influenced by the Doors,' said Erik. 'I believe Jimi Hendrix was important for them, too, and probably also the Beatles – they gave me the book *The Beatles: In Their Own Words*

Essens' Viggo Bondi and Erik Hagelien, circa 1976.

13

for my 17th birthday. I was, and Viggo too, more of a prog rock lover, listening to artists like Rick Wakeman, Emerson, Lake & Palmer, Yes, Genesis and Frank Zappa. We also loved what we called jazz-rock, like Mahavishnu Orchestra. I was a fan of the drummer Phil Collins (both in Genesis and Brand X), Carl Palmer, Billy Cobham and Terry Bozzio.'

It was this combination of eclectic influences that would form the basis of the Bridges sound, which would prove to be more in keeping with the progressive rock genre than the punk and new wave sounds that were coming out of the UK and the USA in the mid- to late 1970s. Prog rock was certainly popular in Norway throughout the decade, with a movement spearheaded by acts such as Aunt Mary, Popol Ace, Saft and Junipher Greene, who released the country's first-ever double album, *Friendship*, in 1971. Cult favourite Frank Zappa, meanwhile, had made something of an impression during Norway's Kalvøyafestivalen [Kalvøya Festival] in 1973, and even enjoyed a chart-topper with the lewd 'Bobby Brown' in 1979. (Indicative of his popularity, Zappa was also namechecked in Lars Kilevold's classic Norwegian No. 1, 'Livet er for kjipt' [Life Is Too Bad], in 1980.)

KNUSLA BRUK

Much to his parents' disappointment, the increasingly music-obsessed Pål harboured little in the way of academic ambition (he was even nicknamed 'the Guest' by his teachers because of his poor attendance record!). However, he certainly found an ally in Tonje, who would spur him on both during this period and throughout his musical career. Elsewhere, Magne's mother, Annelise, was also a constant source of encouragement.

By the time of Bridges' formation, Annelise had remarried. The family moved to Vollen in the Asker municipality, and the basement of this larger home – known as Knusla Bruk, due to its farming origins – provided the rehearsal space during their high school years.

'Viggo played a not-very-sophisticated Shaftesbury bass guitar,' remembered Erik, 'and I played a British-made Premier drum kit with Paiste 2002 cymbals.' In a conscious bid to mimic the Doors' Ray Manzarek, Magne played a Gem Jumbo organ, which was more than capable of emulating the classically trained keyboardist's signature sounds (as is evident from four-track recordings such as 'Bhaki Moti').

While Magne's home was within a commutable distance from Pål's school in Nordstrand, the journey was awkward as it included time spent both on Oslo's subway system and the bus. The round trip would often stretch to four hours, but time on the bus gave Pål the opportunity to fine-tune his lyrics, since original material was the band's primary focus. He also insisted on writing his lyrics in

English rather than his native Norwegian, an early indication that the band were already thinking outside of the box in terms of their musical aspirations. Reading some of the lyrics from the period, it's immediately obvious that English wasn't Pål's first language, but there's a naive charm to some of those early songs, and his language skills would considerably improve within the next few years. 'I was attracted to a more unusual choice of words,' said Pål, 'and would always gravitate towards that if it came my way. Reading mostly literature from 50 to 100 years ago was another influence I'm sure. It certainly didn't always sound like something you'd write on the tube but it fit the songs. But sure, there are a few clunkers but not the ones people tend to bring up.'

It's also interesting to note the lyrical diversity of Pål's writing, evidenced by an amalgam of politics ('Come on and cry for what we have lost / Soldiers born between the battles / Some day the borders are free to be crossed'), unrequited love ('May the last dance be mine / Let it be mine / Cos the love I can't find / Won't escape my mind') and atheism ('Love her till the day you die / Sorry, there's no God / But don't be frightened').

BASEMENT TAPES

'Pål came all the way to Vollen every Friday after school,' recalled Erik. 'He stayed there for the whole weekend. Viggo and I showed up on Saturdays and Sundays. There was a 25-minute walk from Hvalstad – where Viggo and I lived in Asker – to the bus stop and another 25 minutes from the bus stop in Vollen to Magne's house. We practised mostly every weekend and Magne's mother always served us good food – we felt very welcome. It was a big house with a large room in the basement where we played, and my drums stood permanently. Over time I damaged the very nice and brand new wooden pine floor with my drum hardware spikes – I felt very embarrassed!'

I asked Magne to describe a typical session. 'In general, Pål would be the first to arrive,' he replied. 'He and I would start to show each other anything we had written since the last rehearsal, and we would be (or pretend to be) a little grumpy waiting for the other guys who, to our chagrin, did not seem to take it all as seriously as the two of us did. They had a more developed social life than we had in the beginning – meaning they had some kind of social network, whereas we had none – and so they would also often have places to go afterwards. Pål and I would spend most of the evenings playing and writing stuff far into the night, waiting for the next day's rehearsal. This dynamic changed after I moved to a different high school and developed new friendships there.

'Irrespective of whatever other band members we were playing with at the time, Pål and I were in a kind of symbiotic orbit around each other, writing, playing, responding and pushing each other. There was definitely a competitive element involved, but most of all there was a recognition of a really good fit in terms of talents and taste. I rarely challenged Pål's position as the main lyric writer and, as a consequence, he was pretty much in the driver's seat in our relationship – also much later – whenever it came to finishing my songs.'

During the first six months of the band's life, they amassed over an album's worth of songs, and many of these were recorded onto a multitrack machine supplied by Svein Erichsen. Not only was he a neighbour of Magne's, he was also a fan of the Doors and had reportedly seen them perform at one of their final shows at the Isle of Wight festival in 1970. (Viggo said he was impressed by the fact that Erichsen had also witnessed one of Emerson, Lake & Palmer's first shows.) He was also an experienced musician and is credited with backing vocals on *Enda mere rock* [Even More Rock], the third in a series of albums featuring rock and roll covers by a band made up of Elvis Presley impersonators! (Among their members was Trond Granlund, who would later release his career-spanning retrospective, *Fra Manglerud til Manchester*, in 1998.)

'Svein was our nearest and, frankly, our *only* neighbour in the very rural part of Asker where we had moved,' explained Magne. 'My grandfather had known him from long before my family moved out there so, in a sense, I had always known of him. He was a very gentle soul and a nice man. (He was a bit like a hippy stuck in a decade gone by.) He was a musician, a bass player, and he sang backing vocals. But, most important of all, he had a TEAC tape recorder!

'Once he realised I had a band rehearsing in the basement next door, he would start inviting us over to his own basement, at first just to come over and listen to his eclectic record collection on his quadrophonic sound system which he was super-proud of. I remember he would always sing the parts which he enjoyed the most out loud – in particular, nice details in a bassline or in the backing vocal parts. These listening sessions were quite formative, in the sense that we listened to music we had otherwise deemed too square or outside of our interest, and by pointing out parts and arrangements, Svein was instrumental in shaping our way of thinking about arrangements. It also didn't take long before we realised we could record ourselves on his equipment, and thoughts of making an album started forming.'

Under the guidance of Erichsen, the band soon began recording their songs. These early 'basement tapes' have been well preserved, and the audio is of a surprisingly high quality. The performances, while a bit rough around the edges, are also highly accomplished for such a young band. 'Born Between the Battles' was an early six-minute-plus epic, with an obvious Doors influence (evident from Magne's organ parts), while Pål's bluesy guitar parts recalled Peter Green-era Fleetwood Mac. Elsewhere, 'Breath of Wind' displayed a more melancholy aspect to their repertoire, with its mournful piano playing, while the more pop-oriented 'Truths of Love' was evocative of the psychedelic swirl of garage rock acts such as the Strawberry Alarm Clock and ? and the Mysterians.

According to song sheets from the period, most of the tracks were simply credited to 'Paul Gamst and the Bridges'.

IN CONCERT

While songwriting and rehearsing were the band's main priorities during the infancy of their career, they were still keen to make a mark in their native country, and this included live performance. The band performed publicly for the first time on 7 February 1979 in Venskaben, Asker, during a mixed cultural event in aid of the liberation movements in Eritrea, Africa. According to Erik, the event included music, poem readings and 'auctions and sales of strange things'. However, it was the *NM i rock* event at Chateau Neuf in Oslo that provided a genuine opportunity for the band to get themselves noticed. A 'Battle of the Bands'-type competition, it gave new acts – over 40 of them – vital exposure and the opportunity to compete for a place in

the televised final in July. Bridges performed during the preliminary heat on 11 March 1979 but didn't progress to the following day's round. (Broadway News were eventually crowned as the overall winners.)

Following *NM i rock*, Bridges played a private show for family and friends at Erik's home in Hvalstad on 17 March, and also went to the trouble of preparing a small programme for the event. This fascinating document reveals that Pål was still using his original surname of Gamst at this point, while the set list included songs such as 'Born Between the Battles', 'Imagination', 'Face in Mirror' and the mysteriously titled 'Bhaki Moti'. 'We had a pretty intense psychedelic period at 15, 16,' said Pål. 'I think this means "pearl of love" or similar.' (Indeed, the song's opening lines are 'You are the pearl of love / Spread a little love to us all'.)

The following month, the band were interviewed by *Asker og Bærums Budstikke*. Published on 18 April 1979, the short piece confirmed that the band were focusing on songwriting and rehearsing. They also insisted that their future lay outside of their native turf. 'We will not try to make it big here in Norway,' they said. Magne added: 'I said that. I was also the first of us to say I was going to be an artist/ musician when I grew up. It blew Pål's mind!'

The band reconvened for another multi-act show at Chateau Neuf on 27 May, as organised by the amateur band association, IAB. According to the concert poster, other acts on the bill included Hexagon (whose guitarist was well known to Pål), Gummgakk AS and Ski Patrol, plus Villblomst [Wildflower] and Jydske Rev, who later released albums in 1979 and 1981, respectively. According to Magne's mother, Annelise, Bridges performed 'Bhaki Moti', 'Imagination', 'The Endless Brigade' and 'Truths of Love' on the day, but endured something of a shaky start as their guitars needed to be retuned. 'When we started to play, some of the audience left, and others rose up and were about to leave, but then stayed when they understood that this was something special and very different,' said Viggo.

ULTIMATUM

The IAB show proved to be Erik's final live engagement for Bridges. 'Magne and Pål showed up at the family house to have a discussion,' explained Erik. 'They had decided to dedicate themselves 100 per cent to the music to become international professionals. They also had a clear view to grow abroad and not in Norway. The ultimatum they gave me was to commit to their strategy, with the consequence that I had to quit school. At that time this was not an option for me.'

It wasn't quite the end of Erik's association with Bridges, though (as will be explained in the next chapter). He currently works for a battery manufacturer but still sees Viggo occasionally. 'Just for fun, our first band, Essens, were reunited five years ago,' he said in 2017. 'I meet Viggo and the others a couple of times a year, ending up with the same yearly performance at a local reunion party.' (With Jostein Nygard having moved to the US, the current Essens line-up now includes guitarist Tor Tørrissen.)

Erik's place was eventually taken by Øystein Jevanord. 'I was looking for an interesting band to play with,' he said. 'I had played drums since I was 12, had some special skills, and was open-minded to all kinds of music. I saw Bridges live at Chateau Neuf during the IAB concert, with Hagelien on drums, so I knew what they were about . . . and they stood out that night. A good friend of mine ripped out a small ad [dated 4 September] in *Aftenposten* (Norway's biggest newspaper), and I got it a week too late. It sounded interesting, so I called them up. They had already tested two drummers – which didn't work too well – so they invited me to Magne's house the following weekend (15 September 1979). I remember the date because my 20th birthday was the day after. We played all night, slept over, and after breakfast we continued playing. It was magic – interesting music, very nice people. Everything matched. I was very happy and excited, and the others agreed . . . this was it!'

Magne added: 'With Øystein entering the picture, Pål and he would travel to and from rehearsals together, and our sessions became more structured and set, timewise. Pål would stop sleeping over and return to Oslo, and I would go hang out with my new friends, which he hated.'

In terms of Øystein's musical influences, he shared many of his new bandmates' tastes. 'I listened to all kinds of music,' he confirmed, 'but mostly to music with great drummers, such as Frank Zappa, Genesis, Brand X, Yes and Santana. But I must admit that Phil Collins was my biggest influence at the time.'

Following a performance at Asker Gymnasium on 16 December 1979, the increasingly confident band played a show at Oslo's Dovrehallen club on 5

The classic Bridges line-up. Left to right: Pål Waaktaar, Øystein Jevanord, Viggo Bondi and Magne Furuholmen.

February 1980, sharing the bill with future cult favourites Kjøtt [Meat], a local punk rock band who had just released their debut EP, *Et nytt og bedre liv!* [A New and Better Life]. Despite the fact that one of Øystein's drum skins split on the night, the show was largely a success. 'I remember a lot about that evening,' recalled Pål. 'It was perhaps the one concert where we played to our limits. We didn't make any simple choices. There were long songs and very complicated arrangements. It was almost like a theatre performance, from relative silence to full pelt – big fluctuations. Of course, when Kjøtt were playing, it was full pelt the whole time. And although, initially, the audience started waltz-dancing ironically to our songs – as if to make a statement – we felt we got through to people. They weren't impatient. They listened to us.'[6]

Bridges were beginning to make a name for themselves, and the next logical step for the band was to cut a record of their own.

NORSKTOPPEN

In terms of Norway's cultural impact, the likes of Edvard Munch and Henrik Ibsen had certainly put the country on the map. In the classical music world, Edvard Grieg, too, was internationally renowned. (Indeed, his most famous piece, 'In the Hall of the Mountain King', was later covered by numerous mainstream acts, including Erasure, Rick Wakeman and the Who.) But, unlike neighbouring Sweden, who had produced the global phenomenon ABBA, Norway wasn't able to boast a successful pop music export until a-ha's breakthrough in 1985.

To the outside world, Norwegian music was seen by some as a bit of a joke, and this was compounded in April 1978 when Jahn Teigen – the former singer of progressive rock band Popol Ace – became the first act to score 'nul points' with 'Mil etter mil' [Mile After Mile] at the Eurovision Song Contest in Paris. This was repeated in 1981 when Finn Kalvik's 'Aldri i livet' [Never in My Life] finished last, a feat that now sounds absurd, given that the studio recording was not only produced by ABBA's Benny Andersson but also featured the Swedish band's Agnetha Fältskog and Anni-Frid Lyngstad on backing vocals.

While music by Norwegian artists was highly popular, the country's charts during this period in the late 70s and early 80s predominantly featured mainstream acts from the UK and USA. In the singles chart, Irish Eurovision favourite Johnny Logan enjoyed an eight-week residency at the summit with 'What's Another Year', while Chris de Burgh's *Eastern Wind* and Bruce Springsteen's double set, *The River*, were two particularly big sellers in the album market.

The charts also acted as a haven for the more idiosyncratic chart-topper, such as the previously mentioned 'Bobby Brown' (Frank Zappa) and future *Auf Wiedersehen, Pet* star Gary Holton's take on the country classic 'Ruby, Don't Take Your Love to Town'.

For music-obsessed teenagers like Magne and Pål, sourcing exciting new music wasn't easy. Until Norway's state-owned broadcaster NRK's monopoly formally ended in 1981, there was just one TV channel and one national radio station (and certainly no local radio stations).

From 1973 onwards, NRK radio aired the *Norsktoppen* show, a hit list of sorts which showcased Norwegian music. Until a rule change in May 1986, only songs with Norwegian lyrics were permitted to be included in the rundown.

NRK's *Pop Spesial* radio show (presented by Ivar Dyrhaug and Sigbjørn Nedland) did, however, provide something of an alternative, and the Sex Pistols actually gained their first radio plays in Norway via this outlet. The presenters' ethos to showcase a more 'underground' side of music later transcended to TV on the Dyrhaug-presented *Zikk-Zakk* show, which featured a mixture of Norwegian acts (including punk rockers Kjøtt) and contemporary favourites from abroad.

STEPPING STONE

Although Magne and Pål had ambitions that stretched beyond their homeland, they were still keen to make strides within the Norwegian music industry, using it as a stepping stone to greater things. One particularly well-known figure within the industry was Ole Sørli, a former manager at Polydor Records. When Viggo received a call from Sørli a few days after the double-header with Kjøtt, it was perhaps reasonable for the band to enter his office with some degree of expectation.

A former member of 60s band the Cool Cats, Sørli had produced Geir Børresen's big-selling novelty single, 'Smurfesangen' (a Norwegian version of Father Abraham's huge international hit, 'The Smurf Song'), plus a string of albums based on the Belgian phenomenon. He was also making headway as a songwriter, co-writing tracks for a female pop duo named Dollie (later, Dollie de Luxe). And it was around these young protégés of his that he based his proposition – he wanted Bridges to become their backing band! Clutching a copy of the duo's debut album, *Første akt* [First Act], Bridges left the office infuriated. While Dollie's album would later earn the duo a Spellemann award (the Norwegian equivalent of a Grammy), the members of Bridges used the record as a frisbee. 'And I was the cocky kid who started throwing them!' added Magne.

Undeterred by the Dollie incident, Bridges participated in the latest *NM i rock* competition at Chateau Neuf on 13 March 1980. Although they were unsuccessful once more, they did receive a favourable, albeit brief mention in *Klassekampen* [The Class Struggle], a daily newspaper based in Oslo. And, on 27 May 1980, Bridges performed at Chateau Neuf again, co-headlining with Schlappe Waffla. (Their bassist, Jan Swensson, later played with Øystein in rock bands such as Dei Nye Kapellanane and Oslo Plektrum.)

Over the ensuing months, the band made plans to record their debut album.

FAKKELTOG (1980 Album)
Produced by Svein Erichsen

In the summer of 1980, Bridges booked recording time at Octocon Studio, which was essentially a basement in an old factory in Nydalen that had been converted into a recording facility by engineer and musician Tore Aarnes. 'It was a terrible indoor climate, like most studios I've visited,' said Tonje. 'No daylight or fresh air, but they had dedication – Pål never tired! They were great, and so well rehearsed.'

'I think it was Pål that found Octocon,' recalled Øystein. 'Not too expensive for four young lads. And the recording conditions were okay . . . We didn't have much to compare it to since this was our first time in a real studio. I just remember it was exciting and joyful to work there.'

It would take the well-rehearsed band just a week to record the album – at a cost of 500 kroner per day – and the sessions were long and productive. 'We prepared all the arrangements at the rehearsals, so we needed just four days to record the main album,' continued Øystein. 'The rest of the week we did the overdubs, vocals and mix. *Fakkeltog* was finished in one week, in other words. But of

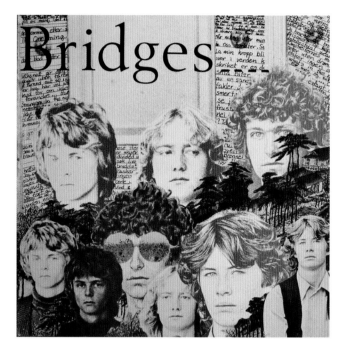

course, some changes were also done here and there in the studio.' (During the overdubbing stage, the band brought in some additional musicians to augment some of the songs, including strings on the beautiful 'Vagrants'.)

'The album was recorded on Svein's TEAC, through a 12-channel Peavey mixer if I remember correctly,' added Magne. 'It was a case of rigging the rehearsal space as a recording space. The writing had started so many years ago – many ideas we had tried in different ways came together in this new setting and everyone added their bits. Both Viggo and Øystein were opinionated, but I think it was clear that Pål and mine's symbiotic relationship had the authority in how it should sound. Recording the album it felt like we were finally ready to present our music to the world, and I remember it as a particularly dedicated and forward-leaning time for everyone involved.'

INSTRUMENTAL INSTRUMENTS

Pål's guitar of choice was a Gibson SG (a model favoured both by the Doors' Robby Krieger and the Beatles' George Harrison), while Magne's keyboard set-up included a Wasp synthesiser and a Moog Polymoog (203A) synthesiser which had been borrowed from Erik Nygaard, who was Tonje's boyfriend at the time. (Erik was later credited as a camera assistant on a-ha's *Live in South America* video.)

The Wasp synth was a quirky but affordable instrument that was launched by EDP (Electronic Dream Plant) in 1978, and is easily identifiable by its yellow and black colours and unconventional flat keys.

Back in the 70s, the almost toylike Wasp had a recommended retail price of £199 and a press advertisement claimed: 'For those who dream of owning a synthesiser, this instrument offers more facilities and better sound than others costing six times as much!' This contrasted sharply with the Polymoog, which was considerably more expensive at over £3,000, and also much bigger and heavier (two people were often required to carry this particular model!). The instrument dated back to 1975 and featured a number of presets (including harpsichord, piano and organ). Like Gem's Jumbo organ, it was capable of emulating some of the Doors' sounds. (The Doors had been one of the first rock bands to use a Moog synthesiser, notably on their second studio album, *Strange Days*.)

'I was not really a tech nerd,' said Magne. 'I just wanted to have something that sounded distinct. The Wasp was an unruly beast, but such an innovative little thing! I bought it in London when Pål and I were on our first InterRail trip through Europe together (the fact that our parents would let a 15- and a 14-year-old do this alone speaks volumes about how mature and sensible we must have seemed!). The Polymoog was a whole different kettle of fish. I was using the Wasp on my set-up for some time before this with this Italian organ – the amazing Jumbo – being my main instrument.

I had gotten quite adept at using all conceivable variations that this organ offered, most notably a super-slow imitation Leslie effect which gave it a druggy, gloriously out of tune feel. Plus, it had some outlandish percussive buttons which, on their own, without any underlying active preset, would sound otherworldly. I still have this organ today. It is one of the few sentimental attachments I have to an instrument. However, moving on to the Polymoog felt like a real decisive shift; never again would an organ be my main instrument.'

CELEBRATION OF THE LIZARD

Though unarguably derivative in places, the resulting album was a perfect representation of where the band were at that point. Underpinned by Viggo and Øystein's formidable rhythm section, *Fakkeltog* was characterised both by Magne's imaginative keyboard playing and Pål's inventive guitar work, with tracks such as 'Somebody's Going Away' veering into Robby Krieger-like blues territory.

Although the album wasn't quite in tune with the musical trends of the day, the band certainly weren't alone in their affinity for the Doors' music – acts such as the Stranglers, Echo & the Bunnymen, the Triffids and even Joy Division were influenced by the Los Angeles rockers. The Doors themselves were back in the public eye by the end of the decade: *An American Prayer*, featuring spoken word and poetry by Jim Morrison set to new music, had been released in 1978, while Pål's favourite track of theirs, 'The End', had been used to great effect in Francis Ford Coppola's 1979 movie, *Apocalypse Now*.

The spectre of the Lizard King certainly looms large, but it would be cruel to dismiss *Fakkeltog* as nothing more than a Doors tribute album. However, 'Death of the Century' and 'Vagrants', signposts of Pål's favoured ballad style with a-ha, certainly echoed the mournful and melancholic side of Morrison's baritone, while the spoken word elements of 'Every Mortal Night' recalled 'The WASP (Texas Radio and the Big Beat)'.

The Doors' own musical manifesto wasn't a million miles away from Bridges' either. 'We wanted a rock band that could play jazz and blues and classical music with poetry floating over the top,' claimed Ray Manzarek in his autobiography. 'An aesthetic little quartet.'[7]

Aside from Morrison, there were some other key literary references on *Fakkeltog*, too: Gunvor Hofmo was a reclusive writer who lived in the Nordstrand area of Oslo, publishing several poetry collections before her death in 1995. *Gjest på jorden* (1971) was one such collection, which later provided the title of Bridges' 'Guest on Earth'. Pål later revealed that the lyrics on *Fakkeltog* were heavily influenced by Hofmo, and that he related to much of her work, which typically featured ruminations on loneliness and mortality. He also claimed that Hofmo was the closest that Norway ever got to the Doors – certainly, her willingness to embrace darker topics was prevalent in Morrison's own poetry. (Pål wasn't alone in his admiration for Gunvor Hofmo either. Many years later, in 2011, a Norwegian singer-songwriter named Susanna Wallumrød would record an entire album, titled *Jeg vil hjem til menneskene* [I Want to Go Home to the Humans], using Hofmo's poetry. Jazz singer Solveig Slettahjell also included interpretations of Hofmo's work on her 2016 album, *Poetisk tale* [Poetic Speech].

Another influence arrived via a book by John Hay, titled *Masterpieces of Chinese Art*. Aside from his passion for music, Pål was also a keen artist and his father had given this book to him as a present in 1979. Two particular pieces in the book, by the Ming Dynasty-era landscape painters Wu Wei and Shen Shih-ch'ung, inspired two song titles: 'Vagrants' ('A universe, a vagrant's dream / You're a Chinese garden / You're a world unseen') and 'Pavilion of the Luxuriant Trees' ('Chinese garden world / View from a pavilion of art'), respectively. Foliage from the book was also sourced for the album's home-made cover, which boasted a striking collage of band photos and a seemingly random patchwork of Norwegian and English text.

SYMPHONIC ROCK

The album was mixed by Svein Erichsen and Octocon's owner, Tore Aarnes. Adopting the DIY ethos of bands such as the Saints and Buzzcocks, the band financed the album's manufacture themselves and released it in October 1980 on their own (unregistered) *Våkenatt* label, the name of which had been inspired by a Gunvor Hofmo poetry collection from 1954 titled *I en våkenatt* [In a Waking Night]. Having blown most of their budget on the studio hire, the band couldn't afford a colour cover but, following negotiations with the printers, they were allowed another colour in addition to black and white, resulting in the sleeve's distinctive purple tinge. With the band constantly thinking outside of the box, they also had a novel way of getting around the problem of presenting a three-part album across two sides of vinyl – by inserting a stop-groove in the middle of one side!

A somewhat optimistic 1,000 copies were pressed, with the band shifting less than half of these units. To promote any record in Norway – let alone a self-financed, independent release – wasn't easy. And, for a band that had largely shied away from live performance, there were few options, so their campaign was largely centred around fly-posting throughout the city, as well as good old-fashioned word of mouth.

'We thought we'd get huge press just from making Norway's first self-financed album,' said Pål. 'That wasn't the case!'

'All the promotion we did was to glue lots of posters all over Oslo wherever we could,' remembered Øystein, 'and we went round to the most popular record shops in Oslo and asked if they would like to buy some of them . . . some of them actually did!'

Two cuts from *Fakkeltog* did get a play on Ivar Dyrhaug's *Pop Spesial* radio show, and it was reviewed by several publications. *Puls* magazine's young writer, Hege Duckert, gave generally good feedback in the December issue of the popular monthly, but was critical of the sleeve design and the vinyl's impractical stop-groove. Writing for *Nye Takter* magazine, Morten Muller praised the 'promising' band for their ambition and the music's timeless qualities, describing it as 'symphonic rock in the punk spirit'. Elsewhere, there were the inevitable Doors comparisons in *Asker og Bærums Budstikke*, but the reviewer also praised the young band for their musicianship. But, tellingly, the same review also stated an opinion that was perhaps indicative of the nation's perception of the Norwegian music scene: 'Bridges are one of the few new Norwegian rock groups that sing in English. They should end this because the lyrics on the record are very good – maybe better than the music – and the message won't reach a broad Norwegian audience with English words.'

Perhaps the most impressive aspect of the recording was that it was cut by a band largely in their late teens and barely out of school (Magne was just 17 at the time). One of the criticisms of the album, however, was its poor sound, which Pål attributed to the length of the album, which strayed beyond vinyl's optimal 40 minutes.

These days, *Fakkeltog* is a highly desirable collector's item, with some copies changing hands for over £500. It was unofficially rereleased by Luna Nera Records as a limited edition in 2012, but the tracks are now easily accessible via vinyl rips on YouTube, giving a fresh generation of a-ha fans the opportunity to listen to this cult favourite. However, Pål hasn't ruled out the possibility of a reissue in the future. 'I did get a transfer of the multitrack last year,' he said in 2017. 'And, who knows, maybe we'll remix this one day. [However], the album was done on eight-track and the main performance is already mixed down on two tracks, so it's limited to what you can do to restore it.'

TORE AARNES

Concurrent to the recording of *Fakkeltog*, Tore Aarnes worked on an impressive progressive rock album by Octopus, released on Octocon Records in 1981. Titled *Thærie Wiighen* and inspired by the writings of Ibsen, this cult release featured Aarnes on keyboards and synths. (A second album, *Sica*, remains unreleased.)

One man that knew Octocon's owner well was songwriter, engineer and producer Robert Alan Morley, who worked in the studio in the first half of the 80s. (He'd also seen Bridges perform at *NM i rock* in 1979.) 'Tore was an old friend of mine that I knew from the early 70s, when he played in a band and I used to play in another band,' he said. 'We became good friends, and I think he was a super guy to work with. We used to hang together for a lot of years, both in Oslo and in a town called Haugesund.'

Aarnes worked on various projects at the studio throughout the decade and even released a pair of singles himself (as Y Me), but the recording facility did not remain on the industrialised site in Nydalen. 'The studio moved to a shipping container,'

Octocon Studio, 1980. Left to right: Magne Furuholmen, Øystein Jevanord, Pål Waaktaar, Tore Aarnes and Viggo Bondi.

said Robert, 'and Tore used to live in that container. I only did one session there because I didn't like it. There was no air and it was very hot in the summertime and cold in the wintertime. Tore got an electro allergy because of all the metal around him, and he sold the studio and moved to Spain.'

Aarnes currently resides in Haugesund, but Robert said he has not spoken to him for several years.

CHAPTER TWO

POEM

By the end of 1980, the band had defected from Octocon's makeshift studio and were ensconced in Sound Art Studio, working on a quick-fire follow-up to *Fakkeltog* with their avuncular producer, Svein Erichsen. With a plethora of bands such as Børres Kork springing up in the wake of the Sex Pistols' Scandinavian tour, many independent single releases had started appearing in 1979. Ischjazz and Fort & Gæli were two other such acts, and they had used Sound Art in the centre of Oslo to cut some singles.

Although it was on the verge of closing down, the facility was a significant step up from what they were used to in the industrialised setting of Nydalen. 'Octocon was a makeshift and always non-functioning studio, where the owner, Tore Aarnes, was an absolute enthusiast, bless him,' said Magne, 'and so he would give us great value for money in terms of time allowed in the studio to record and experiment. But the studio was a makeshift place with all kinds of quirks. Tore would be the sound engineer and often he would argue for or against musical ideas, which we would not always welcome. He had a seemingly very ambitious project involving literature and music of his own going on, and there was definitely a competitive spirit on our part towards him. You meet people along the way and they all play a part in forming who you become, but the decision to move to Sound Art Studio was, in a sense, a move towards professionalism.'

Prior to recording the album, the band practised their new repertoire of songs in the basement of a town hall in the centre of Oslo, away from the home comforts of Knusla Bruk. 'We had been rehearsing in my house for a long time at that point,' continued Magne. 'I think my parents were particularly relieved we moved, and also my family's food budget dropped by about two thirds! Plus, Pål and Øystein had been making the long journey across town and out to our little farmhouse. It was time to move on. The fact that we were now eyeing the possibility of recording in a proper studio was also a factor.'

Pål also persuaded his colleagues to adopt Poem as a new name for the band. 'I liked it,' said Magne. 'Being so closely linked with the Doors was starting to feel a bit tired and restraining.'

And with the change of name there also came a change in musical direction. For their sophomore release, the band would continue to build upon their progressive rock foundations, with the near 10-minute opening track, 'Fakkeltog', weaving in elements from their previous album. But, at the same time, there was a conscious desire to cut a more commercially minded record. The band also had some new instruments to experiment with. 'I think I had already bought my huge Korg

PS-3100 for this album,' said Magne. 'Another unruly beast with a very distinctive sound, and with lots of cables having to be plugged in, trying my patience.'

Additionally, whereas the lyrics on *Fakkeltog* had employed something of a labyrinthine approach, the lyrics on its follow-up were far more focused, and the song structures less sinuous and slightly more conventional. Both 'Waterworks' (prefaced by an ephemeral slice of whimsy in 'What Do You Do') and 'Asleep' (aka 'The Fair Unknown') found the band in familiar Doors territory, with the former of the two cuts featuring a refrain redolent of 'Yes, the River Knows' ('On and on and on it goes / Where it's heading, no one knows'). Elsewhere, the more angular 'Superior' represented something of a departure for the band with its ska-like rhythms, while the accessible, psychedelic pop of 'Faceless City' predated the Coral by 20 years. In addition, there was the beautifully melancholic, Beatles-esque 'Need No Doctor', with Pål's recurring theme of insomnia set to Magne's chord progression.

'I think these songs actually stand as key moments in our musical oeuvre,' said Magne. 'Not only as Bridges, but as a testament and solidification of the songwriting collaboration between Pål and me. There was less and less input from the others, and so the method for writing together between Pål and me – which would continue well into a-ha – had been established here, for good and bad. I would add hooks and motifs and parts to Pål's songs, and he would write lyrics and, in many cases, topline melodies and parts to songs that I brought in. The amalgamation of our talents had started to show real promise, previewing songs like "Scoundrel Days". One of the songs that I had written, "Soft Rains of April", was – and still feels like – some of the best of what our collaboration was all about: creating moments together which would not have been possible separately.'

DARKNESS OF DECEMBER

While both the musicianship and the songwriting were improving, Magne revealed that cracks were beginning to show during the making of their second record. 'There was a lot more dissent and fragmentation in the band this time around,' he said. 'Even though we kept it together, I started feeling the early signs of the band breaking apart. Well, maybe not so much breaking apart as becoming fractured, and with a feeling that perhaps this was not a combination of people that would continue and ride into the sunset together.'

Additionally, there were two incidents in December that would significantly affect the band's mood. Firstly, there was John Lennon's murder in New York on 8 December (coincidentally, Jim Morrison's birthday), a tragic event that was felt around the world. 'I do remember the day John Lennon was shot very well,' recalled Viggo. 'I was together with Pål in Oslo when we saw the headlines in the newspapers. Pål's reaction was complete silence for a long period of time. We spent that afternoon in the restaurant where we used to eat meatballs for dinner. The restaurant was next to the building which hosted the Pingvin Club, where the Sex Pistols played in 1977.'

And then there was the incident that, with hindsight, signalled the beginning of the end for the foursome. The band had been preparing to finish the album, but their plans were derailed when an intruder broke into the recording studio during the Christmas period and stole some of the master tapes and Viggo's prized Gibson Les Paul bass guitar. Understandably distraught by the incident, Pål and Viggo made an appeal for the return of the stolen items via *Aftenposten* in January 1981. 'Those tapes couldn't possibly be of any value to the thieves,' stated Pål. 'But the recordings, the unfinished album, have cost us thousands that we've spent on studio time and work. Those tapes are worth so much more to us than the thieves. Can we please have them back?'

Viggo Bondi and producer Svein Erichsen at Oslo's Sound Art Studio during the making of Våkenatt.

Undeterred by their latest setback, the band regrouped and resolved to rerecord the lost tracks. 'You can imagine what we felt about losing the tapes,' recalled Viggo. 'But, looking back, I think that was actually good for the album, because we had the experience from the first recording session, and also got a chance to improve the material further.' He added: 'We were very efficient, and I think those songs were recorded during three or four evenings. For example, we only needed one take to record "Superior". The owner of the studio was very sorry about what happened, and he offered us new studio time free of charge.'

'The death of Lennon was of course a dramatic occurrence for all who were into music,' added Magne, 'and the way it happened seemed impossible to fathom. For us Beatles fans it was particularly devastating. Having our tapes stolen was also a downer – it made a hard reset necessary, a kind of "shit, let's get on with it, let's start again" kind of vibe. I think the perceived genius of the first recordings grew exponentially in our heads, though. Doing it over was arduous, but clearly things also got better.'

In February 1981, with the bulk of the new album recorded, Pål and Viggo travelled to London, with the primary aim of picking up a new instrument during their one-week stay. 'I think it was a Boss synthesiser bass,' recalled Viggo. 'Unfortunately, it had not yet arrived from the manufacturer when we came to London – bad planning not calling the shop before travelling over!' Rather than going home empty-handed, the pair decided to purchase an expensive set of Pollard Syndrums, which did not go down well with Øystein, who was opposed to the idea of using synthetic drums, claiming they were more a toy than an instrument.

The Syndrum was more synonymous with the disco era, but it was also used by new wave and electronic acts, including the Cars and Yellow Magic Orchestra. One other notable user was Joy Division's metronomic drummer, Stephen Morris, who purchased the instrument during the recording of their debut album, *Unknown Pleasures* (the Syndrum's primitive sounds can be heard on 'Insight').

Joy Division were certainly influential during this period, which is evident on tracks such as 'The Leap' (which would later evolve into a-ha's 'Scoundrel Days'). Like Poem, the band's use of electronics was steadily proliferating and their signature song, 'Love Will Tear Us Apart', seemed to signpost their future, until Ian Curtis's suicide in May 1980. Other Norwegian musicians' ears had also pricked to their unique sound: Firstly, there was the Oslo-based De Press, who would later win a Spellemann award for the John Leckie-produced *Block to Block*. Secondly, there was Fra Lippo Lippi, whose 1981 debut album, *In Silence*, was also heavily influenced by the Manchester-based band. (Fra Lippo Lippi later enjoyed some commercial success in the mid-80s with the single 'Shouldn't Have to Be Like That'.)

'We realised the importance of the shift punk had on the music scene,' said Magne, 'and we did in fact assimilate new things from this into our music, but without fully embracing this new direction.'

UNIQUE SOUND

While its arrangement remained true to Bridges' proggy roots, 'All the Planes That Come In on the Quiet' was something of an acknowledgement of the burgeoning synth-pop scene, and boasted an electronic production that would point towards Magne and Pål's future. 'We were convinced – at least some of us – that synthesisers would be the answer to finding our own unique sound,' confirmed Pål. 'The master plan was that this album would start with "Fakkeltog" (the song) to recap what we were before, and then end with songs only utilising synths. It didn't quite happen that way, but that was the plan!'

By the late 70s, prog rock and disco music were becoming increasingly unpopular. Punk music – despite its fleeting existence – had shaken up the music industry and the three-chord maxim of acts such as the Sex Pistols and the Ramones had given rise to a legion of new bands in both the UK and Norway. In addition, a new 'Blitz Kid' generation of musicians, inspired by the likes of David Bowie, Kraftwerk and Roxy Music, was about to impose itself on a decade that would later be – technologically speaking – defined by Yamaha DX7s, LinnDrums, Fairlight CMIs and Simmons drum kits.

Acts such as the Human League, Gary Numan, Orchestral Manoeuvres in the Dark (OMD) and Ultravox were spearheading a new movement of pioneering electronic acts. In addition, rock behemoths such as Queen, who had famously added 'No synthesisers!' to the credits on a string of albums, were now using synths to augment their sound (particularly on 1980's excellent *Flash Gordon* soundtrack), while other acts such as Sparks were adapting their sound, eschewing their glam rock leanings in favour of more electronic soundscapes. By 1982, the use of synthesisers was so widespread that the Musicians' Union voted to ban them.

Magne and Pål were paying close attention to the technological developments that were taking place. Magne had already invested in a new polyphonic Korg synthesiser, while Pål traded in his beloved SG Gibson guitar for a Roland GR-300 guitar synth, which had been introduced in the late 70s and officially endorsed by the Police's Andy Summers. (Like the Syndrum, it's more of a collector's piece these days.) 'The synth guitar rig Pål had bought was intended to bring about a big change in direction, sound-wise,' said Magne, 'and I think "All the Planes That Come In on the Quiet" is by far the most successful example of this. Having two synths brought a new sonic landscape, and a new way of thinking about parts and intertwining motifs.'

BRIDGES TOO FAR

There was a happy postscript to the break-in drama when *Aftenposten* later reported that the police had recovered both Viggo's bass guitar and the album master tapes. However, by the time the popular paper had broken the story at the end of February 1981, the band had more or less moved on to their next project. While they were waiting for the Poem album to be mixed, work continued apace at Sound Art Studio, with Pål keen to keep the momentum going. One particular session – for the song 'Våkenatt' – included former drummer Erik Hagelien and Erik Nygaard, who plays slide guitar. It's an accomplished production, too, with hints of the Doors' 'Queen of the Highway' in the melody. 'I think it is me playing the flute,' added Viggo. 'The backing vocals are by Svein Erichsen and me.' Unusually, it also features Pål singing wholly in Norwegian, while lines such as 'Alt som kan skje, alt som vil skje, i en våkenatt' [Everything that can happen, everything that will happen, in a waking night] confirmed Pål's continued fascination with Gunvor Hofmo.

Eventually, an acquaintance of Svein Erichsen's did mix three of the album's tracks, but the band were reportedly unhappy with the results. Despite the fact that album artwork had been prepared, the band returned to their routine of songwriting and rehearsing, and worked on some promising new material in the basement of a nursery school just outside Manglerud. Some of these songs, including embryonic versions of 'I've Been Losing You', 'Take On Me' and 'You Are the One', were later taped, with the assistance of Erichsen. One other gem, referred to as 'Wild World', also displayed great potential. 'All four of us rehearsed these songs,' said Viggo, 'but it is Pål who is playing the bass on the recording.'

The recordings confirm that the band were evolving at a frenetic pace, while the melodies were getting stronger. The problem was, both Viggo and Øystein were becoming increasingly frustrated by the lack of live performances. By contrast, Magne and Pål were happy to continue writing and rehearsing, and it was almost inevitable that the band would break up.

'It was a dynamic process,' said Viggo. 'There was no conflict at a personal level – which is common in many bands – and we have been good friends since the band broke up. We had spent very much time together in a period of almost four years, and I think we achieved a lot. At that time, very few bands in Norway had recorded two albums. And very few bands established by teenagers stayed together as many years as we did.'

VÅKENATT (2018 Album)
Produced by Svein Erichsen

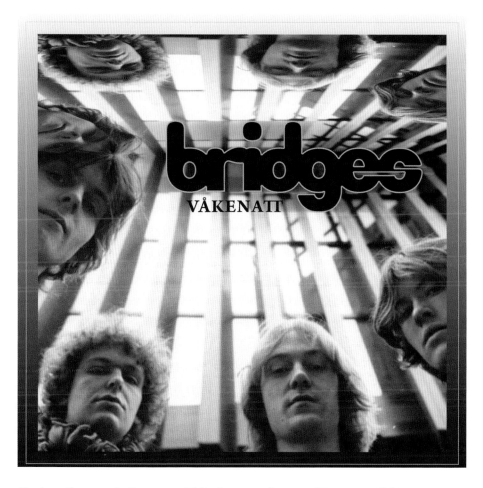

The band's second album would lie dormant for over 35 years until it was eventually mixed in 2016 by Pål and Chuck Zwicky. 'I'm surprised how good it ended up sounding,' said Pål, 'considering the age of the tape and the modest studio we used.'

During the mixing process, equipment from the period was used to add more authenticity to its sound, as Pål explained during a press conference for the album in 2018: 'I didn't feel it was right to use every modern method to mix the album. But at the same time, I tried to work out: "Am I doing this the way it sounded at that time, or do I try to make the songs as best as possible now?" So I thought the coolest way was to make the songs as good as they could be, but only with equipment available in 1981. I could have mixed this album so it sounded very modern, but it didn't feel quite right.'

Magne's take on the album mix contrasts with Pål's, however. 'Viggo started a process to get this album mixed by the original people involved a couple of years ago, and I accepted out of historical correctness,' he said. 'But Pål refused. Pål then took the tapes and corrected a hell of a lot of vocals and added effects and things that were *not* around back then. He did not ask me about any of these changes and I was really pissed off. I hear the result is fine but, make no mistake, this was not how it originally sounded.'

Magne was also not in agreement with the album being released under the name of Bridges. 'I would of course have preferred Poem,' he said. 'I am pretty allergic to revisionism in all its forms, just like I would have preferred the original title of the song "Need No Doctor". This song was titled "Words", never "Need No Doctor". This song is one of my favourites of all the songs we wrote together at the time.'

As for a Bridges reunion, it is highly unlikely. 'I resist the idea of a reunion,' said Magne. 'This eternal need to look backwards and somehow even try to mould the past to suit the present in a better way all seems too self-important and revisionist to me. I can see it would be fun from a fan's point of view, but as an artist I believe it is our solemn duty to leave the past as it was and not start idolising it, but move on . . . I say this knowing full well that we currently celebrate a record from 1985 throughout the world this year, but there is a huge difference in how many people *Hunting High and Low* means something to compared with Bridges.'

TIMELESS

While this 'lost album' hasn't quite attained the mythical status of, say, *Smile* (the Beach Boys) or even *Black Gold* (Jimi Hendrix), the release of the *Våkenatt* album in August 2018 was certainly keenly anticipated by a-ha fans, some of whom were played snippets of some of the newly mixed tracks at a convention in 2016 by Viggo and Øystein.

Like 1980's *Fakkeltog*, the album was issued in limited quantities. To the consternation of some fans, it was released as a lavish (and quite expensive) vinyl-only edition by Rockheim Museum's newly founded RMA label in August 2018. Because of the constraints of the format, two tracks weren't included: 'Wood End' ('a deliberate misspelling of "Would End"', said Magne) and 'Panorama'.

'When we were approached to release it, I was never in doubt,' explained RMA's Terje Nilsen. 'This is an essential chapter in the history of Norwegian popular music. *Våkenatt* documents the transition from the indie band Bridges to the global success of a-ha. And certainly, the album is an artistic achievement on its own – a timeless musical masterpiece, which feels completely natural and relevant to release today, almost four decades after its conception.'

'I have been pushing for the release of the second album for many years,' said Viggo, 'and you can imagine that I am very happy we are finally there. I think the mix is very loyal to the band and I am very proud of the record.'

'I think the songs have timeless qualities,' said Pål. 'We could have recorded them today, with just as much enthusiasm.' Magne added: 'At that time, we felt that Bridges was definitely the most exciting band in Norway. Not many others thought the same, but one did, and that was Morten Harket.'

CHAPTER THREE
A NEW SINGER

Morten Harket was born on 14 September 1959 in Buskerud county's town of Kongsberg (well known due to its mining of high-quality silver), but spent the majority of his childhood in the Greater Oslo area of Asker.

Like Magne and Pål, Morten had come from a stable middle-class background and, like his future bandmates, a love of music had been instilled in him from an early age. 'My first musical experience that blew my mind – blew everything – was seeing a local brass band performing on Norway's National Day,' he recalled. 'The conductor let me sit on his shoulders and the excitement went through me light like lightning. I was three.'[1]

At school, Morten played the trombone in an orchestra, and he was also encouraged by his parents to take piano lessons. However, like Magne, the actual process of learning to play the instrument didn't appeal. 'I took lessons for a number of years, and I never learned to read music. I just copied what [the tutor] played,' he said. 'I got good at faking it. I was never confrontational about it, because I didn't want to let my parents down. But I had this aversion to being taught anything.'[2]

In tandem with the Gamst household in the 1960s, it was classical music that filled Morten's ears during his formative years, but he did recall miming to the Beatles when he was six years old. However, his first proper introduction to contemporary pop music wouldn't arrive until Simon & Garfunkel's 1970 classic, 'Bridge Over Troubled Water' (which he would later perform in concert during his solo career in the 90s). Testament to his musical upbringing, he later latched on to the music of Queen, whose own classical influences were prevalent on classic albums such as *Sheer Heart Attack* and *A Night at the Opera*. (Morten later covered Freddie Mercury's moving ballad 'Love of My Life' in the early 90s.)

Other favourites included Johnny Cash and Uriah Heep, but it was one record, more than any other, that would ultimately cement a lifelong passion for music: the Jimi Hendrix Experience's version of 'Hey Joe'. According to Morten, he had played the single on a turntable at school and was so overwhelmed by the listening experience that he stole it from the common room. 'I did not play the stolen record,' he stated. 'I didn't play anything. For three months I stopped listening to music. The effect of the Hendrix record was so great that everything I had heard before suddenly seemed superfluous. It changed all the rules and values that I had connected to music so far . . . One thing was clear to me, though: I wanted to become a musician.'[3]

A similar musical epiphany occurred when he saw Bridges in concert for the first time at Asker Gymnasium on 16 December 1979. 'It really stunned me when I heard them live,' he said. 'The big change for me was when I heard Pål and Mags and their band. All of a sudden everything changed. It stunned me, right there on the floor. "This is it. This is how it's gonna happen." It was instant, but at the same time I knew they needed me. I had to be a part of it.'[4]

It would be a while before Morten would become involved, however, but he did make a connection with Magne following Bridges' performance at *NM i rock* in 1980 – a particularly spooky one at that. During lengthy conversations on their long journey back home, it eventually transpired that Morten had witnessed the plane crash that had claimed the life of Magne's father. 'The first time I met Morten Harket, we walked home together after a party,' Magne told *Adresseavisen* in 2015. 'It was a long walk, and after we had talked about the important stuff – what music we liked – we needed to find other topics of conversation: what our parents were doing, things like that. I told him that my father died in a plane crash in 1969. Morten remained completely silent for a while before telling me he was an eyewitness to the plane crash in Drammen.' (In December 1995, Morten purchased one of Magne's woodcuts – *Erindringens trompet* [The Trumpet of Remembrance] – at the keyboardist's *Kutt* exhibition, which had been inspired by Kåre Furuholmen's recovered trumpet case.)

Although Morten was sure that their paths would cross again, the official formation of a-ha was still a few years away. Bridges were beginning to make a name for themselves at this stage, and on the cusp of taking their career to the next level. Morten needed to complete his own musical apprenticeship before he could think about joining them.

He'd formed his first band, Laelia Anceps – named after a species of orchid which he was particularly fond of – with his brother, Håkon. However, their repertoire didn't extend past covers of Genesis songs, and the act didn't make it beyond the rehearsal room.

Another prog rock-inspired band, with brothers Per and Dag Lien providing the musical backbone, was another short-lived affair. Their tenure culminated in a failed attempt by Morten to rally his bandmates into raising awareness about the famines in Africa after he'd been moved, Bob Geldof-style, by a TV documentary. (The Lien brothers later released an album as Brother to Brother in 1990, titled *Materialize*. Interestingly, its producer, Geir Holmsen, turned down an offer in 1989 to become a-ha's bass player.)

Prior to this latest failed musical venture, Morten had also recorded some tracks in 1979 with Geir Kolbu, a former member of a local band called Quien Sabe. Using the name Mercy, the duo made some recordings at Cross Studio in Kristiansand, incorporating parts they had recorded on a large church organ at

Oslo's Trinity Church. Sadly, while Morten did design a Gothic-style cover for an album, titled *Spirit Battle*, it's believed that most of the recordings were erased. When quizzed about the album by *Puls* magazine in 1999, Morten described it as a 'concert in his head for a hundred thousand people' and ruled out a release. (Geir Kolbu later created the melody for 'East Timor', which appeared on Morten's debut solo album, *Wild Seed*.)

SOUL MAN

While Morten was enthusiastic about music, the next few years would see him committing to both his theological studies and a year-long mandatory bout of military service. Years later, he laid to rest a common misconception in the press that he had considered a career in the priesthood: 'I was not considering that, that's not true. I embarked on studies in theology after school. But I never considered being a priest. I was just interested in theology, which I still am.'[5] (As conscientious objectors, both Magne and Pål managed to avoid military service.)

Morten's first serious band, the Bluebirds, would not come together until mid-January 1982, and the five-piece combo's origins stemmed from the disbandment of a blues band named Hartvik and the Heartbreakers, who had been together between 1979 and 1981. Among their members were Espen Farstad, Knut Reiersrud (a future Spellemann winner) and Arild Evenby, who had played bass for the Berg Brothers Band.

Hartvik and the Heartbreakers were a popular act in Norway, but they also attracted some interest from abroad, as Espen confirmed: 'We did go to Chicago in 1980, and were offered a contract through Warner Brothers. But, to cut a long story short, we left the USA with nothing.'

In the end, the band (with Øivind Karlsen on bass) recorded a three-track EP, *I Play the Blues for You*, at Oslo's Økorec studio in May 1980, and released it on their own *MacRell* label. By the end of the year, however, the band had split.

Along with Arild Fetveit, Espen Farstad and Arild Evenby quickly put a new band together, recruiting drummer Knut Lie in the process. Both Evenby and Lie were friends from Askim and had been a part of a local ensemble, Blanda Drops, who'd released a double album titled *Vårslipp* [Spring Release] in 1980, while Lie had also played in the progressive rock band, Høst [Autumn].

Employing a singer to front this new band wasn't quite so straightforward, however. Arild Fetveit had been impressed by Morten, whom he'd seen performing as Judas in the Christian musical *Vitnet* [The Witness] at Asker's Østenstad Church in 1980, and had pushed for him to be the band's singer, but Espen was initially sceptical about his appointment. 'I can remember we had an audition to find the best singer,' he said. 'There was a fight between two singers. My opinion was that Bård Kranstad did best in the audition. He was a bluesy, raw type. Arild Fetveit strongly argued for Morten as the vocalist in the band, I think, due to his soul preferences. I did not find Morten as my kind of blues-friend – I did not believe this guy had any future as a singer!'

Morten and Arild Fetveit were relative rookies, but Morten could at least boast some stage experience. Aside from the aforementioned *Vitnet* production, he'd also been a part of the drama group Anthem, who performed a musical version of *Peer Gynt* at the tail end of the 70s. The rest of the band, however, were seasoned professionals and, via their array of music biz connections, were easily able to gain live bookings in various nightspots throughout Norway, which included Trondheim's Bluesklubb, plus Oslo's Hot House, Club 7 and Chateau Neuf venues.

The Bluebirds made their live debut in Askim on 26 March 1982, but later changed their name to Souldier Blue, a moniker which perfectly encapsulated their repertoire of soul and blues covers. A typical set list included songs by the likes of Buddy Guy, Freddie King, Otis Rush and the Spencer Davis Group.

Inevitably, there were murmurs of discontent among the blues purists who were expecting a more weathered voice, but the shows attracted some good reviews in the local papers. Although the aspiring singer was out of his comfort zone, vocally, and not exactly enamoured with some of the set list choices, the shows also provided invaluable opportunities to both develop his voice and perfect his stage craft.

I asked Espen if the band's ambitions extended to the recording studio. 'Souldier Blue was strictly a gigging band,' he replied. 'I had started studying, and the band was mostly for fun.'

Souldier Blue would eventually fizzle out as fate came calling in the form of a struggling duo named Poem.

TAKE HIM ON

When Magne and Pål journeyed to London as Poem for the first time in November 1981, it was the latter member who was still undertaking vocal duties. 'He sounded like Jim Morrison,' Magne said, 'but he didn't sound right. I didn't want him to sing. I figured that out early, but it took him longer to admit he wasn't the right singer for us.'[6]

I asked Magne when he'd first heard Morten sing. 'Morten hummed something the first time he and I met, walking back home through the snow after a Bridges concert he attended,' he said, 'but the first time I heard him really sing was in concert with his band Souldier Blue, together with Pål.' According to Magne, the duo approached Morten to become their singer but were asked to wait while he finished his studies. However, neither Magne nor Pål were prepared to wait and they travelled to London anyway. 'Our strategy was pretty simple: Get out of Oslo and try to find people to form a band with in London,' said Magne. 'We put some ads in the music papers and some musicians turned up at our bedsit in Linden Gardens. But, frankly, those who were any good left pretty quickly. It was more a case of us auditioning for them than the other way round. Pål was on acoustic guitar and whistling the melodies and I was on the Korg synth. We didn't come across as future pop stars!'

One of the duo's ads in *Melody Maker* eventually led to the somewhat unorthodox recruitment of an electrical harp player. 'I can't remember his name,' said Magne, 'but I do remember his family lived in a house they had bought from Van Morrison in Notting Hill.'

In the end, their attempt to both integrate a harpist and make headway in the capital failed. 'After a couple of months, the money we had saved dried up, and I took odd jobs to keep us afloat,' said Magne. 'Due to shyness, Pål did not want to engage with strangers, so we agreed he should sit at home and write music while I worked, firstly as a labourer, cleaning out asbestos, then as a bartender, earning one pound an hour. In the end I said, "Sod this, we're going back home to get Morten on board." Then we hitchhiked to Norway.'

Following his InterRail holiday with Arild Fetveit, Morten mulled over a fresh offer from Magne and Pål to join them. He eventually agreed to join the pair on his 23rd birthday in September 1982. (He would, however, continue gigging with Souldier Blue over the ensuing months.) The newly expanded outfit eventually ruled out an immediate return to London, and instead decided to prepare a demo tape for potential record labels in the UK's music industry. The trio hauled their sleeping bags and instruments onto a bus and retreated to a more rural and aesthetic location, away from the urban sprawl of Oslo.

CHAPTER FOUR
NÆRSNES

With the Norwegian economy thriving in the 70s, it was not uncommon for families to own a holiday home, and both the Harkets and the Gamsts owned summer properties, in Kristiansand and Nærsnes, respectively.

Nærsnes, in Buskerud, was a particularly picturesque location, overlooking the western part of the Oslofjord. Over the ensuing months, the Gamst family's log cabin, situated within the dense forest of this small village, would serve as a recording studio for the as-yet-unnamed band. 'We suddenly went from being a traditional band to something that could be adapted song by song,' said Pål. 'I was playing keyboards, programming drums, etc. The main focus was getting the song done in a satisfying way.'

In addition to some acoustic guitars, the band's equipment included Magne's borrowed Jupiter synthesiser, Pål's guitar synth and Morten's TEAC multitrack tape recorder. There was also a newly purchased Dr Rhythm drum machine, which enabled the band to get around the dilemma of employing a drummer. (Although Morten had some experience in that department, asking him to undertake a Phil Collins-like role was simply out of the question!) Created by Boss, a sub-division of the Roland company, the Dr. Rhythm DR-55 had been introduced in 1980. With just four sounds available (kick, snare, rimshot and hi-hat), it was somewhat limited, but its affordability and ease of programming made it an attractive instrument for both aspiring and established musicians. China Crisis, Depeche Mode, Thomas Dolby, New Order and Soft Cell were all notable users during the 80s, while Gothic rockers the Sisters of Mercy even gave their machine a name – Doktor Avalanche!

In the final third of 1982, the band recorded several demos using their primitive equipment. Some of these demos would later be rerecorded in London (with some eventually making it onto their debut album), but others, such as 'Nå blåser det på jorden' and 'Du og jeg og vi tre', wouldn't make the cut. 'These early sessions were quite innocent and open,' said Magne, 'but personality differences were clear from the get-go. We turned into a unit pretty quickly, though. Unchecked ambition was one thing we all had in common.'

The uninsulated summer cottage gradually became colder as winter started to rear its freezing head, but the band had recorded several songs which, with the aid of Bridges producer Svein Erichsen, were mixed during the festive period. The resulting cassette included embryonic versions of some of the band's future hits, including 'Take On Me'. 'It was something new and different,' said Tonje Waaktaar

Gamst. 'Pål said they now wanted to make pop music. And they were great songs – I liked them right away.'

SELECTED NÆRSNES DEMOS (Recorded 1982)

NÅ BLÅSER DET PÅ JORDEN
Written by Pål Waaktaar-Savoy and Morten Harket
Produced by a-ha

Sometimes written as 'Så blåser det på jorden' [So It's Blowing on the Earth], this demo represented something of a rarity for the band, in that it found them singing in Norwegian. Pål had previously integrated Norwegian lyrics on early Bridges songs such as 'Hvor er ditt ord' [Where Is Your Word] and, later, 'Fakkeltog' and 'Våkenatt', but this was an unusual step for a band who had loftier ambitions beyond their native country.

The track is rather primitive sounding (indicative of the equipment they were using), and more of an experimental piece as they grappled with their new musical set-up. Morten, too, was still in the early throes of discovering his vocal range.

DU OG JEG OG VI TRE
Written by Pål Waaktaar-Savoy
Produced by a-ha

This was an original composition, but both the title and its folk pop sensibilities were derived from a traditional children's song titled 'Du og jeg og vi to' [You and Me and the Two of Us], which outlined a sailing trip in a wooden shoe. It was popularised by Wenche Myhre, who adapted the song in 1972 and sent it to the top of the Norwegian charts, where it stayed for 14 weeks in 1973.

Because of its Norwegian lyrics, it's another track with decidedly novel appeal, but with a depth in the lyrics that's not immediately apparent – a common feature of Pål's writing. There's a plethora of seaside imagery (parasols, beaches, ice cream, seagulls, etc) that give it an almost childlike quality, but, under the surface, it ostensibly casts Pål as an observer of Magne's relationship with his girlfriend (and future wife), Heidi ('I'm here, you're there / Here's where I need to be / You and me and the three of us').

Pål later mentioned both of the songs in an interview with *Smash Hits* in 1987: 'They were good – we'll probably record them. It's funny, when we came to England to try to get a record contract, we had those on the tape and they thought it was a different singer and a different band – the language changes everything.'

CHAPTER FIVE
LONDON

*They had felt the hunger like young figures from a Knut Hamsun novel stranded
in London. They'd searched high and low for food amongst the rubbish and scraps
of the city. They lived in hope and in the certainty that they had something that
was just too big for Little Old Norway. It was like a force that exploded inside them,
driving them far, far away from social-democratic Norwegian self-righteousness.
Sure, they had problems. Difficulties lay in their way. But they tackled them
one by one!*

– Pål H. Christiansen, *The Scoundrel Days of Hobo Highbrow*, 2002

Sans Magne, who would join them a week later, Morten and Pål left Norway for
London on Sunday, 2 January 1983 and set up home in West London. On this day,
Renee and Renato's 'Save Your Love' was perched at the top of a singles chart that
included synth-pop titans such as Blancmange, the Human League, Soft Cell,
Ultravox and Yazoo, while *The John Lennon Collection* sat atop the album chart
for a sixth consecutive week. On terrestrial television, which had stretched to four
channels by November 1982, *Bullseye*, *Tales of the Unexpected* and *Hi-de-Hi* –
staples of evening entertainment in the early 80s – were broadcast. In the football
world, Liverpool led the way in the old Division One, with Stoke City – the club
Magne and Morten had supported in their youth – in 13th position.

RENDEZVOUS
The band's transition to life in London wasn't straightforward. Since they had
entered the country on a tourist visa, they weren't able to work, and there was
some toing and froing as Magne and Morten sought work at home to replenish
their dwindling funds. (The pair both worked at Dikemark, a psychiatric hospital
in Asker.) As part of a three-night residency at the Hot House club in Oslo, Morten
also performed with Souldier Blue for the last time on 9 March 1983, and on the
10th and 11th as a guest – nicknamed Sporty Morty – for the newly formed House
Rockers, a four-piece which comprised Arild Fetveit and Espen Farstad on guitar,
plus the Bøgeberg brothers, Jørun and Dag, on bass and drums, respectively.

'We existed for a short period, around 1983–84,' said Dag, when asked about
the House Rockers. 'Most of the gigs we played were at the Hot House. A couple
of times this guy Morten showed up and sang a song or three. I hadn't seen him
before and didn't know who he was, but he sang great. I was told that he lived in
London and tried hard to make it with this band, a-ha.' (In 2014, Souldier Blue

reformed for a few shows at a jazz club in Askim, featuring original members Espen Farstad, Knut Lie and Arild Evenby. According to Espen, Morten and Arild Fetveit weren't invited.)

'We came to England because it's still the heart of rock and pop music,' said Morten. 'We also wanted to get away from the safe cocoon that Norway was for us. There's no competition, and no strong ambitions there.'[1] They were also inspired by the fact one of their musical heroes, Jimi Hendrix, had arrived in London in September 1966, and within a year had become one of the biggest rock stars in the UK. As it would transpire, the band's journey to stardom would take them a little longer, and their initial attempts to get their demo heard were often met with disappointment. 'We knocked on every door,' said Pål, 'but couldn't get past the doorman usually.' However, when they were turned down by Decca, the record company that had famously turned down the Beatles in January 1962, they took this as a positive sign.

Contact was also re-established with Lionheart (a publishing company whom Magne and Pål had reportedly become acquainted with during their first sojourn to the capital) and a deal of sorts was signed. However, the band would eventually enjoy the luxury of hedging their bets after an advert in the back pages of *Melody Maker* caught their eye.

The ad was for a studio named Rendezvous in Sydenham, South London. The band felt embarrassed by their demo cassette and, following advice from Lionheart, had sought affordable facilities in which to lay down better quality versions of their songs. Although the studio famously boasted a Space Invaders arcade game as one of its features, Magne later conceded that this wasn't the only thing that appealed. In addition to invaluable rehearsal space, Rendezvous Studios – which had listed the then high-flying Dexys Midnight Runners as one of its users – boasted a number of instruments, including a Prophet-5 synthesiser, a LinnDrum machine and a grand piano, plus a Brenell Mini 8 multitrack recorder and a Roland Space Echo unit.

THE MANY LIVES OF RATCLIFF

Rendezvous Studios was owned by John Ratcliff, who, via his YouTube channel years later, recalled receiving a telephone call from Pål in the spring of 1983: 'I remember when he gave me his surname – Waaktaar Gamst – I thought it might be a wind-up. I wasn't too sure until a deposit cheque arrived in the post and, two weeks later, Morten, Pål and Mags all walked through the door.'

Ratcliff himself had, to say the least, enjoyed something of a varied and colourful career. In his formative years, he was a keen sportsman (representing England in both rugby and athletics), as well as a member of the National Youth Theatre. His strong interest in acting transcended to television, where he gained parts in series such as *Play for Today*, *The Many Wives of Patrick* and *Grange Hill*, as well as the 1976 TV movie *The Hunchback of Notre Dame*. Crucially, he had a concurrent interest in music and was a proficient player of several instruments, including piano, guitar and violin.

In an interview with BBC Radio Bristol in 2015, Ratcliff explained the origins of Rendezvous, which had been funded by a bank loan in the mid-70s: 'I'd always been in bands right from the word go, and to rehearse you'd have to hire a rehearsal studio . . . They were quite costly and I put two and two together and thought, "If I've got my own studio, then rehearsing's free". So this is what I did with a very good friend of mine and the bass player of the band I was in at the time. We took over this little club and converted it into a rehearsal studio. Then, as things developed, I decided to go on my own and turn it into a recording studio, which then became Rendezvous.'

Rendezvous Studios' Brenell Mini-8, currently on display at the Rockheim Museum in Trondheim.

Not to be confused with a pre-fame band featuring the Eurythmics' Annie Lennox and Dave Stewart – or indeed a pop duo from the mid-80s – the Catch had Ratcliff as their frontman and primary songwriter, and they'd signed deals with both EMI Music (in the UK) and Atlantic Records (in the US) in 1978. Although Ratcliff was a more than capable singer and songwriter, mainstream success eluded the band. Sounding not unlike a prototype Kaiser Chiefs, the Catch certainly captured the post-punk/new wave zeitgeist of the late 70s, boasting a sound not dissimilar to the likes of XTC (see 'I'm Interested in You') and the Jam (see 'Living a Lie'). However, despite having 'name' producers on board, like Colin Thurston (Duran Duran) and Christopher Neil (who would later work on *East of the Sun, West of the Moon*), their eventual output amounted to little more than a handful of singles, and they were quietly dropped from EMI's roster. (Interestingly, members Robin Langridge and Chris Jarrett later turned up on a hit version of the Doors' 'Riders on the Storm' by Annabel Lamb in September 1983.)

By the time of the band's arrival at Rendezvous in April 1983, Ratcliff was working with new acts such as the Cabinet, in addition to working on solo material (for example, the 'Kerry Girl' single, released in October that year). Enchanted both by the young hopefuls' politeness and the potential in their songs, he soon took the band under his wing. Later, he offered the band free out-of-hours studio time. 'They were fast running out of money and they needed some more time to finish the tracks off,' he remembered. 'Certainly in the last couple of days of their booking I'd been getting my ear closer and closer to the studio door because I was liking what I was hearing. It sounded very fresh, and the vocal sound was something that I hadn't heard before.'[2]

While acts such as Laugh Clown Laugh used the studio during the daytime, the band operated in a different time zone, using the facilities from the late evenings until the early hours.

One of the studio engineers was an Oxford graduate named Martyn Phillips, who would later work with Magne on the post-production of the 'Cosy Prisons' single in 2006. Martyn worked with a number of acts at Rendezvous during

his burgeoning career as an engineer and producer, including the Accursed, Craft and Bernard Padden. 'I also recorded and mixed a thrash album [*Animal People* by Metal Virgins] in maybe half a day,' he remembered. 'One band came from Sweden and left their passports as a deposit while they went to the bank to get the cash for the session. They never came

The anatomy of a hit. The band's old Yamaha DX7, currently under repair at Martyn Phillips' studio.

back! I remember Alan McGee coming in as a producer at what must have been early Creation days, and being very tough on a young indie band he had signed, not letting them rerecord parts that had mistakes in them. "That's what you played", I remember him saying more than once.

'Phil Da Costa used to engineer there as well. He has done well from kids TV among other things. (We then both worked at Paradise Studios in W3; that was well stocked with synths, including the Fairlight CMI and PPG.) Another engineer who worked there occasionally, I think, was Chris Stone and I was very impressed as he had mixed "Windpower" by Thomas Dolby, my favourite artist at the time. Generally, there was a fairly unspectacular clientele but we did well as engineers and the results were always satisfactory. There was precious little gear in the rack so I was forever running tie lines to speakers in the live area, box room, office and stairwell, and miking up those spaces, and got quite nice results that way.'

With regard to the band, Martyn has fond memories of his time with them. 'There was quite a buzz around a-ha,' he said. 'They were so talented, charismatic and proactive, it was clear they were going to do well. (I remember thinking the same about the Spice Girls when I wrote a song with them before they broke.) They slept in the office during the day session and came in overnight, working very hard, and I was quietly envious of the results they managed to coax out of the gear. I was lucky enough to be the first person to hear many of the classics. I recall them playing me the work so far and asking me what I thought, and I made one comment that they needed a downtempo song. The next day I think it was, they had "Hunting High and Low", and I recall thinking it sounded great. The songs were written on guitar, the studio LinnDrum, Juno 60 and my Yamaha DX7 – one of the first in the country – that I had got to grips with programming, so they are likely to be my sounds on the demos. I still have the synth.'

Martyn has slightly less fond memories of his time with John Ratcliff, however: 'I was not that happy with him as my nice 70s Fender Precision that I had lent the studio got stolen from there, and he did not offer any sympathy or compensation!'

BEARDED BEAR

John Ratcliff also secured the band accommodation close to Rendezvous (in Dartmouth Road) and offered to manage them. 'What I didn't realise was that, despite my offer of management and acceptance by the group, the band was still going out seeing other companies and other interested parties,' he recalled. 'They were trying to cover themselves, I guess, for every eventuality. One of the companies was Lionheart.'[3]

Ratcliff himself had, crucially, amassed a number of connections within the music industry, including a former A&R man at EMI who had not only been involved in signing the Catch in 1978, but had also managed them and co-produced singles such as 'Something for Nothing' for them. His name was Terry Slater.

Like Ratcliff, Terry Slater was a vastly experienced musician. He was the lead guitarist in the Flintstones, a band who'd evolved from a Joe Meek-produced combo called the Blue Men. With Meek again at the helm, the band later cut a single, 'Big Feet', as the Stonehenge Men in 1962, with Slater's 'Pinto' on the B-side.

In the early 60s, the Flintstones provided backing for rock and roll luminaries such as Chuck Berry, Fats Domino and Little Richard, who were all grouped together on package tours in the UK and, further afield, in iconic venues such as the Star Club in Hamburg. It was on one of these tours that Slater first met the Everly Brothers. He later became their bass player and wrote or co-wrote several songs for them, including the US hit 'Bowling Green', which a-ha would later perform in his honour.

With the Everlys on hiatus, his keen interest in the business side of the music industry led him to EMI, and he was involved in the signings of several acts, including Kate Bush and the Sex Pistols. By the end of 1980, the label had also signed Duran Duran. 'EMI made sure we got the star treatment,' recalled their bassist, John Taylor. 'The general of the charm offensive was Terry Slater, who ran the A&R department. Terry was a cockney, a bearded bear of a guy who'd been a musician himself . . . Within an hour, we had been swept off our feet by "The Greatest Music Company in the World".[4]

Occasionally, Ratcliff would hand him tapes by aspiring new acts but, by the time he'd taken delivery of an a-ha cassette at his home in Walton-on-Thames, he'd left EMI. 'Things weren't going so well for EMI, and they made some big changes,' Slater recalled. 'As a result of financial difficulties, people were moved into different positions. They split up our team, so I quit.'[5] He soon moved on to other projects, such as overseeing the reunion of the Everly Brothers in 1983.

'Unfortunately, he wasn't as excited as I was,' recalled Ratcliff. 'Far from it. He felt that the tape lacked substance, and really was so unenthusiastic I was beginning to wonder whether or not I'd made the right decision to get involved with a-ha.'[6]

Although unimpressed with the three-track cassette, Slater was persuaded to meet the band in Sydenham. 'Luckily, he was as impressed on meeting them for the first time as I was,' Ratcliff continued. 'He thought they had fantastic looks, he thought they were very charismatic, had great personalities and, above all, they were extremely polite and courteous.'[7]

As Magne later recalled, Slater would become a fiercely protective father figure: 'He treated us as if we were his sons, to the point that he would threaten to break peoples' legs if they took drugs around the band. We spent most of our career without seeing anyone taking drugs. Quite frankly, we thought that was all a bit of a myth.'[8]

Following a number of meetings, Slater and Ratcliff formed T.J. Management Limited, and the band soon signed with them. Loosely interpreted, the division of labour entailed Ratcliff continuing to oversee the band's recordings, while Slater took care of business and contractual matters, using his vast network of contacts within the industry. (Slater would later assume full control, however.) One such mogul was Andrew Wickham, a renowned talent scout who'd been highly involved in signing acts such as Van Morrison and Joni Mitchell to the Warner/Reprise label in the USA.

In addition to his scouting and production duties, Wickham was a keen writer and penned album liner notes for the likes of Marianne Faithfull, the Hollies, the Kinks and the Mamas and Papas during the mid- to late 60s, when such a feature was commonplace. (He also penned notes for two of the Everly Brothers' albums from the Terry Slater era: *Roots* and *The Everly Brothers Sing*.)

While the members of a-ha were unable to hit the gig circuit due to the restrictions of their visas, they could perform privately, and a series of record company showcases were set up at Rendezvous in August 1983. Ratcliff's diary reveals that MCA and Phonogram were slotted in on the 22nd and 23rd, respectively, while Wickham and chairman Rob Dickens – who had just signed Howard Jones – represented Warner Brothers on the 24th. Although Wickham was enthused by the performance, it would be several months before a-ha would officially sign with the label. However, following a meeting in May 1983, the band had at least signed a deal with ATV Music (the publishing giant who had famously acquired Lennon and McCartney's *Northern Songs* in 1969), which had ensured the band could afford to eat properly now, having endured several months of relative poverty. 'My husband, before they were signed, was starving in London,' recalled Pål's then-girlfriend, Lauren Savoy, in an interview with Gry Sinding in 2016. 'I mean, literally. He had to wear suspenders 'cause all of his clothes wouldn't fit, and he's skinny to begin with!'

The band officially signed with Warner Brothers in December 1983, but they wouldn't commence recording sessions for their debut album for several months. In the interim, they continued their routine of writing and demoing material at Rendezvous. Occasionally, Pål tried out new material on his elder sibling. 'Pål would play the instrumental recording of a new song over the phone and sing along, no lyrics finished yet,' said Tonje. 'I could sing along the second or third time I heard a new song.'

By the time they entered Eel Pie Studios in June 1984, the band had amassed a number of songs, some of which would not make the cut. 'Morten's voice is absolutely fantastic on these early demos,' enthused John Ratcliff. 'He sings with a purity and with an emotion that I think, with the passage of time, inevitably disappears through a young and hopeful voice.'[9]

Some songs – including 'Falls Park', 'She's Humming a Tune' and 'They to Me and I to Them' – wouldn't be recorded until several years later, when Pål was reunited with notebooks he'd not seen since the band's Rendezvous period.

Other song titles dating from this period included 'Don't Belittle Yourself', 'Touton Macoute', 'With a Ghost of a Chance' and 'The Worst Little Boy in the World'. Pål added: '"Touton Macoute" was one of the first songs I wrote as a kid that surprised my mum – "you wrote that?!"'

SELECTED RENDEZVOUS DEMOS (Recorded 1983–1984)

ALL THE PLANES THAT COME IN ON THE QUIET
Written by Pål Waaktaar-Savoy
Produced by a-ha

If the Beatles hadn't split up after recording their *Abbey Road* album and continued experimenting with synthesisers, they may well have come up with something that sounded like Bridges' 'All the Planes That Come In on the Quiet', which the Oslo band had recorded during sessions for their second album.

Employing a strong narrative, with Pål immediately setting the scene ('The place, an old airport / A long life, short of great events'), it's a typically ambitious track, and one that stands out due to its strong use of analogue synths and synthetic drums. More than any other song written and recorded during this period, this was the track that would point towards Magne and Pål's future.

Pål later placed the track at the top of a list of 10 a-ha songs 'that should have received more attention'. In truth, however, Bridges had already recorded the definitive version, but a-ha had a go at putting their own spin on the track during the tail end of 1983. Seemingly intent on putting their proggy past behind them, the band jettisoned the original portmanteau production and omitted the original's playful midsection. In addition, lyrics were tweaked and, in keeping with the song's cinematic title, string sounds were added to heighten the drama. While not without its merits, the 80s makeover didn't quite come together, and the drum programming does date it somewhat.

DAYS ON END
Music written by Pål Waaktaar-Savoy and Morten Harket
Words written by Pål Waaktaar-Savoy
Produced by a-ha

While Magne was in Norway, Morten and Pål worked on this beautiful, stark ballad, which had a working title of 'If You Do'. At Pål's disposal at Rendezvous was a grand piano, while Morten had another go at laying down a trombone part, having previously used the instrument during the Nærsnes sessions.

One line, 'another working day', had previously been used on 'The Sphinx', a Nærsnes demo which would later morph into 'Train of Thought'. Magne also states that the song's original melody came from him. '"Days on End" was originally called "Mary Ann" back in the day,' he said, 'and I introduced the triangle-shaped C chord which started Pål on the melody . . . Even though I always saw "Mary Ann" as a co-write, I was never credited.'

While there are some lyrical quirks (for example, 'I hear the clock / Strike so prettily at the hours'), this was an undoubted highlight of the Rendezvous sessions, and indicative of some of the brooding Nordic melancholia that was to come. Morten's vocals are suitably chilling, and you can almost feel his ice-cold breath in the shivery lead-up to the song's opening line, 'Do you know why winter's such a cold and lonely place?'. The singer later recalled that the vocal was a breakthrough moment, claiming, 'It made me see the possibilities in my voice.'

While the musicianship is decidedly amateurish, the combination of piano and trombone is surprisingly effective. In a 1986 interview Morten declared that the track was one of his favourites from that period, while Pål later claimed that the band had a 'special affection' for it. Indeed, it's evident from the number of handwritten lyrics doing the rounds that the band had intended to develop the track further.

DOT THE I
Written by Pål Waaktaar-Savoy, Magne Furuholmen and Morten Harket
Produced by a-ha

This was the very first song the band recorded at Rendezvous in April 1983, and one of five tracks the band prepared for their showcase gigs at the studio.

Initially demoed at the Gamst family's summer cottage in Nærsnes, this was one of a number of energetic tracks that reflected a conscious effort by the band to write more catchy material. Although Pål and Magne were naturally attracted to bands such as the Cure, Echo & the Bunnymen and Tears for Fears (who all fitted in with Bridges' gloomy indie pop aesthetic), they had been exposed to more colourful pop acts on their first trip to London (a typical singles chart from the period included the likes of Bananarama, Bucks Fizz, Modern Romance and Tight Fit). As Magne confirmed in a radio interview with NRK P2 in 2009, both he and Pål were affected by this explosion of new music, and this certainly transcended to songs such as the Caribbean-flavoured 'Dot the I'. 'We discovered and opened up to more commercial music than what we had listened to before,' he said, 'We were rather stuck in the 60s, in a way. We had noticed punk music and thought it was cool, but we tried our best to hold on to the 60s sound in the music we did ourselves.'

The Rendezvous version of this decidedly throwaway piece boasts a tighter arrangement and a less pronounced steel drum sound than its Nærsnes counterpart, but with lyrics such as 'Spot the gag / Tick it, tock it, light a fag', it was wisely consigned to the sidelines. Later in their career, a-ha would draw comparisons with Radiohead, but this was more Kid Creole than *Kid A*.

GO TO SLEEP
Written by Pål Waaktaar-Savoy
Produced by a-ha

This somnolent lullaby saw Pål extending his fascination with sleep (which had manifested fully on Bridges' second album), but this time with a more romantic, featherlight touch ('The night is here now / Hide out in your dreams / Sweetest love of mine') to complement the chiming synths.

In many ways, this charming song can be seen as a companion piece to the title track of *Hunting High and Low*, which includes lines such as: 'She's sound asleep and she's sweeter now / Than the wildest dream could have seen her.'

The line 'So please, let me come to you / And stay this time' was later reused on 'And You Tell Me.'

THE LOVE GOODBYE
Written by Pål Waaktaar-Savoy, Magne Furuholmen and Morten Harket
Produced by a-ha

Originally demoed in Nærsnes and described by Morten as 'archetypal a-ha', this was the second of three tracks that the band laid down in April 1983, before their studio budget ran out.

Like 'Dot the I', which was also prepared for the band's showcase gigs that year, it showed the band were more than capable of writing a catchy melody, even at this early stage. Unlike 'Dot the I', however, there's considerably more substance in the lyrics, with some interesting imagery in the verses ('There's not a soul / In the streets below / She's sitting by the window / Clinging to the phone / Dialling endless numbers').

Unfortunately, despite some fluid synth playing, there's a somewhat clumsy attempt at a middle eight and the LinnDrum's synthetic handclaps do grate after a while.

MONDAY MOURNING
Written by Pål Waaktaar-Savoy and Magne Furuholmen
Produced by a-ha

With the band waiting to formalise their contract with Warner Brothers, they continued to record – and experiment – at Rendezvous. On this occasion, the band experimented with Ultravox-like atmospherics, while the unusual flute effects were achieved by blowing into the rims of beer bottles! As Morten later confirmed, the band were not averse to using makeshift instruments during their early years: 'We were totally confident that we would make it internationally,' he said. 'We had no money or instruments. We used cake tins or bottles with water in them – anything to make sounds.'[10]

Some odd lyrics aside ('Tears are falling down like fluid pain'), 'Monday Mourning' works perfectly as both a showcase for Morten's blossoming vocal abilities and as an indicator of the band's willingness to operate outside of their comfort zone.

NOTHING TO IT
Written by Pål Waaktaar-Savoy, Magne Furuholmen and Morten Harket
Produced by a-ha

While in London, the band decided on a new name: AHA. Morten had discovered the onomatopoeic moniker while rifling through one of Pål's notebooks, which would typically include sketches for songs and artistic doodles. The threesome eventually agreed it was perfect for the international market as it had the same spelling and definition in several other languages. Like the name ABBA, its symmetry also made it appealing to potential marketers. (The hyphen was added later to ease any potential pronunciation issues.)

Coincidentally, the word also formed part of this sprightly but highly repetitive synth-pop song, which was largely built around a refrain of 'Calm down, relax a bit / You've got to get on top of it / Aha, you can do it'. Redolent of early China Crisis, the track unfortunately lives up to its title in terms of lyrical substance, and Pål later dismissed it as 'light fluff'. However, the band were sufficiently enthused to later rerecord it in a far funkier style but, sadly, this superior version was never officially released.

PRESENTING LILY MARS
Written by Pål Waaktaar-Savoy and Morten Harket
Produced by a-ha

Perhaps the closest the band ever got to vaudeville, 'Presenting Lily Mars' was loosely based on a film adaptation of Booth Tarkington's 1933 novel of the same name. Starring Judy Garland in one of her early roles, the musical comedy follows the fortunes of Lily Mars and her struggles to become a Broadway star. (To give the track more of a Hollywood slant, Pål asked Morten to sing with a slight American accent.)

As Pål later recalled, the track presented the band with something of a challenge during their stay in Nærsnes in 1982: 'We put as much energy into this as the more pop-slanted tunes. It was an unbelievable amount of work to record things like this on a four-track machine.'[11] Indeed, the TEAC did limit the number of vocal and instrumental tracks they could record, but it was possible to mix down two or three tracks onto the fourth channel – often referred to as 'bouncing' – so further tracks could be added. This was an often frustrating process, and a high amount of patience was required to achieve the right sound mix. But, considering the limitations of the machine, the band did a credible job of layering the multiple elements over the steady beat of the DR-55.

Somewhat surprisingly, the band opted for a safe and rather pedestrian new arrangement when rerecording the track using the superior equipment at Rendezvous, stripping away some of its effervescent personality in the process. However, the song was deemed good enough to be earmarked for potential inclusion on the band's second album.

UMBRELLA
Written by Pål Waaktaar-Savoy
Produced by a-ha

Although this unique musique concrète experiment wasn't perhaps in the same league as sound collagists such as the Art of Noise, it was proof positive that the band were open to having fun in the studio. Built over a simple LinnDrum pattern are some melodic synth lines and samples of answering machine dialogue from Lauren Savoy, who bemoans the loss of an umbrella ('I lost my umbrella last night / It kept me dry').

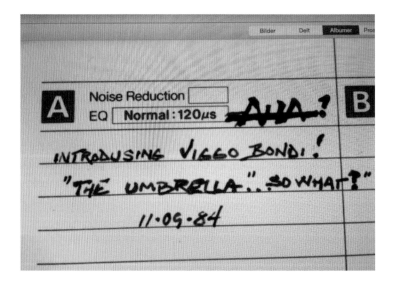

Somewhat bizarrely, the track also features an operatic vocal from one Viggo Bondi, who had popped into the studio during one of his many visits to London. Leaving Bridges had been an amicable experience, and he had kept in touch with his former bandmates over the ensuing period, but his main focus was now law. 'I decided to go to law school more than a year after the band broke up in the spring of 1981,' said Viggo, who currently works at the Norwegian Shipowners' Association.

When it was leaked without permission several years ago, this creative piece was known as 'Telephone', although Pål's handwritten notes from the period confirm that other provisional titles included 'A Certain Umbrella' and 'Miss Savoy's Umbrella'.

WHAT'S THAT YOU'RE DOING TO YOURSELF IN THE POURING RAIN?
Written by Pål Waaktaar-Savoy
Produced by a-ha

Propelled by a catchy synth bassline, this playful number once again displayed the band's openness to experiment in the studio. With its sequenced synth parts and generous use of guitar, it's an accomplished production, too.

Complementing the lyrics are some sampled dialling sounds and a slightly distorted vocal to give the effect of singing through a telephone ('What's that you're saying to yourself in the pouring rain? / Speak up, please, I really can't hear a word you say').

YOU HAVE GROWN THOUGHTFUL AGAIN
Written by Pål Waaktaar-Savoy, Magne Furuholmen and Morten Harket
Produced by a-ha

Boasting a soothing melody – and a percussive intro that is practically identical to the one on 'Love Is Reason' – this was one of the standout demos from the Rendezvous sessions, but it's evident from the way that Morten improvises his way through the intro – which includes a rather flippant cry of 'Carramba!' – that there wasn't enough belief in the song. It's a shame because there's certainly enough punch in the chorus and enough sensitivity in the verses ('I don't know if you are lonely or just con me / And I don't see how you can say / The friends are few and far between') to suggest that it could have been developed further.

YOU'RE SO WHITE
Written by Pål Waaktaar-Savoy
Produced by a-ha

In terms of its musical structure, this jaunty ditty was emblematic of the catchy pop the band were writing and recording during this period but, as Pål confirmed, the melody had actually been derived from one of Bridges' earliest demos, 'Truths of Love'.

The lyrics feature simple observations about falling snow in the midst of a brightly lit city, which includes some quirky couplets ('Gently falling snow / Is melting slower all the time'), but the title was inspired by his bandmate. 'That title sounds a bit racially weird,' said Pål, 'but it was really a direct quote from Morten's girlfriend who visited from Greece sometime in 83–84. She was astonished by how bleached and grey-faced we looked in the London winter – living on next to nothing at that time might have had something to do with it!'

There's been no official reason for the omission of the track from the *Hunting High and Low* reissues in both 2010 and 2015. 'I'm not sure why it wasn't included,' said Pål.

PART TWO

DAYS ON END
1984–1988

I grew up in the sixties
The seventies I betrayed
But the eighties are mine
You can't take them away from me

– Bridges, *Somebody's Going Away*, 1980

CHAPTER SIX

A NEW PRODUCER

Although a-ha had signed their first record deal with Warner Brothers in December 1983, it would be almost a year before the release of their debut single. 'It took six months to negotiate a deal and we had to wait another six months before we started recording,' said Morten. 'For various reasons it took another six months to get the album recorded. It was all very frustrating indeed.'[1]

The reason for this delay was that the record label was struggling to find the right producer for the band. 'I had actually been approached by Warner Brothers and a-ha's manager, Terry Slater, to do the whole album,' said Alan Tarney, who was reportedly the label's first choice. 'At that time, the band were still working at John Ratcliff's studio in Sydenham, so I went to see them there and they did a live performance in front of us all . . . For some reason, after it had been agreed that I would produce the album, it turned out I couldn't do it. So I told Terry Slater this and, at that point, he brought in Tony Mansfield.'[2]

DROWNING IN SOCIETY

A veritable pop visionary, Tony Mansfield had originally fronted the synth-pop act New Musik, in addition to playing guitar for the Nick Straker Band (which essentially included the same personnel). But it was with New Musik that Mansfield made his name, and they cut three albums, which included their classic 1980 debut, *From A to B*.

Coupled with Mansfield's 12-string guitar, the band's bright synth sounds contrasted with the cold electronica offered by acts such as John Foxx, the Human League (MK1) and Gary Numan, while the frontman's thought-provoking lyrics were imbued with a cynicism and world-weariness that may well have appealed to a young Pål Waaktaar Gamst. 'Living by Numbers', the band's biggest hit, featured a somewhat prophetic refrain of 'They don't want your name / Just your number' that was well ahead of its time. And then there was 'This World of Water', which was described by the band's drummer, Phil Towner, as a song about 'drowning in society' ('The water here still rising / It's come to drag me down') and 'Dead Fish (Don't Swim Home)', which depicted Mansfield's fear of nuclear attack in an age when Cold War tensions were still rife ('They play their games with toys / They welcome a war / When will the big fish learn / Just what life is for').

By 1982's *Warp* album, Mansfield was employing a far more experimental approach, which included a somewhat unconventional double-header of songs titled 'All You Need Is Love' (an original composition followed by a cover of the

Beatles' 1967 anthem). 'The thing with New Musik is that, although it's a pop group, there's no reason why you can't produce more experimental music,' he said. 'We call it an experimental band which is literally experimenting with what does and doesn't work.'[3]

MAKING ALL THE MUSIC HE CAN MAKE

A lack of commercial success ultimately resulted in New Musik's demise, but the split meant Mansfield could now concentrate on working in the studio, where he felt more at home. Over the ensuing years, he attracted a plethora of both new and established acts, including the Damned and their moonlighting guitarist, Captain Sensible. 'My girlfriend at the time was a big New Musik fan, who were the acceptable face of 80s synth-pop,' he recalled. 'She played their music all the time, it drove me mad. Then I started really liking it. We went to see them at the Fairfield Halls in Croydon, and I have to admit it was really good, great songs.'[4] The collaboration led to one of the more unlikely hits of the decade: a quirky version of the *South Pacific* show tune 'Happy Talk', which hit the top of the charts in the summer of 1982.

Other clients included Naked Eyes, who released two albums, including *Burning Bridges*, which featured New Musik's Phil Towner on drums. The duo scored a transatlantic hit with 'Always Something There to Remind Me' (a cover of the Bacharach and David standard), but eventually disbanded. Naked Eyes' classically trained keyboardist, Rob Fisher, also formed Planet Ha Ha with the Mansfield brothers (Tony and Lee), and reportedly cut an album's worth of material (including a theme tune for the BBC children's game show *Finders Keepers*). (Fisher later formed Climie Fisher with Simon Climie.)

Mansfield also produced an album for Mari Wilson, registering a memorable UK Top 10 single in the process with 'Just What I Always Wanted'. He also applied a pop glaze to Aztec Camera's 'Walk Out to Winter' single, as their frontman, Roddy Frame, recalled in an interview with the BBC in 2003: 'We used one of the first Fairlight synthesisers – which were one of the first ones in England – and I remember we took it to a rehearsal studio, and a heavy metal band on their way out spat on it! We brought it to *The Old Grey Whistle Test* studios, and people were so kind of taken with this new piece of technology that the camera men wanted to do a special shot of it to start the song, like it was more important than the band. And that was kind of prophetic, in a way, for the 80s, that the equipment became more important than the bands.'

One other notable client was the synth-pop act Vicious Pink, who released the memorable 'Cccan't You See' (a cult favourite on both sides of the Atlantic). Via the band's website, their keyboardist, Brian Moss, recalled encountering a-ha after they had finished working with Mansfield at Ridge Farm Studio in the summer of

1984: 'After the recordings were finished, we had a big party. Free food and booze, with guests including Kirsty MacColl, Captain Sensible, Naked Eyes, a-ha, Tony Mansfield, Speedy Keen [of Thunderclap Newman fame] and our friends and family. We had a big firework display, too. One of the lads from a-ha ended up sleeping in a closet as there were no rooms left!'

ORCHESTRA FOR SALE

In terms of the history of a-ha, there was one instrument advocated by Tony Mansfield that would have a considerable impact on their sound. The Fairlight CMI [Computer Music Instrument] was a highly advanced digital workstation that enabled users to store recorded sounds and alter their pitch via its digital synthesiser. Boasting a light pen that enabled touchscreen control, the machine's futuristic look earned it a spot on the BBC's science and technology show, *Tomorrow's World*, in 1980. 'The scope it offers musicians in being able to create almost any sound you care to name is nearly limitless,' said the programme's presenter, Kieran Prendiville, who competently demonstrated its sampling capabilities.

'Imagine your own orchestra,' began a magazine advert with the enticing tag line, 'Orchestra for sale?'. 'Or just one instrument that offers even greater creative potential. A ludicrous proposition? Not if you owned a Fairlight computer musical instrument. A concept so revolutionary that its capabilities are limited only by your own imagination!'

It's hard to comprehend now, but when it was originally introduced in 1979, the Fairlight cost almost as much as a house, while the Series II model, released in 1982, cost a whopping £30,000! Early users included Kate Bush and Peter Gabriel (who became something of a salesman when he formed a company – Syco Systems – with his cousin to distribute the instrument in the UK), but the instrument soon became a ubiquitous presence throughout the decade. But while acts such as the Pet Shop Boys were huge Fairlight enthusiasts, not everyone was as keen, and Phil Collins' *No Jacket Required* album vehemently declared 'There is no Fairlight on this record' in the credits!

Fledgling producers such as Trevor Horn and Tony Mansfield were keen to jump on the Fairlight bandwagon as well. The Buggles, fronted by Horn, were one of the first acts to use the new technology on their appropriately titled second album, *Adventures in Modern Recording*, and he later produced classic Fairlight-heavy singles for the likes of Frankie Goes to Hollywood and the Art of Noise. Mansfield, too, was a key exponent, and many of his productions were laced with Fairlight flourishes.

LOST IN MUSIK

Certainly on paper, Tony Mansfield was the perfect fit. Aside from being a talented musician and producer, he was a proven hitmaker, and his pioneering use of new digital instruments such as the Fairlight and its rival, the Synclavier, made him an attractive – and exciting – proposition for forward-thinking acts such as a-ha. Initially, the band were impressed by the appointment. 'We were excited to work with Tony,' said Magne, 'and as a person we got on really well. We did, however, get frustrated when he started obsessing over competing with Trevor Horn, who had produced Frankie Goes to Hollywood to great fanfare. This resulted in humongous amounts of equipment being rented, and more and more programmed stuff. Most of the time in that studio, Pål and I worried a lot, and we would anxiously take turns going into the control room to raise our concerns, while mindful we did not bring the whole process to a halt.'

'Tony turned out to be an absolute whizz on the Fairlight,' recalled Pål. 'Up until this point, even though our music sounded electronic, we never used much computer technology to record or perform, even the stuff that sounded machine-like.'[5]

Ultimately, the union with Mansfield proved to be a mismatch, and the band later bemoaned the producer's methods and extensive use of the Fairlight. Captain Sensible confirmed some similar issues with the producer: 'It got a bit machiney,' he said. 'Tony Mansfield wanted to be progressive and pioneering when it came to production ... After *The Power of Love,* Tony decided we needed some changes. He was like, "Third album, Captain, I've got a new concept. You're gonna like this. You've got to be ahead of everyone else in production circles – you can't follow. The new concept is – one word – WEIRD!" I'd had a brilliant career and we'd made some marvellous records together. This time he was wrong, and "weird" wasn't the next best thing. So the whole project was flushed down the toilet.'[6]

Mansfield also had form when it came to scrapped recordings. He had produced *80-f,* an album by the rock band After the Fire, which was then rejected by CBS. Although some of Mansfield's elements were retained, Queen's then-producer, Reinhold Mack, was brought in to finish the 1980 album. There were clear echoes of this scenario when Warner Brothers later voiced their disapproval of Mansfield's version of a-ha's debut album, which would ultimately lead to a similar rescue operation.

Another problem arose when deciding which song to release as a single, since there was no obvious candidate. 'Living a Boy's Adventure Tale' was considered (and a test pressing is even said to exist), but in October 1984, the label eventually went with a song Morten had championed right from the outset.

CHAPTER SEVEN
THE FIRST SINGLE

The origins of 'Take On Me' can be traced back to Magne and Pål's Bridges period and the abandonment of their second album – as Poem – in the spring of 1981. Following their ill-fated recording sessions at Sound Art Studio, the band resumed their routine of songwriting and rehearsing, but at a different venue this time. Pål called a nursery school in Manglerud to see if the band could rehearse there, and they had an early run-through of a riff-based track that was, stylistically, different from anything the band had recorded before.

Inspired by the Doors' 'Light My Fire', Magne had come up with the riff when he was just 15 years old, but it later appeared during sessions for the Poem album, but reportedly attached to one of the out-takes, titled 'Panorama'. 'I referred to it as "Paranoia Panorama", said Magne, 'which was a much better title!'[1]

The riff later resurfaced, with Pål providing the lyrics for an embryonic version of a-ha's biggest hit. 'It started with the verses which I wrote on my parents' mid-century sofa in Manglerud,' he said. 'Magne added his riff at a later stage.'

Magne added: 'Yes, Pål had some chords and the beginnings of a melody for the verses – it was highly embryonic. I immediately – which is not often – heard the riff in my head. I played it over different chords and insisted it was super-catchy. Pål said it sounded like a bubblegum commercial and suggested we lose it. The song was then fashioned around that riff in many different ways in different settings: new choruses, changes to verses, different lyrics and, eventually, it became "Take On Me", with Morten changing the new chorus somewhat. The *one* thing which never changed and was consistent throughout was my keyboard riff.'

According to Pål, the track was originally titled 'Miss Eerie', and the recording reveals a fascinating snapshot of a work in progress. Certainly it's a far spikier song than the one that would evolve into 'Lesson One', boasting an opening riff similar to the Sex Pistols' 'Pretty Vacant'. As is evident from the opening verse, the song bore no similarities to the worldwide smash hit it would later become:

Girl in the air
Two waving hands and
Somewhat near
Two eyes calling me
Do let her be

Her name is Miss Eerie
Couldn't make a sound
Just kept falling
Down, down . . .

TAKE ON ME

Written by Pål Waaktaar-Savoy, Magne Furuholmen and Morten Harket
Produced by Tony Mansfield
Released: October 1984
Chart position: 3 (Norway)

Following the break-up of Poem and the official formation of an as-yet-unnamed new band in September 1982, Magne and Pål ran through their repertoire for their new singer's benefit, which apparently didn't include any of the then unreleased *Våkenatt* songs. 'I don't think we even had a cassette of those songs at that point,' said Pål. 'Anyway, it was too exciting to delve into new stuff.'

One of the new songs was 'Miss Eerie', which has often been referred to as 'The Juicy Fruit Song', since Morten claimed that the catchy melody reminded him of the Wrigley's Juicy Fruit TV commercial that promised 'a packet full of sunshine'. However, Magne said the track was known by that name long before Morten entered the picture.

'[Pål] had a crappy old nylon-stringed guitar with hippy paintings on it and he strummed the chords with Magne playing the riff on piano,' recalled Morten. 'The moment I heard it, I knew it was the one that would break the whole thing open.'[2]

The track was developed further during the trio's sessions in Nærsnes that autumn but the sparse, somewhat half-hearted demo – with a rather cheap-sounding keyboard part – seemed to indicate it wasn't high on their list of priorities. There was also an air of flippancy in the arrangement, too, as Morten – somewhat bizarrely – attempted a cockerel's crow during the second verse! At this stage, the chorus didn't exist, and the bridge part that gave the demo its new title of 'Lesson One' was later removed ('So here's a kid lesson, my number one / All's well that starts well and ends with the sun').

By the time the track was picked up again and demoed at Rendezvous in 1983, the band had, between them, finalised a new arrangement. Morten had dispensed with the chicken impressions, while Pål had fixed the lyrics with Magne's help. 'It is one of the songs Pål struggled to finish lyrics on – it was too upbeat,' said Magne. 'Unusually, I am credited on the lyrics of this song, and it is because I had to come up with some of the lines in the verses as there were holes in it right up until recording, and Pål was stuck.'

As one of the earlier lyric drafts reveals, the song's original opening couplet was 'All I can see now / Is another day of misery'. This was wisely shelved, while the original chorus ('Take on me / Take me on / Love is all I can offer you') was also amended.

'My focus was to give it more than just the sugar rush of the verse and riff,' said Pål, 'like tweaking the lyrics, adding spooky chords from "She's Humming a Tune" for the middle eight, and racking my brains to come up with a chorus that could make you feel something.'

In terms of the vocal, Morten was encouraged by Pål to use the full range of his voice. 'Pål had the idea of really using my vocal range in the chorus, having notes rising in octaves like Strauss's *Also Sprach Zarathustra*,' said Morten. 'As for hitting that last high note, you either have wings or you don't – the voice is not in the throat, it's in the blood. It's what you envisage, what you believe. People think the chorus is the hard part in "Take On Me", but they're wrong. The hard part was making the verses bounce.'[3]

As for the title itself, the band were often asked to explain the song's grammatical quirks. 'When I write lyrics in English, I feel it's an advantage to be Norwegian, because I see the language as something exciting and full of possibilities,' explained Pål. 'I can pick out ordinary words or phrases and make them sound new and interesting . . . Look at "Take On Me". Most people have to think twice about the title before they get to like it. To me, to "take on" somebody means to notice them and take time to find out what they're really like.'[4]

Along one of the banks of the River Thames in Twickenham, the band recorded 'Take On Me' and several other tracks at Pete Townshend's Eel Pie Studios. Acts including Pink Floyd, Marillion and, of course, the Who had recorded there, and the facility was well known to producer Tony Mansfield, as recordings by Captain Sensible and Naked Eyes had been mixed there.

The arrangement of 'Take On Me' was tightened up with the removal of the riff between the first chorus and the second verse, but little else survived from the Rendezvous demo as Mansfield sought to put his own stamp on a track he was reportedly not that impressed with.

While Trevor Horn had used the Fairlight to great effect with his production of Frankie Goes to Hollywood's 'Relax' the previous year, the technology didn't quite have the same transformative impact on a-ha's own debut single. For the instrumental break, the Fairlight's then popular ORCH5 sample was used, which had been popularised by a Horn-produced 'Owner of a Lonely Heart' (by Yes) and, later, the Art of Noise's sleeper hit, 'Close (to the Edit)'.

'He only wanted to program his own thing,' recalled Pål. 'We thought that we had to be open to new ideas, something we regretted once we heard the result. We were very much involved in the album, too, but the recordings were based on his principle that everything had to go through his Fairlight . . . The first version of "Take On Me" was terrible. It sounded like a robot was playing.'[5]

Morten was slightly less scathing but agreed that the band's contributions had become marginalised: 'Tony Mansfield was brilliant. The problem with him was that the whole thing was more of a one-man show. But, as many ideas as Mansfield had, they were his ideas and not ours.'[6] (Mansfield's original recordings were later collated, both on the super deluxe edition of *Hunting High and Low* in 2015 and on a separate vinyl-only edition – titled *The Early Alternate Mixes* – for Record Store Day on 13 April 2019.)

Once their maverick producer had exited the album sessions, several tracks were reworked and 'Take On Me' – backed with 'And You Tell Me' – was released in the UK to a minimum of fanfare in October 1984.

A rather cheap-looking split-screen video – directed by Stevie Price – was shot to accompany the release. As Morten recounted in a TV interview with Carolyn Marshall in 1988, it was a largely disastrous experience: 'On the set, suddenly they appeared one by one – about 12 of them I think – girls, rather lightly clad . . . We realised soon that those clothes were to go during the video. They made them look like prostitutes, somehow. It was a disaster, it was scrapped completely.' In a separate interview that year, Pål added: 'We were new to the business and didn't want to pretend we knew everything about how to sell the product, so we gave them [the label] a chance. After that, we wanted a say in every aspect of the marketing.'[7]

The single did attract some reviews and *No.1* magazine praised Morten for his 'incredible vocal range', but ultimately a lack of promotion sealed the single's fate (it reportedly sold just 300 copies). In the band's homeland, however, it fared far better, peaking at No. 3 (at positions 1 and 2 were Stevie Wonder's 'I Just Called to

Say I Love You' and Wham!'s 'Freedom', respectively). Via *Lørdagssirkuset* [Saturday Circus], the band also made their debut on Norwegian TV with a short interview (with presenter Rita Westvik), followed by a playback performance.

For the UK market at least, it wasn't meant to be, and 'Take On Me' was one of a number of songs that would ultimately belong to 1985, rather than 1984. For example, the Pet Shop Boys' 'West End Girls' would need a Stephen Hague makeover before it eventually became a huge hit, while King's debut single, 'Love and Pride', would need a rerelease before finally securing a Top 10 position.

For a-ha, it was back to the drawing board, in both a literal and metaphorical sense.

STOP! AND MAKE YOUR MIND UP (B-side)
Written by Pål Waaktaar-Savoy
Produced by a-ha with John Ratcliff
Released: October 1984

Tucked away on the B-side of the now super-rare 12-inch format of 'Take On Me' was this playful but repetitive number, which the band had recorded with John Ratcliff at Rendezvous earlier in the year. Lyrics such as 'You've come to my head / I want you / Come back to bed' have ensured its throwaway status, but it's a confident production with some inventive synth work and confident use of the LinnDrum.

CHAPTER EIGHT

HUNTING HIGH AND LOW

The arrangements on our debut were very poppy, but the lyrics were dark – but the attention was not on the lyrics, which was a shame. Because of our commercial sound, we found ourselves in a hailstorm of pop stardom.
– Magne Furuholmen, *Record Collector*, 2009

Released: June 1985
Chart position: 2 (UK), 1 (Norway), 10 (Germany), 15 (US)

A-ha's debut album arrived in US shops in June 1985, while its release in the UK followed in November that year. The bulk of the production credits were attributed to Tony Mansfield but, in truth, many of the plaudits belonged to the band and John Ratcliff who, between them, managed to salvage the album after Warner Brothers had threatened to tear up the contract after hearing the Fairlight-heavy recordings. 'They thought the recording didn't sound like the one we had played for them in the beginning,' Ratcliff recalled in 2015. 'I told them I could save the album. They gave me a few weeks but made it clear that a-ha must be kept out of the process while I finished the job. That was difficult, because I had always been honest with the boys. Everything was at stake: Would they make a career or would they be on the first boat back to Norway? Some of the things I did are still unknown to the boys. They don't know how close they were to the boat back home.'[1]

Since the band didn't have the luxury of scrapping their debut album and starting from scratch like the Smiths had done in 1983, the existing material was simply reworked. Under Ratcliff's supervision, engineer Neill King worked with the band on a new version of the album. 'I had worked many times at Eel Pie, and it was after a-ha had been recording there with Tony Mansfield for a good few weeks that I received a call from the studio manager telling me Tony was leaving the project,' he explained. 'I wasn't told why, but they wanted to know if I would come in. They had done all of the programmed drums and some synths, and since I had engineered there and knew the room, they wanted me to work on the bed tracks, overdubbing guitars, vocals, backing vocals and some extra synths, and then do the mix.'[2]

'Take On Me' was eventually rerecorded with Alan Tarney, while 'Love Is Reason' was recorded in a completely new location. Elsewhere, 'The Sun Always Shines on TV' was added to the album at a very late stage. That the album was completed at all was an achievement in itself but, listened to now, it's a surprisingly cohesive body of work given the veritable piecemeal process.

For the album's front cover, the band purposely aimed for a *Rumble Fish* aesthetic. Francis Ford Coppola's 1983 adaptation of the S.E. Hinton book was reportedly one of Pål's favourite films, and it's evident from Morten's muscly appearance in a white vest that there was an attempt to replicate the look of Matt Dillon's Rusty James character.

In the UK, the album peaked at No. 2 for five weeks but couldn't shake off Dire Straits' huge-selling *Brothers in Arms*. However, due to the enduring popularity of 'Take On Me' and live favourites such as 'The Sun Always Shines on TV' and the title track, *Hunting High and Low* has attained iconic status. It was released as a two-CD set in 2010 and received the super deluxe five-disc treatment in 2015.

The band are currently in the midst of a year-long world tour, performing the album in its entirety for the first time since 2010. 'We're in a situation now where we're looking back and maybe we're able to, in retrospect, enjoy what we created in the '80s,' said Magne. 'We kind of kept running, kept looking forwards. Right now, doing this first album in its entirety is a bit of an exercise that revitalises those first songs for us.'[3]

TAKE ON ME
Written by Pål Waaktaar-Savoy, Magne Furuholmen and Morten Harket
Produced by Alan Tarney
Chart position: 2 (UK), 1 (Norway), 1 (Germany), 1 (US)

> *Something tells me this trio are going to have a hit sooner or later.*
> – *No.1* magazine, April 1985

Although their debut single had flopped in the UK, the band were convinced of the song's commercial potential and persuaded Warner Brothers to bankroll a new version. Alan Tarney – the label's original choice of producer – was eventually persuaded to helm the subsequent session in February 1985. 'Warners wanted the song to sound the best it possibly could, and they were willing to go over budget to get it right,' he explained. 'I was actually involved with David Cassidy's *Romance* album at that time, so I took a day off and the boys came down to RG Jones [Studios] in Wimbledon, which is where I was working, and we recorded and mixed the entire song there.'[4]

Tarney was a vastly experienced songwriter and producer who had worked with the likes of Barbara Dickson, Olivia Newton-John and Bonnie Tyler but, by the mid-80s, his name was largely synonymous with housewife favourites such as Cliff Richard and Leo Sayer who, between them, had enjoyed huge hits such as 'We Don't Talk Anymore', 'Wired for Sound' and 'More Than I Can Say'.

However, what most of his clients had in common was they were all solo artists and, up until this point, he hadn't been able to translate the same studio magic to bands. These included Squeeze and the Lotus Eaters, who both registered flop singles with 'Annie Get Your Gun' (1982) and 'You Don't Need Someone New' (1983), respectively. 'Take On Me' would change all that.

For the new recording, Tarney revisited the original Rendezvous demo and soon decided the band should use that as a template for the revamp. 'To my mind, the original version of "Take On Me" that the boys themselves had recorded in

Sydenham with John Ratcliff was the hit version,' he said. 'So all I did was recreate the original demo, the one from Sydenham. That was the one that had all the charm.'[5]

'It was such a joy to go back to our usual way of recording,' recalled Pål. 'Within a couple of hours at RG Jones, "Take On Me" already sounded very much like itself. Magne and I did some passes, each at our own synth playing off each other, which laid a nice bed for the track. After that, we recreated all the best bits from the demo with improved sounds.'[6]

Since Tarney was concurrently working on David Cassidy's future hit single 'The Last Kiss' (which also featured George Michael), the track had to be recorded quickly and, incredibly, it was completed within just a few days.

With its propulsive LinnDrum intro and dynamic hybrid of programmed and analogue parts, the new version of 'Take On Me' was released in April 1985 and seemed set to conquer the charts. However, although the record label had green-lighted the rerecording, they didn't give it the promotional push required to send it into the all-important Top 40, which in those days was often the difference between *Top of the Pops* and bottom of the pile. The band did secure a coveted spot on BBC's *Saturday Superstore* show, but it wasn't enough.

It was obvious to the band that they didn't have a good enough team behind them in the UK but, across the big pond, Warner Brothers were far more enthusiastic, and this was backed up when the label's Jeff Ayeroff commissioned an expensive new promotional video, based on the innovative rotoscope animation methods used in Michael Patterson's short film *Commuter*. 'Rotoscoping uses live action motion but my drawing style anyway was very loose and sketchy – no one had really drawn anything like that style before,' said the pioneering animator. 'Rotoscope was usually done in a dry kind of way, very static or very sterile looking. But mine is more about just deriving the motion and creating a feeling of energy.'[7]

'*Commuter* was great. I paid Michael Patterson $2,500 to give me a six-month exclusive on his services, so I'd get to use him first,' explained Ayeroff. 'Soon after, I heard a-ha's "Take On Me" and fell in love with the song. Then I saw a picture of the band, and it was like, "Do people actually look like this?" Morten Harket was one of the best-looking men in the world.'[8]

By the time 'Take On Me' was released, MTV was in full swing, and music executives such as Ayeroff were throwing money around like confetti. In the opulent 80s, huge investments in now-iconic videos such as Duran Duran's 'Rio' and Michael Jackson's 'Thriller' were paying dividends. One other artist that benefitted was Madonna, whose provocative video for 'Like a Virgin' went some way to catapulting the singer to global stardom in 1984. 'Madonna was on the cover of *Rolling Stone*,' recalled Ayeroff. 'So we went to Venice, like a bunch of fucking whack jobs. I don't know what we spent – $150,000? $175,000? – but it was way more than we'd ever spent on a video . . . What did I do on the shoot? I sat on the back of the barge and yelled "duck," so Madonna didn't smack her head on the bridges!'[9]

Ayeroff contacted Steve Barron, a former camera assistant who had worked on Richard Donner's *Superman* movie. His vast experience of directing promo clips stretched back to the Jam's 'Strange Town' in 1979, which eventually led to helming memorable videos for OMD ('Maid of Orleans'), the Human League ('Don't You Want Me'), Michael Jackson ('Billie Jean') and many others, before eventually branching out into the world of movies with 1984's *Electric Dreams*. 'I worked with Jeff Ayeroff when he was commissioning videos at A&M, on Bryan Adams and a couple of other things,' recalled Barron. 'Jeff said to me, "I need an amazing video for these guys. You can have as much time as you'd like. And I'm going to give you £100,000 to do it." Which was an unheard of amount, especially for an unknown act.'[10]

With both Patterson and Barron now on board, they could begin work on the part-animated video. 'At the first meeting, I had the feeling that we would get along well and probably work together for a long time,' said Morten. 'I liked his presentation right away – he explained how the animation worked and that he had devised a story for the video that would captivate the viewer.'[11]

However, as Morten recalled in 1985, there were still some ongoing issues with regard to their visas. 'We've only specific permits for the recording sessions and the video shoot,' he said. 'We've been thrown out of England two or three times. We'd stayed here too long and had been here so many times. But we managed to stay because an MP has taken us under his wing.'[12]

The multi-award-winning video – which included a more dramatic musical ending than the single/album version – would take several months to make, but it was an instant hit with MTV viewers in the US, who were captivated both by its groundbreaking visuals and its romantic storyline. Although there were some intermittent shots of Magne and Pål playing, respectively, a Prophet-5 synthesiser and a Rickenbacker 345 guitar, the main focal point was provided by Morten and a former Hot Gossip dancer named Bunty Bailey. Some of the café scenes were shot at Kim's Café in Wandsworth, which still exists today, but with the somewhat appropriate new name of the Savoy Café.

'Morten and Bunty became a couple pretty much straight after the video shoot, maybe even during.' said Magne. 'Did I have the feeling he was trying to flirt with her? I always had that impression when I was around Morten! He had this insatiable curiosity for any of the women who came our way. He was doing a lot of posing and prancing, and the attraction between them made the video irresistible.'[13]

Just a few months after Bobbysocks! had won the Eurovision Song Contest for Norway in May 1985 with 'La det swinge' [Let It Swing], 'Take On Me' quickly gained traction in the US. After a steady ascent, the single eventually climbed to the top of the Billboard chart, earning the band – in the words of John Lennon – their 'top of the mountain' moment and gateway to worldwide success.

The rereleased single also climbed to No. 1 in Norway and was a huge hit in the UK, where it peaked at No. 2 for three weeks. (It was denied top spot by Jennifer Rush's ballad 'The Power of Love', the bestselling single that year.)

But what was the reaction like back home? 'It was massive!' replied Tonje. 'But still pretty much just like before around family and friends. In Norway, a big healthy appetite for humble pie is expected. All the families kept their cool. The parents were calm, collected and polite towards fans and everyone who behaved nicely. Siblings carried on with their own thing as a-ha were out there conquering the world, but when they came home, everything was just . . . normal. I got letters from fans, little gifts, a collect call at 4 a.m. from Australia!'

Dead of the winter. Left to right: Morten Harket, Bunty Bailey and Magne Furuholmen.

To paraphrase one of Pål's lyrics, nothing would ever be the same again.

TRAIN OF THOUGHT
Written by Pål Waaktaar-Savoy
Produced by Tony Mansfield
Chart position: 8 (UK), 14 (Germany)

There was some bemusement during a-ha's *Electric Summer* tour in 2018 when the band launched into a version of 'Train of Thought' that some sections of the audiences weren't familiar with. The band were, in fact, playing the original version of the track, which had been demoed at Rendezvous. But its origins went back even further, when it was taped during the band's sessions in Nærsnes in

1982 and provisionally called 'The Sphinx', a title which had possibly been sourced from Act IV of *Peer Gynt*. 'Morten was very into David Bowie and stuff like that, and he really wanted to do a song in that lower register of his voice.'[14] recalled Pål.

The lyrics to 'The Sphinx' – and, indeed, other songs from this fertile period in the early 80s – represented something of a progression in Pål's writing. While tracks such as 'Need No Doctor' and 'Asleep' hinted at a more introspective lyrical path, other songs occupied more surrealistic territory, as evidenced by the epic 'Waterworks' ('Did it take a scream to get in? / It'll take a scream to get out'), 'The Leap' ('My room drowned in white smoke / I can't breathe no more / I got my head up from the pillows of ashes') and 'The Stranger's Town' ('You don't lose your mind like I do / Those clouds are upside down / This is the stranger's town'). By the turn of the decade, Pål had become an avid reader and, during a gap year in which he waited for Magne to graduate from high school, he spent many hours in Oslo cafés absorbing literary classics. Just as Gunvor Hofmo's work had seeped into many of the lyrics on *Fakkeltog*, the influence of the likes of Fyodor Dostoevsky, Franz Kafka and Knut Hamsun would eventually manifest in future songs, including 'The Sphinx'. Like Kafka's *The Metamorphosis*, 'Train of Thought' features reflections on the mundanity of commuter life ('He grabs a pile of letters from a small suitcase / Disappears into an office / It's another working day'), but the protagonist's mind is perpetually distracted ('And his thoughts were full of strangers').

In the Rendezvous demo, there are pan flute sounds and additional lyrics that would give the song its final title ('A sudden interruption on his train of thought'), but essentially it follows the template of the Nærsnes demo (mercifully, Morten chose not to reprise his sinister laugh!). By the time the band had recorded the song with Tony Mansfield, the bluesy riff had been abandoned (and later recycled for 1990's 'Cold River'), although the pan flute motif was carried forward. There was some noticeable decluttering in post-production with parts of the vocal redone, but the basic track was retained. (For the single version, Alan Tarney and John Hudson remixed the track.)

Although there were some strong arguments for 'Hunting High and Low' being released as the album's third single, a video (by directors Candace Reckinger and Michael Patterson) had already been completed for 'Train of Thought', which completed a trilogy of semi-animated videos. Patterson's groundbreaking *Commuter* animation from 1981, which had inspired the 'Take On Me' video, was sourced for the new black and white promo, which included Pål playing pan pipes. (Interestingly, pan flutist Roar Engelberg recorded a version of 'Hunting High and Low' for his 1999 album, *Har en drøm* [Have a Dream], which included guest musicians such as Marius Müller and Per Hillestad.)

In 2019, H.R. Francis published a sci-fi novella that bore the song's name. '*Train of Thought* follows one man on a journey of enlightenment, as he is forced to explore his thoughts, fears and hopes for a better future,' wrote the author on her website. 'It is based on Norwegian band a-ha's 1985 debut album, *Hunting High and Low*, and is my imagination digging deeper into its well-loved songs and videos, as well as its unreleased tracks. It gives a sci-fi look at the 48 hours before a famous motorbike race leads to a hero's escape from a comic.'

HUNTING HIGH AND LOW
Written by Pål Waaktaar-Savoy
Produced by Tony Mansfield
Single version produced by Tony Mansfield and Alan Tarney
Chart position: 5 (UK), 10 (Norway), 11 (Germany)

Strange things had been happening in Mrs Pepperpot's house. It all began when a little girl came to the door selling penny raffle tickets for a tablecloth. Mrs Pepperpot hunted high and low until she found a penny; it was a nice shiny one, because someone had been polishing it.
– Alf Prøysen, *Mrs Pepperpot's Penny Watchman*

On the eve of their first world tour – which kicked off in Perth, Australia, on 3 June 1986 – the band released the acoustic guitar-driven title track from their debut album as a single. Although Pål would later claim the production was 'too family friendly', it was his favourite song on the album, and easily one of the best ballads released that year.

The song had originally been written and demoed at Rendezvous in the spring of 1984 but, like 'The Sun Always Shines on TV', it had initially formed part of another track. Pål soon latched on to its commercial possibilities and, typical of his working methods at the time, crafted a brand new song. (Another line from the original demo – 'Something dark against the light' – was later used for 'I Dream Myself Alive'.)

The title itself had been inspired by a line in an English translation of one of the books in Alf Prøysen's *Teskjekjerringa* [Mrs Pepperpot] series. However, the lyrics were clearly inspired by Pål's girlfriend, Lauren, whom he'd originally met in 1983 during one of the band's nights out in London. 'We met at the Hippodrome,' Pål told *Dagbladet* years later. 'It was the only place Lauren knew about and the only place where I, Morten and Magne came in for free. We met there and, later, Lauren returned to the States, and I built up a £3,000 phone bill!'

Other hotspots of the band's included Camden Palace (now KOKO), a concert venue that also doubled up as a nightclub. Steve Strange and Rusty Egan from 'Fade to Grey' hitmakers, Visage, often hosted evenings there, while other Blitz Kid luminaries, such as Boy George and the Kemp brothers from Spandau Ballet, were known visitors of the trendy nightspot. *Smash Hits'* Deborah Steele described it as 'a place full of famous people trying to look ordinary and ordinary people trying to look famous'. The members of a-ha may not have liked this generalisation, but they were certainly keen to make themselves stand out while out and about in the capital, with Pål seemingly happy to allow Morten to apply make-up to his face. The singer, meanwhile, was keen to make an impression himself. 'He'd have white Dulux paint in his hair and he'd hang out at the Camden Palace,' recalled Magne. 'He'd get invited to all these parties and clubs, and Pål and I would just tag along. As long as you could get in for free and steal people's drinks behind their backs, that would be a pretty successful night out!'[15]

Lauren later claimed that Pål was the most intelligent person she'd ever met, but the Boston-born student – who was doing a film studies semester at the time – eventually had to fly back to the States after her stepfather became ill.

Like other songs composed during this period, 'Hunting High and Low' documents both Pål's affections for Lauren ('She's the sweetest love I could find') and his struggles with their lengthy separations ('And now she's telling me she's got to go away / . . . Watch me tearing myself to pieces'). 'There's always this underlying fear that [love] can never last,' said Pål, candidly. 'I mean, months can go by without our being able to meet. All the songs on the album were written in an attempt to secure a place in her heart for me. I wanted to put so much of myself into her that she couldn't live without me. I admit I used every musical trick in the book to get her to love me. Every single song is a prayer for attention.'[16]

It's evident from the early version of the track recorded at Eel Pie Studios how restrained the production is in comparison to other tracks on the album, as if both a-ha and Tony Mansfield were aware of both its pan-generational qualities and commercial possibilities. Morten's impassioned vocal was his best to date, while emotional tension was heightened by Magne's symphonic synth parts. Elsewhere, some effective seagull sounds gave it a pleasingly nostalgic touch.

Although the band could easily have released the finished album version as a single, Alan Tarney was hired to add his magic, which largely entailed adding some string parts – recorded at Abbey Road Studios – which had been scored by the Art of Noise's Anne Dudley.

In their review, *No.1* described it as 'a nice break from the frenetic songs', but *Record Mirror*'s Jim Reid wasn't quite as kind: 'Happy, healthy, smiling Scandinavian chappies singing washing up liquid commercial pop, I can live with. Poster mags of happy, smiling, singing Scandinavian chappies, I can live with. But this, the first sign of a curled lip and a furrowed brow, is where I pass

the smorgasbord. The angst, the strain, the melodrama, the syrupy background – it can't be serious can it?'

The snow-capped video was directed by Steve Barron and included Morten morphing into both an eagle and a shark to depict a hunt. A shot of a shark being harpooned – presumably added to signify the writer's pain of separation – may not have gotten past today's censors, but it was certainly eye-catching, and the band later received a Spellemann award for it. (Indicative of the band's popularity at the time, a segment featuring the making of the promo was also broadcast on the BBC's long-running TV show *Blue Peter*.)

Although the heartfelt ballad provided the band with another big hit in the UK – and a first appearance, on volume seven, of the popular *Now That's What I Call Music* series – the track failed to chart in the US. According to Pål, Warner Brothers didn't want to release it as a single as it was 'too atypical'.

The song – which was inexplicably banned by the BBC during the Gulf War in the early 1990s – was later covered by the Bergen band Poor Rich Ones, who released it as a single in 1998. A decade later, Chris Martin – who was a well-known admirer of a-ha's – performed the song during a Coldplay encore at the Oslo Spektrum in September 2008, accompanied by Magne on keyboards. (Coldplay also covered 'The Living Daylights' at the same venue in 2002, but considerably less successfully.)

Nearly 30 years after its original release, Morten recorded a new, acoustic version of 'Hunting High and Low', for inclusion in the short film *Hemland* [Homeland], by the Swedish film-maker Sara Broos, which formed part of a documentary series titled *Fans*. Morten also appeared in the episode, which aired in Sweden in May 2015. The film revolves around a refugee named Raghad Kanawahti, who cited the a-ha classic as the song that meant the most to her when growing up in war-torn Syria. 'I had no idea there were people there who were listening to what we were doing, and that it mattered to them,' said Morten on his official website.

THE BLUE SKY
Written by Pål Waaktaar-Savoy
Produced by Tony Mansfield

An exercise in introspection, rather than an observation about the weather, this track took its inspiration from a coffee lounge named the Blue Sky in affluent Westbourne Grove – hence its working title of 'The Coffee Lounge' – although Pål observes it wasn't such a prosperous area back then ('it looked pretty ragged in those days,' he said.)

En route to its finished Eel Pie version, the song went through a series of lyrical (and musical) changes. Within the context of a Central London café, various fears and insecurities are played out. The narrator anxiously craves a cigarette ('I'm dying for a cigarette in the coffee lounge') and ponders asking the lady at his table for one. But at the same time he's self-conscious about his accent ('Would she laugh at my accent and make fun of me?'). He goes into daydream mode. His 'paper cups of coffee' grow cold while he looks around at the 'faces that surround' him. He feels the intimidatory glances from the posters on the walls. It could almost be a character from a Kafka novel, but we assume it's Pål ruminating on his anxieties, as well as his concerns about having an old head on young shoulders ('I'm older than my looks and older than my years / I'm too young to take on my deepest fears').

Not only are Pål's skills as an interpreter of emotions evident, it's also clear from placing the lyrical drafts back to back that he was also a dedicated song craftsman, constantly tweaking the lyrics until coming up with a set of words he was happy with – the removal of odd couplets (for example, 'The only risk I'm running is a runny nose / She's got such a bad, bad cold') was just part of the process. Pål made one further tweak (reportedly at Andrew Wickham's insistence), removing the opening line about the cigarette and replacing it with something far more startling ('I find it hard to breathe as life just eats away'). It later came as no surprise that Morrissey was a fan of the band.

Fairlight doyen Tony Mansfield applied a suitable – if somewhat mechanical – pop gloss to proceedings, and also experimented with the interpolation of Norwegian dialogue that was, presumably, designed to emulate café chit-chat (sadly, it was edited out).

LIVING A BOY'S ADVENTURE TALE
Written by Pål Waaktaar-Savoy and Morten Harket
Produced by Tony Mansfield

Like 'The Blue Sky', this pocket-sized escapist drama went through a series of changes before its final tweaks in the summer of 1984, but its origins went all the way back to 1982's cabin sessions. A handwritten set of lyrics from the period also reveals that two particular lines ('You get lost in so many places / Seeks love in so many faces') were sourced from an untitled song that opens with the somewhat harrowing line of 'Couple died in a blazing flat'.

According to Pål, the chorus melody had partly been inspired by Soft Cell's epic electro-ballad 'Say Hello, Wave Goodbye', while the song's title had reportedly been sourced from Dostoevsky's *The Idiot*.

What's interesting about the Nærsnes demo is that the bulk of the lyrics were already in place before it was later worked on at Rendezvous, including the scene-setting opening couplet ('I've fixed my dwelling for the night / Lights in pairs come passing by where I hide'). Other lines – including the Kinks-referencing 'Where have all the good times gone' – were later trimmed away.

When it came to demoing the track at Rendezvous, the band wisely didn't attempt to replicate Morten's trombone part and the chipmunk-like noises, which Magne later referred to as 'the mouse voice'.

Like other memorable songs from the period, such as Madonna's 'Crazy for You' and China Crisis' 'Wishful Thinking', the subtle use of oboe proved to be extremely effective, perfectly complementing the song's dreamlike narrative. 'The first song that grabbed me was "Living a Boy's Adventure Tale"', stated Pål. 'It had a catchy chorus and, at the same time, something strange about it . . . I was very proud when we signed our first contract with ATV Music, the publishing company. The guy who signed us there had heard that song and, after a few seconds, at the onset of the oboe, he suddenly said, "That's a hit!"'[17]

Warner Brothers' Andrew Wickham was certainly impressed by Morten's falsetto when the track was performed during the band's series of showcase gigs at Rendezvous in August 1983, while the studio's owner, John Ratcliff, also shared his enthusiasm for it. 'I remember the first time I heard Pål play this song,' he recalled on his Facebook page in 2015. 'It sent shivers down my spine.'

It was understandably earmarked as a potential single in the UK, but sadly never got beyond the test pressing stage. In the Philippines, however, it did receive the 45 rpm treatment, albeit in an edited version.

The song has since been sampled by Lifelike ('Adventure') and Gotye ('Eighties Bonanza'), and it was also covered by US synth-pop act Color Theory, who included it on their eighth album, *The Sound*, in 2010.

THE SUN ALWAYS SHINES ON TV
Written by Pål Waaktaar-Savoy
Produced by Alan Tarney
Chart position: 1 (UK), 2 (Norway), 5 (Germany), 20 (US)

The band's strong rapport with Alan Tarney resulted in the jobbing hitmaker being hired to produce 'The Sun Always Shines on TV'. A very late addition to the album, the track had reportedly been tagged on at the insistence of Andrew Wickham's secretary at Warner Brothers.

The track had evolved from a Rendezvous demo titled 'Never Never', which included an intriguing refrain of 'I won't give you shadows'. Sadly, the promising track wasn't developed further, but Pål lifted the midsection ('Hold me / Give all your love / Touch me / Give all your love to me') and began to craft a new song, whose title was inspired by something Pål had heard a TV presenter say while he and Magne were reportedly holed up in a UK hotel. '"The sun always shines on the telly" were the words he said,' said Pål. 'I had it like that for a bit, but it felt too "local" in the end.'

Pål presented the new song as a ballad to his band colleagues, but was soon persuaded to up its tempo. When it came to recording the track at RG Jones Studios in the spring of 1985, Tarney once again used the previous year's Rendezvous demo as a template. 'The production lifts what was already a really cool song,' recalled Pål. 'It was a ballad, like a torch song at first. All the parts fit together so well. It really rolls. But when we recorded it, Magne and Morten had a fever and there were beds in the studio.'[18]

Despite the ailments, the band managed to pull off their best – and most dynamic – production to date, creating a wall of sound that contrasted beautifully with the lightweight pop of 'Take On Me'. Magne's stunning intro showcased the band's classical influences, while Pål's riffing gave it a robustness that would carry forward into live performance. The guitarist's considerable LinnDrum skills didn't go unnoticed either, with Magne later stating that his programming 'has never been surpassed'. Programming the machine was something that seemed to come naturally to Pål. 'We booked three days in Rendezvous to make a better demo and that was the first time I saw a LinnDrum,' he said. 'It just made sense to me, and drums was my first instrument so I imagined myself behind the kit.'

For the single version, the track was edited slightly for radio purposes and a video was filmed in October 1985 while 'Take On Me' was riding high in the charts. With an obvious eye on the MTV market, director Steve Barron was rehired, and the opening shots established a segue between the two videos. However, the bulk of the memorable promo was largely performance-based, with the band playing to an audience (of several hundred showroom dummies!) in a disused church in Teddington. (The drummer simulating Pål's drum parts was Lindsay Elliott, who'd played on Midge Ure's debut solo album, *The Gift*, in 1985.)

Although 'The Sun Always Shines on TV' couldn't quite match the gargantuan success of its predecessor in the US, it did give the band their first – and, to date, only – UK No. 1 during a quiet post-Christmas period (it was displaced by Billy Ocean's 'When the Going Gets Tough, the Tough Get Going').

Years later, the band released a live version of the song as a single (to promote the album *How Can I Sleep with Your Voice in My Head?* in 2003).

The song has been covered and sampled several times over the years, particularly by Europop acts (for example, Interactive, Milk Inc. and Mario Lopez). Lauren Savoy directed a video to accompany a cover by the Eurodance duo Diva in 1994, while a-ha later reportedly endorsed the release, in 2011, of 'Touch Me' by Denmark's Electric Lady Lab, who sampled elements of their classic track.

Following the release of 'Beautiful Day' in 2000, U2 were accused of plagiarism as their No. 1 hit included a brief snatch of 'The Sun Always Shines on TV'. 'In Norway there was a big scandal,' Magne told *The Scotsman* a few years later. 'People reacted a little bit like they'd touched the crown jewels!' In an interview with *Dagbladet*, the Irish band's guitarist, the Edge, acknowledged the similarity: 'It's positively creepy how alike they are. We first became aware of it when we read about it in *Q*. It isn't intentional but, somehow, deep down in the subconscious, a-ha must have been lying around and smouldering away while we were cutting our record. Regardless, it doesn't involve more than a couple of notes and a few words.'

More recently, the song was included in the soundtrack for *Blinded by the Light*, which had been inspired by journalist Sarfraz Manzoor's infatuation with the music of Bruce Springsteen.

AND YOU TELL ME
Written by Pål Waaktaar-Savoy
Produced by Tony Mansfield

> *Many romantic songs fall apart because they're not real. I could never write a song like 'Hunting High and Low' or 'And You Tell Me' if I thought it sounded soppy, but to me they sound honest.*
> – Pål Waaktaar-Savoy, *Smash Hits*, 1987

Originally tucked away on the B-side of the Tony Mansfield version of 'Take On Me' was this plaintive ballad. While many of a-ha's songs were developed over time, this particular track came to its writer almost immediately. According to Pål, the Beatles-flavoured track had come to him during a taxi journey. After paying the driver, he had run into his flat to pick up a guitar while the melody was still fresh in his mind.

Like 'Love Is Reason', 'Hunting High and Low' and other songs from this period, there's an endearing honesty about the lyrics. The original lyrics for 'And You Tell Me' depict a man struggling with a long distance relationship ('It's so hard / Love drives me crazy / When you're away'), but there's also a near-desperation about some of the lines ('I'm trying hard to make you jealous / Thinking maybe it will make you stay'). Pål later revealed the emotional turmoil he was in during his time in London: 'A week before we went to England, I actually met a girl in Norway with whom I had a halfway relationship. So I was in some way, in a relationship, when I met Lauren. You can imagine the scenario; at first I had nothing to do with women, and now I was in the midst of this situation . . . my head was about to explode!'[19]

The track was duly demoed at Rendezvous, but some lyrics were changed before cutting the track with Tony Mansfield at Eel Pie Studios (including the addition of a few lines from 'Go to Sleep').

It's arguable that this ephemeral slice of Nordic melancholia may have benefitted from a more sparse arrangement, but its folk-pop qualities nevertheless cut through any machinizations. During their first tour, the band played a stripped-back version with just an acoustic guitar as accompaniment, while years later, on the *Foot of the Mountain* tour, the arrangement was reduced to just vocal, guitar and xylophone.

Anneli Drecker, who worked with a-ha during the noughties, also performed the track, backed by just piano and cello, during a 2015 session for NRK's P13 radio station, in which Norwegian artists covered several of the band's songs.

LOVE IS REASON
Written by Magne Furuholmen and Pål Waaktaar-Savoy
Produced by John Ratcliff with a-ha

To capitalise on the momentum that was building in their homeland and the Top 5 success of the Tony Mansfield version of 'Take On Me', Warner Brothers released this track as a single in Norway in the spring of 1985. (The track was placed on the B-side of the second release of 'Take On Me' in the UK, but in the Philippines the record label, somewhat bizarrely, went with 'Love Is Reason' as the A-side, with the Alan Tarney-produced 'Take On Me' on the flip side!)

Featuring sequenced bass and some rather over-used brass-like synth stabs, this fast-paced synth-pop track was originally demoed at Rendezvous and scheduled to be recorded at Eel Pie Studios but, as the album had already gone over budget, a cheaper alternative had to be sought. The band's new co-manager, John Ratcliff, found a solution in Sheffield's Vibrasound Studios, which had been built by Stuart Skinner, his former bandmate in the Catch. Ratcliff and the band travelled up to Yorkshire in August 1984 and the track was cut with a minimum of fuss. 'We left with a very pleasing piece of work,' recalled Ratcliff on his Facebook page.

It's immediately noticeable in the demo that Pål's guitar playing is prominent, while the slightly laboured intro recalls the Police. There are some very subtle lyrical differences in the final product, but it's essentially a song stemming from the early throes of Pål's relationship with Lauren. The message in the repetitive chorus intimates that love is reason enough to stay together, but the narrator also lays bare some of his insecurities about the relationship, desperately declaring: 'I'll be what you want me to be / I'd die at the thought of the loss of your heart'.

The unique single release featured the band as cartoon characters on the sleeve, a foretaste of what was to come with the 'Take On Me' video. It was sketched by Henrik Haugan, who would later design a logo for the band in 2000.

I DREAM MYSELF ALIVE
Written by Magne Furuholmen and Pål Waaktaar-Savoy
Produced by Tony Mansfield

Arguably the album's weakest track, the origins of 'I Dream Myself Alive' were firmly rooted in a Poem track titled 'Wildfire', which was eventually released in 2018. True to the band's level of ambition, it was a somewhat complex production and exemplified the band's prog rock roots with its 'song within a song' arrangement. Most of the lyrics from the track's wistful midsection were reused on *Hunting High and Low*'s penultimate track, but producer Tony Mansfield reportedly took exception to the opening lines ('Rain, go away / My little girl wants to play / She wonders why / The rain would like to see her cry') and insisted on a rewrite. According to the book *Så blåser det på jorden*, Magne was inspired to pen the amended verse following a death back home, although one line ('Something dark against the light') appears to have been sourced from a demo version of 'Hunting High and Low'.

As for the finished recording, there's certainly an element of self-indulgence about the mechanised production, and the inclusion of a section of speech from a 1981 Conservative Party conference certainly raises eyebrows. The earlier 'NYC Mix', featuring the original lyrics, has an interesting Latin freestyle vibe to it, but the finished version sounds more like the Pet Shop Boys than a-ha. Certainly, it's evident from listening to New Musik cuts such as 'A Train on Twisted Tracks' (from 1982's *Warp* album) that the 'West End Girls' hitmakers were fans of Mansfield's work. And, according to Mansfield's brother, Lee, he had once been approached by the synth-pop duo's manager, Tom Watkins, about working with them.

The track was later sampled by Junior Sanchez in 1999 (on the double 12-inch release of '2Morrows Future 2Day'), while a-ha themselves dusted it off for their *Foot of the Mountain* tour in 2009, having not played it regularly since a-ha's inaugural world tour.

During their *Hunting High and Low* world tour, which commenced in October 2019, the band performed a version of the song that was closer to the original demo, before it was blighted by Mansfield's production trickery. 'The demo is where this song's at,' stated Pål. 'It's one of my personal favourites.'

HERE I STAND AND FACE THE RAIN
Written by Pål Waaktaar-Savoy
Produced by Tony Mansfield

Fresh from signing one of their first record deals in 1983, Morten and Pål used part of their respective advances to fund a celebratory package holiday. The duo's chosen destination was the Spanish island of Tenerife, whose sunny climes offered a welcome contrast to the dankness of their South London abode. But, with Pål's songwriting head still on, it proved to be something of a busman's holiday. And, in spite of the sun-drenched setting, he managed to pen this miserabilist classic. 'I remember Morten was in the room while I was writing the song,' recalled Pål. 'He tried to sing along a bit, which completely panicked me . . . So I asked him to be quiet.'[20]

A throwback to Pål's Bridges days, in terms of its musical complexity and different time signatures, the lyrics saw its writer perched on a pre-fame precipice. Like other lyrics from the period, worries for the future ('I know that nothing's gonna be the same again / I fear for what tomorrow brings') and relationship insecurities ('I need your love / Don't walk away / The dark scares me so') were brought to the fore once more, while there was an unusual turn of phrase in the title itself.

Boasting a further demonstration of the songwriter's exemplary drum programming skills, the track was duly demoed at Rendezvous in a considerably poppier version than the one that would eventually close the band's debut album. At Eel Pie Studios, the track was given a suitably Gothic twist by producer Tony Mansfield, with an effective monastic intro (which was later edited) that recalled OMD in their pomp, while the stacked vocals had a soaring, Sting-like quality about them.

During the early phase of their career, the song was a staple of the band's live sets, but it was also performed during the *Cast in Steel* tour, with Anneli Drecker on joint lead vocal duties.

DRIFTWOOD (B-side)
Written by Pål Waaktaar-Savoy
Produced by a-ha

In the relative calm before the storm – with the global success of 'Take On Me' just around the corner – the band spent some time in Oslo during the summer of 1985, and booked time at Tore Aarnes' Octocon Studio in Nydalen, where Bridges had recorded the *Fakkeltog* album five years previous. The band worked on demos of 'Scoundrel Days' and 'I've Been Losing You' (which Bridges had worked on in

1981, when they were known as Poem) and a brand new track, titled 'Driftwood', which would eventually find a home on the B-side of 'The Sun Always Shines on TV'. Although the tracks were produced by a-ha, the session was reportedly overseen by Bridges' producer, Svein Erichsen. (Under the pseudonym of Y Me, Tore Aarnes released 'Dance with the World' on Octocon Records in 1985. The catchy Europop single was supposedly remixed by Pål, though he claims he never worked on the song.)

On the surface, 'Driftwood' is a generic slice of mid-80s sophisti-pop, but this unusual track saw Pål steering his songwriting ship through some seemingly murky waters. There's an unsettling introduction, featuring a groaning woman and a crying baby that suggests an Ibsen influence (*The Lady of the Sea*, in particular), and an almost sea shanty-like feel to the lyrics, which are clearly folk-inspired ('Oh come pity me a poor mad sailor / Stranded on this love'). Less visceral than some of the lines on *Hunting High and Low*, its writer is seemingly pondering the question of whether love can transcend from youth to old age ('So I ask in fading innocence / And all my youthful rage / Will your hands still touch me / When my face has fallen in with age').

The song was performed during a-ha's world tour in 1986–87, while a version of the song by Kristiansand band Tørst [Thirst] – who won the *NM i rock* competition in 1996 – was released as a single in 2000.

CHAPTER NINE
SCOUNDREL DAYS

We want to be respected musicians. We want to do an album that's much better than the current one.
– Magne Furuholmen, *LA Times*, 1986

Released: October 1986
Chart position: 2 (UK), 1 (Norway), 4 (Germany), 74 (US)

By the time of the release of their sophomore record in October 1986, a-ha were partway into a lengthy world tour that had, until that point, taken in a considerable number of dates in Australia, Canada, Japan and the US. The rest of the year had, similarly, been extremely busy for the band. By the time of the release of the 'Train of Thought' single in March 1986, a-ha's popularity had reached fever pitch, and Magne, Morten and Pål were in the midst of a seemingly endless cycle of photo sessions and TV and radio interviews, not just in the UK and US, but also Australia and Japan. By the turn of the year there were already two books – by *Aftenposten* journalist Tor Marcussen and Magne's mother, Annelise Furuholmen Nøkleby – in Norwegian shops. In the UK, with Duran Duran on hiatus and its members split into two camps (the Power Station and Arcadia), teen magazines such as *Just Seventeen*, *Smash Hits* and *No.1* had now found new pinups to adorn their glossy pages, while a plethora of cash-in publications had hit newsagents up and down the country. That a-ha managed to release any new music in the midst of this maelstrom of promotional madness was an achievement in itself, but the fact that they also managed to turn out such a high-quality product bordered on the miraculous.

By clambering aboard the Trojan Horse that was 'Take On Me', the band had achieved their goal of breaking into the international market, but even they couldn't have foreseen its gargantuan level of success, which had been consolidated by significant sales for both its parent album and attendant singles. But where could a band who had, in football parlance, scored a cup-winning goal within the first minute go from here? Their debut album had provided a platform to work from, but now the band had to deal with a record label who wanted more of the same. 'People would say, "There's no 'Take On Me' on this record", and we'd say, "Yeah, great!", reflected Magne. 'We knew that the expectation was to regurgitate our own success and that wasn't what we were about.'[1] Morten added: 'We wanted the freedom to be playful with music, to experiment and do what we felt like doing, but we were heavily affected by the type of success that the first record gave us.'[2]

Although the band felt the pressure, they certainly didn't have a shortage of songs, and these had been stockpiling since Magne and Pål's Bridges period. 'After the first album, we were literally brimming with material, both new and old,' recalled Magne. 'We had lots of stuff left over, which was written before *Hunting High and Low*, but was, perhaps, of a darker and more complex nature and had not really tickled producer Tony Mansfield's fancy.'[3] Certainly there was a darker tone to the new body of songs and, in many respects, *Scoundrel Days* can be viewed more as a prequel than a sequel to *Hunting High and Low*.

Although many of the new songs had already been demoed, time was against them, so the album had to be completed quickly. However, choosing a producer this time round was a relatively painless process. Alan Tarney had had a hand in all of the band's hit singles to date, so enlisting his services on the follow-up was a no-brainer. Although Magne and Pål had to self-produce some late additions due to their touring commitments, the album was completed within a reasonably short time frame, with the bulk of the work being done at RG Jones Studios in Wimbledon in the spring of 1986.

For the album's sleeve, a striking shot of the volcanic landscape of Haleakala in Hawaii – one of the stops on the US leg of the tour in August – was used, overlaid with a photo of a rather tired-looking band traversing its surface. Both the photography and the handwritten band name and album title signified the album's more organic dircction. It was ccrtainly less electronic than its predecessor, and the use of real bass and drums ensured a much thicker sound.

NME's David Quantick ungenerously labelled *Scoundrel Days* 'pretty standard 80s fare', describing it as 'a contemporary clatter of modern drums and tootling swathes of synthesiser', but at least recognised its melancholic qualities. At the other end of the music press spectrum, however, *Smash Hits* described it as 'much rougher and more ambitious than their first LP'. In Norway, *VG*'s Morten Stensland described it as 'a surprisingly varied LP' and singled out the title track, 'Cry Wolf' and 'Manhattan Skyline' as having hit potential. 'Songwriters Pål Waaktaar and Magne Furuholmen show greater breadth and more imagination on *Scoundrel Days*,' he wrote. 'Furthermore, it displays a marked difference between the two songwriters. Furuholmen's songs, "Cry Wolf", "We're Looking for the Whales" and "Maybe, Maybe" are light and relatively simple, while Waaktaar's songs – especially "The Weight of the Wind" and "The Swing of Things" – are more melancholy and introverted.'

While sales weren't commensurate to those of its predecessor, the album was another big seller. (In the UK, the band were denied top spot once again; this time by Paul Simon's *Graceland*.)

Morten was later asked if things would have turned out differently had they released *Scoundrel Days* first. 'No, I think it would have been the same,' he replied, 'but we wouldn't have exploded on to the scene like we did. It would have been more of a slow burning thing. It would have given us an ability to enter the scene at some level and work it from there. As it happened, we went in at the top and worked hard to stay there.'[4]

SCOUNDREL DAYS
Music written by Magne Furuholmen and Pål Waaktaar-Savoy
Words written by Pål Waaktaar-Savoy
Produced by Alan Tarney

With its imaginative chord changes and an intro evocative of horror film-maker and musician John Carpenter, the title cut of a-ha's second album served as a statement of intent from a band who – like 'Too Shy' hitmakers Kajagoogoo before them – were keen to up the average age of their fan base. The opening line ('Was that somebody screaming? / It wasn't me for sure') instantly draws the listener in, transporting them into a Kafka-like world of mystery and mortality. Pål's lyrics are both vivid ('I can feel the sweat on my lips / Leaking into my mouth') and slightly offbeat ('I cut my wrist on a bad thought'), while there's an ambiguity at play that leaves the work open to interpretation.

Like much of the band's material from this period, the track had gone through several lyrical and musical evolutions to reach this point. The riff itself had predated Bridges and had been composed by Magne using a jazz guitar that his grandfather, Kaare Aasen, had given to him as a child. During the Poem album sessions in 1980, the riff was resurrected for the 'The Leap', which embodied a Joy Divison-like vibe in the verses, while the whimsical musical interludes, featuring a series of 60s-inspired la-las, added an interesting contrast to the lyrics' dark hue.

At Rendezvous, the band retained the basic lyrical hub of 'The Leap', but applied both a motorik drive and a soaring new chorus, the melody of which had been lifted from a very early version of 'This Alone Is Love' (also known as 'Bergman Suite'). (To complicate things further, a discarded section from the original 'Scoundrel Days' demo was later reused in the coda of 2015's 'Shadow Endeavors'!)

In the summer of 1985, with *Hunting High and Low* already in US shops, the band worked on a new version of 'Scoundrel Days' at Octocon Studio. Aside from some minor lyrical tweaks, the arrangement was virtually identical to the finished version that was cut at RG Jones Studios the following year.

Partly for sentimental reasons, Magne declared in 2010 that it was his favourite a-ha song, and it's been a virtually immovable part of the band's set lists since its inception. While its subject matter may not have appealed to radio programmers, it was certainly worthy of release as a single. Had the band not been offered the opportunity to cut the theme song for *The Living Daylights*, it's highly probable it would have been scheduled as the album's fourth single.

THE SWING OF THINGS
Written by Pål Waaktaar-Savoy
Produced by Alan Tarney

I was always afraid of large groups and crowds. I was very much a loner, and that was one of the reasons I began writing songs at a very early age.
– Pål Waaktaar-Savoy, *Look-in* magazine, 1988

Whereas 'Scoundrel Days' had presented a more cinematic side to a-ha, 'The Swing of Things' was more akin to an internal monologue, with the recording occupying a more introspective terrain. Certainly there's a gamut of emotions threading through its tapestry of complex rhythms. Aside from an early insight into Pål's well-documented social anxieties ('There's a worldful out there of people

I fear'), familiar ground is covered in both his affection for his girlfriend ('When she glows in the dark / And I'm weak by the sight / Of this breathtaking beauty') and his separation struggles ('How can I sleep with your voice in my head / With an ocean between us / And room in my bed'), but there's an underlying tension as the writer describes how he is 'losing the grip' as he desperately tries to get back into 'the swing of things'. Years later, Magne declared that this was the best set of lyrics on the album, while Morten's praise was considerably more pronounced: 'It isn't necessarily my all-time favourite. But yeah, if I had to choose, that would be the one,' he gushed. 'The whole thing. The atmosphere and excitement in the song. It's a song that gets you moving. It would have been possible to make a fantastic single out of it, with a new recording.'[5]

During the demo stages, the band did experiment with a heavier, more guitar-based version – with some Depeche Mode-like keyboard flourishes – but settled on a less robust and more Japan-esque take, with its soupçon of light funk. The final version was, however, beefed up with some live drums, courtesy of Michael Sturgis. (The American-born drummer was part of a-ha's live set-up that year, along with bassist Leif Karsten Johansen and keyboardist Dag Kolsrud who later, as one third of One 2 Many, had a chart-topper in Norway with the excellent 'Downtown' single.)

I'VE BEEN LOSING YOU
Written by Pål Waaktaar-Savoy
Produced by Magne Furuholmen and Pål Waaktaar-Savoy
Chart position: 8 (UK), 1 (Norway), 15 (Germany)

The origins of 'I've Been Losing You' went all the way back to 1981 when Bridges – who were then using the Poem name – had recorded an early version of the track. The fascinating near-six-minute recording reveals a song in proggy transition – replete with a two-minute instrumental midsection – with just glimpses of the melody that would appear in the hit version.

The track was later demoed by a-ha at Rendezvous, and some of the lyrics from the Bridges version were carried over. (One of the lines, 'Life is a place you will remember well', was also used on a demo of 'Touchy!') The band had another run-through of the track during sessions at Octocon Studio in the summer of 1985, but they weren't quite able to pull off an effective transition from verse to chorus. The track remained a work in progress until the band flew out to Australia for the start of their world tour in the summer of 1986.

While the bulk of their second album had already been recorded by this time, they were still lacking a few songs and an obvious lead-off single. Since the band were over 9,000 miles away from the UK, some late additions to the album had to be recorded on the fly, and without their regular producer. The band had a limited window in which to work, but there was a week-long gap between their final Sydney show and the start of the Japanese leg of the tour. It was seemingly the perfect opportunity to dust off the song.

'The music was written and recorded in the same day, and then I did the lyrics the next night and Morten sang it the day after,' said Pål. 'I guess it's the song we've recorded under the most pressure – Morten sang the last lines shouting from the lift waiting to take us to Japan. You can also hear in his voice that we'd just done [several] concerts. It has a very rough quality which I thought suited it.'[6]

According to Pål, the verse melody came to him while the band were recording 'Cry Wolf'. 'I could hear the rumble of the bottom end blaring through the glass in the studio,' he explained. 'I wrote "I've Been Losing You" on top of that. It's in the same key. I'd had a chorus with a different verse before, but the new verse was written on top of "Cry Wolf".'[7]

Additionally, the band's live rhythm section was on hand to give 'I've Been Losing You' some added bite. 'It was an attempt to capture the live sound and show how we came over as a band on stage,' explained Morten. 'This was all new to us, and it would take years for us to feel like a real live band.'[8]

The song begins with a single drum hit – to perhaps signify a gunshot – and its protagonist is a killer. He can't quite believe what he's done ('I could have sworn it wasn't me'), but nevertheless accepts his part in the crime ('Yet I did it all so coldly / Almost slowly / Plain for all to see') and awaits retribution ('I want the guilt to get me / Thoughts to wreck me / Preying on my mind').

The detail in the noir-infused vignettes is certainly vivid, and the alchemised song included one of the decade's most memorable couplets ('I can still hear our screams competing / You're hissing your esses like a snake').

There have certainly been some interesting interpretations of the song over the years. '"I've Been Losing You" is a soliloquy addressed to a corpse,' declared *Melody Maker*, 'a pleading with a murdered lover to say something "useful", a hopeless staring into eyes "rinsed of colour". It's nasty stuff, not very pop . . . Howard Deveto could easily have written any one of their lines. What he couldn't have done is give them such a magnificent context, such stark, overwhelming melodic motifs.'

As a follow-up to the considerably more tender 'Hunting High and Low', it was certainly a brave choice of single (for the benefit of radio programmers in territories such as the US, the song's false ending was edited out), but *Smash Hits'* Ian Cranna was certainly impressed: 'As someone who previously couldn't have cared less either way about a-ha, it came as something of a shock to find this is actually a very good record. Sounding tougher and meaner than before . . . A lot of people will have to reshuffle their prejudices.'

The band were rewarded with another Top 10 placing in the UK and a second chart-topper in Norway, but it's arguable its commercial performance could have been improved with a video that lent on the song's vividness. However, time constraints meant that a clip had to be assembled using footage from a live show in the US. (For 1991's *Headlines and Deadlines* compilation, the clip was replaced with a live version recorded at NRK that year.)

In 2011, the track featured in Joachim Trier's award-winning film *Oslo, August 31st*.

OCTOBER
Written by Pål Waaktaar-Savoy
Produced by Alan Tarney

Featuring an ambient intro that conveys the atmosphere of a cold and misty city, 'October' served as some light relief after the album's tension-filled triumvirate of tracks. According to Pål, the soothing track had been written in London while

Magne and Morten had travelled to Norway and Lauren had returned to the US. Certainly it's his girlfriend who provides the lyrical inspiration, with the musician pondering over her movements in the different time zone ('Wherever you may be right now / It must be getting late / You're probably asleep already / I am wide awake'), but while he obviously misses her, he's clearly in a far more comfortable headspace ('Loneliness can be ignored / And time has shown me how'). The sparse, jazz-like arrangement, featuring some brassy keyboard parts redolent of Burt Bacharach, perfectly complements the lyrics, while Morten's near-whispered vocals provided further evidence of his increasing versatility as a singer.

The song was later covered by Pål and Lauren's band, Savoy, and included on the B-side of their 1996 debut single, 'Velvet' (a Norwegian chart-topper that was later covered by a-ha), but presented in a slightly slower, more 60s-influenced arrangement.

The song was also covered in 1996 by Sigurd Køhn, a jazz musician who had been part of a-ha's live set-up in the 1990s. The beautiful instrumental take on the track was included on his album *More Pepper, Please*.

MANHATTAN SKYLINE
Music written by Magne Furuholmen and Pål Waaktaar-Savoy
Words written by Pål Waaktaar-Savoy
Produced by Alan Tarney
Chart position: 13 (UK), 4 (Norway), 28 (Germany)

> *'Manhattan Skyline' alternates soaring melodrama with avant-garde rock figures to better effect than Radiohead's 'Paranoid Android.'*
> – Steven Poole, *The Guardian*, June 2002

Like the Beatles' classic 'We Can Work It Out', 'Manhattan Skyline' can be defined as a deft exercise in cut and paste songwriting, and one that features a canny composite of clearly distinct parts that deftly alternate between nostalgia and angst. Unified by Pål's eloquent but near-schizophrenic lyrics, the track fuses the beauty and whimsy of Magne's waltz-time verses with the guitarist's more raucous, rock-based choruses. While the lyrics were once again open to interpretation, they essentially centred around the contrasting emotions of saying goodbye to a loved one.

The band were so impressed with the track that they insisted on its release as a single. However, Warner Brothers were reportedly unhappy with releasing a near five-minute track as a single and the band were forced to edit the track for the benefit of radio. In his autobiography, Ray Manzarek described Paul Rothchild's edit of the Doors' 'Light My Fire' as 'disembowelment with a dull blade'. While perhaps not on the same level, the single version of 'Manhattan Skyline' certainly bordered on butchery and included the removal of a key couplet ('You see things in the depths of my eyes / That my love's run dry'). However, the accompanying Steve Barron-directed video – which had partly been influenced by Terry Gilliam's dystopian cult classic, *Brazil* – did offer an interesting perspective on the newly truncated set of lyrics, with the band cast as dot-to-dot characters in a post-apocalyptic void, and the mocked-up *Aftenposten* newspaper, featuring the harrowing image of a devastated city, was certainly striking.

The reaction to the single was mixed, with some reviewers confused by the collision of swaying harpsichord notes, muted power chords and sinister synth stabs. 'The gentle musings about umbrellas flying are interrupted and a Slade record suddenly appears from nowhere,' said *Smash Hits'* Lola Borg. '. . . This is really very strange indeed, jumping about madly between quiet bits and lots of crashing drums. What has come over them?' Elsewhere, *Record Mirror*'s Eleanor Levy was considerably more scathing: 'If a-ha weren't so pretty, they'd be on the cover of *Q* and treated as the new Tangerine Dream. And that's something none of us need.'

Although the release gave the band their lowest chart placing to date since they'd exploded onto the scene in 1985, the song has since attained classic status among fans, as well as attracting a series of high-profile admirers, including fellow countrymen Kings of Convenience, who released a gorgeous stripped-back version of the track in 2001. (Erlend Øye from the revered indie folk duo revealed that the first album he ever bought was *Hunting High and Low*.)

CRY WOLF

Music written by Magne Furuholmen
Words written by Magne Furuholmen and Pål Waaktaar-Savoy
Produced by Alan Tarney
Chart position: 5 (UK), 2 (Norway), 20 (Germany), 50 (US)

Although Pål cites Raskolnikov – the protagonist of Dostoevsky's *Crime and Punishment* – as a major influence on his lyric writing, the impact of the Doors on a-ha's music, which had previously been evident on brooding cuts such as 'Here I Stand and Face the Rain', would also manifest itself on *Scoundrel Days*. Certainly, the bloodstained imagery on cuts such as 'I've Been Losing You' and 'Scoundrel Days' had more than a whiff of Jim Morrison about them, while the use of Lauren Savoy's scene setting 'Night I left the city, I dreamt of a wolf' as a preface to the lupine drama of 'Cry Wolf' was certainly evocative of the psychedelic rockers (the song's actual title was sourced from one of Lauren's film school manuscripts). For many years, the band also regularly included a snatch of the 'cocktail jazz' element of the Doors' 'Riders on the Storm' during performances of the song.

"'Cry Wolf" was quite easy to write,' said Magne. 'I also had the line, "He came from where the winds are cold, and truth is seen through keyholes". When I presented it to Pål, he gave it the title.'

Building upon the foundations of the demo, the band faithfully recreated the track at RG Jones Studios, but an old friend, who had been staying at Magne's flat in Kensington, was on hand to help out. 'We first did a demo version of "Cry Wolf" in Oslo,' remembered Bridges' former drummer, Øystein Jevanord, 'and then some months later I was asked to come to London for a week in 1986. We started from scratch with "Cry Wolf", using a drum machine on bass drum, snare and cowbell. Then I did all the cymbals and fills, using a full drum kit with lots of toms – my take took about 20 minutes to do, so the rest of the one-week session I was just present and watched!

I remember that, after a couple of test takes, Pål told me to "go bananas"! And I did – that's the take they used on the record!'

The following year, Øystein was also recruited as a percussionist in a-ha's live band, which included Mike Sturgis (drums), Ian Wherry (keyboards) and Leif Karsten Johansen (bass). A photo from the tour also captured a reunited Bridges, prior to Viggo Bondi's wedding. 'The picture is taken on the stage in Nîmes in the south of France,' said Viggo. 'Magne was my best man and the bachelor party took place in Nice on the same tour.' (Leif Karsten Johansen later produced *First Breath*, the 1997 debut album by Morten's future wife, Camilla.)

One of the band's most underrated singles, its release coincided with a lengthy UK tour which, indicative of their popularity at the time, included a six-night residency at the Hammersmith Odeon and three nights at the Royal Albert Hall. A Steve Barron-directed video, featuring footage shot in and around the Castle of Couches in Burgundy, France, was interspersed with concert footage and some shots of the band as book pop-up characters. (The band received an award for the video at the International Music & Media Conference gala in Montreux in May 1987.)

Writing for *No.1*, TV presenter Phillip Schofield wrote: 'There seemed to be an infectious buzz about a-ha a while back but, after hearing this and the last single which are both on *Scoundrel Days*, I'm not so impressed . . . It seems to just drift in and out.' *Smash Hits* were equally dismissive, writing: 'It is with great disappointment that I have to report that "Cry Wolf" is definitely a non-starter,' wrote Ro Newton. '. . . Catchy, but repetitive, and quite tiresome after a few plays.'

However, despite the criticism, the single returned the band to the UK's Top 5, and it even cracked the Top 50 in the Billboard chart.

WE'RE LOOKING FOR THE WHALES
Music written by Magne Furuholmen
Words written by Pål Waaktaar-Savoy
Produced by Alan Tarney

> *Well, Spock, thanks to your restored memory and a little bit of luck, we are in the streets of San Francisco looking for a pair of humpback whales.*
> – William Shatner, *Star Trek IV: The Voyage Home*, 1986

'We're Looking for the Whales' had, of course, not been written to tie in with the November release of a new *Star Trek* film, but was in fact one of Magne and Pål's earliest co-writes. The soundtrack work would come later.

Like many of the tracks on *Scoundrel Days*, its origins went back to the duo's Bridges period, and the band worked on a version of the track with Pål on bass guitar. '"We're Looking for the Whales" was my song,' said Magne. 'I was particularly proud of having written it – the changes from the major verse to the insistent minor chorus, etc, kind of felt like an accomplishment. As usual, however, I had no lyrics. From a band perspective, Pål and I had already set our sights on moving to UK at this point. Pål had finished his schooling a year before me and he was literally just waiting for me to finish school and go. The other members were dragging their feet, and so we just thought, "Fuck it, let's spend the time writing and developing material getting ready for our departure".'

The track was later deemed worthy of a run-through during a-ha's sojourn in Nærsnes, and it's certainly an interesting sonic capture of the band's songwriting development, and further evidence of Magne's knack for a catchy melody. Pål's lyrics are quirky ('One left low left two who left high'), though often lost in translation ('Echoes lost in waterland / It seems like man has won to lose again'), but there was enough potential in the demo to suggest it was worthy of developing further, and the lyrics were slightly reworked during the band's time in Sydenham.

A near-permanent fixture in the band's early live repertoire (preserved for posterity on the B-side of 'Manhattan Skyline'), the perky pop song was brought out of retirement for the band's 'farewell' shows in 2010, while Morten continued to perform it during his subsequent solo career. 'There's one particular song which has a special importance for me,' he said during one such show in Berlin in 2012, 'because it's the first song as a demo that Pål, Magne and I did together in the early days, and we were waiting for something that actually sounded good, and this one did.'

THE WEIGHT OF THE WIND
Written by Pål Waaktaar-Savoy
Produced by Alan Tarney

Against a dainty, light jazz backdrop, the hushed tones of 'October' had cleverly diffused some of the percolating tension at the start of the album. On 'The Weight of the Wind', much of this tension resurfaces, with the tormented narrator seemingly burdened by raging jealousy and paranoia ('You see their snakey arms entwined / So clear and so cruel / In your jealous mind'). Musically, the track shares the propulsive drive of 'The Sun Always Shines on TV', replete with some suitably sorrowful harmonies and some gnarly guitar work that recalls the claustrophobic fadeout of Bridges' 'Faceless City'.

Somewhat surprisingly, Pål revealed that he preferred the version the band had cut at Rendezvous. 'I don't like the official released version,' he said in 2011, 'but the demo gives a better impression of what this song could have been.' The rhythmic complexities of the track are certainly more to the fore in said demo, but it lacks the escalating tension of the finished version (not helped by Morten's exclamation of 'Sock it to me!').

On tour, the band have experimented with different versions of the track over the years. During their inaugural world tour, it was given a much slower, more symphonic treatment, while a stripped-back, more acoustic take greeted audiences on the *Memorial Beach* tour.

MAYBE, MAYBE
Written by Magne Furuholmen
Produced by Pål Waaktaar-Savoy and Magne Furuholmen

Although Magne had written songs independently before, in terms of penning lyrics, he was largely reliant on his creative foil, Pål. This catchy but disposable track broke with tradition, but it was originally conceived as something far less quirky than the playful skit that eventually materialised both on the album and as the B-side of 'Cry Wolf'. A clear tribute to his teenage sweetheart, Heidi Rydford (whom he eventually married in August 1992), the original lyrics are, by turns, sincere and jocular ('But if I ever write a word that hurts you / I shall break this pen in two million pieces'). However, by the time of its reworking, the song's idiosyncratic, almost Morrissey-esque line ('Maybe it was over when you chucked me out the Rover at full speed') was in place, rendering it one of the band's most throwaway numbers. 'It isn't the only time I've wound up disappointed with one of my own contributions,' Magne later lamented, 'but looking back in the rear-view mirror, maybe it wouldn't have been so brilliant as a sad song.'

Magne would of course pen better songs, but 'Maybe, Maybe' was at the time deemed worthy of release as a single in Bolivia, of all places, while even more bizarrely, a list of Top 100 B-sides by the entertainment website, *TV Cream*, actually placed the song at the top, ahead of flip-side classics such as 'Rain' (the Beatles) and 'Please, Please, Please, Let Me Get What I Want' (the Smiths). 'If a-ha had arrived on the pop scene a decade or so later,' they wrote, 'chances are that they would have been marketed, not as teen heartthrob pop sensations, but as charming European indie eccentrics in the manner of the Cardigans or the Wannadies. Their hit singles were often weird enough, but their B-sides were weirder still.'[9]

SOFT RAINS OF APRIL
Music written by Magne Furuholmen and Pål Waaktaar-Savoy
Words written by Pål Waaktaar-Savoy
Produced by Pål Waaktaar-Savoy and Magne Furuholmen

One of Magne and Pål's greatest compositions, 'Soft Rains of April' had originally been recorded by Poem during sessions at Sound Art Studio, but in a noticeably different, more guitar-oriented take that included some slightly different lyrics. As the band's former bassist confirmed, another version was also cut: 'It was recorded in the same session as the *Våkenatt* album and called "Soft Rains of April (Reprise)",' said Viggo. 'It is a version with electric instruments and it is much faster than the acoustic version on the record. There are no vocals on this version – Pål is playing the melody on electric guitar. In the last part, Pål is playing his best solo ever . . . It is a great version.'

The track was later refreshed during sessions at Rendezvous, with the band trying out different versions, just as Poem had done. In one of the early demos, the band experimented with a more rhythmic version that included some different lyrics ('All I want to say is / They'll be back someday next year / Wait and see'), as well as synthesised vocals. A stark, piano-based take of the track was far more successful, while a so-called guitar version was awash with swathes of synth bass that predated Berlin's 'Take My Breath Away'. But it's the final version, with its ethereal New Age aesthetic, that impresses the most. With its spectral synth sounds and harpsichord flourishes, it's a veritable masterclass in baroque synth-pop and a suitably chilling bookend to the album, embellished by a harrowing 'over' as the song reaches an abrupt climax.

Lyrically, the epic track emits an aura of Kafka-like mystery. It's implied in the somewhat opaque lyrics that the song's central character is holed up in prison ('Well they gave me four years / Three more to go'), and there are echoes of *The Trial*, whereby the details of the crime aren't divulged to the reader. Once again, the lyrics are open to interpretation but, essentially, the protagonist dreams of returning home and is desperate to hear a voice on the phone, but in the end has to appease his boredom in other ways ('Keep writing letters / Time's passing so slow').

THIS ALONE IS LOVE (B-side)
Music written by Magne Furuholmen and Pål Waaktaar-Savoy
Words written by Pål Waaktaar-Savoy
Produced by Magne Furuholmen and Pål Waaktaar-Savoy

Just as a-ha had exploited a gap in their touring schedule to cut 'I've Been Losing You', they also managed to cut its non-album B-side in between shows in Japan and the US in July/August 1986. In Hawaii, the band played at the outdoor venue Waikiki Shell on 8 August and, during their stay on the volcanic island, also fitted in both an album cover shoot with photographer Knut Bry and a recording session at Maui's Lahaina Sound, which is currently described as a 'studio in the clouds'.

The band once again delved deep into their past, with Pål, the band's resident music mosaicist, piecing together this intriguing – though lyrically slight – track that had roots in Bridges' *Fakkeltog* album. It had originally been demoed at Rendezvous and, befitting of the band's level of ambition at the time, had provisionally been titled 'Bergman Suite', on account of both its musical complexities and the fact it was laced with samples of Swedish dialogue from an unidentifiable Ingmar Bergman movie which Pål had recorded from the TV.

The soaring chorus ('It will make my last breath pass out at dawn / It will make my body dissolve out in the blue') had been sourced from Bridges' 'May the Last Dance Be Mine', which itself had evolved from much longer, proggier takes of the track at Magne's Knusla Bruk home. Additionally, fragments of lyrics from the same album's 'Every Mortal Night' ('Travel by trapdoors / Our souls are a myriad of wars / And we are losing every one') were also recycled for the verses. The multifaceted track also featured a section ('And see / That's just one of those feelings / It's free / It's the air on which your wings / Cross the sea') that was later reworked for the chorus of 'Scoundrel Days'.

The newly abridged version of the song, titled 'This Alone Is Love', retained the chorus and verses, but the Bergman dialogue didn't survive the cull. Given its fragmentary history, it's a remarkably cohesive work, but the song's potential was arguably unrealised on this unadventurous take. It was later repurposed for the band's third album, thus rendering this particular version a fascinating document of a work in progress.

PÅL H. CHRISTIANSEN

The title of 'Scoundrel Days' also inspired the name of the English translation of Pål H. Christiansen's 2002 book, *Drømmer om storhet* [Dreaming of Greatness]. The protagonist of *The Scoundrel Days of Hobo Highbrow* is an aspiring writer who loses his proofreading job, his girlfriend and, amusingly, his sofa, but a chance meeting with Pål proves to be creatively inspiring. While the book is not centred around a-ha, there are occasional references to their history, and some subtle uses of some of their song titles – such as 'Driftwood' and 'The Blue Sky' – within the text.

***Both a knowledge of a-ha's history and a passion for their music comes
across in your book. Were you a fan of theirs right from the start?***
I liked their music and their attitude right from the start, yes. They made
music that touched me on several levels – it was catchy and soulful at the
same time. This was when I was starting a career as a writer, and it inspired
me to move on. I also liked that their thing was not about being naughty
boys and sex and drugs and rock and roll. They were kind of serious artists
drifting into the world of pop. But I kept a-ha mostly to myself at that time.
Liking a-ha wasn't cool for upcoming writers in Norway in the 80s and 90s,
so I didn't go to concerts or collect a-ha-stuff or anything like that.

Have you ever met them?
When the Norwegian edition of the novel was published in 2002, the
marketing manager with my publisher succeeded in getting Pål to appear
at a meeting with the Norwegian press. After that, we have bumped into
each other once in a while and kept in touch through email and Facebook
whenever needed. I haven't communicated directly with the other guys in
any way. A person I do see regularly is Viggo Bondi from Bridges. We have
been living in the same neighbourhood for ages and bump into each other
quite often in the grocery shop or in the suburban streets of Høvik. Then
we always chat about a-ha and Bridges.

Has Pål read the book? And, if so, what was his opinion of it?
Yes, Pål read the book not long after it was published in Norwegian. My
publisher sent it over to him in order to see if there were any problem
there. He let Lauren check it out first. Then he read it himself and he said
some nice things about my writing to me and in the Norwegian media, and
I think he meant what he said.

***The Norwegian title seems to perfectly encapsulate the essence of
the book. Why did you decide to change the title for the English
translation?***
As far as I remember, this was a suggestion from the translator, Jon Buscall,
who thought a title playing on the a-ha theme would sound better in
English. He gave me some alternative titles, and I liked *The Scoundrel
Days of Hobo Highbrow*. I think I told Pål about the title at that time, and
I remember he said that Lauren disagreed about it. Pål liked it but Lauren
didn't that much. My German publisher also changed the title, but they
went in the other direction, away from the a-ha theme, probably because
they wanted to reach a broader audience.

What inspired you to write the book initially?

Hobo Highbrow appeared in my first novel from 1989, and later I wanted to write a new novel with him as the main character. At the same time I was eager to write an essay or something about a-ha. At a point I found out that making Hobo an a-ha fan would really make the right twist to my novel. When Pål, Magne and Morten started up again after the break in the 90s, it made the project more interesting to complete.

How much of yourself did you pour into the character Hobo Highbrow?

There will always be bit of yourself in all characters, but Hobo is much more extreme in most ways than me. Writing for me is much about taking a little piece of yourself and blowing it up to enormous proportions. Hobo's dream of greatness is like a teenager pretending to be a pop star before the mirror. What is a fact is that I had a similar experience in 1992 as Hobo had in the book, spotting Pål and Lauren in the street for the first time. That episode was lingering in my brain for years before I found out what to do with it. I also lived for many years in an apartment just like Hobo in the Frogner area of Oslo. And I can admit that the reason I made Hobo a proofreader in *VG* was that I wanted to make fun of an actual proofreader at *VG* that was allowed to write book reviews now and then at that time. He was also a not-so-very-successful poet, and he made an attempt to kill my prize-winning novel, *Humle & Honning* [Bumble & Honey], in a review, obviously as a kind of statement about what he thought about contemporary writers. So I had my revenge by making him an important part of Hobo. I still think that was a very good idea.

Have you ever considered writing a sequel to the book?

I have been working on and off on a sequel for many years. Whether it will ever be finished I'm not sure about. I concentrated on writing children's books for many years, and published 12 books between 2006 and 2018. Now I'm in a period where I'm more involved in the real world than in fiction. Time will tell if Hobo returns.

CHAPTER TEN
THE LIVING DAYLIGHTS

The offer of recording the theme song for the 17th James Bond film, *The Living Daylights*, was a strong indicator of just how far a-ha's stock had risen within the space of less than 18 months. By the end of 1986, the band had registered five Top 10 hit singles – including a No. 1 with 'The Sun Always Shines on TV' – and that was just in the UK. Both *Hunting High and Low* and *Scoundrel Days* were a perennial presence in the worldwide album charts, while the band also played to enthusiastic audiences in Australia, France, Germany, Japan and the US, as well as the UK. By the end of the year they had played well over a hundred shows.

While it was generally big-name singers such as Shirley Bassey, Matt Monroe, Lulu and Tom Jones who landed the James Bond theme job, there was the occasional opening for a more pop-oriented act, and Paul McCartney and Wings delivered the memorable George Martin-produced 'Live and Let Die' in 1973. Over a decade later, Duran Duran – who, like a-ha, were very much on trend at the time – also demonstrated that a popular band could provide a credible theme song for a Bond movie. A-ha's popularity was a given, but their music also had considerable cinematic appeal, as well as an inherent rock classicism that made them a natural fit for the franchise. Or so it seemed.

'We were actually in the middle of our second album then,' said Pål, 'and were starting to release singles for that and heard there was a competition to try and get this next Bond song. And we were invited to submit a track.'[1]

According to Morten, the producer of the James Bond films, Albert Broccoli, wanted the band to submit a proposed song first, which was steadfastly rebuked by their manager, Terry Slater. 'In fact, the production team came to us again and asked us to send a song,' he recalled. 'Terry once again told them that they would have to decide whether they wanted a-ha or not.'[2] However, the band did eventually cave in and sent Broccoli and his team a rough demo, which was apparently met with enthusiasm.

THE NAME'S BARRY, JOHN BARRY

John Barry, whose name was synonymous with James Bond, reportedly first met a-ha after a show in Croydon in January 1987, and rumours soon circulated that they were on the verge of landing this major coup, which Jeremy Paxman later referred to in a BBC Breakfast news report as 'one of the highest accolades the music industry can offer'.

For both a-ha and Duran Duran, however, the experience of working with the multi-award-winning composer wasn't a particularly enjoyable one. In the case of

Duran Duran, the sessions that produced the Billboard chart-topping theme for *A View to a Kill* in 1985 were fraught with tension. 'It wasn't an easy song to write,' recalled the band's bassist, John Taylor. 'Nick [Rhodes] and John Barry didn't click. They found it hard just being in the same room. They were very stubborn and had very specific visions of how things should get done. I was caught in the crossfire: friend to Nick, adjutant to John. Many times I received late-night phone calls from John, admonishing me to "sort out this bloody bullshit". It was a negotiation, and I did what was required in order to get my dream realised.'[3]

Similarly, there were tensions during the making of 'The Living Daylights', as Morten recalled: 'Pål had composed a song together with Magne that we thought was appropriate, but then John Barry insisted on changing the song. Barry had been working on the music for the Bond films for years, and we were told very clearly that we had to involve him, too. I didn't get the impression that the song needed any changes; we liked it the way it was. But it was obvious to us that it was the usual procedure and, before we knew it, Magne's name was removed from the credits and replaced by Barry's name (including a share of the royalties). That was not nice, and it became a political thing.'[4]

THE LIVING DAYLIGHTS (Single Version)
Written by John Barry and Pål Waaktaar-Savoy
Produced by Jason Corsaro, Magne Furuholmen, Pål Waaktaar-Savoy
and John Barry
Chart position: 5 (UK), 1 (Norway), 8 (Germany)

According to Pål, the first germ of an idea for the song was played to his band colleagues backstage at BBC's *Top of the Pops*. 'I was very happy when I heard the title because it immediately seemed to suggest that melody for me,' he said, 'The chorus came superfast.'[5]

'The song started as a co-write between Pål and me,' added Magne, 'and Pål begged me to let him remove my name after John Barry insisted he be credited – stupidly, I agreed. To be fair, John Barry did totally change the verses so, contract or not, his credit is absolutely warranted. Only I had changed the choruses drastically to what they are today, and Pål never even mentions that I wrote the chant part that in many ways has become a signature.'

The original demo, which was put together for the benefit of the film's production team, reveals a track in a very early, transitional stage. While the key chant of the chorus was in place, there were just a bare outline of lyrics. 'The song radiated a good amount of energy, and I was satisfied with it,' said Pål. 'All hell broke loose when I was supposed to write the lyrics. The only thing I had was the title, and I had no idea what the movie was about . . . I remember Lauren being in

Boston at the time and I called her five times a day and asked, "How about this, or how about that?" I sat until three or four in the morning trying to get the lyrics finished.'[6]

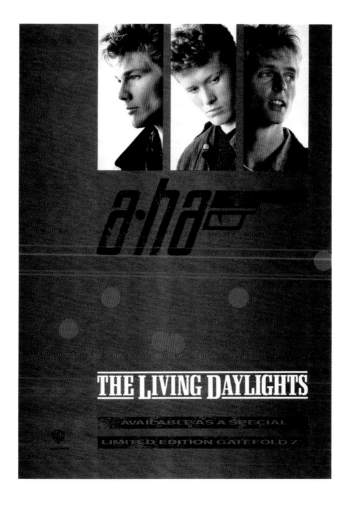

However, although the original demo's verses were sketchy at best ('We've walked on virgin soil / You don't believe it'), the chorus was nailed, and the band were also happy with one of the synth motifs. 'John Barry added his strings and changed a note in this melody by a semitone,' explained Morten. 'When we went to the studio to mix the song, we changed it back.'[7] Magne added: 'This was on one of my riffs in the bridge parts.'

'After we finished the basic track, John Barry added a wonderful dark and droning string score with heavy brass stabs that just reeked Bond,' said Pål. 'Then we went to New York for the mix with Jason Corsaro, who also added some exotic percussion tracks that further strengthened the Bond vibe.'[8]

The theme, featuring Barry's signature Bond embellishments, was eventually completed to the satisfaction of both parties. However, tensions between a-ha and the Bond camp resurfaced when they were unable to attend the film's premiere in Leicester Square on 29 June 1987. Morten recalled that the band were expected to cancel their show at Osaka-j Hall, despite their touring commitments in Japan: 'They couldn't believe that we would not show up, and so it turned into a bit of a [media] circus with everybody wondering why the band who did the theme tune weren't at the opening of the movie,' he said. 'Some people said that we didn't care, but that wasn't true. We would have been there and wanted to be there but our conscience wouldn't let us cancel our shows in Japan and disappoint all those people. That wouldn't have been right.'[9]

The single, backed with an instrumental version of the track, returned the band to the Top 10, but not everyone was struck by it. 'It's unmistakably a-ha,' said *Smash Hits'* Tom Hibbert: '. . . But is there a proper tune? No. Can you twist to it? No, you jolly well cannot.' Elsewhere, *Record Mirror*'s Robin Smith wrote: 'Mort and the boys belt out something that might have stood a better chance as the theme for a gardening programme. The world tour seems to have well-knackered them. Licensed to thrill? I think not.'

Despite the criticism, the band proved they could produce a song to order, with Pål coming up with some memorable couplets under pressure ('Set your hopes up way too high / The living's in the way we die'). It's also proved to be a popular singalong during live shows, with both Magne and Pål integrating parts of Monty Norman's distinctive 'James Bond Theme'.

CHAPTER ELEVEN
STAY ON THESE ROADS

The real problems started with this one. It opened a can of worms. It felt like we
were going backwards.
– Magne Furuholmen, *Record Collector*, 2009

Released: May 1988
Chart position: 2 (UK), 1 (Norway), 4 (Germany)

By the time a-ha's 15-month world tour had concluded in August 1987, the band
had performed over 170 shows. But there was little opportunity for a break as they
almost immediately began working on what Pål called their 'difficult third album',
the final segment of a triptych of teen-oriented long-players. (Morten also found
time to finish filming scenes for the film *Kamilla og tyven* [Kamilla and the Thief],
which he had a small part in.)

Although the band felt they had made the album they wanted to make with
Scoundrel Days, the record label weren't exactly enamoured with their efforts
and, given that their first album had been such a spectacular success for both
parties, its release was treated almost like a concession. The band had taken

huge musical strides, but they were still being pigeonholed – and marketed – as a teenybopper band. 'If we'd grown up in the UK I'm sure we would have had a different approach to becoming famous and been much more conscious of the mechanisms,' said Magne. 'But we sort of embraced it all, letting [ourselves] be photographed in every stupid way, not really questioning anything, thinking the music's going to shine through, that everybody's going to see it for what it is. But it doesn't happen like that.'[1]

Testament to their strong work ethic, the band had indeed posed dutifully for every photo and gamefully answered the same tired questions several times over, but the fact that they had songs such as 'Here I Stand and Face the Rain' and 'I've Been Losing You' in their repertoire counted for nothing as they struggled to up the average age of their audience. But, with *Scoundrel Days* not performing as well as its predecessor, the band were now under pressure to revert to a catchier, pop-based sound.

Giorgio Moroder – whose impressive CV boasted clients such as Blondie, David Bowie, Freddie Mercury and Donna Summer – had reportedly showed an interest in producing the band during this period. 'I usually don't work with rock groups,' he said years later. '. . . I want to come in, be in charge and have the songs ready. Do you remember a-ha? They came to Los Angeles to record with me. They were supposed to come to the studio at one o'clock to start, and at six o'clock, they still were not there. The next day, same thing. So I left. Life is too short to work with bands.'[2]

I asked Magne about Moroder's claims. 'Well, there was a meeting set up with Moroder which fell apart,' he said, 'but to my knowledge we did not know about any recording session. If there was one set up, I can understand how he would think of us as arrogant, but truthfully we really loved his work on David Bowie's "Cat People (Putting Out Fire)", so we were quite keen to meet him. I think this is one of those things best described as a cock-up!'

In the end, the band settled once again with Alan Tarney, who had just enjoyed big hit singles with Cliff Richard's 'My Pretty One' and 'Some People', but it was a move that Pål later described as 'a big mistake'. Earlier in the year, the musician indicated that the band favoured self-production: 'We have to prove to ourselves that we're good,' he said. 'At the moment we're developing in a positive way. We'll produce our next album ourselves. We've started recording already . . . *Scoundrel Days* was a step in the right direction, but now we're ready to take the giant step forward from being pop stars to rock stars.'[3]

As it transpired, it would take a few more years for this pop-rock transition to occur, and the band would have to toe the line for the time being, which included the reinstatement of their original logo, as if to further emphasise that they had come full circle.

Another problem facing the band, aside from their perceived image in the music press, was a lack of new songs, and the fact that they ended up revisiting some of Bridges' songs did indicate they were desperate for material. However, all things considered, the album did hold together reasonably well. In Germany, the long-running *Pop/Rocky* magazine was certainly impressed, declaring that the album included 'many soulful and romantic songs with clever melodies, beautiful arrangements and accomplished vocals', while in the UK, the normally unforgiving *NME* recognised the band's growing maturity: 'A-ha are not a kiddy pop band after all – they are a slick CD vehicle with a big, full sound . . . This band will, in time, develop a serious back catalogue'. However, *Smash Hits*' Tom Doyle noticed a dip in quality: 'In lots of ways this is their most consistent LP yet, but the problem is that it's consistently average'. *Record Mirror*, too, were disappointed: 'A-ha are far from inarticulate, but their previous effortless grasp of the English language seems to be foundering somewhat,' wrote Lesley O'Toole. 'They can still teach our natives a thing or two about pop, and Morten Harket remains the best overgrown choirboy in the business, but something, somewhere is missing.'

In Norway, *VG*'s Morten Stensland singled out 'This Alone Is Love', 'Touchy!' and the title track for praise but couldn't hide his disappointment. 'Unfortunately, this is not an LP that lives up to expectations after the fine previous LP, *Scoundrel Days*,' he wrote. '*Stay on These Roads* contains far too many uninteresting songs.'

'Terry Slater's claim that reviews, good or bad, were tomorrow's fish and chips paper became our motto, too,' reflected Pål on the band's mixed reviews over the years. 'The English press always dismissed us as foreigners, while Norwegian ones had a mission to bring us down to earth. We were, with Morten and Magne, too handsome for our own good, so that was also obviously annoying to reviewers. I think the only positive angle is that, since we never relied on good reviews to be successful, it was never given much attention – record companies wouldn't [factor] that into their campaigns. We adapted the attitude we still roll by: If they like it, great . . . If they hate it, fuck 'em!'

In spite of the mixed reviews, *Stay on These Roads* provided the band with another strong-selling album and even a Spellemann nomination for Best Album in the pop category. However, cracks were already starting to show by this stage. As Morten later recalled, the novelty of fame was beginning to wear off: 'We enjoyed the attention and success at first. It was fun and there were some great moments. But we were never after success simply for its own sake. The music was important to us. We were saddened that we were not allowed to develop. Too many people became dependent on us and we became like a pop factory, churning out records like hamburgers.'[4]

STAY ON THESE ROADS
Written by Morten Harket, Magne Furuholmen and Pål Waaktaar-Savoy
Produced by Alan Tarney
Chart position: 5 (UK), 1 (Norway), 7 (Germany)

By the time it came to making their third album, the band's days as a close-knit trio were a distant memory. Two years had now passed since the closure of John Ratcliff's Rendezvous Studio, which had served as a-ha's nerve centre during their pre-fame period, while Octocon Studio had also run its course. Back in London, it was no longer necessary to demo songs in a hired studio, since both Magne and Pål could now afford the luxury of working from home.

One such demo was 'Sail on My Love', as Magne explained: 'I had made a song and a makeshift demo. I had these chords, the keyboard riff and the vocal lines of the chorus melody, with the first one being "sail on my love".'

Featuring just a bare outline of lyrics, the writing session for the track reveals that the song originally included the melody from the ambient section of Bridges' 'Wildfire' suite (which also spawned many of the lyrics for 'I Dream Myself Alive'), but this was soon changed.

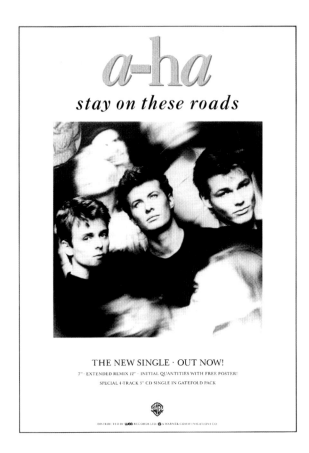

'We were all in Pål's flat,' continued Magne, 'and I was excited and wanted Pål to hear it, but he was on the phone for a long time. I said to Morten we should write something together sometime. He came over to Pål's piano with me and he changed my melody for the second line (it had no lyrics at the time, but it is the one that goes "we shall meet, I know" on the finished record). It was way better with his input, so this was the first time Morten and

I had written together. Pål came in later and heard us play it and he applauded, but not looking happy. Pål did, however, suggest I keep the underlying keyboard riff on the choruses going through the verses and also that I use an instrumental part that I had written for the song "Hurry Home" (which became the part underneath "old man feels the cold"). Recognising a hit, Pål further suggested changing the lyrics and wrote new ones for the song.'

The inspired keyboardist recorded most of the basic tracks on a Macintosh home computer, and much of this groundwork made it to the final version, which included some overdubs from Øystein Jevanord, who recorded some cymbal parts at Rainbow Studio in Oslo. (In addition to working with the band during their *Scoundrel Days* period, Øystein had maintained a high musical profile in his home country as a member of the very popular deLillos, whom he recorded two albums with.)

The end result was another piece of collaborative magic, with each member of the band adding vital elements to the track, just as they had done with 'Take On Me'. Although Magne later labelled the production as 'poodle-rock', this tender slice of glacial melancholia has certainly aged well, and its wintry timbres made it perfect single fodder back in March 1988. (The video for the song, shot on location in Aldeburgh, Suffolk, was directed by the vastly experienced Andrew Morahan, who had helmed promos for many of a-ha's contemporaries, including the Human League, Pet Shop Boys and Thompson Twins.) It was the first a-ha single to be issued on CD format (a three-inch with an adaptor) and provided another big hit for the band in the UK. (A heavily edited mix for the US market fared less well, however.)

Guest reviewer Vince Clarke told *Smash Hits*: 'It's far too manufactured and overproduced,' while Andy Bell, his partner in Erasure, agreed: 'I was really looking forward to this, but I'm disappointed now . . . It's much more bland than anything else they've written. There's no tune to it, nothing that makes you want to sing along to it. I couldn't make out a single word he was singing.' In Bell's defence, the lyrics were unusual ('The cold has a voice / It talks to me / Stillborn by choice'), but there was certainly nothing wrong with Morten's beautiful, crystalline delivery.

Elsewhere, European industry magazine *Music & Media* were far more generous: 'This song needs repeated plays to fully appreciate its impact; after that, you can't get it out of your head. A ballad with a slow and commanding build-up, sporting a subtle melody.'

Since its inception, the band have experimented with several different versions of the song over the years, including an excellent Radiohead-esque interpretation during the *Analogue* tour, which featured both Magne and Pål on electric guitar.

MATTHEW LETLEY

The release of the single coincided with the start of a year-long world tour, and a new-look live band included future Status Quo drummer Matthew Letley.

How did you get the job as a-ha's drummer?

It was all word of mouth as many things are in the music business. Early in 1988 I was on tour with Bob Geldof in Australia when the guitarist in the band, Gerry Moffett – whom I'd recommended to Bob having toured with him in Kim Wilde's band – received a call from Ian Wherry saying a-ha were looking for a bass player and drummer for a world tour over the next year. (Just to complete the circle, Gerry and Ian played together in David Essex's band and I went on to join that band in 1990.) On our return, Gerry and I went to the auditions in London and both of us got through to the final round. After a tense audition playing through 'The Swing of Things' and (I think) 'I've Been Losing You', the guys decided to go with Randy [Hope-Taylor] and me. I'd not met Randy before, but he is a superb bass player and a great chap to have on the road. I seem to remember he did a fantastic impersonation of Eddie Murphy – he'd have everyone in fits on the tour bus!

Were you a fan of the band's music before you joined?

Well, when the video for 'Take On Me' exploded onto our TV screens I think everyone sat up and took note! There was an edge to their sound that I really liked, and so when the opportunity to play with them came along I grabbed it. They are, of course, great songwriters and the first two albums were carefully crafted and well produced. I believe Alan Tarney was their producer at the time and I liked some of the other albums he'd worked on, notably Cliff Richard's *Rock 'n' Roll Juvenile* and the subsequent albums he did with Cliff. Alan always produced great records.

As well as live shows, there were obviously a lot of playback performances during this period. What did you think of the Stay on These Roads album?

All the drums on the *Stay on These Roads* album were programmed and it can be strange having to mime to parts that aren't always what a drummer would naturally play. However, I did my best, and it was a lot of fun to be included in so many TV appearances. I even got to play at the Royal Variety

Show with them that year! Any band's third album can be tricky as it really needs to be a step up from previous releases. *Stay on These Roads* was good, but possibly not as strong as the first two, in my opinion.

What were Magne, Morten and Pål like to work with?
My initial impression was that they were extremely polite guys – not always the case in the music business. Pål was the quiet one but always listening and writing down ideas in a notebook he had on him at all times. I often wonder how many songs came out of that book! Mags was the outgoing comedian often fond of a practical joke or two, and Morten was a little more on the eccentric side and passionate about ecology and saving the planet – a subject he was very knowledgeable about. The guys were great fun to work with and certainly on a roll. What could be better than playing to packed houses all around the world? We went to Japan for a month playing to 10,000 fans a night and went on to play five stadium gigs in Brazil – up until then, the biggest shows the band had done. It was crazy! Brilliant musicians in the band, too, with Ian Wherry on keyboards (certainly one of the best musicians I've worked with), the talented Randy Hope-Taylor on bass and fantastic American percussionist Rafael Gayol, who has become a good friend. Raf went on to tour with Leonard Cohen (Morten's hero!) and Randy got the gig with Jeff Beck! I look back on my time with a-ha with great fondness and on my list of career highlights.

THE BLOOD THAT MOVES THE BODY
Written by Pål Waaktaar-Savoy
Produced by Alan Tarney
Chart position: 25 (UK), 23 (Germany)

With its acute sense of foreboding, 'The Blood That Moves the Body' marked a return to the leitmotifs of Bridges' *Fakkeltog* album, and appropriately featured Øystein Jevanord (credited as 'Einstein Jevanord') on drums.

The lyrics had been inspired by Japanese literature that Pål had picked up during a-ha's tour of the Far East in July 1986, which included the work of Yukio Mishima, a Nobel Prize-nominated author who had committed suicide by seppuku in 1970. The reference to *Eyes of a Blue Dog*, a collection of short stories by the Colombian writer Gabriel García Márquez, was added later.

There was also speculation that the song had been inspired by a proliferating number of teen suicides in Japan. Indeed, the death of 18-year-old *Star Tanj!* winner Yukiko Okada in April 1986 and the resulting spate of copycat suicides –

dubbed the 'Yukiko Syndrome' – would certainly have been big news during that period. 'It is scarcely the stuff from which great pop songs are made,' wrote journalist Martin Townsend in his review of the album, 'but a-ha are hardly a normal pop group. Alongside a string of lightweight hit singles, they have used their albums to explore serious issues such as alienation, loneliness and the politics of love.'

Underpinned by Anne Dudley's cinematic score, the track shares many of the attributes of 'The Living Daylights' and, in spite of its morbid undertones, was selected for single release in June 1988.

'It's a typically spooky and dramatic affair . . . But there's not much of a tune to speak of,' wrote *Smash Hits*' Richard Lowe. 'The mental stability of Pål must be called into question at this point, too. For, let's face it, lines such as "Red stains on 'Eyes of a Blue Dog' / My pains fade as interiors fog" are not the work of an altogether sane man.'

The single was later branded a flop as it failed to reach the Top 20 in the UK, but Pål was quick to point out that the band had missed out on potential *Top of the Pops*

appearances due to their touring schedule. (The promo video, which was filmed while the band were on tour in Paris, was shown, however.)

Curiously, the song was later used in a commercial advertising the Mandom Corporation's new range of Gatsby grooming products, which was filmed during the Japanese leg of a-ha's world tour in September 1988. (A *Making of Gatsby* documentary was later released on VHS video in Japan.)

The single also enjoyed another lease

of life in 1992 when it was rereleased to promote the band's compilation album, *Headlines and Deadlines: The Hits of a-ha*. Alan Tarney's more percussive 'Gun Mix' didn't include the original version's
eerie intro, but Pål's guitar was far more prominent this time round. It failed to chart, however.

TOUCHY!
Written by Morten Harket, Magne Furuholmen and Pål Waaktaar-Savoy
Produced by Alan Tarney
Chart position: 11 (UK), 13 (Germany)

The band debuted 'Touchy!' during their world tour in 1987, and later performed it during an appearance on ITV's *Surprise Surprise* show in the UK in December. The TV appearance indicated that the catchy song had been pencilled in as the album's forerunning single, and the band later confirmed to *Smash Hits* that it was one of the contenders.

The song had actually been demoed by the band several years previously at Rendezvous, and the original inspiration behind the lyrics was hay fever, which all three members of the band suffered from ('Sound and sensation, pollen everywhere . . . Mother reads me what the papers say / Two thousand pollen in a cubic metre air'). When the track was dusted down for inclusion on *Stay on These Roads*, the lyrics were changed and a character named Donna – wrongly assumed to be Donna Summer – became the song's new focal point ('Donna found me in her slow and dreamy way / Now she reads me what the papers say'), but some of the decidedly oddball lyrics were retained ('Both of us together in a room by ourselves / I sneeze to look around / There's no escape').

On account of its carousel melody and slightly hackneyed chorus, 'Touchy!' has been labelled as one of the cheesiest tracks in the band's canon, but its production, featuring a polyphony of synths, guitars and harmonica parts, wasn't as simple as it sounded. '"Touchy!" took us ages to perfect because it's an old type of swing rhythm,' said Pål, 'and it took ages to get right, even using computers and things to syncopate the beat.'[5]

Boosted by a promotional video featuring synchronised swimmers, the band were rewarded for their efforts with another Top 20 hit in the UK, but the reviews at the time weren't positive. 'That old a-ha magic just isn't there,' wrote DJ Mark Goodier for *No.1*. 'It will be a small hit with their following, but I'm sure they can do better than this.' Elsewhere, *Smash Hits*' William Shaw thought the song was contrived: '"Touchy!" is just too manic. It sounds like they're trying to regain some of the pop froth that first set them on their way with "Take On Me".'

In concert, it was a different beast altogether, however, and a more muscular performance of the track during the band's shows in the 90s merited a re-evaluation of this highly underrated group composition.

THIS ALONE IS LOVE
Music written by Magne Furuholmen and Pål Waaktaar-Savoy
Words written by Pål Waaktaar-Savoy
Produced by Alan Tarney

Indicative of the fact that the band were scrambling for material for their third album, the B-side of 'I've Been Losing You' was rescued from relative obscurity and given a new lease of life. During the fruitful 80s, it wasn't uncommon for bands to do this. The Smiths' signature song, 'How Soon Is Now?', for example, had started life as the B-side of 'William, It Was Really Nothing' in 1984, before its promotion to A-side status the following year, while two of OMD's *Architecture and Morality*-era B-sides – 'The Romance of the Telescope' and 'Of All the Things We've Made' – were later included on the band's fractured fourth album, *Dazzle Ships*.

For its killer chorus alone, 'This Alone Is Love' was certainly worthy of inclusion on *Stay on These Roads*, and the new version certainly does the job of building upon the original preparatory take. It's a far more polished and indulgent affair, however, distinguishable by Morten's final cry of 'Oh baby, what can we do?' during the climax of an unnecessarily elongated coda.

HURRY HOME
Written by Magne Furuholmen and Pål Waaktaar-Savoy
Produced by Alan Tarney

In many respects, 'Hurry Home' represented much of what was bad about the overproduced *Stay on These Roads*. It starts off promisingly enough with an intro redolent of Talk Talk, while the train-emulating percussive effects are certainly a nice touch, but it soon evolves into a plodding clutter of synths and processed guitar sounds. Certainly, the overall sound of the album had been dictated by the technologies of the period, and the band later criticised Alan Tarney's impregnable production methods.

Its original demo did at least spawn one of the key synth motifs for the album's title track, but the finished version lacked invention while, unusually, the lyrics also lacked Pål's usual enigmatic spark. (The 'Freight train running' line may well have been a subliminal pick-up from Bruce Springsteen's 'I'm on Fire'.) In essence,

'Hurry Home' was devoid of personality, and had more in common with the mid-80s sophisti-pop of acts such as Go West and Living in a Box.

THE LIVING DAYLIGHTS
Written by John Barry and Pål Waaktaar-Savoy
Produced by Alan Tarney

Back in the 1980s, releasing stand-alone singles was commonplace. The likes of Big Country, the Cure, Depeche Mode, Duran Duran, Madness, New Order, the Smiths, Soft Cell, Tears for Fears and many other bands used the 45 rpm medium to keep the momentum going in between album releases, and often came up with the occasional classic song. So it was something of a disappointment when a-ha chose to include a song that was almost a year old on their third long-player. It was the equivalent move of, say, Duran Duran including 'A View to a Kill' on their *Notorious* album (thankfully, this didn't happen). Pål claimed that the band were worried about the accessibility of the track. 'This is before online streaming days,' he said. 'For us, back then, it felt that with a single you could buy them for a certain period and then they were out of the shops. So we thought we should get it on the album, so people would have a place to pick it up.'[6]

There was a problem, though: The band didn't own the recording. Rather than license the track, which would have been expensive – particularly given the James Bond connection – the band decided to rerecord it in a more contemporary style, using the lavish array of synths they were using at the time. The result was a reasonable replication of the original, but it lacked the tension and Hollywood sheen of its celluloid counterpart.

The original version of 'The Living Daylights' was included on the band's *Headlines and Deadlines* compilation in 1991, but was curiously omitted from both the VHS and DVD formats.

THERE'S NEVER A FOREVER THING
Written by Pål Waaktaar-Savoy
Produced by Alan Tarney

Following some of the more convoluted productions on the album, this comparatively sparse track offered some welcome relief, plus a further display of the band's more sensitive side. Originally demoed at Rendezvous using a more bossa nova-like rhythm, this touching song was written in 1984 for Lauren Savoy in the wake of her stepfather's death (hence its provisional title of 'Lauren . . . There's Never a Forever Thing'), and was considered for inclusion on *Scoundrel Days*. Pål's lyrics are both tender and sincere ('It's alright, dear / I'll be here through the night / With you till the first signs of light'), while the level of emotion in Morten's vocal is perfectly judged. Even better was a more stripped-back acoustic version, which wouldn't have sounded out of place on the band's next album.

The track was also issued as a promotional single in Brazil in 1989, while Lauren later directed a tasteful black and white video to accompany the track's inclusion on 1991's *Headlines and Deadlines* VHS compilation (evocative of Phil Collins' 'Another Day in Paradise' clip, it featured shots of the homeless).

OUT OF BLUE COMES GREEN
Written by Pål Waaktaar-Savoy
Produced by Alan Tarney

With a production evocative of *Notorious*-era Duran Duran and a percussive intro that recalled *Tin Drum*-era Japan, *Stay on These Roads*' masterly near-seven-minute centrepiece was conceived during the making of the album.

Just as Lauren's film studies had provided the inspiration for cuts such as 'Cry Wolf', such was the case with this fan favourite, whose title was derived from his future spouse's graduation film. Lyrically, the box-fresh song was inspired by the songwriter's relationship with his parents and their grounding influence on him ('Like a river I'm flowing / And there's no way of knowing / If I'm coming or going / I need something to chain me down'). Musically, it recalled the epic, autumnal soundscapes of *Scoundrel Days*, but it also served as a foretaste of the rockier tones of *Memorial Beach*, with its more prominent guitar work and gutsier vocals. An alternative take of the track – in a much tighter arrangement that seemed tailor-made for single release – does flow better, however.

The track was also played on selected dates on the attendant tour and, years later, following a set list contest, Morten also performed a version of it during the *Out of My Hands* tour in 2012.

In 2019, a more piano-based cover version of the track was released as a single by Per Ohlson.

YOU ARE THE ONE
Written by Magne Furuholmen and Pål Waaktaar-Savoy
Produced by Alan Tarney
Chart position: 13 (UK), 30 (Germany)

Like many of the songs stemming from a-ha's imperial phase in the mid- to late 80s, the origins of 'You Are the One' went back to Magne and Pål's Bridges era, and an embryonic three-minute version of the track was later rehearsed and recorded by Poem in 1981. What the recording reveals is that the riff was originally played on guitar – with Magne's fairground keyboard sounds providing a counter melody – and only a few of the lyrics from the final version were in place then, including the key line, 'You are the one [that] has done me in'.

It was later dusted down during sessions at Rendezvous, with both Morten and Magne contributing vocals. The slightly sluggish demo reveals that the catchy, cyclical refrain was in place, but the updated lyrics needed some work ('You are the one who can make life fun / You're the best pain that I ever had').

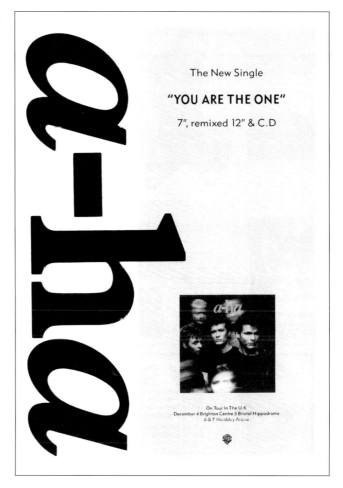

The New Single

"YOU ARE THE ONE"

7", remixed 12" & C.D

On Tour In The U.K
December 4 Brighton Centre 5 Bristol Hippodrome
6 & 7 Wembley Arena

By the time of its completion at RG Jones Studios, the song had undergone something of a sprightly transformation, which was in marked contrast to the melancholia of the song, which oscillates between jealousy ('I call again, but there's no one in / Don't know where, with whom you've been') and unrequited love ('I fought for you, did you let me win? / You don't even care, you don't care where I've been'), before getting slightly stalkery ('I call your friends, but there's no one in / Catching you is so hard'). 'We've been doing an a capella version recently on tour to bring out the harmonies heard on the recorded version,' said Magne in 2016, 'and also to bring out the sadness in the song. It's a song with the ability to sound conflicted.'[7]

'It was one of those songs which sounds really simple, yet was a real brain-twister,' added Pål, who cited the middle eight as the best part of the song. 'Every time we had the chorus and the verse it came out another way, in a different key.

Magne and I would go back and forth. It sounds like three or four chords, but there is a lot more.'[8]

The track was embellished with brass, courtesy of the appropriately named Kick Horns. Although it signalled something of a change in style for a-ha, these overdubs were very much on-trend at the time. In fact, a host of established artists had already employed the services of the jobbing musicians during this period, including Bronski Beat, China Crisis, the Communards, Erasure, Nik Kershaw and many others.

In the UK, a Justin Strauss remix of the track was released as a single in November 1988, which tied in neatly with an arena tour the following month. The accompanying promotional video, featuring shots of the band camping it up in sailor outfits, was filmed in New York.

YOU'LL END UP CRYING
Written by Pål Waaktaar-Savoy
Produced by Alan Tarney

Formerly titled 'You'll End Up Crying With Your Mother's Eyes', this stunning closing track had originally been written for Poem. An entry in Pål's diary dates the song to 22 April 1981, and the lyrics included two verses that would make it to the finished version (other lines, such as 'Reasons to run / Too young to remember how life begun', were culled).

'Back in the pre-album days, it was a song that Morten always wanted to do when there were pretty girls in the room and an acoustic guitar lying around,' said Pål. Indeed, the song was later demoed by a-ha at Rendezvous, and the recording reveals a more classical influence, with its Bach-like arrangement. The band later adopted this blueprint, featuring the stacked harmonies, but the intro was tweaked: Some rather sinister strings were added (which recalled OMD's chilling *Junk Culture* out-take, '(The Angels Keep Turning) the Wheels of the Universe'), while a trumpet part added something of a mariachi flavour. 'It's definitely me playing,' said former Kick Horns member Steve Sidwell. 'I also played on "You Are the One". I seem to remember it was at Roundhouse Studios, and I was brought back into the studio on my own to do the solo.'

As well as showcasing the band's gift for harmonisation, 'You'll End Up Crying' exemplified the band's knack for writing melancholic pop music, as well as adding some welcome contrast to the more complex (and, arguably, overproduced) tracks on this transitional work.

SOLO WORK

During their commercial peak, a-ha were attracting offers to write theme songs for James Bond movies, while Morten himself was in demand, not only as a vocalist but also as an actor, appearing in *Kamilla og tyven* (1988) and its sequel the following year. He also contributed 'Kamilla og Sebastian' to the Ragnar Bjerkreim-composed soundtrack, a sentimental ballad that encapsulated the movie's friendship between an orphan and a reformed thief. (The track was later released as a promotional single in 2005.)

'The reason I did the film is because I like the people who are doing it and I like what they're trying to do,' said Morten. '. . . It has standards. It follows morals that one used to have in that era, because it's set [around 1913]. I think we have a very cold society and I think the main reason for that is that family life has broken down. I was rebellious in an introverted way when I was a teenager. But I had discipline and respect for my parents and I think the problems that exist with drugs – which is the worst disease to hit our society – and violence amongst young people is because these things have been lost.'[9]

Morten's high profile also accorded him the opportunity to indulge in other musical endeavours. One such project was an appearance on 'Det er ennå tid' [There Is Still Time], an uplifting track that was used to promote a 1989 Scout convention in Skaugum. The promotional single was credited to Bjørn Eidsvåg with Morten Harket and the Oslo Gospel Choir. Eidsvåg was a well-known Norwegian songwriter, musician and Spellemann winner who shared his interest in theology. Known affectionately as 'Rockepresten' [the Rock Priest], the ordained minister later conducted the ceremony at Magne's wedding in August 1992.

During this busy period in the late 1980s, Morten also contributed backing vocals to 'Merciful Waters', an atmospheric – though unremarkable – single released by Jan Bang in 1989. (The song featured both on Bang's *Frozen Feelings* album and the soundtrack to an Icelandic film named *Foxtrot*.) An accomplished musician and producer, Bang later worked on projects involving the likes of David Sylvian and Brian Eno, and also co-founded the annual Punkt music festival, which Magne performed at in 2007. Both Magne and Bang also contributed to Nils Petter Molvær's 2005 album, *er*.

PART THREE
AMERICANA
1989-1994

CHAPTER TWELVE

EAST OF THE SUN, WEST OF THE MOON

What might turn out to be a-ha's finest work comes at a time when their natural audience is less inclined to listen.
– *Q* magazine, 1990

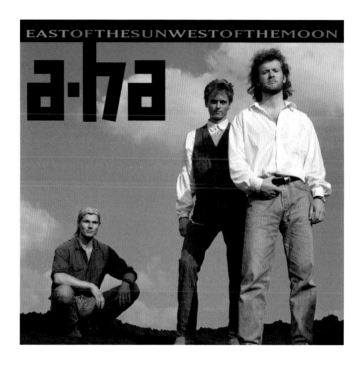

Released: October 1990
Chart position: 12 (UK), 1 (Norway), 6 (Germany)

While *Stay on These Roads* represented the sound of a band coming full circle, their next album would see them striving for a more organic and guitar-based sound, deliberately steering away from the *koldtbord* of synths and drum machines that had defined much of their output to this point. They were also aware they had lost ground in the US since their debut album, and what followed was an arguably conscious effort to Americanise their sound for this potentially lucrative market. To achieve this, the band needed to hit the reset button and devote more energy to the recording studio, curtailing their touring and promotional commitments in the process. 'We had been on tour for about three years, practically without stopping,' said Morten. 'We absolutely needed to make a stop, to disconnect. So we said enough, for a while.'[1]

The year-long *Stay on These Roads* world tour had ended in São Paulo on 19 March 1989, but the band had reportedly, by this time, already done some preliminary work on the next album, which had an intriguing working title of *Beginning Middle End*. 'We've proved ourselves now, and soon we'll be taking a lot of time to get the vision of a-ha back into shape,' said Morten the previous summer. 'Because we really have great potential. And we need to spend more time, just the three of us together to achieve that and sit down and write our masterpiece. We are not a pop band anymore; that is just one part of what a-ha is about.'[2]

There would be a considerable gap between the release of 1988's 'You Are the One' hit and the band's next single, and there was a report in Norway's *Aftenposten* newspaper that this gap would be plugged with a compilation titled *So Far*, which was originally pencilled in for release at the end of 1989, but ultimately back-burnered as work on a new album continued apace.

RHYTHM DIVINE

Intent on going back to their roots and forging a more live sound in the studio, the band recruited a new Norwegian-speaking rhythm section. 'The reason why we chose Norwegian musicians for the recording of *East of the Sun, West of the Moon* was simply the language,' said Pål. 'When we talked at length in the studio, in Norwegian, the musicians we had used in the past would sit there, not understanding a word. We knew that we would continue to speak Norwegian with each other, so we wanted someone who could be more in the loop.'[3]

Jørun Bøgeberg was both a bass player and songwriter, and he had played on some of the final recordings by veteran prog rockers Junipher Greene. He was also well known to a-ha, having performed with Morten during some shows at Oslo's Hot House club in 1983 (as Sporty Morty and the House Rockers). He'd even seen Bridges perform at Chateau Neuf and bought a copy of their *Fakkeltog* album from a street seller who he said was likely to have been Magne. Additionally, he'd also played on the *Rock vs. Opera* album by Dollie de Luxe, whose producer had once tried to enlist the services of Bridges as a backing group for the duo.

'I knew quite a bit about the band and their progress towards fame,' said Jørun. 'I met Morten sometimes at Club 7 in Oslo in the period before the breakthrough. Maybe I heard some songs they were working on as well. But we were all quite stunned when they made it big with the final version of "Take On Me". I remember sitting in a taxi the first time I heard "Hunting High and Low" coming through the radio, and from that moment I was really impressed and touched by the mood, the voice, the melody and the song in general. I guess I became a fan from then on, even though I never saw them live before my joining.'

Jørun eventually joined after receiving what he termed a 'weird phone call from a guy calling himself Morten something' in September 1989. Eventually, Jørun worked out that he was in fact speaking to Norway's biggest pop star, and gratefully accepted the offer to become a-ha's new bassist.

Taking his position on the drum stool was Per Hillestad who, since 1977, has been a member of the Spellemann award-winning jazz-rock band Lava (*Rockipedia* describes them as 'a Norwegian Toto'). Per was also an in-demand session player and had previously worked with Jørun on albums by Jonas Fjeld and Ottar 'Big Hand' Johansen.

According to Jørun, the new five-piece line-up played together at a rehearsal space in Oslo in November 1989, and there was an immediate rapport.

HOOKS AND MOTIFS

The new band started working on demos at a Shepherds Bush studio in January 1990, but the actual album was recorded at various other locations in London, including Air Studios in Oxford Street. Once again, there were a number of co-writes, with Magne and Pål contributing highly rated songs such as 'Rolling Thunder', 'Slender Frame' and 'Waiting for Her'. 'I could not have finished them without Pål,' said Magne, 'but each of these were songs I had developed and brought to him. Pål would accept my hooks and motifs on the songs he was writing, but he would call my contributions arrangement, not songwriting. Since I did not complete lyrics at the time, I would always need lyrics from Pål in order to finish my songs, hence they were always co-writes.'

Overseeing the sessions this time round was not one but two new producers – Chris Neil and Ian Stanley – who were allocated half an album each. According to Pål, they each chose five different songs to work on, and there was surprisingly no overlap.

Chris Neil was an experienced musician and producer who, prior to working with a-ha, had helmed the albums *American English* (Wax) and *The Living Years* (Mike + the Mechanics), but he'd also worked with many other acts, too, including Dollar, Sheena Easton and Toyah. Though arguably tenuous, he also had links with a-ha: He'd previously worked with John Ratcliff's band, the Catch, and had co-produced Leo Sayer's *Have You Ever Been in Love* album with Alan Tarney.

Ian Stanley's CV was also impressive. As a key member of Tears for Fears during their imperial phase in the mid-80s, he'd co-written big hit singles such as 'Shout' and 'Everybody Wants to Rule the World', before leaving the band during the painstakingly slow production of their third album, *The Seeds of Love*.

Both producers had contrasting working methods. Neil was described by Magne as being 'very pragmatic', while Stanley was considerably more technically minded. 'We got along best with Chris Neil,' wrote Jørun Bøgeberg on his website, 'simply because he let us play.'

PREMIUM POP

Morten would later claim he didn't fully identify with the music, but this was an assured and mature collection, and critics tended to agree. *Smash Hits* described the Spellemann-nominated album as a 'premium pop package' in their 8/10 review, while *Q* magazine awarded four stars. 'What separates this particular trio from their fellow teen cover stars is their overwhelming air of melancholia,' wrote Barry McIlheney, 'a distinctly Scandinavian emotional worldview which works to impressive effect on their less uptempo songs.' Elsewhere, *Music & Media*'s writer declared: 'This is a remarkable album with echoes of U2 and Roy Orbison in a sophisticated, but never sterile, mix. Melancholy and sadness-ridden but not depressive or annoyingly dramatic.'

'Even *Melody Maker* liked *East of the Sun, West of the Moon*,' said Pål, 'but I found out about this afterwards. I came across a lot of newspaper clippings and reviews, and I almost felt cheated. Why hadn't I seen this before?'[4]

There were some negative reviews in the UK, however. *No.1*'s Jeremy Mark cluelessly suggested that the band had 'made very few changes to their sound', before concluding that the album was 'Samey, and very wailing'. Writing for

Vox magazine, Karen Doughwaite criticised 'Crying in the Rain' for 'the most nauseating Simon & Garfunkel type staged harmonies you've ever heard', and then bizarrely went on to suggest that the band had previously been inspired by Stock, Aitken and Waterman!

Writing for *VG* (Verdens Gang) in Norway, Catharina Jacobsen praised the band for their more adult-oriented sound: 'On the one hand, you have songs like "Slender Frame" and "Sycamore Leaves" that have something American about them and are considerably heavier than you are used to from a-ha, but the ballads are fortunately also in place. Both "Waiting for Her" and "(Seemingly) Nonstop July" show that the group has not forgotten their old tricks, and Pål Waaktaar's composition, "East of the Sun", could slide straight on to one of a-ha's first LPs.'

VINTAGE

When a-ha returned to the public eye in the autumn of 1990, they were almost unrecognisable, with both Magne and Morten sporting a considerably more hirsute look. And, as if to further emphasise the fact that they'd moved on from their leather wristband days, the album cover featured both a moody black and white shot of the band and a chunky new band logo.

While the attempt to broaden their fan demographic was admirable, sales were disappointing, and the failure of its lead single, 'Crying in the Rain', to crack the UK Top 10 indicated that a significant percentage of a-ha's audience had moved on since the band's heyday. 'Perhaps we have lost some of our teenage fans, but I don't think that all of them wanted to live with me. There were a few who didn't,' said Morten the following year. 'Those people who don't like us any more were probably only fascinated by a look or an image, and not the music. It is only in England we have this problem.'[5]

However, it wasn't just a-ha who were struggling to adapt to a fast-changing musical landscape, as the sliding fortunes of contemporaries such as Duran Duran, the Human League and Spandau Ballet would attest. Indeed, 80s bands were becoming increasingly unfashionable, and the charts were now being dominated by music of a more manufactured ilk. Artists gliding along the conveyor belt of Stock, Aitken and Waterman's 'Hit Factory' continued to permeate the charts, while dance and hip-hop music was becoming increasingly popular, as the significant sales of singles by the likes of Adamski, Beats International, MC Hammer, Snap! and Vanilla Ice would confirm. Following the emergence of the so-called Madchester movement at the turn of the year, alternative music was also on-trend with record-buyers, and acts such as Happy Mondays, Inspiral Carpets and the Stone Roses were crossing into the mainstream with increasing prolificacy.

However, there was still a market for music of a more 'vintage' persuasion, as the triple chart-topping success of Jive Bunny & the Mastermixers the previous year had already confirmed. At the time of the release of a-ha's comeback single in October 1990, Status Quo were riding high in the charts with a hits medley of their own in 'The Anniversary Waltz', while the Righteous Brothers' 'Unchained Melody' (1965) and Bobby Vinton's 'Blue Velvet' (1963) were both enjoying renewed success. Sadly, a-ha's version of an old Everly Brothers hit didn't quite have the same resonance, and the knock-on effect was that subsequent singles from the album would fail to chart in the UK's Top 40. 'This marked the point where a-ha became fuzzy for people, and we started to drop off the map, although ironically we went to South America and became huge around this time,' said Magne. 'We weren't pushing ourselves shamelessly into the limelight anymore; it was the start of us withdrawing, which we did completely in 1993.'[6] (During the *Rock in Rio II* festival on 26 January 1991, the band played to 198,000 people at the Maracanã stadium, which was then a world record.)

CRYING IN THE RAIN
Written by Howard Greenfield and Carole King
Produced by Chris Neil
Chart position: 13 (UK), 1 (Norway), 6 (Germany)

A one-off collaboration between Howard Greenfield and Carole King (two key frequenters of New York's songwriting office/studio, the Brill Building), 'Crying in the Rain' had originally been recorded by the Everly Brothers in 1961 and released as a single while the pair were undertaking military service in the US. It was a Top 10 hit on both sides of the Atlantic, as well as Norway.

A-ha's manager, Terry Slater, had close ties with the American duo, of course. He'd been their bass player and had co-written songs such as 'Bowling Green' before working with Phil Everly on solo projects during a decade-long hiatus in the 1970s. An Everly Brothers reunion, which culminated in the release of a new Dave Edmonds-produced album in 1984 (which included the Paul McCartney-penned 'On the Wings of a Nightingale' single), was overseen by Slater, while a concert at London's Royal Albert Hall on 23 September 1983 was witnessed by the members of a-ha. 'Crying in the Rain' was the third song on the set list that night. (In 1985, Phil Everly presented a-ha with three custom-made acoustic guitars which the band would later show off on the cover of a German-only limited edition picture disc version of the *Stay on These Roads* album. As recently as November 2018, Magne and Pål played these guitars during a special symphonic performance of 'Take On Me' on BBC's *The One Show*.)

'When we saw the Everly Brothers at the Albert Hall, "Crying in the Rain" was a song we loved,' said Pål. 'When we listened to the original, we were surprised it was done in that almost-cheerful, 50s way [of] underplaying it. We had felt it could be made into a darker song.'[7] There were some slight lyrical amendments (for example, 'Raindrops falling from heaven / Could never wash away my misery'), but a-ha's version was largely faithful to the original, and lines such as 'Some day when my crying's done / I'm gonna wear a smile and walk in the sun' perfectly fitted in with a-ha's melancholy mantra.

The decision to cover the song had come about because the band didn't feel there was an obvious first single. As Magne confirmed, Trevor Horn was mooted as a producer of the track. 'We were really stoked to work with him,' he said. 'The meeting took place in his studio and we had a nice chat. However, he was very clear that he wanted to make a Donna Summer version of "Crying in the Rain", and we did not feel this was the version we wanted to make, so we left the studio and immediately telephoned our manager to call it off.'

According to Pål, Chris Neil loved the band's arrangement of 'Rolling Thunder' and suggested using the same tempo on the recording of 'Crying in the Rain', which is adorned with sampled sounds of thunder and some subtle slide guitar. 'It was a very unusual experience recording it, because it's only drawing on the strengths of our sound, not on our writing skills,' Magne told *Going Live!*'s Sarah Greene. 'All of a sudden there was this challenge, whether or not we could put our personality stamp on somebody's else song.'

A Steve Barron-directed video was filmed in Big Timber, Montana, although two different cuts were produced, with the second version deviating from the storyline and focusing more on Morten.

For the benefit of US radio, the intro was edited, and the track actually cracked the Top 30 of Billboard's Adult Contemporary chart in 1991.

EARLY MORNING
Written by Pål Waaktaar-Savoy and Magne Furuholmen
Produced by Ian Stanley
Chart position: 78 (UK), 52 (Germany)

According to the Human League's Susan Sulley, the Doors were Ian Stanley's favourite band, so it was little surprise that the album's co-producer latched on to 'Early Morning', a song that perhaps embodied the Venice Beach campfire spirit of

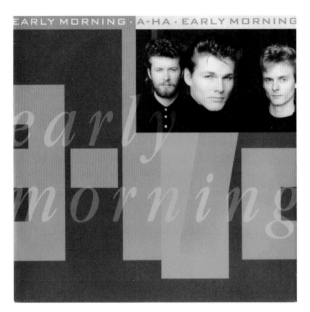

Jim Morrison and co more than any other. (During their 'farewell' tour in 2010, the band encapsulated this vibe with a stripped-back version, featuring Magne on glockenspiel). Recalling the serpentine groove of 'Riders on the Storm' and the jazz-like dexterity of earlier cuts such as 'Twentieth Century Fox' and 'Take It as It Comes', 'Early Morning' was, in the words of Magne, 'practically custom-made for old Doors fans'.

The dark undertones of the lyrics certainly occupied familiar Morrison-like terrain, marking a return to the thought-provoking vignettes of *Scoundrel Days*, with its strong narrative and intriguing plot lines ('I climbed all the stairways / To find the rooftop clear / Got the shotgun lying with me here'). An audio snippet exists of Morten humming the melody of the song (and a line that sounds like 'There's a world out there'), which does seem to date the song to this period. '"I've Been Losing You", "Sycamore Leaves" and "Early Morning" all share a lyrical topic,' said Pål. 'I was looking for a chorus for "Early Morning" for a while but decided in the end that it didn't need one.'

In an issue of *New Musical Express*, guest reviewer Julian Cope declared it was one of his singles of the week. 'A-ha are a great band,' said the former lead singer of the Teardrop Explodes. 'I bought that first single, "Take On Me", and loved it. It was like something from a different age. Like 1962 and Del Shannon and all that. He has such a brilliant voice. And in all their records, there's this underlying sorrow, as if something has been lost. I just wish people were open-minded enough to admit they're good. This could be from the second Doors album.'

The timing of the release of the single was impeccable, since the Doors were now the focus of a new Oliver Stone-directed movie, and a rereleased 'Light My Fire' would also hit the Top 10 that year. 'Early Morning', which also tied in with a short tour of the UK, fared far worse, however, entering the chart at No. 87 and peaking at No. 78, a clear sign of just how far the band had faded from the public's attention. (An unimaginative video, which included footage culled from the band's *Rock in Rio II* show, did little to bolster sales.)

I CALL YOUR NAME
Written by Pål Waaktaar-Savoy and Magne Furuholmen
Produced by Chris Neil
Chart position: 44 (UK), 37 (Germany)

> *A-ha have gotten mature but still have few equals when it comes to writing sterling pop melodies.*
> – *Smash Hits*, December 1990

While the 'Crying in the Rain' single had given a-ha another Top 20 hit in the UK, sales of its parent album were disappointing, and it marked the beginning of the band's commercial decline. This was compounded in December 1990 when 'I Call Your Name' gave them their first flop single in over five years. In an effort to link the modern-day a-ha with the teen-oriented band of yore, Warner Brothers issued an EP that included three of their old hits, but the marketing ploy proved to be in vain.

On account of its strong melody and memorable saxophone part, it seemed like an obvious choice for a single. Pål's lyrics, too, were impressive, and saw him writing from the viewpoint of a man reflecting on both the enormity of his wedding vows ('Those pronouncements had such weight / I guess they made us hesitate') and the ensuing marital journey and all of its ups and downs ('Through the fire and rain / Through the wilderness and pain / Through the losses, through the gains / On love's roller coaster train'), before intimating that the relationship has run its course ('Is the fire dying, babe? / It hurts to ask'). Sadly, record buyers didn't latch on to its charms, and the single languished outside of the all-important Top 40.

For the recording, the band brought in Phil Todd to play the song's distinctive saxophone motif. Todd was a prolific session musician throughout the 80s, having played on numerous recordings by the likes of Alphaville, Kajagoogoo, Marillion, Swing Out Sister, The The and countless other acts. 'It was the time of the pop record brass section and sax solo,' he wrote on his website. 'It seemed to be compulsory for every single in the charts at that time to have one or the other, or both, so who was I to refuse to help out and do my bit?!'

For the benefit of radio programmers, the song was wisely edited down from its near-five-minute length, while a black and white video, directed by Lauren Savoy, featured the band performing the track at Abbey Road Studios. 'Here, we look like an ordinary band,' said Pål. 'Of course, we got a lot of crap for that, and partly because Lauren had directed it. While the other vids, with the corniest ideas you can think of, just sailed on by.'[8]

In order to replicate Todd's part during their forthcoming tour, the band had to bring in a new saxophone player. 'When the album was about to be released in November 1990, things started getting busy,' wrote Jørun Bøgeberg on his website. 'At some point, the boys asked Per and me who we thought should be the saxophone player in the band, since the song "I Call Your Name" had an important tenor sax part. Per and me looked at each other and the same thought popped into our minds: It must be Sigurd, of course. Mr Køhn, who we both had worked with in Lava and the Heavy Gentlemen.'

Sigurd Køhn was a one-time member of Hartvik and the Heartbreakers and had played on a plethora of albums by high-profile Norwegian acts such as deLillos and Trond Granlund. It was the perfect fit, and Køhn would become a permanent fixture in the band's live set-up in the 90s.

SLENDER FRAME
Written by Pål Waaktaar-Savoy and Magne Furuholmen
Produced by Chris Neil

Written in the same key as 'Early Morning', this masterful co-write has become a firm fan favourite since its release, as evidenced by its inclusion on the *25* compilation in 2010. The combination of Pål's unshowy guitar work and Magne's bright piano motifs and organ swirls is certainly effective, while Chris Neil's laid-back production is suitably restrained and faithful to the original demo version.

In terms of the lyrics, they're typically cinematic, but the overall theme of the song seems to centre around a couple who are plagued with doubts about leaving town and starting afresh ('What's stopping you is stopping me / One moonless night we'll make it right / And vanish in the dark of night'), but the ambiguity in lines such as 'Run down the road, they'll never know' ensures an element of mystery.

EAST OF THE SUN
Written by Pål Waaktaar-Savoy
Produced by Ian Stanley

The album's stunning title track represented a conscious effort from Pål to return to his Norwegian roots, slipping back through the 'Take On Me' portal to more familiar pastures. In essence, 'East of the Sun' was an acknowledgement of both his heritage ('Where I came from / I forgot too soon') and mental state following the recording of *Stay on These Roads* ('Another day leaves me aching / I try to wake up / But something's breaking / Here inside me'). Certainly the song's 40-second ambient intro and plaintive strum serves as an antidote to the mechanical contrivances of the band's third album, while the title itself is steeped in the nostalgia of an old Norwegian fairy tale.

The musical sea change was also marked by a noticeable difference in Morten's vocal delivery, which saw him singing in a much deeper register before going up through the gears mid-song. But the frontman was seemingly unimpressed with the change: 'I had to sing in a different way for the songs that Pål and Magne had come up with,' he said. 'An integral part of the a-ha sound was the unmistakable characteristic of my voice. It was a challenge to adapt . . . it did not feel like it was me.'[9]

Before settling with the final version, which included a gorgeous string arrangement from Magne, the band tried out an electric version of the track in a slightly higher tempo. 'That was an attempt at a single release,' said Pål. 'Ian Stanley produced it . . . I sat in Abbey Road Studios for a whole day playing acoustic guitar, again and again, and he spent hours chopping up the guitar track from a hundred different takes. I didn't understand what he needed so many takes for.'[10]

SYCAMORE LEAVES
Written by Pål Waaktaar-Savoy
Produced by Chris Neil

In marked contrast to the pop melodrama of 'Slender Frame' and the estranged melancholia of the title track, 'Sycamore Leaves' saw the band branching out in a heavier and more strident direction. With a general air of malaise floating across its gloomy rock soundscape, the track pointed towards Pål's future with Savoy, but also established a connection with the autumnal subtexts of *Scoundrel Days*.

A veritable microcosm of Kafka-esque drama, the song is laced with a palpable terror and paranoia, which is perfectly complemented by Pål's grungy basslines and dirty licks. The protagonist has convinced himself there's a corpse lying below woodland foliage ('It fills me with unease / Out there by the roadside / Something's buried under sycamore leaves'), and is unable to erase the imagery from his mind ('I could never break out / And shake its grip on me').

With its generally surrealistic undertones, it seemed logical that Pål would later send the track to film-maker David Lynch – whom he was a big fan of – with a view to the famed *Eraserhead* director possibly working on one of a-ha's videos in the future. Lynch replied that he was too busy working on his supernatural murder-mystery series, *Twin Peaks*, which had begun airing in April 1990. However, when Pål noticed a track that was, coincidentally, titled 'Sycamore Trees' playing during the finale of the second series in June 1991, he was reportedly incensed.

In a version that reinforced the song's grunge-like vibe, the song was later recorded by Savoy and included on their second album, *Lackluster Me*, in 1997. The indie rock version of the track was also played during a-ha's *Lifelines* tour, with Pål on lead vocals.

WAITING FOR HER
Written by Pål Waaktaar-Savoy and Magne Furuholmen
Produced by Ian Stanley

In terms of the quality of their melancholic orchestral pop music, a-ha continued to raise the bar with this showstopping ballad, which acted as something of a palate cleanser after the more raucous tones of 'Sycamore Leaves'.

Proving they'd picked up a trick or two by listening to the likes of the Everly Brothers, the production featured some soothing harmonies, as well as a suitably tender string arrangement by David Bedford, whose myriad of clients then included ABC, China Crisis, Ian McCulloch, Madness and Mike Oldfield. (Bedford also had a significant hand in the stunning 'Movement 2' mix of Frankie Goes to Hollywood's underrated seventh single, 'Watching the Wildlife').

On drum duties this time round was producer Ian Stanley's former Tears for Fears bandmate, Chris Hughes, who had also been a member (known as Merrick) of Adam and the Ants and produced two of their hit albums, *Kings of the Wild Frontier* and *Prince Charming*.

The demo version of the song reveals that the arrangement was largely in place, but the lyrics were not yet complete, as is evident from the repetition of some of the lines (for example, 'You know it's true / It's been a week or two'). According to Magne, he struggled with the lyrics and asked Pål to finish them for him.

In the lead-up to the release of 2010's *25* compilation in Japan, the public were invited to vote for their favourite a-ha songs, and a unique tracklisting was created. Deep cuts such as 'Living a Boy's Adventure Tale' and 'Out of Blue Comes Green' were included, but the popularity of the band's fourth album was evident with the inclusion of both 'Rolling Thunder' and 'Waiting for Her', which had also been released as a single there. Unlike the version released worldwide, the tracks weren't sequenced chronologically, which made it doubly interesting for collectors.

COLD RIVER
Written by Pål Waaktaar-Savoy and Lauren Savoy
Produced by Chris Neil

In October 1987, in between the release of 'The Living Daylights' and the band's next single, 'Stay on These Roads', Norwegian viewers got a foretaste of some new a-ha material during 'Hjerte for livet' [A Heart for Life], the latest in a long line of annual fundraising events broadcast on NRK. A short clip of the band being interviewed at Pål's London apartment was shown, interspersed with footage of the band performing 'Cold River', which was then a work in progress (and later dropped from the *Stay on These Roads* shortlist). At this embryonic stage, the track had recycled the guitar riff from the original version of 'Train of Thought', which was known as 'The Sphinx' when it was demoed in Nærsnes in the autumn of 1982.

However, the provenance of the subsequent original demo of 'Cold River' could be traced back even further. One particular couplet, 'Don't let me die in an automobile / I wanna lie in an open field', had been lifted verbatim from an elongated version of 'The End', which the Doors had performed at the Hollywood Bowl on 5 July 1968, but it was later substituted for 'I took a ride in an automobile / Pushed my hands out against the wheel'.

Something of a filler, 'Cold River' combined perfunctory rock shapes with some of the album's weakest lyrics. Pseudo-macho lines such as 'Asked a girl if she needed a ride / She said, "Sure, babe, but I wanna drive"' certainly didn't suit the band, and the track represented something of a misstep on an otherwise solid album. According to Pål, there was a tight deadline and Lauren had helped him finish the lyrics.

THE WAY WE TALK
Written by Magne Furuholmen
Produced by Ian Stanley

Clocking in at just over 90 seconds, the deliciously jazzy 'The Way We Talk' was not just a-ha's shortest song to date, but it also marked Magne's debut as a lead vocalist for the band, which he described as 'my first little rebellion'.

It's a sparse arrangement, featuring little more than piano and a soupçon of light percussive brushes, but with a sidewinding bass part dictating the groove. The lyrics, too, are sparse, while the stacked vocal parts have a Prince-like feel to them, recalling tracks such as 'Let's Go Crazy'.

Aside from an acknowledgement of Magne's jazz lineage, it further exemplified the band's knack for transcending genres, but it was one particular direction the band wouldn't actively pursue in the near future. (As a solo artist, Morten did flirt with the medium in 2016, contributing a version of 'The Boy from Port Manteau'

ROLLING THUNDER
Written by Pål Waaktaar-Savoy and Magne Furuholmen
Produced by Chris Neil

The centrepiece of the album, this brooding number found the band at the top of their game, in terms of both its grandiose production and lyrics. Suffused with weather-based metaphors, the overall message of the song seems to be one of patiently riding out hard times ('The rain keeps falling / But I won't be leaving your side / Until all is over'), and Morten delivers a suitably sonorous vocal to complement the inclement drama. Elsewhere, the use of sampled storm sounds wasn't just a throwback to the Doors' 'Riders on the Storm', it also acted as something of a bookend to the opening track, 'Crying in the Rain', which includes the same samples.

Its epic qualities can certainly be evinced from the original demo, even if the lyrics weren't quite complete at this stage. Some of the gaps were plugged with do-do-dos and na-na-nas, but some lines – for example, 'It's the weight revolving / As our guilt's evolving' – were later cut.

What is also evident from 'Rolling Thunder' is a strong U2 influence – which would unravel more fully on the band's next album – and the track certainly has shades of *Rattle and Hum*'s 'Hawkmoon 269', which employs both a similar tempo and drum sound.

When it was performed on tour, the band turned in a blistering version of the track, with an unshackled Pål adding some exemplary guitar embellishments. In terms of the band's development as a live act, it was certainly a standout tour. 'We had a band we felt really solid with,' said Pål. 'It felt like a natural progression to the album, and that was the tour when we really learned how to play live. We had relaxed into playing live. With big audiences we certainly had to make more of ourselves.'[11]

A new-found confidence was certainly evident when the band performed in an intimate setting at NRK's Marienlyst studio in May 1991. The unique show, which was broadcast in September that year, included a set list which was interspersed with readings from Scandi writer Lars Saabye Christensen. 'That NRK recording ended up really great,' said Pål. 'Until then, everything had been playback, playback and playback again when it came to a-ha and television. To stand there, to be filmed and to play live, and not least to play well, felt thrilling.'[12]

(SEEMINGLY) NONSTOP JULY
Written by Pål Waaktaar-Savoy
Produced by Ian Stanley

Although the title of a-ha's 2010 farewell tour – *Ending on a High Note* – proved to be something of a misnomer, audiences were at least treated to a rare outing for this fine acoustic ballad which, at the time, had increased emotional resonance, due to its reflective lyrics ('It's hard to conceive it all comes to an end'). The recorded version that closes the album largely features acoustic guitar and piano (both played by Pål), although its meditative ambience is enhanced by some studio chatter and some street dialogue – as sampled by Lauren Savoy – in the coda, with the 'Endless pain or endless pleasure' line being the most audible (these were replaced by some mood-enhancing saxophone work from Sigurd Køhn during the *East of the Sun, West of the Moon* tour).

TREES WILL NOT GROW ON SAND (Demo)
Written by Magne Furuholmen

Featuring a composite of acoustic and electric guitars, this period demo with the somewhat proverbic title was both written and earnestly sung by Magne. Although some of the lyrics are a little clunky ('Come on over, baby / We were meant to be'), it's an interesting piece, with the band's penchant for West Coast rock and late-period Beatles – notably the much-covered B-side 'Don't Let Me Down' – both in evidence, and it's a track that, arguably, wouldn't have sounded out of place on the band's *Analogue* album.

MOVE TO MEMPHIS (Single Version)
Written by Pål Waaktaar-Savoy and Magne Furuholmen
Produced by a-ha
Chart position: 47 (UK), 2 (Norway), 39 (Germany)

Once the *East of the Sun, West of the Moon* tour had wrapped up in South America in June 1991, the band almost immediately began working on their fifth studio album. During the summer, they not only demoed some promising new tracks but also recorded a brand new song – at the record label's request – for a new compilation album. 'We're just trying to lay our past to rest before we move on,' Magne told MTV. 'It's called *Headlines and Deadlines*, which fairly accurately reflects what our career has been about the last six years.'

According to Pål, 'Move to Memphis' had been written on tour in South America and tried out during one of the band's soundchecks. While the recording represented a continuation of the band's more rock-oriented direction, its laid-back groove and Bach-influenced keyboard solo also added an exciting new dynamic. 'The idea came from Pål,' said Magne. 'We were going in a rocky direction. It was part of an overall nod to Americana then, and, I think, the only time I've heard Pål play funky guitar.'[13]

The funkiness in the recording could partly be attributed to Prince, whose musicianship had already influenced a plethora of other recording acts (for example, Duran Duran, the Go-Betweens and the Icicle Works), and it was certainly no coincidence that a-ha's next album would eventually be recorded at the diminutive musician's Paisley Park Studios.

It was described in layman's terms by Magne as 'a song about departure,' but Pål may well have been referring to his move to the US in the lyrics ('This old town brings me down / You were the one who told me / You've got to move to Memphis'). Pål had been living in New York with Lauren since 1988 and, as he recalled that year, London life no longer appealed to the established musician. 'New York's my home now . . . We were totally big fans of England when we came over the first time and everywhere we went looked just like a movie scene! We had very romantic views of England, but I think that's worn off a bit over the years.'[14]

Aside from freshening up their sound, the band also green-lighted an unusually sexualised video that was in stark contrast to their portfolio of largely clean-cut promos. While the focal point was undoubtedly Morten, who seductively tosses his long locks at every opportunity, the Erick Ifergan-directed video also featured shots of bare-chested male models and a star turn from *Betty Blue* actress Béatrice Dalle. 'We've never done anything that blatantly sexual before,' Magne told MTV '. . . As Scandinavians, we are terribly paranoid about using girls in our videos.'

However, in spite of the arguably cheap gimmickry, the single, which was released in October 1991, wasn't able to end a run of flops in the UK and it peaked outside of the Top 40, while *Headlines and Deadlines* stalled at a disappointing No. 12. (The video wasn't included on the VHS version of the compilation.)

But while their chart performances were certainly indicative of a lull in the band's popularity, a-ha had not lost their creative spark, as their next album would confirm.

CHAPTER THIRTEEN
MEMORIAL BEACH

Our heads are in a different place now than they were five years ago.
– Magne Furuholmen, MTV, 1993

Released: June 1993
Chart position: 17 (UK), 1 (Norway), 17 (Germany)

According to Pål, many of the tracks that ended up on *Memorial Beach* had already been demoed in New York, before being knocked into shape at two studios in Southern Norway during the album's pre-production stage, namely Cross Lydstudio in Kristiansand and Studio Nova in Østfold.

Since the touring line-up of the band had gelled so well, the services of bassist Jørun Bøgeberg and drummer Per Hillestad were retained. Following the reaction to their shows in South America, the band had also developed something of a stadium rock swagger, which would result in a proliferating use of guitars and a far thicker sound on their next album.

Although the work was interrupted by the band's promotion of their *Headlines and Deadlines* compilation, they were at least able to offer a glimpse of their work in progress during a slot on MTV, in which snippets of 'Dark Is the Night for All' and 'Memorial Beach' were played. Also in 1991, 'Where You Are', Morten's duet with Silje Nergaard, was released, via the popular jazz vocalist's *Silje* album.

THE WEST IS THE BEST

Work on the album recommenced in the new year of 1992. The band laid down some more demos, including a late addition in 'Angel in the Snow'. Due to various individual commitments – which included some art exhibition work from Magne – the band weren't able to start recording their album properly until October 1992. In a surprise move, the band opted for Prince's Paisley Park Studios in Chanhassen, Minnesota, a facility which Pål described as 'a square box on a field outside Minneapolis'.

Co-producing the album was David Z – aka David Rivkin – a former member of 'Funkytown' hit-makers Lipps Inc. and the older brother of Prince's former drummer, Bobby Z (aka Robert Rivkin). He'd not only played a key part in both Prince's and his affiliates' recording careers, he'd also worked with several other acts, including Fine Young Cannibals, whose huge hit, 'She Drives Me Crazy', had featured his unique – and instantly recognisable – drum sound. According to Magne, he was someone they'd wanted to work with since the musician's work on the classic 1986 hit 'Kiss'.

According to the band, Prince showed no interest in meeting them, but they were certainly aware when he was recording and filming on-site.

Since their new co-producer wasn't fond of doing multiple takes and both parties were keen on capturing more of a live sound, the band rehearsed the songs several times. 'David Z was a different producer than what we were used to,' said Pål. 'He focused mostly on the rhythmic elements, and the feel of the songs. We cut all the basic tracks live on the floor inside a huge hangar with live vocals and all.'[1] But, as Jørun later recalled on his website, there was also an element of 'cut and paste' methodology during production: 'A good deal of live recordings happened in the studio – uncountable takes of "Cold as Stone" – but most of the songs came together in bits and pieces. Even demos from an early session were thrown on tape and built further from there.'

THE CHAMBERLIN

Aside from the fact that David Z had instilled some new working methods, he also introduced the band to a new instrument, the Chamberlin. While it was often prone to overheat, it added some welcome colour to the album's sepia palette. Something of a forerunner to the mellotron – and, indeed, the Fairlight CMI

– the 1940s-patented keyboard allowed users to experiment with different pre-recorded sounds and effects via its built-in tapes and somewhat complex spooling mechanisms. Early exponents of the unique instrument included the Moody Blues and the Beach Boys (who had experimented with it during their post-*Smile* period), while it was later used on classic albums such as David Bowie's *Low* (see 'Warszawa', the track that inspired the name of a pre-Joy Division Warsaw) and XTC's *Skylarking* (see 'Dying'). In an interview with *Hot Rod* magazine in 2003, Magne declared that it was his all-time favourite instrument.

THE ANIMAL AND THE POET

During the recording of the album, the band invited *Aftenposten* to the studio. They not only reported that the album was scheduled for release in February 1993, they also announced that it had an intriguing working title of *The Story of a-ha*.

In terms of the reflective nature of the lyrics, it was certainly the band's most thematic and introspective collection to date, and a feel for the band's emotional headspace could certainly be garnered from tracks such

Down to the tracks. The band at Prince's Paisley Park Studios, with producer David Z.

as 'Cold as Stone' and 'Lamb to the Slaughter'. 'It feels like a requiem,' reflected Magne, years later. 'It was clear that we wanted to get out of the pop business, for musical and personal reasons . . . We weren't propelling ourselves forward, and consequently the album has a sombre feel.'[2]

Described by Morten at the time as 'a mix between the animal and the poet', the renamed *Memorial Beach* album wouldn't arrive in UK shops until June that year (the delay was likely to have been caused by the fact it had to be mixed several times before all parties were satisfied). The album was housed in a fiery sleeve that perfectly complemented its contents, but an up-to-date shot of the band wasn't used for the front cover. Instead, a two-year old photo of the band on a Brazilian beach was sourced.

TOUGHER, HEAVIER, DARKER

'We've never felt that strongly as we do now, actually,' Morten told MTV. 'This is an important album for us – internally, certainly – but I think it will be to the public as well.' The reviews were favourable, too, and it was later included in *Q* magazine's end-of-year list of favourite albums. In Norway, *VG* praised the band for their 'tougher, heavier, darker and more guitar-oriented' direction. 'The guys have finally grown up,' said Espen A. Hansen, 'and they have allowed themselves to mature with dignity.'

But although the band were rewarded with yet another chart-topper in their homeland, the public response elsewhere was tepid, to say the least, and the album could only muster a four-week run in the UK. According to Pål, the buck stopped with him. 'I got blamed for *Memorial Beach* not selling more than it did,' he said. 'You do your best to give the guys a little weight, and you wind up in the dock as the accused.'[3]

What is certain about *Memorial Beach* is that it has aged well, and there's a tonality about the recordings that mark it out as one of the band's most consistent and satisfying bodies of work. In spite of its dark overtones, a change of environment had clearly inspired Pål – who is credited with writing 85 per cent of the songs – but having a settled rhythm section and a producer who was on their wavelength certainly helped. 'The record perhaps hasn't sold that much, but it is important to me and I'm proud of it,' Pål later reflected. 'There are such different things on it, and I'm so glad we made this album.'[4]

'There are good songs on the album,' said Magne, 'but the dynamic inside the group was signalling some sort of ending.'[5] Indeed, it would be seven years until the band released their next album.

DARK IS THE NIGHT FOR ALL

Written by Pål Waaktaar-Savoy
Produced by David Z and a-ha
Chart position: 19 (UK), 4 (Norway), 46 (Germany)

Underpinned by a celestial lustre of keyboard work and more-than-faint echoes of *The Joshua Tree*-era U2, the opening cut of *Memorial Beach* marked a continuation of the band's more mature sound, but the lyrics also signalled the start of a creative rebirth for its writer, who had by now moved to the US ('It's time we moved out west / This time will be the best'). As Pål would clarify in the album's press release, it wasn't a break-up song: 'It is actually the opposite,' he said. 'It's about breaking away, taking a risk.'

The song was also selected for worldwide single release, but retitled 'Dark Is the Night' (presumably because it had less negative connotations). In the US, where the band hadn't performed live since 1986, the single merited some significant radio exposure, and hovered just outside of the Billboard Hot 100. 'That song did very well in the US,' confirmed Pål, 'but still lacked the push to drive it all the way up.'[6] (The campaign wouldn't have been helped by the fact that an early version of the Erick Ifargan-directed video was banned by MTV for its supposedly disturbing content.)

Elsewhere, the band were now competing for chart space in the UK with Europop acts such as Ace of Base, Haddaway and 2 Unlimited. When the band appeared on BBC's *Top of the Pops*, they had to adhere to a new policy, instated in 1991, which meant that Morten would have to sing live in the studio. But, while the practice often exposed less technically proficient singers – which would often have a detrimental effect on their chart positions – there were no such problems for Morten, who competently delivered the single's soaring vocal. It climbed into the Top 20 the following week.

MOVE TO MEMPHIS
Written by Pål Waaktaar-Savoy and Magne Furuholmen
Produced by David Z and a-ha

During promotional work for the single version of 'Move to Memphis' in 1991, it was intimated that the track was not just a means of promoting the band's *Headlines and Deadlines* compilation, but also a foretaste of the band's fifth album. However, when *Memorial Beach* eventually arrived almost two years later, it had a noticeably different coating, which *VG* described as 'a bit rougher and more rustic in shape'. Morten's skyward vocal from the original lead-in was cut and the intro now had a less winsome, more Depeche Mode-esque feel to it, with the extra guitar parts ensuring a more dense sound.

While the majority of Morten's vocals were retained, some new backing vocal parts were added, courtesy of Jevetta and J.D. Steele – who had both contributed to Prince albums such as *Diamonds & Pearls* and *Graffiti Bridge* – and Kathy Wilson.

'I love the animal feel of it,' declared Morten. 'It stands out as one of the strongest band songs we have.'[7] The view wasn't shared by Magne, however, who later described it as 'boring', and he had a point. Although the backing vocals added a gospel-tinged veneer, which was in keeping with the band's new direction, the somewhat leaden album version lacked excitement, while the pulsating groove of its 1991 counterpart was noticeably absent.

COLD AS STONE
Written by Pål Waaktaar-Savoy
Produced by David Z and a-ha

This is a vital track for the band and it's interesting that we have ended up using a
version we cut live. I am very proud of this track.
– Morten Harket, 1993

At the time of writing, the epic 'Cold as Stone' was the longest track in a-ha's back catalogue, and it was then the longest track that Magne and Pål had recorded since their Bridges days ('The Endless Brigade', 'The Stranger's Town' and 'Fakkeltog' all clock in at over eight minutes). But, according to Pål, the album's existential centrepiece wasn't originally intended to be so lengthy: 'I remember standing in the dark at Paisley Park, playing and playing – we just kept going,' he recalled. 'The long jam at the end of the song was not originally planned. It was created in the studio, and that was something we had never allowed ourselves to do before. And it's perhaps also the only song where Morten's vocals were recorded while we were playing live. The whole thing became a performance.'[8]

On the deluxe edition of *Memorial Beach*, you can hear one of the song's multiple takes, which also includes a noticeable use of the band's hired Chamberlin keyboard in the intro, which certainly adds some otherworldly ambience. 'When we were laying down the basic tracks, we would set ourselves up on this huge stage, the size of an airplane hangar,' said Pål. 'We worked on getting the sounds right during the day and then came back and attempted the actual recording at the end of the evening. It was one of the first songs we did and it felt like a cornerstone – something to build on. It set the tone for the rest of the album.'[9]

Although the song was, ostensibly, recorded live, several guitar parts were added during the overdub stages. 'In the past we used to add keyboards, but this time we often added several layers of guitar, said Pål. "Luckily I didn't have to suggest it myself; David Z wanted to go in the same direction as I did."[10]

Lyrically, 'Cold as Stone' was a companion piece to 'East of the Sun', detailing not only a comedown after years in the spotlight ('Emerald green neon lights above / Sapphire red falls on you below') but also a loss of identity in the writer's homeland ('Standing here in the town / Where you were born / It's not your home'). According to Pål, the idiomatic title of the song was a reference to how he felt he was being perceived by certain people: 'People are constantly trying to figure me out and find out what's wrong with me. "What's up with him? Why is he so moody?". . . It's a bit of self-analysis.'[11]

Reinforcing the song's Doors-like credentials, the song featured an interpolation of 'Sycamore Leaves' during the subsequent *Memorial Beach* tour. A truncated version of the song was also created for potential single release, but it ended up as the B-side of 1994's 'Shapes That Go Together' single.

ANGEL IN THE SNOW
Written by Pål Waaktaar-Savoy
Produced by David Z and a-ha
Chart position: 41 (UK)

Featuring clear echoes of U2 in its arrangement and a drum break that seemed to mirror James Brown's often-sampled 'Funky Drummer' track, this tender, more acoustically driven song provided some welcome respite following the smouldering intensity of 'Cold as Stone'.

Its origins went back to December 1991, when Pål was on the cusp of marrying his long-term girlfriend, Lauren Savoy. However, for the famously taciturn musician – who often appeared aloof during interviews and said very little during the band's concerts – the prospect of delivering a wedding day speech wasn't particularly appealing. But the future *brudgom*'s social anxiety would soon be alleviated by a novel – and highly creative – solution: 'Everyone who knows me, knows that I can't hold a speech,' he said. 'Then, out of nowhere, "Angel in the Snow" arrived, four days before the wedding – that song became my wedding speech. We recorded it in Magne's studio the day before the wedding.'[12] (In the album credits, the song includes the dedication 'For Luchie', a reference to Lauren's nickname – her middle name is Lucia.)

On the deluxe edition of the album, released in 2015, it's Pål's voice that can be heard on the demo, and in retrospect it's disappointing that his vocals weren't included on the final version, especially since it was such a personal song. Pål responded that it wouldn't have felt like a-ha without Morten's voice.

As both a vow and an expression of love ('Wherever you may go / I'll follow / And always I will be there / Shake worries from your hair'), it certainly delivers, but the decision to release it as a single was arguably questionable. The release was limited to the UK and German markets and, like its predecessor, 'Dark Is the Night', the title of the song was changed (to 'Angel'). Typical of the music industry's marketing strategy of the period, a two-CD set was issued in the UK – which would often give a single a leg-up in the charts – but the single failed to crack the Top 40, and there was very little promotional work done to support its release.

For the video, which was filmed in the Silvertown area of London, a new director, Howard Greenhalgh, was employed to put a fresh spin on the track, with model Jasmine Lewis cast as Morten's lover, who becomes the victim of a car crash. Two videos were produced by the prolific director (who had previously worked with acts such as Big Country, INXS, Marillion and Sting), with one version featuring a cameo by an MTV competition winner.

LOCUST
Written by Pål Waaktaar-Savoy
Produced by David Z and a-ha

One of the band's most cinematic and captivating songs, 'Locust' captured the band at their most poetic and blissfully bleak. 'This song is a film,' enthused Morten, prior to the album's release. 'It blew me away . . . I am still out there.'[13]

The ambient intro and the sound of a rattlesnake sets the tone, and there's a spectre of foreboding doom threading through the track that makes for both a chilling and unsettling listen at times. The drama is perfectly complemented by Pål's lugubrious guitar flourishes, while the combination of Jørun Bøgeberg's gently rumbling bass work and Per Hillestad's skeletal framework of percussion authenticates the atmospherics. 'Making a record is a lot like mixing colours on a canvas,' declared Magne. 'This track has a rich texture and a very abstract solo section.'[14]

Compounding the mood was a rare spoken word vocal from Morten, in which a post-apocalyptic world is envisioned by its writer ('My dream was this / Across the sky / A slate-grey cloud / That filled the eye'). Pål declared that it was his favourite track on the album, and he would later recycle a section of its lyrics for Savoy's 'Whalebone' in 2004.

While it hasn't been performed live in recent years, 'Locust' was a fixture in the set list on both the *Memorial Beach* and *Lifelines* tours.

LIE DOWN IN DARKNESS
Written by Pål Waaktaar-Savoy
Produced by David Z and a-ha

In terms of its sonic aesthetic, this strutting funk-rock workout picked up where 'Move to Memphis' left off, but the version that made the final cut was significantly different from the original demo, which is notable for its synth stabs and synthetic brass – in fact, it could almost have passed off as a demo from the *Stay on These Roads* era. The final version, however, features a far subtler use of keyboards – courtesy of the ubiquitous Chamberlin – while layers of guitar were added behind the scenes. 'I always found it inhibiting to do guitar overdubs in the studio, with everybody standing around,' said Pål, 'so halfway through the recording of this album, I took a few tapes to New York, booked a studio at random with an engineer I'd never met before and went in and tried to blow him away . . . It's a method that worked on a lot of songs, including this one.'[15]

In their review of the album, *VG* described the song as 'the album's most danceable moment, but not particularly good.' While the production is slightly indulgent, the song certainly boasts a memorable chorus, which was elevated by the same backing singers who had graced the 'Move to Memphis' session.

It was selected for single release in the US, but was only issued in cassingle format, paired with a live version of 'I Call Your Name'.

HOW SWEET IT WAS
Written by Pål Waaktaar-Savoy
Produced by David Z and a-ha

According to Pål, the title of 'How Sweet It Was' had been derived from a sweet shop he'd spotted while honeymooning in the US. Additionally, some of the lyrics appear to have been inspired by his then-recent wedding ('Just about a month ago / You made a promise, babe / Not to go'), and the chorus does seem to play out like a series of toasts ('One to the nightfall / One to the stars / One to the haunted fools we are').

With its expansive arrangement and huge drums, the song arguably represented the band at the peak of their stadium rock pretensions, but it included one of Pål's most memorable choruses and was bookended by some effective keyboard work from Magne. 'I like this song a lot,' said Pål. 'It's both slow and fast at the same time. Magne plays great piano and I also like the fact that no two verses are alike.'[16]

LAMB TO THE SLAUGHTER
Written by Magne Furuholmen
Produced by David Z and a-ha

With its mellow, waltz-time aura and lilting bossa nova beat, 'Lamb to the Slaughter' stood out as one of the best productions on the album. But beneath the song's gently swaying groove, there was a palpable tension as Magne put into words his disillusionment with the music industry and its concomitant trappings.

The opening verse immediately sets the tone: 'I went down to the water / Like a lamb to the slaughter / Didn't know what was waiting for me there'. It's easy to forget that Magne was just 22 years old when 'Take On Me' was beginning its ascent to the top of the Billboard chart and, while the band had considerable ambitions, they certainly wouldn't have been prepared for that level of success. In a further verse, Magne addresses fame head-on ('You polluted my head / With the things that you said / I became what you wanted to see'), before candidly revealing a pent-up bitterness in the song's denouement ('All of these years / Have built up this hate').

Magne was reportedly unhappy with Morten's vocal delivery, which does lack some much-needed bite, and it's arguable that the song should have been sung by its writer. But, in terms of both its melody and lyrics, it certainly delivers a punch. (The song was rarely performed live by a-ha during their career but, along with 'How Sweet It Was', it did appear on set lists during the *Analogue* tour.)

In retrospect, it's clear that the band were on the verge of imploding, and lines such as 'We go down / We go down, it's the only way out' practically became a self-fulfilling prophecy. 'At this point, we had been going full-on for ten years,' said Pål, 'and I think there was an element of burnout as well as a desire to discover who we were as individuals.'[17] Indeed, while the band would limp on for a while, its members would soon drift into solo work.

BETWEEN YOUR MAMA AND YOURSELF
Written by Pål Waaktaar-Savoy
Produced by David Z and a-ha

'We did this one just to clear the air,' said Pål. 'It was fun to write and to play.'[18] Certainly, this was the album's most light-hearted number, and it featured lyrics that had partly been inspired by Mike Nichols' classic movie *The Graduate*. In the multi-award-winning film, Benjamin Braddock (played by Dustin Hoffman), is seduced by an older woman, Mrs Robinson, before falling in love with her daughter, and there are certainly echoes of the storyline in the lyrics ('I've been meaning to tell you a long time ago / And today's that day / I'll put it straight'). Ostensibly, though, the song is built around an imaginary love triangle ('Between your mama and yourself / Forced to choose and without help . . . / The one I love / Well, it's probably you').

While it was criticised in some quarters for its throwaway lyrics, there was no doubting the quality of the chorus. In concert, the song was embellished by some excellent piano work from Magne and a suitably energetic sax solo from Sigurd Køhn, which resulted in a marked improvement on the slightly dense album version.

MEMORIAL BEACH
Written by Pål Waaktaar-Savoy
Produced by David Z and a-ha

The title of the album's stunning closing track had been inspired by a trip to the Sarasota area of Florida, where Pål chanced upon its name. 'A grey day, an abandoned beach – I instantly knew that I had the story for a song,' he said. 'The same thing with "Locust"; it's like a book that you never want to end.'[19] The ballad's lyrics are certainly strong, with the narrator reminiscing about a relationship that had prospered during its honeymoon phase ('Honey days and nights without sleep / Lost in the sand') but ultimately failed ('We never found / A place to hide / Some peace of mind / God knows we tried'). 'I feel I've known this song all my life,' said Morten. 'It's got every reason to be the title track. For me, it's a classic.'[20]

With its slightly lower pitch, there's a definite Doors-like feel to the demo, which evokes the brooding melancholia of songs such as 'Blue Sunday' and 'Indian Summer'. The wistful vibe was carried over to the final version, which certainly benefits from a less-is-more approach, with Magne's trickling piano parts working perfectly in tandem with Per Hillestad's gently shuffling percussion.

During season six of *Baywatch* in 1996, the song was played during the finale of the 'Last Wave' episode.

BAR ROOM (Demo)
Written by Pål Waaktaar-Savoy

It was back in December 1992 when *Aftenposten* exclusively revealed a preliminary tracklisting for the band's imminent new album, but the list did not include 'Lie Down in Darkness'. In its place was a track titled 'Bar Room', which didn't receive an airing until the 2015 rerelease of the album. 'When I heard it again, I thought it was awesome,' said Pål. 'I don't remember why it didn't end up on the album.'[21]

In terms of both its pace and overall sound, 'Bar Room' doesn't really fit in with the other tracks, while the lyrics are unusually hedonistic ('There's a bar room down the street / Where we meet / Where we pick up girls and take them dancing') and occasionally bordering on trite ('It's alright / Dance all night / Never gonna see the morning light'). But there's much to admire about this fascinating period piece, which recalls the Doors during their *LA Woman* period, with the honky-tonk keyboard work calling to mind Robby Krieger's 'Love Her Madly'.

SHAPES THAT GO TOGETHER (Single)
Written by Pål Waaktaar-Savoy and Magne Furuholmen
Produced by Chris Neil
Chart position: 27 (UK), 57 (Germany)

With the 1994 Winter Olympics just around the corner, a-ha somehow managed to find the time to submit a prospective official song to the games committee in Lillehammer. But there was reportedly some stiff competition, and soprano singer Sissel Kyrkjebø eventually prevailed. Kyrkjebø performed the winning song, 'Se ilden lyse' [Fire in Your Heart], during the opening and closing ceremony, and it also topped the Norwegian charts.

There was some consolation for the band, however, as their song, 'Shapes That Go Together', was selected as the official song for the Paralympics that year. The song was recorded at Studio Nova in January 1994, but Jørun Bøgeberg and Per Hillestad were not involved. 'I was never part of that session,' confirmed Jørun. 'I think bass and drums were programmed on that track.'

The recording also doubled up as a rare stand-alone single, and the band were rewarded with another Top 30 hit in the UK. 'We weren't really sure whether we should connect it up with the Paralympics,' Magne told MTV. 'The song is supposed to have a life of its own outside of this event, so we treated it as just a normal a-ha thing and made a video.'

With Chris Neil once again at the helm, the band were able to move away from the dense, introverted rock of *Memorial Beach* and produce something that was considerably jauntier and poppier than much of their recent output. But this was the sound of a band going through the motions and, following the conclusion of their tour in June 1994, a period of uncertainty ensued. Magne's disillusionment with fame had already been documented on 'Lamb to the Slaughter', while Morten, the band's main focal point, was also burnt out. 'It got to the stage where I was exhausted by it all,' he said in a candid interview the following year. 'My body was covered in boils. I lost all sense of taste and I went colour blind. Everything sort of dried out and I felt like an ashtray. I felt 96 years old and I was through with life. It can kill you, you know. It's what killed Elvis – the demands of the public and the media. If you don't understand it and when to pull away, it will get you one way or another. I needed the breakdown to get myself sorted out.'[22]

PART FOUR
END OF THE LINE – THE SOLO YEARS
1993–1999

CHAPTER FOURTEEN
WILD SEED

Over the years, Morten's versatile and adaptable voice has lent itself to several musical genres, including synth-pop, Christian pop, rock, jazz, folk and even drum 'n' bass, while his interest in theology, nature, environmental issues and politics has frequently seeped into his recordings, giving much of the material a spiritual – and often philosophical – slant. With his finely chiselled features and distinctive voice, Morten was certainly the most marketable member of a-ha, but the transition to a successful solo career wasn't without its challenges.

MORTEN HARKET – POETENES EVANGELIUM (1993 Album)
Produced by Erik Hillestad
Chart position: N/A

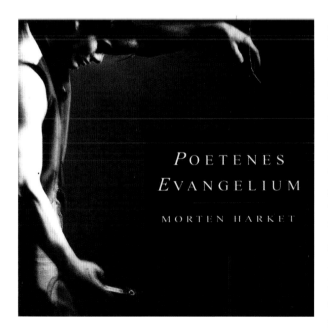

Although a-ha were beginning to implode by the time of the *Memorial Beach* album, Morten was at least able to distract himself with other projects, which included a faithful version of the much-covered Frankie Valli hit 'Can't Take My Eyes off You', which was included on the soundtrack for *Coneheads* (1993), Steve Barron's poorly received directorial follow-up to the box office hit *Teenage Mutant Ninja Turtles* (1990). The track, which was a personal favourite of Barron's, was recorded at Bearsville Studios in Woodstock and produced by Stephen Hague, who would later work on the *Lifelines* album.

More significantly, once the German leg of the *Memorial Beach* tour had ended in September 1993, Morten was able to take advantage of a break in the touring schedule and switch his attention to the promotion of *Poetenes Evangelium*.

157

Set to music composed in the early 90s by former music teacher Øivind Varkøy, this challenging album was based on *Poetenes evangelium: Jesu liv i norske dikt*, a 191-page anthology of 20th-century poetry, published in 1991, which depicted the life and death of Jesus. (Roughly translated as 'The Gospel of the Poets: Jesus's Life in Norwegian Poetry', the book had been edited by Morten's future collaborator, Håvard Rem.) The ambitious project was masterminded by Erik Hillestad, a well-known musician and producer (particularly among the church community), and released through his Kirkelig Kulturverksted label at the end of the year.

As Morten told *Treff* magazine that year, he was certainly ready for a change of direction: 'I have always had control of things, but lately I have found this to be more and more of a hindrance. Now I feel the strong need to get rid of the control. I want to get away from any predictable and well-known situation . . . I have been walking for too long on well-trodden paths.'

The studio band included keyboardist Kjetil Bjerkestrand (who would later play a major role in both Morten's and Magne's side projects), Dance with a Stranger guitarist Frode Alnæs and Per Hillestad, a drummer that Morten was already well acquainted with, both in a-ha's live set-up and on their previous two albums.

'I had no idea what would happen when I sat down in front of the microphone to sing these songs,' Morten told *Treff*. 'I didn't know anything. I didn't know anything about how I should sing. I didn't even know the melodies – they were just as unknown to me as the lyrics. When I heard the piano chords, I didn't think that they fitted together with the lyrics.' While Morten found the recording process challenging, similar challenges were to be found for the album's listeners, particularly a-ha fans who weren't used to the vocalist singing in his native language.

As far removed from a-ha's synth-pop as you could possibly expect, it's an intriguing collection of songs. The stories are familiar, but they're simply and eloquently interpreted, without ever being preachy. What really shines through, though, is the quality of Morten's versatile voice, allowing the material to smoothly transcend the language barrier. *Vårt Land*, a popular Christian newspaper, certainly agreed: 'Even if the album isn't perfect, Harket's voice acts as a gateway to the words,' wrote Pål A. Berg, 'and is much more than just an intriguing celebrity gimmick.' The *Haugesunds Avis* newspaper offered a somewhat contrasting review, however: 'Morten Harket has never sung better than on *Memorial Beach*, this summer's highly underrated a-ha album. Therefore, it's sad to suffer through *Poetenes Evangelium*. Harket sings in a way-too-contrived and fumbling manner, on top of non-melodies so pretentiously serious that they border on parody.'

While it's certainly a challenging listen (and not exactly brimming with immediate, catchy songs), it's nevertheless a beautifully produced collection. The use of strings, particularly on tracks such as 'Sviket' [The Betrayal] and the opening

'Natten' [The Night], give some of the songs a haunting, ethereal quality and, while the arrangements are largely sparse, there's enough musical adventure to sustain the listener's interest. 'Salome' adds contemporary beats and programming to the mix, while there are some beautiful choral flourishes on 'Rytteren' [The Rider].

Despite the fact that it's Morten's name and image emblazoned on the cover, the singer modestly claimed he was simply a guest on *Poetenes Evangelium* and didn't regard it as a solo album. 'Far from it,' he told *Treff*. 'The album wasn't planned. This whole album is a gift, not just to us, but to those who get their hands on it.'

Those who did get their hands on the record were in a minority, however, despite Morten's best efforts to promote it. Two promotional videos – for 'Natten' and 'Salome' – were filmed during a trip to Israel in October that year and later shown (as trailers) in cinemas throughout Norway. It was a trip that seemingly had a profound effect on the singer: 'I met 17-year-old girls and boys with guns in their hip pocket,' he told *Treff*. 'They would show their love for each other, but knew at the same time that a bomb could go off anytime. I experienced that same intensity in Rio – life was decaying and blossoming at the same time.'

Having originally met in 1980, Morten reconnected with the award-winning, Oslo-born writer Håvard Rem, during the trip, forming a bond that would eventually lead to a songwriting partnership. 'He appeared at the right time and was the fire I needed,' he later told *Aftenposten*. 'I knew I needed someone to sharpen me, because I knew I had come to some point . . . and I knew I had powers in me that only Håvard could get out.'

MORTEN HARKET – WILD SEED (1995 Album)

> *I don't feel under any pressure to match [a-ha's] success. I'm not interested in competition or comparison. As long as this album works well enough for me to be able to carry on, I shall be satisfied.*
> – Morten Harket, *Daily Express*, 1995

Produced by Chris Neil
Chart position: 89 (UK), 1 (Norway)

In between Morten's promotional duties for the *Poetenes Evangelium* album, a-ha resumed the *Memorial Beach* tour in mid-December 1993. A few months later, in March 1994, the band released 'Shapes That Go Together', which reunited Morten with Kjetil Bjerkestrand, who co-arranged the song. Also released that month was *Millimeter*, a Spellemann-winning album by Norwegian rock singer Anne Grete Preus, featuring Morten performing backing vocals on the funky title cut. (*Millimeter* also included contributions from a-ha's bassist, Jørun Bøgeberg.)

At the other end of the musical spectrum, Morten contributed a track to a Kjetil Bjerkestrand-produced collection of Norwegian evening prayers titled *Nå lukker seg mitt øye* [Now My Eye Is Closing]. Set to a beautiful piano accompaniment, the singer's contribution was a plaintive version of 'Me slår framfor oss krossen din'

[We Cross Ourselves]. It was originally released on cassette, but eventually released on CD in 2001.

While a-ha did not officially split up, the first phase of their career came to a natural end, following the conclusion of their tour in June 1994. 'There were no new disagreements – they were the same ones we always had,' Morten explained. 'When we stopped we were fed up with the media – I certainly was . . . We were just fed up because the take on a-ha was that we belonged to 1985 and we had never embraced that – we just accepted it for a while. So we pulled the plug and let everything go [down] the drain.'[1]

With a-ha's future in the balance, Morten was still intent on launching a solo career, but there would be something of a false start prior to the recording of *Wild Seed*. Under the terms of the contract that a-ha had signed in 1983, Warner Brothers had exercised their right to release a solo album by Morten. In collaboration with manager Terry Slater and Andrew Wickham (the man who had originally signed a-ha to the label), they hired the band's original producer, Alan Tarney, to oversee an album of largely original material at RG Jones Studios. However, the new songs were neither penned by Morten nor the Cliff Richard hitmaker. Instead, the writing was, somewhat bizarrely, entrusted to two relative rookies: Tarney's son, Oliver – who would later gain recognition for his work as a sound editor in the film industry – and his childhood friend Robert Carr. (Oliver Tarney is also credited with playing additional keyboards on the Alan Tarney-produced version of Pulp's 1995 hit, 'Disco 2000'.)

At Wickham's behest, the secretly recorded album included a cover of the Everly Brothers' 'Devoted to You', which established an obvious connection between both a-ha and Slater. Elsewhere, 'Sounds of Rain' and 'A Place I Know' – which were later leaked onto the internet – continued in the same polished and radio-friendly vein, deviating significantly from the dusty synth-rock of *Memorial Beach*. Initially, Morten was enthusiastic about the new songs but, as he later confirmed to *Aftenposten*, there was a change of heart. It wasn't the album he wanted to launch his international career with after all: 'At first, I recorded the album Warners wanted to have. It's there, finished and all,' he said. 'But I didn't want them to have this one, so I had to give them something else. Little by little, I gave them my own thing; songs I'd written myself . . . It was necessary for me that the record company threw away the old in favour of the new, that they changed their minds in my favour. Not because I argued for something they didn't want, but because my music convinced them.'

BIT BY BIT

While Morten had co-written a handful of a-ha's songs – notably 'Take On Me', 'Living a Boy's Adventure Tale', 'Stay on These Roads' and 'Touchy!' – he was certainly more renowned for his vocal skills than his songwriting abilities. He'd only just started playing the guitar seriously and was heavily reliant on creative foils such as Håvard Rem to supply the lyrics. 'After we'd been to Jerusalem, I sent a few texts to Morten in England,' Rem told *Aftenposten*. 'On the plane home, I wrote my first poem in English. Two weeks later, the melody to it was on my answering machine.' Later, the pair went on a working holiday to the Maldives, where the ideas for songs such as 'Los Angeles' germinated. According to Morten, part of the lyric-writing process involved him translating some of Rem's Norwegian poems into English.

'I am actively a songwriter now,' Morten told VH-1's Paul King in 1995. 'I started to write at the beginning of last year, and at that point I had no experience with any of that process, so I've learnt quickly as I've gone along. And I've changed my methods on how to do it as I've gone along . . . I started looking for songs and very quickly I started to write instead. And then I started recording in the way that I'm used to recording with a-ha, but I kind of felt my way through it and put pieces together bit by bit.'

Aside from Håvard Rem, other collaborators on *Wild Seed* included a close childhood friend of Rem's named Ole Sverre Olsen, whose lyrics for 'Half in Love Half in Hate' had reportedly been inspired by his recently broken marriage. The words were duly faxed to Morten, who was sufficiently enthused to build a melody around them. (Olsen would later contribute lyrics to future songs of Morten's, both within and outside of a-ha).

Elsewhere, the Norwegian poet Henning Kramer Dahl co-wrote 'East Timor'. It dealt with a subject that was close to Morten's heart: East Timor's fight for independence. Morten was subsequently able to use his high profile to highlight

161

the plight of the Timorese people, who had endured decades of oppression from the Indonesian armed forces, and he was involved in a Max Stahl-directed documentary titled *Sometimes I Must Speak Out Strongly*. (Henning Kramer Dahl, who went to the same high school as Magne, had co-written the *Så blåser det på jorden* book with Morten's brother, Håkon, which chronicled the band's origins. Prior to that, the pair had collaborated on *Nådens bok*, a Norwegian translation of a Leonard Cohen poetry collection, titled *Book of Mercy*.)

'Spanish Steps' was sourced from Ole Edvard Antonsen's 1992 album, *Tour de Force*. Produced by *Wild Seed* engineer Bjørn Nessjø, the song was originally known as '5000 Miles' and had been written by Torstein Flakne, the lead singer of the Norwegian rock band Stage Dolls. New lyrics were added, and it eventually became the album's second single. (Flakne, who also added backing vocals to the track, had originally been a member of the Kids, who'd taken part in the *NM i rock* competition in 1980. Their 'Forelska i lærer'n' [In Love With the Teacher] single topped the Norwegian charts, and the accompanying promotional video was reportedly the first of its kind in the country.)

READY TO BEGIN

Aiding Morten during the recording sessions (in Norway and the UK) was Chris Neil, who had worked with a-ha on both the *East of the Sun, West of the Moon* album and 'Shapes That Go Together' single. 'It was my luck that he had the time to do it, because he has been very successful and everyone wants to work with him,' Morten told Radio Signal One in July 1995. 'I invited him to Norway. I wanted to let him come over to listen to some of the songs I had been working on and that I myself had written. He loved the idea. He came and the material was completely different from what he had expected . . . He was totally excited about the whole process. One song after another surprised him.'

Chris Neil had also introduced Morten and his bandmates to 'Ready to Go Home' in 1994. It was a 10cc song that had featured on the 'I'm Not in Love' hitmakers' final album, *Mirror Mirror* (1995), before being rerecorded in a more electronic version on Graham Gouldman's solo album, *And Another Thing* (2000). The track was credited to both Gouldman and singer-songwriter Andrew Gold, who had recorded a handful of albums as the duo Wax in the 1980s. The lyrics were inspired by the death of Gouldman's father in 1991: 'I suppose I was trying to put a positive slant on his passing,' Gouldman later revealed. 'Remembering all the things we had done together and his artistic legacy to me. The last verse of the song best reflects my feelings on this.'[2]

The recording of *Wild Seed* would take several months. The musicians included keyboardist Kjetil Bjerkestrand, guitarists Frode Alnæs and Eivind Aarset, bassist

Øyvind Madsen (who, due to Jørun Bøgeberg's imminent parenthood, played on the South African leg of the *Memorial Beach* tour) and a-ha's future drummer, Per Lindvall, an experienced Swedish musician who'd played on some of ABBA's recording sessions in the early 80s. (Both Bjerkestrand and Madsen formed part of the live band on the subsequent *Wild Seed* tour.)

TIME WILL PRONOUNCE

A taste of Morten's new solo venture arrived in June 1994, via an exclusive feature on MTV's Vote Europe Weekend. 'I read this poem by Joseph Brodsky, a Russian writer and poet, called "Bosnia Tune" or "Time Will Pronounce", explained Morten. 'It's called "Bosnia Tune" but I don't really see it as about Bosnia, it's more about the West . . . I just ended up doing this piece to it. It's not really a call for action or anything, it's just a comment really.'

The title 'Time Will Pronounce' had already filtered into popular culture, via Michael Nyman's 1993 album of the same name, while Joseph Brodsky himself was a huge literary influence, as well as a winner of the Nobel Prize in Literature in 1987. Morten was clearly impressed by Brodsky's 'Bosnia Tune' (published in 1992), relaying the abstract piece word for word via his own effective three-chord strum. It was eventually retitled 'Brodsky Tune'.

Some of the album's out-takes followed a similar political trajectory, tracks that would have undoubtedly given *Wild Seed* a much harder edge had they made the final shortlist. These included 'The World Outside Waco', which concerned 1993's Waco siege in Texas that resulted in over 80 deaths. Until Warner Brothers' intervention – they reportedly informed Morten that the song would kill his career – it was considered to be a central part of the album. And then there was 'Gospel from a Heathen', which had been sourced from Håvard Rem's 1993 poetry collection, *Øvelser i grensesetting* [Exercises in Boundaries]. Despite Morten's assertion that it was 'a song about love', lines such as 'I'm not an atheist / But I'll be an atheist for you' and 'Well, I'm not a fascist / But I'll be a fascist for you' ensured its place in the archives. Similarly, 'Ape Angel' was culled due to its opening couplet, 'I'm not clean / I've never been clean', which ostensibly didn't fit with Morten's clean-cut profile. (Both 'Gospel from a Heathen' and 'Ape Angel' were performed in concert – to little consternation – during some live shows in 1995.)

BURNING OUT AGAIN

During radio promotion in the UK in July 1995, Morten showcased some of his new songs, including 'A Kind of Christmas Card', which was released as a single the following month. It included a live version of Sam Cooke's 1964 civil rights movement anthem, 'A Change Is Gonna Come', which Morten had previously performed as a member of Souldier Blue in the early 80s. (The track was also included on the Japanese version of *Wild Seed*).

The origins of 'A Kind of Christmas Card' can be traced back to 1994 and a chance encounter in Trondheim with a Norwegian band named Locomotives, who had been active since 1991. Morten picked up the story several years later, telling Ando Woltmann: 'I was on the way home. It was late. I was at a relatively early stage when it came to preparing my first solo record. I was also in the process of searching as a songwriter. So that's when I met them . . . I invited them into the studio where they played the song ["My Woman"] that was to become "Movies". At once, I thought that it was my song – I want a song like that! Then I drove right home and composed "A Kind of Christmas Card" as an answer of sorts.'[3]

The actual lyrics stemmed from a visit to Los Angeles, and a meeting with a friend who had relayed the story of a girl who had journeyed from Norway to LA to become a film star. 'That was her dream,' Morten explained to VH-1. 'And then very quickly she started doing X-rated movies, porn films – which has become a very big industry there – and got deeply involved with drugs. When my friend realised what was happening to her, she contacted the Norwegian consulate and got her put on a plane back to Norway – hopefully in time. This prompted Håvard [Rem] to write the lyrics.'

VG were certainly impressed with the single: 'Morten Harket may be about to make an ingenious turn in his career because, on "A Kind of Christmas Card", he appears with a brand new style. And it sounds very promising,' wrote Stein Østbø. 'A new haircut, a new voice and a new sound are important keywords. Harket's voice has become noticeably lower and more raspy; like a cross between a young and potent Rod Stewart and a focused Feargal Sharkey.'

In Germany, the single was retitled 'Burning Out Again (A Kind of Christmas Card)', since the record label in that territory were uncomfortable with releasing a song with 'Christmas' in the title at the height of summer.

In 1996, an interesting lounge-pop version of the track by Penthouse Playboys was released as a promotional single, and it was also included on the novelty band's album *Sånn skal det gjøres* [That's How It Should Be Done].

WIDER RANGE

Wild Seed's front cover, which displayed an ocean-traversing Morten carrying a typewriter, certainly symbolised his rebirth as a songwriter. And, as a document of where he was at that stage in his career, both in terms of the development of his songwriting and the musical direction in which he was heading, the album certainly does the job. In interviews, Morten name-dropped artists such as Crowded House and Sting, and you can certainly feel their influence as the album occasionally lapses into safe, MOR territory. Indeed, *Haugesunds Avis* commented that 'the music lacks soul . . . There is something a little too safe and complacent about *Wild Seed*.' In the UK, the *Today* newspaper's James Bennett remarked: 'He sounds like Sting on a bad day, on this gloomy and pretentious solo effort.'

On the whole, though, *Wild Seed* was largely lauded by the music media, particularly in Norway. *Vårt Land*'s Lars Navestad declared it an 'impressive solo effort', while *VG* praised the album for its songs and vocals: '*Wild Seed* is first and foremost a triumph for Morten Harket as a songwriter and vocalist,' wrote Stein Østbø. 'He's using a wider vocal range than before, and that's to his benefit.'

Harket? Alene?

Ja, – og du finner ham på toppen av hitlistene.

«Wild Seed» er Morten Harkets internasjonale solo-debut. Albumet er hovedsaklig spilt inn i Norge, med norske musikere og bakmenn.

Inneholder selvfølgelig storslageren «A Kind Of Christmas Card»

There are indeed some wonderful moments on the album. 'Brodsky Tune' is simplicity itself, with Morten delivering an almost David Sylvian-like vocal to convey Brodsky's wordy meditations on Bosnia. Elsewhere, 'Los Angeles' and the chilling, funereal 'Lay Me Down Tonight' both evoke a-ha's seemingly effortless melancholia, while 'Spanish Steps' drifts along in a pleasing 'Streets of Philadelphia' kind of way. What the album lacked were the big soaring choruses and pop hooks that Messrs Furuholmen and Waaktaar-Savoy were able to provide, and there are some tracks which are best described as fillers, notably the lyrically slight 'Tell Me What You See' and 'Lord', a dull 'Dear God'-type monologue.

CONTRASTING FORTUNES

In terms of the album's chart performance, there were some contrasting fortunes in Norway and the UK. Both the single and album hit No. 1 in Morten's homeland, and *Wild Seed* went on to become the year's biggest seller, eventually selling over 180,000 copies. In the UK, the lead-off single and album fared less well, reaching a disappointing No. 53 and No. 09, respectively. In fairness, a-ha were already past their commercial peak in the UK, and several of their more recent singles – namely, 'I Call Your Name', 'Early Morning' and 'Angel' – had all failed to reach the Top 40 and, arguably, Morten's profile had tapered off in recent years. Despite doing plenty of TV and radio promotion, the release of his debut solo single at the height of Britpop had been mistimed, with the attentions of the British record-buying public swaying more towards Oasis and Blur's battle for the No. 1 spot that month.

While success in the UK would elude him, Morten was kept busy in his homeland until the end of the year. Aside from the release of the 'Spanish Steps' single (featuring the non-album track 'Girl', on the B-side), there was a new compilation album released, titled *Kom ut og lek!* [Come Out and Play]. Recorded in co-operation with the *LO* (Norway's largest employee association), the album featured several greats of Norwegian music, including Lars Lillo-Stenberg (of deLillos) and Magnus Grønneberg (CC Cowboys). Morten's contribution was 'Evig ung', a Norwegian-language version of Bob Dylan's 'Forever Young'.

Earlier in the year he had also guested on an album by *Kamilla og tyven* composer Ragnar Bjerkreim, titled *Missa Caritatis* (proceeds from the February release went towards the Norwegian Missionary Society). Morten also contributed vocals to 'Hymne til kjærleiken' [Hymn to Love] and 'Sanctus', a largely choral piece.

The year was rounded off with a Norwegian tour that included performances of several new and unreleased songs. While the new year would provide Morten with some fresh challenges, his interview with VH-1 in the summer of 1995 seemed to sum up his contentment as a solo performer: 'I've never had it better than I have now,' he said. 'These are by far the best two years I've had, without a doubt.'

MORTEN HARKET – VOGTS VILLA (1996 Album)

Singing in Norwegian is a completely different challenge. It is no more and no less challenging than singing in English. But it requires something completely different and new from me.
– Morten Harket, *Dagbladet*, 1996

Produced by Kåre Christoffer Vestrheim and Morten Harket
Chart position: 21 (Norway)

The critical and commercial success of *Wild Seed* was acknowledged during the Spellemann awards ceremony in February 1996, with Morten winning in both the Best Song ('A Kind of Christmas Card') and Best Album categories, as well as Best Male Artist and Spellemann of the Year.

Around this time, Warner Brothers also released 'Los Angeles' as a single, and Morten duly performed the track during the awards ceremony. However, the lack of any new bonus tracks made it an unattractive purchase. 'Spanish Steps' was released as the UK's second single, but a lack of promotion ensured it wouldn't chart. Sensing that the label weren't keen to heavily invest in the album abroad, a prescient Morten sought to extricate himself from his contract, even threatening to quit the music business if he didn't get his way. 'I could see dangerous signals about dissolution within Warner Music internationally,' he told *VG*. 'I understood that the album was going to be lost, so I withdrew.'

In March 1996, he performed two new songs – 'Queen of Stormy Weather' and 'End of the Western World' – at a show at the Rockefeller in Oslo, songs that had, reportedly, been penned during a working trip to South America (the filming of an arts programme called *Safari* for Norwegian TV). All the signs were pointing towards a quick-fire follow-up to *Wild Seed*, and this appeared to be backed up by the release in May of a brand new single on the Arista label, the Steve Lovell-produced 'Heaven's Not for Saints (Let It Go)'. In a smart marketing move, the track – co-written by Håvard Rem and Ole Sverre Olsen – was performed at the Eurovision Song Contest in Oslo, which was also hosted by Morten (along with journalist Ingvild Bryn). Boasting his most epic production to date, with a suitably soaring chorus to match ('The night is calling you / Close to the edge / Who knows the distance / The distance when light fades away'), the single was another Top 10 hit in Norway. It failed to chart in the UK, however.

The summer of 1996 was spent performing several indoor and outdoor shows in Norway, as well as working on new material with Ole Sverre Olsen. One concert during the *Skagerrak Kulturfestival* in August featured an unusual 'pop and poetry' set from Morten that included English-language songs interspersed with poetry readings from both Olsen and Håvard Rem.

The same month also saw the release of *Songs from the Pocket*, the debut album by Jørun Bøgeberg. Morten's vocals can be heard on the mournful and elegiac 'Never Hear That Laugh'. In the liner notes, Jørun described it as 'a song for my grandma's sister, my mamma for some years, written on a silent night as she went walking home to her heaven, the shores unknown', and recently added some insight into the recording of the track: 'I asked Morten if it was possible that he

would contribute on this particular track, and he said yes. I think he liked the song. When he came to the studio late one night with only him and me around, he was just humming along with what he heard in the headphones, not really into the microphone, but quite out of distance and focus, and I wondered when we would start to nail it for real. Suddenly he had to leave, and luckily I had recorded all the humming, and ended up with some unfocused Harket

vocal tracks that, after some editing, worked nice and cool as a shadow next to my own vocal, even though the sound quality was kinda crappy. You can hear the difference in sound quality, especially in the line that Morten sings by himself in the second verse. I am very happy it came out this way. He probably knew what he was doing, and he also gave me some helpful guidance on how to approach the song, vocally. I guess I tried to sing it in a Harket kind of way.'

HOLIDAY HOME

While Morten had stockpiled a number of new songs, there would be a change of direction for his next release. By September, he was committed to recording a new Norwegian-language album for BMG, which would eventually appear on its subsidiary label, Norsk Plateproduksjon.

Provisionally titled *Gammel gris* [Old Pig], the album was recorded during a productive 12-day period on the remote Norwegian island of Dvergsøya, which was notorious for its links to a local resident named Maren who was reportedly tortured and then burned as a witch in 1670 for her alleged part in the sinking of a boat bound for Jutland.

Vogts Villa, an old country house on the historic island, was temporarily converted into a recording studio, while Morten's hastily assembled new band included multi-instrumentalist Geir Sundstøl (who would later play on sessions for both a-ha and Savoy), plus Thomas Tofte and Kåre Vestrheim from Locomotives, the band he'd met in 1994. (To Morten's surprise and disappointment, Kjetil Bjerkestrand chose not to be involved in the project.) The remote recording location certainly appealed to Morten, but there was no electricity on the property and diesel generators had to be shipped over.

Lyrically, the songs drew heavily from the poetry of Håvard Rem (who had published *Taksameteret går* [The Meter Is Running], an anthology of his work, in 1996), but Ole Sverre Olsen also provided some interesting material, including 'Himmelske danser' [Heavenly Dancer], which concerned a dancer who had succumbed to the ecstasy drug. 'It hits me right in the chest,' Morten told *Dagbladet*. 'It is beautiful and full of life, full of love and full of sorrow.' (Both Rem and Olsen joined Morten and his band during their fortnight on the island, although it was claimed that Olsen spent most of his time there working on his debut novel.)

For 'Fremmed her' [Stranger Here] and 'Jeg kjenner ingen fremtid' [I Know No Future], Morten recycled the melodies of the previously unreleased songs 'Gospel from a Heathen' and 'All of You Concerned', respectively, while 'Vuggevise' [Lullaby] was a new Norwegian-language – and country-tinged – version of 'Lay Me Down Tonight'.

Morten and his new band – along with Håvard Rem, who also read some poetry – previewed some of the new songs during a concert at Oslo's Bredtveit Prison in October. To the outsider this would have seemed like an unusual move but, in addition to the likes of Simon & Garfunkel and Queen, Morten had grown up listening to Johnny Cash, who had famously played at San Quentin and Folsom Prison, so the chance to play a handful of songs at a women's prison would no doubt have appealed greatly to the singer.

FALLEN STAR

'Tilbake til livet' [Back to Life] and 'Herre i drømmen' [Lord of the Dream] were released as promotional singles, with the album *Vogts Villa* arriving in shops at the end of November 1996. Without a big hit single to bolster its sales, however, the album peaked at a disappointing No. 21.

In terms of the reviews, *Vårt Land*'s Lars Navestad declared that it was 'a good follow-up from one of our very best artists. It's clear that Morten and his buddies have enjoyed their cabin trip. *Vogts Villa* displays a musical playfulness and relaxed atmosphere that our former superstar probably needed to travel a far distance outside the regular studio walls to find.' Elsewhere, *Haugesunds Avis* were equally enthused: '*Wild Seed* was the most overrated Norwegian album last year. I much prefer *Vogts Villa* – it's more introverted, melancholic, stripped-down and honest. Choosing to work with young and energetic musicians – led by the brilliant Geir Sundstøl – has been a smart move.'

However, *Dagbladet* criticised the album for its lack of ambition, and in 1997 they sensationally declared that Morten was 'a fallen star with an audience reduced to a tenth'. The paper had, somewhat unfairly, compared the 180,000-selling *Wild Seed* to *Vogts Villa*'s somewhat more modest sales of 18,000, even going to the lengths of asking the record label's Per Østmark to comment on the album's poor performance. 'There was never the intention that this would be a great deal like *Wild Seed*,' Østmark told the popular newspaper,' but we hoped it would sell a little more, of course.' Østmark also admitted they would have considered advertising the album on TV during the lucrative festive period if initial sales had been better.

While, in some quarters, *Vogts Villa* was viewed as a suicidal career move in light of the success of *Wild Seed*, it would be foolhardy to dismiss the album as merely a vanity project from a musician who was harbouring major record label disenchantment. Instead, it's easier to view the album more as a stop-gap release, with Morten still honing his songwriting skills. And, besides, there is plenty to enjoy on *Vogts Villa*, with Morten's latest studio band utilising a number of instruments (mandolin, harmonica, mellotron, pedal steel guitar, etc) to great effect. Like the similarly styled *Poetenes Evangelium*, its appeal isn't immediately apparent, but there are a number of standout tracks. 'Tilbake til livet' and 'Herre i drømmen' boast decent hooks, 'Jeg kjenner ingen fremtid' features a typically haunting vocal that recalls Chris Isaak in his pomp, while there's a welcome folky style employed on the playful 'Gammal og vis' [Old and Wise].

REUNION

By the end of February 1997, Morten had concluded his Norwegian tour in support of the *Vogts Villa* album and his focus would soon switch to the writing of a new album for the international market. But a-ha's reformation the following year would mean the English-language follow-up to *Wild Seed* wouldn't be released for at least a decade.

In between working trips to China and Jamaica with Håvard Rem, Morten also found the time to perform some (largely low-key) shows throughout the year, and also appeared on a compilation album titled *Kvirre virre vitt!*, which was released in May. Featuring childhood favourites by both new and established Norwegian artists, the album included Morten's contemporary version of the popular children's folk song 'Kråkevisa' [The Crow Song], while other notable contributors included Bjørn Eidsvåg, DumDum Boys and Bel Canto, whose singer, Anneli Drecker, would later work with a-ha.

Also released in 1997 was *First Breath*, the debut album by Morten's then-wife, Camilla (with whom he had three children), but the couple would announce their divorce the following year, after nine years of marriage. Aside from the change in Morten's personal life, there was to be a significant change in his professional career, too, with the announcement that a-ha were to reform for the Nobel Peace Prize Concert in December 1998.

While plans for a new solo album had to be put on the back burner, Morten kept busy during the lead-up to the reunion show and the subsequent recording of the *Minor Earth Major Sky* album. The summer of 1998 saw the release of the soundtrack of the musical *Sophie's World*, which made its world premiere in Germany in June 1998. Morten contributed 'A Jester in Our Town', a quirky and theatrical track that further displayed his musical versatility. It was later released as a promotional single.

Within the same soundtrack medium, Morten also contributed the mid-paced 'Jungle of Beliefs' to the Swedish TV series *Cultures Span the World*. The project saw Morten reunited with Ragnar Bjerkreim, who had masterminded the *Missa Caritatis* project. Aside from its appearance on the accompanying soundtrack album, the track – which featured lyrics by both Morten and Ole Sverre Olsen – was also released as a single in 1999.

There was also a rather unusual collaboration, with Morten dipping his toes into the world of dance music and working on a number of tracks with a Sweden-based drum 'n' bass duo named Boolaboss, who had released an album titled *Nature Will Be Satisfied* in 1998. One track from these sessions, 'The Secret', was scheduled for release as a single in 1999, but this was abandoned as a-ha became Morten's primary focus following their well-publicised reunion in December 1998. (The duo's unusual name was seemingly derived from the Irish term, bualadh bos, meaning 'clap your hands'.)

CHAPTER FIFTEEN
UNDERGROUND

If Morten had decided that a-ha had run its course by 1994, Pål certainly didn't know about it as he and Magne both did some preliminary work on the follow-up to 1993's *Memorial Beach*. But it soon became obvious to him that Morten's top priority was a solo career, which had already been kick-started with the release of *Poetenes Evangelium*. Following this relatively low-key project, Morten had signed a major recording deal with Warner Brothers and started working on his debut solo album for the international market. 'Towards the end, Morten would say, "Warner Brothers now believes I can sell more than a-ha", said Pål. 'I couldn't bear to listen. Why couldn't he just say, "Okay, I'm now making a solo album"? Our manager, Terry Slater, suddenly became the manager of Morten, and I happened to discover, through a Warners secretary, that the album was finished . . . So I'd wasted half a year on the follow-up to *Memorial Beach*. One expects some respect after a collaboration of ten years.'[1] The clearly unimpressed musician famously vented his frustration in the song 'Daylight's Wasting':

> *The singer was fair but got it wrong*
> *He never did justice to my songs*
> *He did more for me and that's a fact*
> *When he went and stabbed me in the back*
> *So I've gotta do now, don't you know*
> *What I should have done five years ago*

Once it had become clear to Pål that there wasn't going to be a follow-up to *Memorial Beach*, the songwriter pondered various options, which included working with luminaries such as Morrissey and Talk Talk's Mark Hollis (in the case of the latter, he received a polite letter turning him down). Other options included starting a new band with Magne, while there was even the serious proposition of reforming Bridges (former bassist Viggo Bondi even began practising old songs in readiness). But, after much deliberation, Pål eventually formed a new band with his wife, Lauren. The couple would both sing and play guitar, with drummer Frode Unneland completing the line-up. While Lauren's syrupy vocals would often divide opinion, Pål's rougher vocal tones would prove the perfect fit for the new band's blend of 60s-influenced indie rock. (An established musician on the Norwegian music scene, Frode Unneland had played in bands such as Chocolate Overdose, Pompel & the Pilts, the Rub and Unge Frustrerte Menn [Young

Frustrated Men], but he'd also worked on a-ha demos with Pål in 1994.)

In January 1995, *Dagbladet* reported that the new band was called Savoy and they'd commenced work on their debut album, provisionally titled *Fade*.

SAVOY – MARY IS COMING (1996 Album)
Produced by Savoy
Chart position: 1 (Norway)

Savoy's debut album, featuring songs co-written and produced by the husband-and-wife team, was completed in 1995, but it wouldn't be released until February 1996. (The Norwegian media speculated that the record company didn't want it to clash with Morten's *Wild Seed* album.)

While 'Velvet' was scheduled as the band's debut single, the first song to be officially released by Savoy was 'Foolish', which appeared on a nine-track compilation CD affixed to copies of Norway's now-defunct music magazine *Beat*. Pål later described it as his most aggressive song to date.

Shortly afterwards, the band's debut single, 'Velvet', reached the top of the Norwegian charts. One of the slower numbers on the album, the track featured Simone Larsen from the Oslo-based pop band D'Sound. Her backing vocals, which ghost in and out to great effect, provided the song's memorable hook, while there was a slight hint of the Cure's 'Just Like Heaven' in the melody. 'Velvet' did not chart in the UK but the song would prove to be a perfect fit for a-ha, and it enjoyed a new lease of life as the third single to be lifted from their comeback album, *Minor Earth Major Sky*.

Evidence that Pål had lost none of his pop sensibilities was displayed on catchy tracks such as 'Underground' and 'We Will Never Forget', while the likes of 'Daylight's Wasting', 'Get Up Now' and 'Foolish' demonstrated some lyrical and musical bite. Elsewhere, 'Half an Hour's Worth' featured some pleasing Paul McCartney-esque melodic touches, while the daring title cut – which was also released as a promotional single – exhibited a whole new side of Pål's writing, with its overtly sexual lyrics ('Mary never blows you / But that's alright / 'Cause what I like is when / Mary is coming / . . . And it looks like I'm coming too'). 'No one believed that such a thing would come from me,' Pål later recalled. 'But for us it was clear, and on the album cover are the two legs and everything. Nobody got it!'[2]

Without the recognisable voice of a-ha amidst their ranks, Savoy were always likely to struggle to emulate the success enjoyed by Morten, and their odds of global success were slashed considerably when Danny Goldberg, the man who had originally signed them to Warner Brothers, left the label. Without Goldberg's support, Savoy's album soon disappeared from public attention, despite some promising sales in Norway. However, the band were nominated for two Spellemann awards (eventually losing out in both the Best Band and Best Newcomer categories), and managed to secure a new recording deal with EMI.

SAVOY – LACKLUSTER ME (1997 Album)
Produced by Pål Waaktaar-Savoy and Lauren Waaktaar-Savoy
Chart position: 12 (Norway)

The sessions for Savoy's second album, which was largely recorded at Lauren and Pål's New York home, now included bassist Greg Calvert, whom the couple had seen playing in a band named Soup. Following his appointment in the autumn of 1995, he performed with the band several times the following year, and even played on a new – and almost unrecognisable – version of a-ha's 'October' for the B-side of 'Velvet'. The band also incorporated the likes of 'I've Been Losing You' and 'Sycamore Leaves' into the set lists, and a more rock-based version of the latter track would later find its way onto the new self-produced album. 'Some people thought I wrote differently for Savoy than a-ha, but really it's mostly down to the arrangement and instrumentation,' explained Pål. 'It was fun to showcase that by covering songs from, shall we say, the other side.'[3]

The serviceable ballad 'Rain' was issued to Norwegian radio as a promotional single and was somewhat indicative of the largely downbeat feel of the band's second album, the title track being a case in point ('Lackluster me / Stands before you / What can I be / To make you want me'). The bleakness continued apace with 'Unsound', with a grungy bassline complementing the biting lyrics ('No point asking me to stay / I'd rather walk away'). Elsewhere, 'This, That and the Other' featured some more indie rock grit, recalling Eels' breakthrough hit, 'Novocaine for the Soul'.

With the recruitment of Calvert effectively freeing up Pål to utilise a broader sonic palette, Lauren was also accorded the opportunity to add a touch of art-house pop to the mix with a daring double-header: Future promotional single 'Foreign Film' saw the band experimenting with electronics and mellotron sounds, while the more esoteric and ambient 'Flowers for Sylvia' served as an interesting tribute to the prolific Boston-born poet and novelist Sylvia Plath, who'd committed suicide in 1963. Against a backdrop of unsettling sound effects, Lauren recites a select list of Plath's poems in a spoken word homage. 'Pål had written "Flowers for Sylvia" as an instrumental to use as a soundtrack to an art film I made after film school, a surrealistic montage of arty street scenes,' explained Lauren. 'I spoke Sylvia Plath poem titles over the instrumental – partly out of tribute, but mostly because her words are so much better than mine!'[4] (Lauren would later reference Plath's only novel, *The Bell Jar*, on 2004's 'Girl One'.)

The album included several other gems: The beautifully wistful 'You Should Have Told Me' rates as one of Pål's best ballads, while the faster-paced rock workout 'I Still Cry' (which was also released as a promotional single) was another standout. Other tracks worthy of note included 'If You Tell', which featured some Beatles-esque melodic touches, and 'Hey Luchie', a sequel of sorts to 'Angel in the

Snow,' which had been penned while a-ha were on tour in South America. (On the 1993 *Live in South America* video, directed by Lauren, Pål can be seen practising the song.)

CREEPY

Featuring a creepy sleeve depicting the cracked face of a doll, which had been purchased from a Manhattan flea market, *Lackluster Me* hit Norwegian record stores in October 1997 and peaked at No. 12. (A promo CD featuring the festive non-album track 'Xmas Time (Blows My Mind)', was given away with copies of *Lackluster Me* during the Christmas period.) While it lacked some of the pop hooks prevalent in its predecessor, it was, sonically, a more eclectic and satisfying album, a companion piece of sorts to Radiohead's highly rated *OK Computer*,

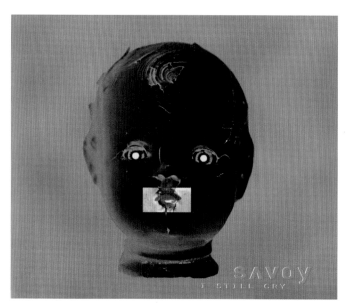

which had been released just months earlier. (Frode Unneland later revealed that Savoy had been listening to the Oxfordshire band's second album, *The Bends*, during the making of their own record.)

While the album enjoyed only modest sales, critics were certainly impressed. *Stavanger Aftenblad*'s reviewer called it 'an astonishing masterpiece: dangerously catchy and unpredictably intellectual in its gloomy, monumental beauty', while *Dagbladet*'s Håkon Moslet wrote: 'It is simply a pleasure to hear what Savoy has achieved on their second album. Here, it ranges from naive indie pop to dark and warm quality pop, with the same gorgeous production all the way.' It also earned another Spellemann nomination (for Best Rock Album).

As part of a Savoy reissue programme, the album was re-released by the Bergen-based Apollon Records in December 2016, including a limited edition vinyl that marked its first release on the format.

SAVOY – MOUNTAINS OF TIME (1999 Album)
Produced by Pål Waaktaar-Savoy and Lauren Savoy
Chart position: 1 (Norway)

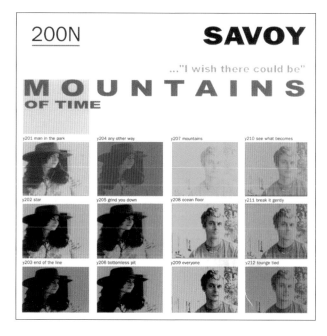

The first half of 1998 saw Savoy performing some of their songs at showcase gigs in the UK and the USA. Pål also busied himself with other ventures, firstly exhibiting a collection of his oil paintings – titled *Rammer* [Frames] – at a gallery in Lillehammer and, secondly, producing a single by deLillos, titled 'Tyve null tre' [Twenty Zero Three], which was also included on the band's compilation album, *Gamle sanger om igjen* [Old Songs All Over Again].

By the time a-ha had reformed for the Nobel Peace Prize Concert in Oslo in 1998, Savoy had already released two albums and attained a respectable level of success – both critically and commercially – in Norway. Despite a-ha's reformation and intentions to release new material, plans were already in place to release a third Savoy album. Indeed, by the time a-ha had signed with WEA Germany in July 1999, both acts were working concurrently. 'To run the two bands alongside each other was of course madness,' said Pål. 'To juggle records, recording dates, release plans, tour plans, and promotional plans from two different record companies makes everything spin for me. The place of freedom that Savoy had been, became, in the end, pretty stressful.'[5]

However, it was a confident band that entered the recording studio to cut their third record, and Savoy were undoubtedly buoyed by the enthusiastic response to their previous album. 'The songs kept coming – recording it was easy,' recalled Pål during a Facebook Q&A. 'Lauren was pregnant. We were giddy and excited!' (The album had originally been pencilled in for an April 1999 release – four months before Lauren was due to give birth – but it wasn't finished in time.)

MOUNTAINS OF SONGS

At the time of its release, Savoy's third album, *Mountains of Time*, arguably represented Pål's best set of songs since 1986's *Scoundrel Days* and attracted some of the best reviews of his career, but credit also belonged to Lauren and Frode, who both raised their game during the production. Lauren was certainly keen to make an impression this time round. 'It's hard starting a band with your husband,' she said. 'The assumption is that [Pål] does everything and you're along for the ride. That drove me to write more original material.'[6]

Like its predecessor, the album was self-produced. Pål also resumed bass-playing duties following the departure of Greg Calvert, but Jørun Bøgeberg was also brought in to play on two tracks.

Pål's songwriting prolificacy during this period also meant the band were able to set aside songs for a fourth album. And, inevitably, there were some Savoy songs that would eventually make it onto a-ha's comeback album, *Minor Earth Major Sky*, such as 'Mary Ellen Makes the Moment Count' and 'Barely Hanging On'.

With both a-ha and Savoy running in tandem, both acts' new albums inevitably ended up featuring some of the same musicians. Drummer Per Lindvall – a mainstay of a-ha's recording and performing team in the noughties – guested on 'Man in the Park', while Frode Unneland featured on a-ha's 'Minor Earth Major Sky' and 'The Company Man'.

One notable guest on *Mountains of Time* was Magne, who added a gorgeous clavichord part to 'Bottomless Pit'. 'Magne can pick up any instrument at all and play it as if he's been doing it all his life,' said Pål. 'I'll never forget when he walked in and laid down a fantastic part on "Bottomless Pit" in the space of two hours . . . I used to challenge him, and the only time I've been surprised was when I asked him to play the saxophone part on "The Living Daylights" live at a concert. Magne bought a sax, went out in front of a packed arena, and totally screwed it up! The shock was that he couldn't pull it off. It was the only time.'[7]

STAR

Released as the album's first single in July 1999, 'Star (I'm Not Stupid Baby)' provided a taste of what was to come: well-produced songs with a clear 60s flavour and catchier pop sheen, an antidote to the previous album's more sombre inflections. Featuring Lauren on lead vocals, the song was a hit with radio listeners and later earned the band another Spellemann nomination. 'I'd never heard myself on the radio before,' Lauren told *Dagbladet*, 'so when I heard "Star" on the car radio the other day, it was just, *wow*!' (A remix of the song was created for the German market the following year, while a second Lauren Savoy-directed promotional video featured a cameo from Anneli Drecker.)

Lauren's vocals could also be heard on another of the album's standouts, the extremely catchy four-chord pop track 'Grind You Down', which also included some infectious arpeggiated guitar. It was also released as a promotional single, and *VG*'s Stein Østbø described it as 'an amazing pop song with handclaps, tambourine and doo-wop in the chorus. Pop art!'

Elsewhere, the more sombre 'Bottomless Pit' found itself in similar Beatles-influenced territory, subtly evoking the melodic craft of *Rubber Soul*. Other highlights included 'End of the Line' (which has shades of Burt Bacharach) and 'Any Other Way', which included some terrific keyboard work from session player Preben Grieg-Halvorsen, who had also played on the deLillos single 'Tyve null tre'.

Whether by coincidence or by design, the album seemingly takes the listener on something of a seasonal journey. The opening 'Man in the Park' – which was also released as a promotional single in 2000 – evokes images of springtime walks in Washington Square Park, with its tale of the 'flower shop girl' and the 'man that knows'; summer is clearly represented by 'Grind You Down' ('You wait all year / Then the summer comes'), and there's some lovely wintery imagery on the nostalgic 'See What Becomes' ('I'm walking through a snowfall / I'm just a little kid'). Lauren's original 1960s-style sleeve design, featuring individual shots of the band, also seemed to embody the album's many moods, via its array of Warhol-esque colour filters.

MAGICAL

The album – which actually sold more copies in Norway than a-ha's *Memorial Beach* – was released by EMI in August 1999, with initial copies including a bonus five-track EP (titled *The Bovarnick Twins*). Reviews were unanimous in their praise. *Dagbladet*'s reviewer wrote: 'John Lennon would have been hailed as a god if this were his solo album,' while *VG*'s critic gushed: 'If the legendary Phil Spector had heard Savoy's *Mountains of Time*, we would probably have seen tears behind that eccentric's sunglasses.'

And there were celebrations aplenty in the Waaktaar–Savoy household throughout August and September 1999, with the couple heralding the arrival of their son, True August, and the album hitting No. 1 in the Norwegian charts. The celebrations continued in February 2000 when Savoy were awarded a Spellemann award for Best Pop Group. 'This album was so much fun to make, and we enjoyed it so much,' Lauren said during her brief award acceptance speech. 'It's so nice when you guys like it as well!'

A-ha's comeback album, *Minor Earth Major Sky*, would attract similar plaudits, and it was no surprise when Pål later described this period as one of the highlights of his career. 'We got two-page reviews in all the Norwegian newspapers,' he later reflected. 'That's never happened with a-ha. The summer we had [our son] Augie and released *Mountains of Time* almost at the same time was totally special. It was magical. It's never been better.'[8]

Like its predecessor, the album was reissued on both CD and vinyl by Apollon Records in 2017, although the sleeve and booklet were revamped as the original artwork couldn't be sourced.

CHAPTER SIXTEEN
TIMBER AND SOUND

By the time of a-ha's final stop on the *Memorial Beach* tour in June 1994, the band's members were burnt out, both physically and emotionally, following years of almost relentless recording, touring and media work. While Magne often came across as the most gregarious and loquacious member of the band, he was perhaps the one most deeply affected by fame's pressure cooker, as the lyrics for 'Lamb to the Slaughter' would illustrate. 'As a member of a-ha, I was submitted to an enormous amount of attention directly on me as a person, something that can be quite taxing,' he reflected in 2004. 'Of course, there are perks to selling 29 million albums and touring sell-out stadiums worldwide – I will not pretend I did not relish it at times – but gradually the feeling of chasing your own success eroded my conviction in what I was doing.'

As the release of the somewhat formulaic 'Shapes That Go Together' in March 1994 would suggest, creativity was also at a low point. They'd been signed to Warner Brothers for a decade by this point, but the hits were starting to dry up and tensions within the band had still been unresolved. 'It was like a car,' reflected Magne. 'We ran it for so long but never serviced it properly. Then it broke down and died.'[1]

As it would transpire, the demise of the band wasn't instant, but it had become obvious that they needed a break. The problem was, no one had told the New York-based Pål, who had laid down a series of new demos with Echobelly's producer, Simon Vinestock. But while it was intimated in the Norwegian media that a new album was on the way, both Morten's and Magne's interest in the band had dwindled. Morten, who'd already released the low-key *Poetenes Evangelium* album in Norway the previous year, now had his heart set on an international solo career, while Magne – who had sold his Kensington apartment and moved back to Norway – now craved a quieter life with his newly expanded family (he and his wife, Heidi, were raising two young sons by this point). 'I feel increasingly restless about living in a city as big as London,' he told the *Daily Express* in 1991. 'Oslo just doesn't compare as a city, since growing up there I was able to play out on the street without any fear. I would like to be able to give [my son] Thomas some of the happiness and freedom I had as a child.'

Pål eventually conceded defeat and, after much deliberation, found a new vehicle for his songwriting talents in Savoy, while Morten forged ahead with his solo career. As for Magne, he would release new music during the 90s, but it was a medium which he would describe as being more of a hobby than a profession as he prioritised an art career that decade. 'When we moved to London, I tried to sell drawings on the street to make some extra money. A-ha found success, and I gradually became more and more tired of fame,' he explained. 'I sensed a need to start creating artwork again – as a form of therapy. A gallerist I knew from earlier had run into Morten Harket and asked, "When is Magne going to give up this music nonsense and start doing what he's destined to do?" When Morten told me that, it hit something in me, because I had already been thinking the same thing.'[2]

CONSCRIPTION

Like Morten and Pål, Magne – who shared his birthday with L.S. Lowry – had been a keen artist during his formative years, and he continued to draw while holed up in hotels during promotional duties with a-ha in the mid-80s. Prior to this, he received an eye-opening introduction to the world of art during his teens, while working at the Henie Onstad Art Centre. 'It had a recording studio in the basement and great artists coming from abroad like David Hockney and Yoko Ono,' he recalled. 'I got to meet them – I was one of the assistants running around, sorting every little thing that needed to be done for their exhibitions. They gave me the odd kind word, but what I found most exciting was peeking into their world. It made me realise one's hobby could be a way of life. I found that quite informative and inspirational.'[3]

The venue, which overlooks the Oslofjord in Høvikodden, currently exhibits over 4,000 works of art, and it would become very familiar to Magne during the post-*Memorial Beach* years.

As a conscientious objector, Magne had evaded the country's compulsory military service, but the terms of the Military Refusal Act of 1965 dictated that he would have to undertake *Siviltjenesten* [Civil Service] as an alternative to military conscription. In the mid-90s, Magne completed this compulsory service at the Henie Onstad Art Centre which, in addition to showcasing the work of both national and international artists, has also doubled up as a concert venue for music acts of a more left-field and experimental persuasion. The progressive jazz-rock band Soft Machine played there in the early 70s, and so too did local punk acts such as Kjøtt and Oslo Børs. In addition, both the German composer Karlheinz Stockhausen and the more avant-garde composer John Cage had performed at the prestigious venue. Magne was entrusted with the task of digitalising the centre's live recordings. 'The idea was to activate the sound treasures that were in the archive,' he said, 'but the people working at the centre couldn't agree on how the CD releases should be done. It was supposed to be the start of a series of *Arkivalia* releases. Instead, it became the starting point for [*Electra 96*], a large exhibition of electronic multimedia art.'[4]

Arkivalia, Volume One, featuring Stockhausen, Cage and other renowned composers such as Arne Nordheim, was eventually released in 1996, but many of the live recordings were later released separately. (Soft Machine's 1971 show received a release both on CD and vinyl, in 2009 and 2010, respectively, while John Cage's 1983 visit was immortalised on 2010's *In Norway* CD, via the centre's own Prisma Records imprint.)

NORWEGIAN WOOD

By the time of his civic duties, Magne had also reactivated his own art career – under the continuing mentorship of the renowned visual artist Kjell Nupen – and exhibited a number of paintings at a gallery in Tvedestrand in 1992. By then it had been three years since his debut exhibition, *Maleri* [Painting], at the Sølvberget gallery in Stavanger. Because of a-ha's exhausting work schedule, he'd had to wait until 1989 – a relative gap year by the band's standards – before he could showcase his artwork. However, Magne was somewhat critical of his initial efforts: 'The pictures at this time functioned mostly as a diary or journal,' he recalled. 'When I look back, it's clear that I was more of a drawing artist than a painter.'[5]

Much of his early work was inspired by the Norwegian painter Edvard Munch – two of Magne's paintings were even titled 'Munch Landskap I' and 'Munch Landskap II' – but the inspiration for his woodcut exhibition, *Kutt* [Cuts], in 1995 was to be found much closer to home. 'I used personal memories from my father's plane crash as a starting point,' he said. 'He was a jazz musician and every picture in *Kutt* reflects jazz song titles from a handwritten list I found in his destroyed trumpet case. Every title is cut up and changed into form and colour.'[6] The exhibition, which opened at the Henie Onstad Art Centre, was seen as something of a breakthrough for the aspiring artist and received a favourable write-up in *Aftenposten*.

There would be further exhibitions – both solo and collaborative – throughout the decade, plus other commissions, such as the illustration of Henning Kramer Dahl's jazz-inspired poetry book, *Blåtoneboulevardene* [Blue Note Boulevard] in 1997, and the woodcut design that formed the front cover of Jørun Bøgeberg's 1996 debut solo album, *Songs from the Pocket*.

'As far as I remember, I must have asked Mags if he had an idea for a cover,' said Jørun, 'just as a shot in the dark, without any expectations really, and he came up with this woodcut graphic which was a small part of a bigger piece. I liked it very much, as did the record company. Mags pointed out that it was a coincidence it showed four strings and something that could be interpreted as a hand. The idea of making 200 special numbered and signed versions of the album with Mags' print on the cover of a booklet with lyrics, photos and a music CD inside came from Mags himself. This was kind of new in 1996, combining art, photography and music this way. This led to some attention for the release – a little spot on the

Norwegian broadcasting news. I still find this special edition for sale on Discogs for an incredibly good price.'

MAGNE FURUHOLMEN AND KJETIL BJERKESTRAND
– TI KNIVER I HJERTET (1994 Album)

Produced by Magne Furuholmen and Kjetil Bjerkestrand
Chart position: N/A

Although Magne's burgeoning career as a visual artist had seemingly reduced his musical endeavours to more of a pastime, he remained active as a musician, particularly in his homeland. Aside from delving into the world of modern ballet, which saw him composing the music for an Anderz Døving-choreographed performance of *Støt* [Shock] at Oslo's Black Box theatre, he also teamed up with Kjetil Bjerkestrand – under the name of Timbersound – for a number of soundtrack projects, including *Ti kniver i hjertet* [Ten Knives in the Heart], which was created during a period of great uncertainty within the a-ha camp.

Kjetil Bjerkestrand was already well known to the band. In addition to co-arranging the 'Shapes That Go Together' single in 1994, the highly accomplished keyboardist had also played on Morten's *Poetenes Evangelium*. He was also an in-demand session musician and had previously worked with an array of luminaries from the Norwegian music scene, including Bjørn Eidsvåg, Jonas Fjeld, Sissel Kyrkjebø, Rune Larsen, Marius Müller and Jahn Teigen, as well as popular bands such as Dance with a Stranger, DumDum Boys and Stage Dolls. His skills as both a musician and an arranger also led to work with a number of international artists, including Dee Dee Bridgewater, Ray Charles and Keith Emerson. In recognition of his studio work, he received a Gammleng Award from Norway's Fund for Performing Artists in 1988.

Bjerkestrand was also an experienced film soundtrack composer. Along with Nils-Aslak Valkeapää and the Manglerud-born Marius Müller, he'd written the music for Nils Gaup's acclaimed *Veiviseren* [Pathfinder], which was nominated for Best Foreign Language Film at the 60th Academy Awards in 1988. In 1993, he provided the music for the Gaup-helmed *Hodet over vannet* [Head Above Water], and its title track – featuring DumDum Boys' Prepple Houmb and the September When's Morten Abel – hit the Top 10 hit in Norway. Both films earned Gaup an Amanda Award at the annual Norwegian International Film Festival in 1988 and 1994, respectively.

'Kjetil and I were an odd match,' said Magne, 'but we really enjoyed each other's strengths. It was a very free and easy collaboration to start with. Kjetil brought a lot of experience and knowledge – making music for film, for example. He is also a very talented composer and arranger. I think maybe what I brought to the table was to be somewhat more radical and experimental.'

Ti kniver i hjertet – which was marketed as *Cross My Heart and Hope to Die* outside of Norway – was loosely based on Lars Saabye Christensen's coming-of-age novel *Gutten som ville være en av gutta* [The Boy Who Wanted to Be One of the Guys], which centres around a shy young teenager named Otto who befriends an interesting character named Frank during a dramatic, life-changing summer holiday. (Christensen, who co-wrote the screenplay, had previously performed with a-ha during the *Østenfor sol vestenfor måne* show in 1991, doing poetry readings in between some of the songs.)

Marius Holst's first major feature film as a director earned some very favourable reviews upon its release in August 1994, and has since been hailed as a classic of Norwegian cinema. 'Exciting, subtle and dramatic, without resorting to cliché,' wrote *Morgenbladet*'s Kjetil Korslund. '… one of the year's best films.' Elsewhere, *Nordlandsposten*'s Rune Nilsen wrote: 'All in all, a good movie experience for anyone who has been a teenager. A movie that should be seen twice.' The film also received worldwide recognition, earning a Blue Angel award at the 45th Berlin International Film Festival in 1995 and a Golden Zenith award at the Montreal World Film Festival the same year.

NORDIC FOLK

While the original music on the soundtrack does include some dialogue from the film, it's largely an instrumental work. Tracks such as 'Den blinde pianostemmeren' [The Blind Piano Tuner] are true to Kjetil Bjerkestrand's classical training, but there's also a strong Nordic folk feel to the album in places, which is characterised by the beautiful flute work of 1990 Spellemann nominee Hans Olav Gorset. Elsewhere, the guitar playing of Eivind Aarset adds a touch of jazz to the mix.

There's also a recurring motif threading through the work, which would later be recycled for a-ha's 'What There Is' (released in 2009). The melody is certainly recognisable in the opening cut, 'Ti kniver i hjertet (Ottos tema)' [Otto's Theme] – which was also released as a single – while tracks such as 'Guttestreker' [Boyhood

Pranks], 'Styrkeprøven' [Trial of Strength] and 'Farvel Til Johnny' [Farewell to Johnny] are essentially variations on a theme, but with noticeable differences in both pace and mood. 'Guttestreker', with its combination of fast-paced acoustic guitar and block flute, was certainly a highlight, while other standouts included the eerie shuffle of 'Blindebukk' [Blind Man's Buff] and the closing theme, 'Avslutningstema', which has shades of Mike Oldfield.

In addition to the original material, other tracks were added to complement the nostalgic 60s setting, including two contrasting versions of Adriano Celentano's 'Il ragazzo della via Gluck' [The Boy from Gluck Street]. Swedish singer Anna-Lena Löfgren's take on the Italian pop classic 'Lyckliga Gatan' [Happy Street] was a huge hit in Norway in 1968 and stayed at No. 1 for 12 weeks, while 'Barneselskap (Lyckliga gatan)' – with vocals from Nina Helene Andersen – offered a new, Norwegian interpretation of the much-covered song. Elsewhere on the soundtrack were two recordings by the Swedish tenor Jussi Björling: 'Tonerna' [Tones] and 'När jag för m ig själv i mörka skogen går' [When I Walk Alone in the Dark Forest].

It's certainly an eclectic mix, and the soundtrack deservedly received some favourable notices from film reviewers.

MAGNE FURUHOLMEN AND KJETIL BJERKESTRAND – HOTEL OSLO (1997 Album)

Produced by Magne Furuholmen and Kjetil Bjerkestrand
Chart position: N/A

In the years following his work on the *Ti kniver i hjertet* soundtrack, Magne completed his compulsory civil service and forged ahead with his career as a visual artist, gaining critical acclaim for his woodcuts at the *Kutt* exhibition, which ran via several galleries throughout Norway in 1995. Although he would contribute keyboards to 'Grå' [Grey] on the self-titled album for Det Gode

Selskap [the Good Company] that year, new music wouldn't appear until the end of the following year.

Kjetil Bjerkestrand, meanwhile, had completed session work on various projects, which included Morten's *Wild Seed* album, and had also released the 1995 album *Gull, røkelse og myrra* [Gold, Frankincense and Myyrh], in collaboration with saxophonist Tore Brunborg. (Like its 1997 follow-up, *Prima Luna*, it included versions of various hymns and carols.) Additionally, there was further soundtrack work, which included the short film *Eremittkrepsen* [Hermit Crab].

In 1996, Magne and Kjetil Bjerkestrand reactivated their Timbersound project and completed a soundtrack for *Hotel Oslo*, a new four-part TV series which interwove the stories of six young people who had met at a run-down hotel in Oslo. The series starred the Amanda Award-winning actor Reidar Sørensen, who had also appeared in *Ti kniver i hjertet*.

The series began broadcasting on Norwegian TV in January 1997, and the titles of the songs on the accompanying soundtrack were listed as 'rooms'. The project reunited Magne and Bjerkestrand with guitarist Eivind Aarset and cellist Bjørg Lewis (née Værnes), who had also played on Morten's *Poetenes Evangelium* and *Wild Seed* albums. Other guest musicians included future a-ha drummer Per Lindvall (who had also worked with Morten) and D'Sound bassist Jonny Sjo.

According to the series' director, Karin Julsrud, the resulting soundtrack ticked all the boxes for her. She told *Dagbladet* in October 1996: 'We wanted music that reflected a mix of the young and modern, which the people stand for, and the old and dilapidated, which the hotel represents. We've got that.' Magne also stressed that there was a concerted effort to produce a stand-alone body of work, rather than just a soundtrack.

Preceded by an edited version of 'In the Hands of Fools', which was issued as a promotional single in December 1996, the *Hotel Oslo* soundtrack was released the following month, via Ivar Dyrhaug's Norsk Plateproduksjon label, which had previously issued both *Vogts Villa* (Morten Harket) and *Songs from the Pocket* (Jørun Bøgeberg), as well as albums by Åge Aleksandersen, Ole Edvard Antonsen, Dance with a Stranger, Bjørn Eidsvåg, Jonas Fjeld and many others.

DREAM POP

The fact that the *Hotel Oslo* series was a Nordic co-production was emphasised by the appearance of Swedish singer Freddie Wadling on the accompanying soundtrack. His distinctive vocals – which have often been compared to artists such as Tom Waits – appear on several of the accompanying tracks and were, arguably, a perfect fit for Timbersound's abstract soundscapes.

A relative veteran of the Swedish music scene, Wadling had been a member of several bands, including post-punk acts such as Liket Lever [the Corpse Lives], Cortex and the Leather Nun. By the time of his work on *Hotel Oslo*, he'd released four albums as part of the duo Blue for Two and had guested on albums by Fläskkvartetten [Flesh Quartet], including the Grammis award-winning *Flow*. (The Grammis was the Swedish equivalent of a Grammy award.)

There was also a significant guest turn from Anneli Drecker, who would later work with a-ha during phase two of their career. The Tromsø-born singer had come to prominence as an actress in the 1983 film *Søsken på Guds jord* [Siblings on God's Earth], which featured a soundtrack by Popol Ace's Pete Knutsen. She would later star in 1992's *Svarte Pantere* [Black Panthers], but it was the 4AD-influenced dream pop act Bel Canto, formed in 1985, which would ultimately gain her the most success, both critically and commercially. Indeed, both the *Shimmering Warm & Bright* and *Magic Box* albums would earn the band Spellemann awards.

Bel Canto's stellar reputation also meant they were able to attract renowned musicians such as Jaki Liebezeit (Can) and Jah Wobble (PiL) to guest on their albums, while Drecker herself was in demand as a vocalist for a plethora of other acts. The *Song of Joy* album by Tsunematsu Matsui, the former bassist with Japanese rock band Boøwy, features her distinctive vocals, which were pitched somewhere between the ethereal pop of the Cocteau Twins and the Gothic-rock of Siouxsie and the Banshees. (Curiously, the single 'In the Maze' sounds like Siouxsie Sioux fronting Ultravox!) Drecker's vocals could also be found on the album *The North Pole by Submarine* by Geir Jenssen, who was then recording music under the Bleep moniker. (A former member of Bel Canto, Jenssen would later record under the name of Biosphere.)

ANNELI DRECKER

Bel Canto formed in the same year that 'Take On Me' broke worldwide. Were you a fan of a-ha's music from the start?

I was, of course, a fan of a-ha back in the earlier days. I remember having their music on my Walkman the summer the three of us in Bel Canto took a train through Europe and visited record companies with our demo, shopping for a record deal. A-ha was in many ways our mental Columbus: If they could conquer, well, then so could Bel Canto! I also saw them play live in my hometown, Tromsø, back in 1987. My friends and I skipped school to get first in line. We found places all the way up front, but then the girls in the crowd started screaming hysterically when the band started playing, and I got frustrated and embarrassed on behalf of them and basically any other girl my age, since I could barely hear the music. I remember escaping from the screams and sitting down all by myself in the very back of the big hall, to enjoy the concert undisturbed. I really wanted to meet the guys after the concert, since my band had just recorded our first album in Brussels. So, I felt more like a colleague, rather than a fan. But of course, that did not happen. I did not know how to get in contact with them at that time.

Would you say they've been an influence on your own music?
As a singer and composer, I must say that, indeed, a-ha's songs have been a great influence. I cannot say otherwise because their music has been a part of my life for so long.

There's a lovely version of you singing 'And You Tell Me', accompanied by piano and cello. Was this a particular favourite of yours?
Thank you very much, I appreciate that. I always hoped they would do 'And You Tell Me' live but it never happened, so I thought, 'Well, then I will make my own version'. That being said, the radio recording that is available is not really that good. I was very nervous when it was broadcasted live.

Are there any other songs that stand out for you?
Well, 'And You Tell Me', 'Soft Rains of April', 'Here I Stand and Face the Rain' and 'The Blue Sky' were my favourites from their first two albums. These songs had such an impact on me because they were, well, odd and quirky but, at the same time, simple in their complexity. There are so many – it's like asking which flower I like the most! Also, some of the songs sound better live than on the album – because the production is updated – so it's hard to say. It's the combination of many songs; they enhance each other's beauty. Like an exotic bouquet with flowers.

How did you end up working on 'We'll Never Speak Again'? And what can you remember about the session?
A common friend, Norwegian jazz musician Nils Petter Molvær, put me and Magne in touch. I truly loved that track and I was excited, of course, to finally meet and work with one of my musical heroes. At that time I was an established artist myself so it was, in a way, natural since the popular music scene in Norway is not that big. Since this first meeting was work-related, and in the studio, which is one of my favourite places on earth, I soon forgot who I was dealing with. And I cannot recall being nervous at all

since Magne is very relaxed and unpretentious. I remember laughing a lot. I really love Wadling's vocals on this song, so it was inspiring and fulfilling to sing on the choruses.

CITY VIEWS

It's arguable that 'We'll Never Speak Again' – which was also released as a promotional single in Norway – was the most immediate and accessible track on the album, and a version of the track was later taped during sessions for a-ha's *Minor Earth Major Sky* album. (It was eventually adapted by Morten for his *Letter from Egypt* album.) The lyrics also seemed to capture the essence of the series ('All of us have stories / All more or less the same / Though some of us have spoken / We'll never speak again'), while Drecker's silky vocals provided a welcome contrast to Wadling's gravelly tones.

While there was the occasional burst of melody, which was in keeping with Magne's pop lineage, this was a largely downbeat work which would point less towards a-ha's future and more towards the avant-garde indie rock of Radiohead. But while tracks such as 'Witchi Tai To/The Sharp Canopies of Your Broken Heart' ensured a challenging listen, the album was not without its highlights. Aside from 'We'll Never Speak Again', the ephemeral 'City View', with its spectral electronics and frenetic percussion, was one of the standout instrumentals, while 'I Remember You', which recalled *Zooropa*-era U2, was one of the more memorable vocal tracks. There was a Bridges connection, too, in the form of 'A Room for Thought', whose melody recalled 'Scared, Bewildered, Wild'.

However, while the album may have left some a-ha fans confused, it was certainly a hit with critics: 'If the TV series has been described as unusually good, the music that accompanies the production is even better!' wrote *Pan Music Guide*'s Paul Nordal in his 5/6 review. 'The music is alluring and convincing through and through, with a good sound and lively arrangements.'

The soundtrack was also nominated for a 1997 Spellemann award, but went one better when it earned its makers a prestigious Edvardprisen [Edvard Award] in its inaugural year (1998).

FURUHOLMEN / BJERKESTRAND / WADLING – HERMETIC (1999 Album)
Produced by Magne Furuholmen and Kjetil Bjerkestrand
Chart position: N/A

By the turn of the year 1998, a-ha were still officially on hiatus. However, in an interview the previous year, Magne had hinted that a reunion was on the cards. This eventually came to fruition in December 1998 but, in the interim, it was business as usual for Magne. There were further art exhibitions but also more soundtrack work, which would include the delivery of his most sonically challenging album to date.

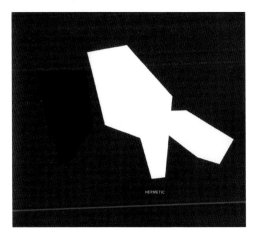

In addition to his work on *Hermetic*, Kjetil Bjerkestrand also composed most of the music for the popular animated film *Solan, Ludvig og Gurin med reverompa*, which was based on Kjell Aukrust's 1991 book, *Gurin med reverompa* [Gurin with the Foxtail]. The accompanying soundtrack, which featured Per and Sven Lindvall – a-ha's future rhythm section – also included a songwriting contribution from Magne on one of the album's bonus tracks, 'Ein strek – nokon fargar' [A Line – Some Colours]. The song was co-written with Bjerkestrand, while the lyrics were penned by Bjørn Eidsvåg and sung by Herborg Kråkevik. An English version of the track, featuring completely different lyrics, was later recorded by Jan Werner Danielsen.

BLOODY ANGELS

Timbersound's third album saw them teaming up once more with Freddie Wadling – with equal billing accorded to the Swedish singer this time around – and the trio's left-field leanings would be taken to new extremes for the soundtrack to Karin Julsrud's debut feature film, *1732 Høtten*. The film, which was titled *Bloody Angels* outside of Norway, starred Reidar Sørensen as a detective who is tasked with investigating the rape and murder of a 13-year-old girl in the remote village of Høtten.

The film attracted some comparisons with both *Twin Peaks* and *Fargo*, but the reviews were mixed. 'As a thriller, it fails to enthral,' stated the BBC's Sandi Chaitram, while *The Guardian* was equally unimpressed: 'Nothing about the movie is particularly novel,' wrote Peter Bradshaw, 'and there's an overwrought finale to distract us from the loose ends.' But in the US, the *Austin Chronicle* was slightly more generous: 'It's not the most gripping police procedural I've ever seen, but *Bloody Angels* still manages to unnerve,' wrote Marc Savlov. 'Like the frozen northern forests it's set in, the film has a stark, chilling beauty.' *Variety* magazine's David Stratton was even more impressed, writing: 'A crisply made crime thriller that makes excellent use of wintry locations in rural Norway. *Bloody Angels* is filled with sardonic humour and sharp observation.'

As for the soundtrack, it was a largely instrumental work. The 12 tracks – which were simply listed as 'Solve et coagula' (01–12) – saw the trio dabbling with electronics, abstract sounds and tangential vocal experiments (Wadling's unpredictable vocals were notably utilised on two idiosyncratic versions of 'When the Saints Go Marching In', a track that features prominently during the horror-tinged thriller). However, while it was a largely unsettling and discordant collection, it wasn't wholly devoid of melody. 'Solve et coagula 04' was conventionally structured and featured a satisfying mix of acoustic guitar and theremin sounds, plus industrial drum loops that recalled *Sacrifice*-era Gary Numan. Unsurprisingly, the track was selected for promotional single release (though renamed as 'Wash Her Off Your Hands'). Elsewhere, the piano-based 'Solve et coagula 10' boasted a memorable melody, which was reprised during 'Solve et coagula 12', which played during the film's end credits.

The album was picked up for release by Rune Grammofon, which was founded by Fra Lippo Lippi's former bassist, Rune Kristoffersen, in 1997. Described as 'a record label dedicated to releasing work by the most adventurous and creative Norwegian artists and composers', the boutique outlet has released albums by an array of acts over the years, including Biosphere, Chocolate Overdose, Anneli Drecker, Arne Nordheim, Motorpsycho and, of course, Fra Lippo Lippi.

Like all the releases on Rune Grammofon, it featured artwork by the musician and graphic designer Kim Hiorthøy. However, a special edition of the album, which boasted an exclusive handmade lead cover design by Magne, was issued prior to its main commercial release. The reviews were mixed. 'Large parts of *Hermetic* can best be described as diffuse sound collages', wrote *Dagbladet*'s Beate Nossum. 'The exception is the Flesh Quartet vocalist Freddie Wadling's exquisite versions of "When the Saints Go Marching In" and the radio single, "Wash Her Off Your Hands", the only commercially-based song.' Elsewhere, *Motion*'s reviewer wrote: 'Not one of the more cohesive records in recent memory, though there's quite a bit of intriguing weirdness here, and that alone is enough to suck you into the morass.'

PART FIVE
SUMMER MOVED ON
1998–2007

CHAPTER SEVENTEEN
MINOR EARTH | MAJOR SKY

Having had the sort of success we've had, we don't really have anything to prove in the commercial sense. Rather, this is about us finally proving what we're capable of as artists and musicians. And the astonishing thing is that, in every way you could think of, we're simply better than ever.
Morten Harket, 2000

Released: April 2000
Chart position: 27 (UK), 1 (Norway), 1 (Germany)

By the summer of 1998 it had been just over four years since a-ha had honoured their final touring commitment at the White Nights Festival in Saint Petersburg. All three members of the band had subsequently immersed themselves in various musical, artistic and environmental projects and, while an a-ha reunion had been hinted at in various interviews during their hiatus, work continued apace on their individual endeavours.

In addition to his ongoing visual art projects, Magne had started work on the soundtrack for the *1732 Høtten* movie with Kjetil Bjerkestrand, while Pål's well-established new band, Savoy, had committed to recording their third album. While Morten's musical activities in 1998 had been restricted to the odd guest appearance, there were still plans in place to record the follow-up to the *Vogts Villa* album. These plans were put on ice when a-ha were invited to perform at the Nobel Peace Prize Concert at the Oslo Spektrum in December 1998. 'At that point, we didn't know whether that would be a farewell thing for us or the start of something new,' Morten told TV presenter Gloria Hunniford in 2000, 'but we knew that if we were going to do anything together again, this was really the time.'

The Nobel Peace Prize Concert is an annual event which takes place a day after the awards ceremony on 10 December (the anniversary of the death of the revered Swedish inventor Alfred Nobel). By 1998, the concert was in its fifth year. Wide-ranging musical acts from all over the world, including Mariah Carey, Ofra Haza, Youssou N'Dour, Nusrat Fateh Ali Khan, Sinéad O'Connor and Joan Osborne, had all previously performed at the event, as too had Norwegian acts such as Ole Edvard Antonsen, Nils Petter Molvær and Anne Grete Preus. Morten himself had appeared at one of the prestigious concerts in 1996, performing a beautiful string-accompanied version of 'East Timor'.

Having accepted the invitation, Magne, Morten and Pål now had to decide which two songs to perform on the night. In the end, they opted for both a celebration of their past in 'The Sun Always Shines on TV' and a brand new song. Morten suggested 'Back to the Senses', an English-language version of 'Tilbake til livet', while Pål brought in the stunning 'Summer Moved On', which reportedly evoked an enthusiastic response from Magne. (Morten later performed 'Back to the Senses' during a show in Stavanger in 2008.)

Other established acts, including Phil Collins, the Cranberries, Alanis Morissette and Shania Twain, performed on the actual night of the concert. A-ha's new-look line-up included Kjetil Bjerkestrand and the Lindvall brothers, Per and Sven, on drums and bass, respectively. 'It was Kjetil Bjerkestrand that recommended me and Per for the guys,' said Sven. 'I had only heard the hits on the radio, so I came in with fresh ears.'

Although footage of a-ha's performance was controversially omitted from TV screens in some territories, the positive reaction across the board was difficult to ignore. 'We were, in reality, way too busy with our own projects,' Morten told *VG* in 2007. 'There was nothing to indicate that we would reform. We were tricked back together in a peculiar way. The response from the audience was totally unexpected – it had such a warmth, a feeling of them reaching out to us, like an attempt to make contact.'

YOU WANTED MORE

Prior to the concert, the band announced plans – at a press conference in Oslo on 4 December – for both a new studio album and a world tour. 'This new album could be the biggest thing a-ha has ever done,' Magne told *VG*. However, the road to its actual release would be considerably bumpy. Further down the track there would be interference from the band's new record label, but getting the project off the ground presented its own problems. Morten had financial conditions that needed to be met before he would sing a single note. This, ostensibly, revolved around the division of the band's income, which he insisted should be more commensurate to his considerably higher profile. As the band's frontman and main focal point, he had arguably undertaken significantly more media work during the band's initial 10-year run, and he felt that an adjustment needed to be made to his percentage of earnings, particularly in light of the fact that Magne's and Pål's publishing income was much higher than his. 'I'm unquestionably the one who has earned the least, because of the way things have been set up,' he said. 'I wasn't interested in going back into it and earning money for the other two by selling my body, to put it that way . . . I had very clear criteria for going along a second time around and, to be honest, I had very little faith that my conditions for that would be met. But they were, in fact. Now we are – for the first time – starting to approach a division of income in which the contribution of each of us is considered equally valuable.'[1]

In addition to the financial tweaks, there would also be significant changes to the writing credits. On *Memorial Beach*, Pål had written the bulk of the songs, but subsequent albums would prove to be more democratic affairs, with both Magne and Morten making significant songwriting contributions. With the decline of vinyl and the popularity of the considerably more capacious CD format, the band could also now include more songs on their albums, without having to worry about space constraints. However, this was something that would raise quality control concerns further down the line.

DEMOS

The initial demos for *Minor Earth Major Sky* were completed by Magne and Pål in the new year of 1999. Pål was in a rich vein of songwriting form during this period and had written a vast number of songs, for both a-ha and Savoy. 'We had just finished Savoy's third album and I was enjoying making music,' he said. 'That attitude was brought into the making of the first a-ha album in seven years.'[2]

Morten was evidently very happy with the results from these New York sessions, too: 'It was unthinkable for me to see a-ha back together,' he said, 'but when I heard the demos, that changed it for me, because it felt real, genuine. I hadn't liked what we were; I didn't feel like I fitted in; I felt like I was a hindrance to a-ha during *Memorial Beach*.'[3]

The resulting album featured several guest musicians, including the Lindvall brothers, Lauren Savoy and Frode Unneland from Savoy, plus Jørun Bøgeberg and Per Hillestad, who had both been a vital cog in the machine during the band's

Americana phase. 'Pål sometimes called me up to get some bass playing down in his studio just up the road in Oslo,' said Jørun. 'He always worked on songs, so I wouldn't know whether a particular song was intended for Savoy, a-ha, a demo or whatever. He probably didn't know himself! There was no session with more musicians around – just me and Pål, and maybe a technician every now and then.' I asked Jørun if he was disappointed not to be more involved. 'No, not really,' he replied. 'Four years had gone by and I had noticed that they had been collaborating with other musicians in other projects – all three of them – so I did not take it for granted that they would gather the "old" band.'

CHANGING LANES

Continuing his association with a-ha was Kjetil Bjerkestrand, who had also played at the Nobel Peace Prize Concert. In addition to co-producing the album, he also worked on the string arrangements with Magne and Pål. (Bjerkestrand had previously worked with Pål on the string arrangement for the title track of Savoy's *Lackluster Me* album.)

Although Magne and Morten made significant songwriting contributions, most of the songs on the new album were credited to Pål. But, true to form, it wasn't an all-new collection. For example, 'Velvet' had previously been recorded by Savoy, while Magne said that 'Little Black Heart' had been around a while.

The second phase of a-ha's career was also heralded by a change of management, with Brian Lane (born Harvey Freed) replacing a disappointed Terry Slater. Lane was a former accountant who had entered the music industry in the mid-60s. 'London was buzzing, the Beatles had arrived, the world looked bright,' he said. 'I wanted to go into the music industry, but being totally unmusical, I did the next best thing: research and development into what made the industry tick. It was all about the charts and originality. I created my own template of how I would pick artists I wished to manage.'[4]

He initially started out as a record promoter, plugging key hits such as 'The House of the Rising Sun' (the Animals) and 'Arnold Layne' (Pink Floyd), before entering artist management later in the decade. In 1970, he began a decade-long association with prog rockers Yes, before working with a number of different acts, including Asia, former Marillion frontman Fish, and Vangelis. (According to Bill Bruford, the original drummer with Yes, Lane had also plugged 'Hey Joe', the Jimi Hendrix record that had had such a profound impact on a young Morten Harket.)

By the time Lane had started working with a-ha, he'd already managed Norwegian acts such as the Tuesdays and Espen Lind (whose future No. 1 hit 'Scared of Heights' would later be covered by Morten). According to Lane, he'd first met the band during one of the Spellemann award ceremonies. 'I spoke to them and was impressed at how intelligent and well they appeared. They told me they had never actually broken up; they'd just stopped working for several years.'[5]

GOOD DEAL

With their new manager in place, the band signed a contract with WEA Germany in the summer of 1999, and Lane reportedly secured an advance of almost 20 million Norwegian kroner. 'In reality, such advance payments do not mean so much,' Pål later told *Dagbladet*. 'We must sell records, that's what matters. The agreement we have received is very good, because it shows that Warners takes us seriously. The contract commits the company to work hard.'

However, while the new label had offered a decent financial package, the actual album that received its world premiere in Paris in March 2000 was somewhat different from the one the band had originally conceived. 'We laid down the whole album before we went to a record company,' recalled Pål. 'We had all the songs ready . . . Magne came to New York, and we laid down the songs in ten days. We did one song each day. Finished eighty per cent of each song. That became the album, and then the Germans remixed it, making it a little more [dancey] or whatever.'[6]

The Germans in question were Andreas Herbig and Roland Spremberg, who were both highly experienced within their respective fields. Andreas Herbig was a prolific writer, musician, producer and remixer, whose association with Hamburg's renowned Boogie Park Studio had earned him the moniker of Boogieman. By the end of the 90s he had worked on numerous recordings from the world of dance, R&B and hip-hop, and credits included tracks by the likes of Bootsy Collins, Brandy, Busta Rhymes and LL Cool J, while German hit singles included Del Tha Funkee Homosapien's 'Mistadobalina' (No. 9, 1992) and Lucilectric's 'Mädchen' [Girl] (No. 2, 1994).

Roland Spremberg, meanwhile, had studied piano and double bass at Detmold's prestigious music academy before plying his trade in bands such as the Land and the internationally renowned World Music fusionists, Dissidenten [Dissidents]. By the end of the 90s, he had begun working with other acts, including German actress Ina Paule Klink.

Although the post-production work on songs like 'I Won't Forget Her' was, arguably, over the top, the German duo's contemporary flavours certainly freshened up the band's sound for the new millennium, and the album's mixture of electronics and guitars ensured that a-ha's wide-ranging fan base was well catered for.

BLAME IT ON THE BOOGIE

The cover of the new album – which included a striking shot of a plane cockpit in an airplane graveyard – also featured a new band logo, which had been designed by Henrik Haugan, who had provided the illustration for the 'Love Is Reason' single in 1985. With the band clearly prioritising product over image, the release of *Minor Earth Major Sky* also marked the first occasion that a photo of the band hadn't appeared on the front cover of an album. According to Magne, this was a conscious decision on the part of the band.

The band's comeback single, 'Summer Moved On', was a hit all over Europe, while the album reviews were generally positive in the UK. 'Unexpectedly, Norway's finest are back,' wrote *The Independent*'s Glyn Brown. '. . . There are swooping great numbers of filmic intensity, troubling confidences and sombre, Beatles-esque observations on loneliness and quiet desperation.' Elsewhere, the NME's reviewer wrote: 'Still looking Faustian fresh-faced seven years after "retiring", they're doing a pretty good job of growing old gracefully. Admittedly they were never exactly wild, but this comeback record is still older, wiser but crucially just as melodic.'

In Norway, *VG*'s Espen A. Hansen described the songs as 'dangerously catchy and uplifting', but *Dagbladet*'s Håkon Moslet wasn't so keen, and was highly critical of Boogieman's involvement in the album: 'The man who was supposed to take a-ha into a new era has given the band a soundscape that is so backwards and outdated, that our boys might as well forget the dream of a new career peak on old prestigious hunting grounds such as the United States and England right away.'

Given that the album was being released by a German label, it was perhaps unsurprising that a-ha were pushed into doing a lot of promotional work in Germany, including appearances on popular shows such as *Wetten, Dass..?* The workload was so intense that Pål had to persuade Lauren to fly out with their young son, who was barely six months old at the time. 'I said they had to come out now, otherwise Augie would not see his father much during his upbringing,' he told *Dagbladet*. 'The last time I came home, he didn't know who I was.' However, the band were rewarded for their efforts with a first-ever chart-topping album in Germany. In Norway, too, the album reached the summit of the *VG-lista*, staying there for five weeks. But UK record buyers weren't so receptive, and the band's big comeback album had slumped to No. 90 by its third week of release, prompting *VG* to brand *Minor Earth Major Sky* as 'a flop in England'. As it would transpire, the band were still a long way off from re-establishing themselves in one of Europe's most important marketplaces.

In 2019, a double vinyl version of the album was released, as well as a two-disc CD which included demos, alternative versions, remixes and live tracks.

MINOR EARTH MAJOR SKY
Written by Magne Furuholmen and Pål Waaktaar-Savoy
Produced by Boogieman and Roland Spremberg
Co-produced by a-ha and Kjetil Bjerkestrand
Chart position: 73 (Germany)

According to some reports, songs such as 'Minor Earth Major Sky' were in the frame for the aborted follow-up to *Memorial Beach*, which Pål had worked on, largely independently, in 1994. However, Magne said it was a song he showed to Pål around the time of their reunion in 1998. At this stage, the track didn't have a chorus, but it was eventually completed during the New York demo sessions in 1999. 'I had the title and idea of what the verse could be and Pål really liked it,' he recalled. 'He came in and added the breakdown sections. We were really collaborating intimately, throwing balls back and forth. We hadn't really seen each other for a long time and it was the starting point for the album.'[7]

The original a-ha/Kjetil Bjerkestrand production confirms that the song employed a far greater use of electronics during its chrysalis, while the guitar work was also far more prominent. (It was this arrangement of the song that was utilised during the band's *Electric Summer* tour in 2018.) Although the icy synth motif wasn't retained, the album version, featuring Frode Unneland on drumming duties, did benefit from a more groove-based approach, while the scratchy percussive effects – which, arguably, were more in keeping with Boogieman's hip-hop roots – added a contemporary element.

While 'Summer Moved On' had affirmed Pål's hit-making credentials, the album's opening track re-established Magne and Pål as a potent songwriting force, and it was justly selected for single release in July 2000. It was edited for radio purposes, while an array of different mixes were created. Among the most accessible versions were the rock-based 'Black Dog Mix', which contrasted with the considerably more laid-back 'Millenia Nova Remix'.

In terms of the lyrics, Magne later confirmed it was 'a play on the Scandinavian way of life, of everything being in a minor key', but the eye-catching video for the single – which depicted Magne, Morten and Pål as Apollo astronauts – repainted the song as an existential space rock epic. The promo, which utilised dialogue from the Apollo 11 mission in the intro, was directed by Philipp Stölzl, who had previously worked with acts such as Faith No More, Garbage and Rammstein. The reason the spacesuits looked so authentic was that they had previously been used in Ron Howard's 1995 blockbuster *Apollo 13*. 'The one I had was much too small,' said Pål, 'so I had to pad my shoulders with Augie's diapers because the helmet was cutting into my shoulders! I'm sure it was Kevin Bacon's costume.'[8]

LITTLE BLACK HEART
Written by Magne Furuholmen and Pål Waaktaar-Savoy
Produced by Boogieman and Roland Spremberg
Co-produced by a-ha and Kjetil Bjerkestrand

'Little Black Heart' had reportedly been demoed during a time when the band were on the verge of splintering, and the lyrics to the song seem to offer an insight into the lyricist's mindset during this period. But while the narrator of the song is seemingly going through a period of great sadness ('Raindrops on my window / I can't tell them apart') and self-doubt ('You say it's getting better / You say it's alright / But I never felt darkness / Like I feel it tonight'), an optimistic beacon, in the shape of a middle eight, offers a welcome counterpoint to the melancholy ('One day we will shine / Like the moon in the morning / Like the sun when it's dawning').

Although the final version of the track was slightly let down by some heavy-handed percussion and a stuttering stop-start production – signalled by the William Orbit-esque echo drum effects that had characterised Madonna's *Ray of Light*-era recordings – this was, largely, a sonically satisfying composite of electronics, strings and gently picked acoustic guitar. (An alternative mix of the track reveals a brief a capella moment following the instrumental midsection, as well as a different ending that reprises the 'You say it's getting better / You say it's alright' couplet.)

The song was also performed during the *Minor Earth Major Sky* tour (less the modish adornments), while the title itself was also reprised in 'Spare Me Your Passion', one of the poems from Magne's *Payne's Gray* project in 2004 ('The moment before you stop yourself / The things that you hide / The things that you fear / That self-serving part of your little black heart').

VELVET

Written by Lauren Savoy and Pål Waaktaar-Savoy
Produced by Boogieman and Roland Spremberg
Co-produced by a-ha and Kjetil Bjerkestrand
Chart position: 48 (Germany)

For the second time in their career, a-ha decided to record a track that had previously been recorded by another group. However, this was no ordinary cover version: The song had in fact been written by Pål and Lauren Savoy and subsequently released as Savoy's debut single in 1996. It had topped the charts in Norway but hadn't made an impact internationally, so the chance to introduce the song – which Magne described as 'a gem' – to a wider audience seemed too good to pass up. The original take, featuring Simone Larsen's distinctive backing vocals, was used as a template for the new recording, but Frode Unneland's place on the drum stool was this time taken by Per Lindvall. Additionally, two musicians who were well known to producer Roland Spremberg from his days in the Land – namely Stephan Gade and Jörn Heilbut – were also brought in to play bass and additional guitar, respectively. While the arrangements were similar, the versions were markedly different in tone. The a-ha version of the song, which Pål describes as 'wimpy', certainly lacks the indie rock grit of its Savoy counterpart, but its more romantic vibe made it a hit with fans.

For the single release – which featured a striking monochromatic cover design by Magne – the track was edited so Larsen's breathy vocals came in slightly earlier during the acoustic introduction. Like the preceding single, 'Minor Earth Major Sky', several mixes were created, with De-Phazz's trip-hop treatment easily the most creative.

'Velvet' did not set the charts alight in any country, but its accompanying video certainly made an impression. The promo, helmed by Harald Zwart – who'd previously directed the Swedish action film *Hamilton*, starring *Star Wars* actor Mark Hamill – depicted the band lying lifeless in a morgue. Apparently, each member of the band had chosen the manner of their fictitious murders prior to filming. In the clip, Morten is found electrocuted in a bathtub, Pål is found sitting upright in a chair with a gunshot in the head, while Magne's lifeless body is discovered humorously clutching a guitar in a chest freezer. The ensuing embalming scenes, featuring voluptuous nurses in a series of sexual poses, resulted in accusations from the Norwegian media that the band were flirting with necrophilia, but Magne told NRK's daily news show, *Dagsrevyen* [the Daily Review], that the video – which actually won a Spellemann award the following year – was meant to be both tongue-in-cheek and experimental.

Years later, Morten defended the video, which was censored in places by NRK: 'I don't find it that disturbing. It's meant to be a murder scene. The director wanted a little juice so he instructed that old lady to kiss me. And she went for it. I was lying there with my eyes closed and she just stuck her tongue down my throat.'[9]

Although Pål felt the video offered an edge that was missing from the actual recording, he did concede that the director had probably gone too far: 'We were really satisfied, both when the idea was presented to us and with the result . . . But Zwart did manage to make the whole thing look rather unsettling. And, in retrospect, I see that it's not very kid-friendly.'[10]

While the controversial single did little chart-wise, the song did gain valuable exposure via the soundtrack of the Harald Zwart-directed comedy *One Night at McCool's*, which starred Liv Tyler and Matt Dillon. (Both Magne and Morten attended the film's premiere in London in April 2001.) The song also formed part of the band's live sets during this period, with Anneli Drecker singing Simone Larsen's parts. Further down the live track, the band performed the song acoustically (with Morten on guitar) during the *Foot of the Mountain* tour, while a rare lead vocal from Pål greeted concert-goers during the *Cast in Steel* tour.

SUMMER MOVED ON

Written by Pål Waaktaar-Savoy
Produced by Boogieman and Roland Spremberg
Co-produced by a-ha and Kjetil Bjerkestrand
Chart position: 33 (UK), 1 (Norway), 8 (Germany)

The original inspiration behind a-ha's big comeback song was the band itself, and lyrics such as 'Friendships move on / Until the day / You can't get along' certainly offered a glimpse into the members' strained relationships during the mid-90s. 'I wanted to say something about the band in the lyrics, about where we were at,' said Pål. '. . . In songs like that, half of the lyrics will be about Morten and Magne, and I know that no one other than them understands what I mean.'[11]

The demo features only a bare lyrical outline of the song with its writer humming the melody, but the recording offers a fascinating insight into its creation, and even at this embryonic stage, both the musical and vocal arrangement were in place. By the time of the Nobel Peace Prize Concert in

December 1998, the lyrics had been completed and the song's final arrangement more or less nailed, right down to the dramatic orchestral sweeps. By the time of its official release in March 2000, however, there had been some tweaks during production, with the most noticeable of these being the addition of a flamenco-style guitar solo and some more dramatic strings, plus some drifting keyboard flourishes that recalled Seal's classic 1990 hit 'Crazy'.

In terms of the vocals, Morten was encouraged by Pål to really hit the high notes, and the singer duly obliged with some incredible falsetto parts and a then-record-breaking 20-second sustained note during the tail end of the song, something that would wow live audiences over the ensuing years.

There was, however, a somewhat drab and unimaginative sleeve for the single, featuring a moody out-of-focus shot of the band, but it was a big hit all over Europe. According to the industry magazine *Music & Media*, it was at one point the fifth most-played single in that continent.

The accompanying video, filmed in Southern Spain, was directed by Swedish director Adam Berg, who had previously helmed clips for compatriots such as the Cardigans, Grass Show and Kent. (Berg's older brother was Joakim, the lead singer of Kent, whose songwriting credits would later be found on Morten's 2012 solo album, *Out of My Hands*.)

In March 2011, a live version of 'Summer Moved On' was issued as a single in Germany, prior to the release of the *Ending on a High Note: The Final Concert* album.

THE SUN NEVER SHONE THAT DAY
Written by Lauren Savoy and Pål Waaktaar-Savoy
Produced by Boogieman and Roland Spremberg
Co-produced by a-ha and Kjetil Bjerkestrand

Pål and Lauren's prolificacy as songwriters in the late 90s meant that songs which had originally been earmarked for Savoy often overspilled into the work of a-ha.

'The Sun Never Shone That Day' was one such track. Other material that was left over from this fruitful period eventually made it onto Savoy's *Reasons to Stay Indoors* album, but this catchy track – which shared the same rhythmic drive as Garbage's breakthrough hit, 'Stupid Girl' – was deservedly set aside for *Minor Earth Major Sky*.

One thing that lets it down slightly is the title's repetition, which is accentuated in an earlier version of the song by its use of alternating vocal parts. The album version would certainly have benefitted from a tighter arrangement, and this was eventually put into effect when two unique edits were created for the Norwegian and German markets. Unfortunately, the single never made it past the promotional stage, and its commercial availability was restricted to the release of the Minor Earth Major Box set in February 2001, which housed the album's four singles.

TO LET YOU WIN
Written by Morten Harket and Håvard Rem
Produced by Boogieman and Roland Spremberg
Co-produced by a-ha and Kjetil Bjerkestrand

This beautiful, chiming ballad marked Morten's creative return to the band, having seemingly signed off on 1988's *Stay on These Roads* album. Having felt sidelined during the band's Americana phase, Morten grew increasingly confident as both a songwriter and guitarist in the mid-90s, and while he was reliant on creative foils such as Håvard Rem and Ole Sverre Olsen to supply lyrics, he did bring some worthy material to the table.

This particular song had originally been debuted during the NRK1 programme, *Tekst/Melodi: Morten Harket*, in November 1997. Morten told the show's presenter, Karoline Krüger, that it had been penned during a trip to Borneo, while the subsequent demo had been put together with Kjetil Bjerkestrand's assistance. (Morten also performed the song, acoustically, during an appearance on the TV show *God kveld Norge* [Good Evening, Norway], in September 1999.)

The final version, with all its modern-day accoutrements, features a touch of Bristolian trip-hop in its percussive framework, but an earlier mix also reveals an effective counter vocal in the chorus that was sadly removed.

In terms of the lyrics, 'To Let You Win' was something of a soul-baring exercise, with the seemingly resigned narrator ruminating on the end of a relationship ('You know I always had the strength to fight / But I got tired of the wars at night / Thinking they would end if I gave in').

THE COMPANY MAN
Written by Magne Furuholmen and Pål Waaktaar-Savoy
Produced by Boogieman and Roland Spremberg
Co-produced by a-ha and Kjetil Bjerkestrand

Throughout the history of pop music, a vast number of songs have been inspired by the music business itself, ranging from the subtle to the somewhat more polemic. Two of the most famous examples are Pink Floyd's 'Have a Cigar' (1975), which cynically pointed fingers at the industry's fat-cat moguls ('I've always had a deep respect and I mean that most sincere / The band is just fantastic, that is really what I think / Oh, by the way, which one's Pink?') and the Smiths' often-quoted 'Paint a Vulgar Picture' (1987), which provided some astute commentary on marketing (Reissue! Repackage! Repackage! / Re-evaluate the songs! / Double-pack with a photograph / Extra track [and a tacky badge]') and artist exploitation ('At the record company meeting / On their hands – a dead star / And ooh, the plans they weave / And ooh, the sickening greed').

Elsewhere, the Sex Pistols famously took a swipe at their former record label, EMI, who had released the band from their contract after just one single ('And blind acceptance is a sign / Of stupid fools who stand in line / Like EMI'), while fellow punk rockers the Clash questioned the merits of their contract on their 1977 hit 'Complete Control' ('They said we'd be artistically free / When we signed that bit of paper / They meant, let's make a lots-a-money').

Magne's general disillusionment with the music industry had already been documented on 1993's 'Lamb to the Slaughter' of course, but 'The Company Man' delved deeper, recounting the signing of the band's first Warner Brothers contract ('Andy was the company man / Responsible for signing the band / Songs came out of our mouths / And into his hands') and its financial implications ('Legal help, oh yes we had plenty / Bank accounts are easy to empty'). It also offered a somewhat cynical insight into the demands of record label executives ('Give us something easy to sing to / Give us something simple to cling to / Something we can all understand / Said the company man').

'"The Company Man" was my kind of tribute/critique of Andy Wickham, which Pål thought was quite ballsy and loved the idea of,' said Magne, who had previously revealed that his bandmates had helped him tone down the song. Certainly, this mid-paced, acoustic guitar-driven song boasts a fascinating narrative, but it's let down by a slightly pedestrian chorus. It wasn't performed during the subsequent tour.

THOUGHT THAT IT WAS YOU
Written by Morten Harket and Ole Sverre Olsen
Produced by Kjetil Bjerkestrand

Featuring one of the strongest vocals on the album, this gorgeous slice of celestial electronica saw Morten once again teaming up with Ole Sverre Olsen, who had previously worked with the singer on the *Wild Seed* and *Vogts Villa* albums, plus stand-alone singles such as 'Heaven's Not for Saints (Let It Go)' and 'Jungle of Beliefs'. The pair were close friends, sharing an apartment in Oslo while Morten had reportedly funded Olsen's ongoing treatment for drug addiction.

In the build-up to the release of a-ha's new album, Olsen had also co-written 'En fremmed jeg har møtt' [A Stranger I've Met] and 'Ruby' for Silje Nergaard's fifth album, *Hjemmefra* [From Home]. In 1996 he published a collection of poetry, titled *Til søvnens arbeidere* [To the Sleepworkers], while his debut novel, *Den døde mannen* [The Dead Man], followed two years later.

The protagonist of this fascinating song appears to be embracing God ('My soul's split in two / Lord, I thought that it was you') and awaiting some sort of spiritual transition ('You know my deepest sin / You've seen me deep within / So fill me now like wind / And let the miracle begin'). During live performances of the track – which featured Pål playing a double neck guitar – Morten included the additional lyrics, 'I hear an angel calling / I hear an angel cry'.

It's certainly a subjective work, but also consistent with Olsen's ruminations on mortality, which had certainly come to the fore in *Den døde mannen*. 'Death is one of the last taboos left in society,' Olsen told *Dagbladet*. 'However, I don't see death as just tragic. I also think it has an adventurous aspect.'

LIFE'S NOT FAIR
Written by Magne Furuholmen

I WISH I CARED
Written by Magne Furuholmen
Produced by Boogieman and Roland Spremberg
Co-produced by a-ha and Kjetil Bjerkestrand

With its towering falsetto and bright, otherworldly afterglow, 'I Wish I Cared' marked a continuation of the album's flirtation with contemporary electronics, which in this instance were bordering on the supernatural.

Originally, the song had started out as 'Life's Not Fair', and the John Lennon-influenced recording reveals a set of lyrics that were certainly befitting of its miserabilist title ('Love me sister or let me go / In between I don't wanna know / Put me out of my misery / No more us and no more we'). However, according to Magne, both Pål and Lauren felt that the lyrics were 'too pretentious', and he was eventually talked into changing them. 'When Morten sang "Life's Not Fair" in full falsetto, it was a bit much,' said Pål. 'Our suggestion, "I Wish I Cared", gave the text a totally different angle.'[12]

Although Magne later regretted the decision, an edited version of the revamped song was deemed worthy of single release. However, it was in a format that was, at that time, very new to both the band and the music industry. With the internet still in its relatively early throes and Flash technology in its infancy, Magne and Henrik Haugan created what was reportedly the first-ever Web-accessible music video, using some painstaking animation techniques. The video was created in conjunction with the Oslo-based design company Rayon, whom Haugan was working with at the time, and featured footage of Morten – which had apparently been filmed at the designer's apartment – and a series of random multilingual phrases. (Magne and Haugan later collaborated on the design of *XO Contemporary*, a limited edition cognac, for the Braastad company.)

The pairing of 'I Wish I Cared' with the similarly paced 'Thought That It Was You' was also carried forward to the subsequent tour, but with Anneli Drecker replicating the chorus parts. The song also featured in an episode ('Dichotic') of the US TV series *Smallville*, which was broadcast in November 2002.

BARELY HANGING ON
Written by Pål Waaktaar-Savoy
Produced by Boogieman and Roland Spremberg
Co-produced by a-ha and Kjetil Bjerkestrand

> *I'm an introverted person, and I write songs that lean in that direction.*
> – Pål Waaktaar-Savoy, *The Independent*, 2000

This more acoustically driven number saw its writer laying bare some of the anxieties that had been building up since the band's sudden rise to fame in the mid-80s. On 1985's 'The Blue Sky', Pål advised 'I'm too young to take on my deepest fears', but on 'Barely Hanging On' some of these anxieties are tackled head-on. The listener is informed that he's been ground down by fame ('I used to be so confident in a crowd / Now I can't say my own name aloud') and was now far more comfortable in the studio, using music as therapy ('I used to be so sensible on my own / Now I'm so sensitive it's a joke / I'm getting by on decibels like a drug').

In their preview of the album, *VG* unfairly described the chorus as being 'quite pompous'. It's arguable that the main refrain was a touch repetitive but, overall, this was a deft exercise in waltz-time introspection, and worthy of a place on the album.

A slightly different version of the song, featuring a crisper intro, was included on the 'Summer Moved On' CD single.

YOU'LL NEVER GET OVER ME
Written by Pål Waaktaar-Savoy
Produced by Boogieman and Roland Spremberg
Co-produced by a-ha and Kjetil Bjerkestrand

Described by *VG* as 'soft and melodious pop in semi-acoustic packaging', this classy break-up song clocked in at over six minutes. With its heady blend of guitars and strings, it was also a track which could so easily have slotted in on a Savoy album from this period. Adding credence to this view was the fact that the song's suitably ethereal harmonies came courtesy of Lauren Savoy, who was making her debut as a vocalist on an a-ha record.

Although motherhood had restricted her workload, Lauren remained active as a musician. While 'Summer Moved On' was hitting European record stores in March 2000, so too was *Tundra*, the debut solo album by Anneli Drecker, which included Lauren's distinctive spoken word vocal on 'Trinitron', which had been co-produced by the fledgling electronic duo Röyksopp. 'Lauren is a gifted person in so many ways,' said Anneli. 'She is, among other things, a fantastic storyteller! I wanted this track on my album but I only had the melody for the choruses and the sample ready. The rest? Well, I gave the track to Lauren and told her to just "talk". It turned out brilliantly – she should make a whole album just telling stories! I've always been a fan of Laurie Anderson and her way of communicating through her storytelling so, in a way, "Trinitron" turned out to be Anderson-like, I think.'

I WON'T FORGET HER
Written by Pål Waaktaar-Savoy
Produced by Boogieman

While songs such as 'The Sun Never Shone That Day' and 'You'll Never Get Over Me' could easily have been released by Savoy instead of a-ha, there was one particular song on the album that, arguably, didn't belong to either camp. According to Pål, 'I Won't Forget Her' had originally been envisaged as a 'blues piece'; he was justifiably disappointed when Boogieman applied something of a schlager-like gloss to the song. Had it been released as a single in Germany, it may well have topped the charts, but it just didn't sound like a-ha.

An embryonic version of the track – sans the Europop keyboards – reveals a funkier and more groove-based approach but, like the equally lengthy album version, it may well have benefitted from an earlier fade.

MARY ELLEN MAKES THE MOMENT COUNT
Written by Pål Waaktaar-Savoy
Produced by Pål Waaktaar-Savoy

Closing the album in suitably melancholic style was this plaintive, acoustic guitar-based ballad which, mercifully, wasn't tainted by German production. It's feasible that the name Mary Ellen was subliminally derived from the high-profile child abuse case of New Yorker Mary Ellen Wilson, who was subjected to child abuse by her foster parents in the 19th century, but Pål can't remember the source. 'I must have liked how all the Ms made it roll off the tongue,' he said.

What is certain is the quality of the narrative, which is evocative of the cinematic style of tracks such as 'Train of Thought' and 'Early Morning'. The lyrical vignettes are certainly enticing, drawing the listener into the protagonist's world of loneliness ('As she's walking out the laundromat / Down the street and it's the short way home / Feeling special cause she's so alone') and nostalgia ('As she's looking through old photographs / Pictures taken from an early age / Faces look back at her from the page').

On account of its 'lonely people' refrain, the song has often been compared – some might say, lazily – to the Beatles' 1966 classic 'Eleanor Rigby'.

WE WILL NEVER SPEAK AGAIN (Demo)
Words written by Magne Furuholmen
Music written by Magne Furuholmen and Kjetil Bjerkestrand

Previously known as 'We'll Never Speak Again', this interesting track had originally appeared – in not-dissimilar form – on Timbersound's soundtrack for *Hotel Oslo* in 1997, retaining both its percussive template and arrangement.

It had originally been sung as a duet between Freddie Wadling and Anneli Drecker, but later considered for inclusion on *Minor Earth Major Sky*. It's Morten covering much of the vocal ground here, although it's Magne doing his best Wadling impression in the midsection, with the couplet, 'All of us have stories / All more or less the same', recapturing the vibe of the TV series it had been written for.

Although it seemingly never made it past the demo stage, Morten was so impressed with the track that he later adapted it for his *Letter from Egypt* album in 2008.

CHAPTER EIGHTEEN

LIFELINES

There just isn't an easy way to go in this band – it's a constant struggle.
– Morten Harket, *Lifelines* tour programme, 2002

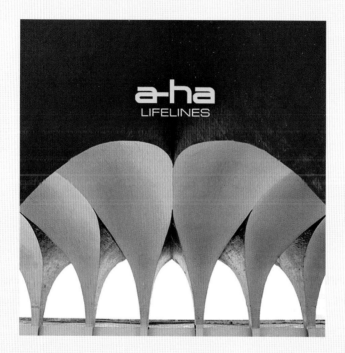

Released: April 2002
Chart position: 67 (UK), 1 (Norway), 1 (Germany)

Minor Earth Major Sky was a hit with both critics and fans, and its success was followed up with a string of live dates throughout 2000 and 2001. Featuring an all-Swedish backing band that included Christer Karlsson (keyboards), Per Lindvall (drums) and Sven Lindvall (bass), a-ha took their show to Denmark, Estonia, Germany, Japan, Norway, Russia and Switzerland.

Joining the band on the tour was backing vocalist Anneli Drecker, who recalled her recruitment: 'My band Bel Canto and I were signed to the same record label as Savoy, and we had been introduced to each other at a label party – I think it was in 99. I was a huge Savoy fan and Lauren and Pål liked my first solo album, *Tundra*, which had just been released, so it was really the music that brought us together. I started hanging out a lot around their house/studio, since my husband

[Jon Marius Aareskjold] – and very fresh boyfriend at that time – was working with Pål on the *Minor Earth Major Sky* album. I was asked to join the tour by Lauren, I think, but if you ask Magne, he will say it was his idea! Either way, I am really happy they did ask me and I believe I said yes on the spot, mainly because I felt I could bring something to the table. Of course, on the very first rehearsal and my first-ever meeting with Morten, I arrived an hour too late, because the clock was set from winter to summertime. But that's all water under the bridge now!'

While the tour was relatively low-key by their standards, the reaction was positive. 'We were met with open arms everywhere,' said Pål. 'People seemed genuinely happy to have us back.' He added: 'It was the same everywhere. We thought we'd have to start from scratch and build up. We had a totally new audience, with a big spread in demographics, from our age and older to really young.'[1] (One of the Oslo dates was captured for posterity on the *Homecoming – Live at Vallhall* VHS video and DVD, released in 2002.)

A more far-reaching tour, taking in key territories such as Brazil and the UK, would follow, but the most important thing at this stage was that a-ha still had an audience, and they were understandably keen to consolidate their recent successes with a second comeback album. However, since Magne and Pål were concurrently working on other projects, the process of recording a new album would prove to be logistically challenging.

TRENCH WARFARE

Magne later described *Lifelines* as 'an important learning experience', but the fact that the band didn't play a single song from the album during the subsequent *Analogue* tour spoke volumes about the tensions within the band during this stage of the band's career. Tensions would no doubt have been exacerbated by Pål's proposal of expanding the band to accommodate both Lauren Savoy and Frode Unneland. 'That was after the *Minor Earth Major Sky* album,' said Pål. 'I sat down with Magne and said, somewhat naively, that I thought a-ha needed some fresh impetus. And, instead of using all the good songs for Savoy, I could accommodate all of them in a-ha. "What do you think?" I asked. It did not go down well.'[2]

By the time the band had concluded a festival date in August 2001, both Magne and Pål were on the verge of releasing new music via their respective side projects. In October, Savoy released their fourth album, *Reasons to Stay Indoors*, while Magne – in partnership with Kjetil Bjerkestrand – issued the soundtrack for the Norwegian film *Øyenstikker* [Dragonfly].

By this time, work had already begun on a-ha's seventh studio album, but there was a much tighter deadline to meet this time around. And, owing to both the band members' geographical spread and their work on other projects, the album had to be recorded in various locations and with several producers. On top of this, there was some unfortunate infighting as each member of the band battled to get his material included on a body of work that would eventually sprawl to 15 tracks. The album was eventually titled *Lifelines*, but it was more like battle lines. On a positive note, Magne was blossoming as a songwriter, both individually and collaboratively, and brought in a number of excellent new songs, including the title track and 'Forever Not Yours'.

Pål, too, had somehow managed to come up with a plethora of new songs under pressure, including future fan favourites such as 'Did Anyone Approach You?' However, his contributions weren't exactly met with enthusiasm by his bandmates. Morten was particularly critical of Pål's new material, suggesting that many of the songwriter's ideas were 'unrealised'. Additionally, he accused Magne of self-interest. 'Magne went too far in pushing for songs,' he said. 'It became his private project. He was going to have his own way and, in the end, he didn't give a fuck about me.'[3]

There were also tensions during the actual recording sessions, as Pål confirmed: 'There were too many producers and they were engaging in trench warfare. Everybody went paranoid. We recorded things three, four times, and in the end we didn't know what was good . . . It took only two weeks before they got our whole history right in their faces. They went real shifty-eyed and were afraid to say anything wrong. They went from following their natural instincts to acting as arbitrators.'[4]

A perennial presence at the sessions was the band's drummer, Per Lindvall, who observed: 'The communication between them is remarkable. There's not much quarrelling, just weird energy. Everyone takes care of his own songs. It's really watertight. Both in rehearsal and in the studio. Now and then you get the feeling that they're sitting there thinking, "Can we finish this number now, so we can get onto my own song?"'[5]

'I can sort of agree with my brother's words,' added Sven Lindvall. 'I suggested that, if they did an equal split of the royalties, the songs would come out better – a win-win situation.'

Anneli Drecker's take on the sessions was slightly different: 'I was only in the studio once or twice,' she said, 'and then they were all there and the atmosphere was good I recall. It was a studio in downtown Oslo they had rented to record the vocals. So, whatever went on behind the scenes, I did not notice. When I was there, it was all about the music and the songs and making me feel relaxed in front of the mic – so good vibes and great laughs as usual!'

ROCK SOLID

The fact there were so many songs presented another problem. With their egos seemingly in overdrive, whittling down a near-double album to, say, 12 tracks, with each band member contributing a third of the songs, Teenage Fanclub-style, was optimistic to say the least, and the resulting hour-long set appeared to be the best compromise during a time when tensions were rife. However, in spite of its length and some obvious quality control issues, *Lifelines* was generally well received by the music press. In Norway, *Panorama*'s Paul Nordal described it as a 'step in the right direction' in his 4/6 review, while *VG*'s Stein Østbø praised the album for its 'rock solid' songwriting. But, elsewhere, *Dagbladet*'s Håkon Moslet was disappointed with Pål's contributions, and also claimed that the band were 'their own worst enemies'. In Sweden, *Release Magazine*'s Niklas Forsberg bluntly claimed there were too many fillers. 'It ruins the whole listening experience when masterpieces are followed by downright bores,' he wrote.

Over in the UK, *Q* awarded the album three stars: '*Lifelines* has the sort of gleaming production normally found on a Pet Shop Boys album,' wrote Nick Duerden, 'but the sense of maudlin reflection is more prevalent than ever. Harket is windswept and wistful throughout, often barely able to keep the lump from his throat. "Time and Again", in particular, makes Leonard Cohen seem positively perky.' Elsewhere, *musicOMH* agreed that the album was darker in tone, but they also picked up on its disjointedness: '*Lifelines* picks up, to an extent, where *Minor Earth Major Sky* left off and marks an evolution of a-ha's sound, rather than a revolution,' wrote Michael Hubbard. 'Harket's trademark vocals sound virtually unchanged and there are still dramatic orchestral sweeps in various tunes, coupled with pop beats and a willingness to experiment with technology. But the mood is darker, more pensive and less immediate . . . At 15 tracks it weighs in on the long side, but this is an obvious manifestation of cramming as many ideas into one album as possible.'

Like its predecessor, the front cover of the album did not feature a photo of the band; in its place was a shot – described by Magne as 'angry teeth' – of the interior of Havana's oceanside Parque José Martí stadium, which also doubled up as a location for the video shoot of 'Forever Not Yours'.

The album was released in April 2002 and performed well in Europe, hitting the top of the charts in both Norway and Germany. In the UK, however, where it appeared two months later, it was very poorly promoted, spending just one week in the chart. This was in spite of the band's triumphant live performance – their first UK show in almost a decade – at London's Royal Albert Hall on 25 June. In his review for *The Guardian*, Steven Poole wrote: 'It is obvious to any rational human that a-ha are some of the greatest unacknowledged geniuses of pop's past two decades'. The reaction was later acknowledged by Magne, who remarked: 'It was very special for us because it was our first reintroduction to the UK audience. But it was also the beginning of a very frustrating time for us because we could see that there was an audience there – as people were coming to the concerts and later the Wembley shows and UK tour – but our records weren't getting released.'[6]

Like its predecessor, a double vinyl version of the album was released in 2019, in addition to a two-disc CD which collected various demos, out-takes and alternative mixes.

LIFELINES
Written by Magne Furuholmen
Produced by Martin Landquist and Stephen Hague
Chart position: 78 (UK), 18 (Norway), 32 (Germany)

Although the making of a-ha's seventh studio album was laced with tension, there were many positives to take from the experience, not least the emergence of Magne as a major songwriting force within the band, as the sweeping symphonic pop of the title track would attest. Although he'd written a number of songs on his own, many songs – for example, 'Waiting for Her' – were simply handed to Pål to complete, ostensibly due to a lack of self-confidence. 'At the outset of our career I didn't write lyrics,' he said, 'and it was frustrating all the time because every co-write was always held hostage to Pål finishing a song with the lyrics, and they always . . . took a long time to come. Also, it felt to me that if he had a song that he felt was more important, he would always finish those lyrics and my song would be left by the wayside!'[7]

The demo of 'Lifelines,' which had been put together with the aid of Kjetil Bjerkestrand, reveals a song in transition, and some of the lyrics were wisely culled (for example: 'One chance / A chance of a lifetime / Please baby, please / . . . It feels like the first time / Down on my knees'). However, there was enough magic in the recording to suggest that the improving songwriter was on to a winner. According to Magne, the lyrics had been written in one sitting. 'It was a "what if" song, imagining what could have happened,' he said. 'It was the idea of someone getting thrown overboard and deciding whether or not to use the lifeline.'[8]

The track was recorded at Oslo's Lydlab Studios, with the aid of the production team of Martin Landquist and Stephen Hague. Landquist was a Swedish musician and producer who had not only released two albums under the pseudonym of Nåid but had also worked with high-profile compatriots such as the Cardigans and Kent. Stephen Hague's CV was considerably more expansive, however. The Portland-born musician's first major hit as both a co-writer and producer arrived in 1983 with the Rocksteady Crew's transatlantic hit, '(Hey You) the Rocksteady Crew', but it was the following year's astonishing pop/opera crossover hit, 'Madame Butterfly (Un bel dì vedremo)', by Malcolm McLaren that caught the attention of other musicians, particularly from the synth-pop fraternity. His first major project was OMD's sixth album, *Crush*, which provided a platform for their success in the US. He then went on to produce classic singles such as 'West End Girls' (Pet Shop Boys), 'True Faith' (New Order) and 'A Little Respect' (Erasure).

Hague's hands-on approach occasionally led to fallouts with his clients, but his wealth of experience in the symphonic pop field made him the perfect fit for a-ha.

For 'Lifelines', both Landquist and Hague had a solid demo to work with, which included lead and backing vocals from Morten and Anneli Drecker, respectively. 'That usually makes my job easier, having a solid starting point,' said Hague, 'though sometimes the artist can become too attached to the work they've done on their own. It's a double-edged sword . . . With the artist's demo. It's a good way to figure out what's working and what needs to be changed. Song structure is very important to me and I'll often chop up the demo into a form that works for me, then mess around with groove ideas and other basic stuff.'[9]

I asked Anneli if she was aware of how special a song 'Lifelines' was during its recording. 'This is of course hard to foresee when you are in the studio and being a tiny part of the making,' she replied. 'One cannot really know these things in advance. When we recorded my vocals for "Lifelines" and I had to dub Mags, we had such a big laugh because the lyrics are really hard to remember – they change on every chorus!'

The new recording included the band's then well-settled rhythm section of Per and Sven Lindvall, while the symphonic parts were delivered by Stockholm Session Strings, Sweden's renowned classical ensemble, whose work had appeared on tracks by pop acts such as Atomic Kitten, Roxette, Steps and Westlife.

The finished track was justly selected for single release (in a slightly edited version) in July 2002, although it was only a minor hit in Europe. Several remixes of the song were also commissioned for inclusion on the various formats. Martin

Gretschmann's 'Console Remix' was, by far, the most left-field version, with Morten's vocal getting the full vocoder treatment on an all-electronic outing.

The accompanying Spellemann-nominated video, shot in Stockholm in May by Swedish director Jesper Hiro, incorporated footage from Morten Skallerud's award-winning short film *Året gjennom Børfjord* (aka 'The Year Along the Abandoned Road'), which utilised time-lapse techniques.

While the song hasn't been a regular feature of the band's live sets since the *Lifelines* tour, it has featured prominently in recent years, and a version sung by Magne greeted concert-goers on the *Cast in Steel* tour.

YOU WANTED MORE
Words written by Magne Furuholmen
Music written by Magne Furuholmen and Morten Harket
Produced by Martin Landquist and Stephen Hague

With Pål on Savoy duties, Magne and Morten were accorded the opportunity to write songs together for the first time since the creation of *Stay on These Roads'* classic title track, and the result was four new songs, including 'You Wanted More'. With its near-tribal rhythm and slightly bombastic arrangement, the song was reminiscent of the Pet Shop Boys during their *Bilingual* era, while the spoken word element ('But in the end, what is a friend') recalled the hitmaking duo during their imperial phase in the mid- to late 80s. Unsurprisingly, the credits reveal Stephen Hague as the song's producer, but it was a rockier take that emerged during the demo stages, as well as a middle eight ('Hey, it's not your game / You don't know how to play it') that was eventually discarded.

An alternative version, meanwhile, reveals a slightly more restrained version. 'This mix could easily have gone on the album,' said Magne. 'The two are quite close, but Morten felt his vocals cut through more on the mix that ended up on the album. This mix has a more airy and perhaps a smoother, more panoramic European sound.'[10]

In terms of the lyrics, at face value they are bitter and confrontational, with the protagonist seemingly admonishing a partner for wrecking a relationship ('We had it all / You gave it up / You wanted more'), and there's an urgent quality about Morten's vocal that seems to authenticate the mood. The song, however, worked on many levels. *Lifelines* is, to date, the only album in the band's back catalogue that doesn't contain a collaborative song by Magne and Pål, and there was some speculation that the keyboardist was ruminating on the breakdown of the pair's creative relationship ('You loved the way it used to be / The way it was with you and me'). Pål certainly thought so, as the lyrics for Savoy's 'Rain on Your Parade' (2004) seem to confirm: 'Damn right I wanted more / Like everything we worked for / I don't want to rain on your parade / But there's just something 'bout your face / That rubs me the wrong way').

'I never stopped writing songs with Pål,' said Magne. 'I said I would no longer contribute things on Pål's songs without being credited, and as a result he stopped writing lyrics on my songs. So, yeah, the relationship had broken down. In a way, I should thank Pål as this indirectly pushed me to finish my own lyrics. Even so, I think we both lost out – as did a-ha – because of this.'

FOREVER NOT YOURS
Words written by Morten Harket and Ole Sverre Olsen
Music written by Magne Furuholmen and Morten Harket
Produced by Stephen Hague and Martin Landquist
Chart position: 1 (Norway), 18 (Germany)

The deliciously melancholic 'Forever Not Yours' saw Magne and Morten collaborating once more to great effect, delivering one of the highlights of the album. A companion piece of sorts to the previous album's 'To Let You Win',

which dealt with a relationship that had faltered due to a lack of strength on the protagonist's part, 'Forever Not Yours' elaborated on the hurtful impact of separation ('Memories / They keep coming through / The good ones hurt more / Than the bad ones do'), before delivering an emotional uppercut in the chorus ('I'll soon be gone now / Forever not yours / It won't be long now').

Morten and Ole Sverre Olsen had come up with the foundations of the song, and an early version reveals some unused lyrics ('Loneliness is like a lamp I guess / When the light is on / You know somebody's gone'). The chorus element of the song was entrusted to Magne. 'Morten came to me and wanted me to look at one of his songs,' he said. 'It was a conscious effort to write together. I had written the chorus part and there was discussion of what the lyric was about, and he said the title has to be "Forever Not Yours".'[11]

With its archetypal melancholic thread and soaring chorus, 'Forever Not Yours' was the perfect choice for the album's lead-off single – except in the UK, where the title track was released instead – and the band were rewarded with another chart-topper in their homeland. 'With Magne Furuholmen as a musical engine, a-ha have come up with a single that gives you a wistful craving in the stomach,' wrote *Dagbladet*'s Håkon Moslet. 'You are filled with fragile grandeur as the classic melancholic melody of the chorus washes over you.'

The promotional clip saw the band reunited with Harald Zwart, who had helmed the controversial 'Velvet' video. 'The video is based on an idea that Harald wanted to do for a while,' explained Magne during its filming. '. . . There's this kind of traditional biblical ark story that starts off with the animals and people going on board, and you sort of get the idea very quickly, but I think it will be very watchable because of Harald's visual style.' Filming took place in and around the Parque José Martí stadium in the Cuban city of Havana, and a vast number of extras and celebrity lookalikes were employed for the ambitious production.

THERE'S A REASON FOR IT (A BREAK IN THE CLOUDS)
Written by Pål Waaktaar-Savoy

THERE'S A REASON FOR IT
Written by Pål Waaktaar-Savoy
Produced by Ian Caple

The uniformity of the Hague/Landquist production partnership was broken up by this largely downbeat track, which marked Pål's entry point on the album as a songwriter. A very early version of the track, fascinatingly, reveals a completely different chorus, later repurposed as 'A Break in the Clouds', which was initially recorded during sessions for Savoy's eponymous fifth album and, later, a-ha's *Summer Solstice* project in 2017.

The final version was produced by former Abbey Road Studios trainee Ian Caple, whose name was synonymous with acts such as Tindersticks and Tricky. As both an engineer and producer, Caple brought a wealth of experience with him and, prior to *Lifelines*, his numerous clients included the Boo Radleys, Manic Street Preachers, Mansun, Shriekback, Spiritualized and Suede. Like Stephen Hague, he was also used to working with acts of varying temperaments. 'From experience, the only artists with whom it is difficult to work are those who are not listened to by their label or their producer,' he recalled. 'During all these years I worked with many artists – some of whom sometimes have the reputation of being difficult – and I discovered that, in fact, the only problem is that no one around them pays attention to what they want. The most important thing in my job is to listen.'[12]

Like 'You Wanted More', it's a subjective work, but at first glance it appears to be a rumination on Pål's relationship with his bandmates ('Everyone is worlds apart / It must have been this way right from the start') and the disintegration of the band in the mid-90s ('Don't know how it got away from me / Don't know how I let things go, you see / Don't know why it took a sudden turn'). However, it's a less accusatory song than, say, 'Daylight's Wasting', and more an acceptance on the 'hot and bothered' writer's part that things happen for a reason, and that people simply drift apart.

An earlier version of the track, with the keyboards higher in the mix, was also cut, but it's the album take that impresses the most. It does get a tad repetitive towards the end, and there are some noticeably quirky lyrics ('And everything is all too fast / Just add water / Nothing's built to last'), but the lovely McCartney-esque chorus saves it from becoming a perfunctory filler.

TIME AND AGAIN
Written by Pål Waaktaar-Savoy
Produced by Pål Waaktaar-Savoy

While many of the songs that Pål had written for *Lifelines* were completed within a short time frame, this tender ballad had been written at the start of the decade. However, it had never been intended for a-ha and, along with 'The Living Daylights', marked one of the few occasions that Pål had written a song to order. The singer Sissel Kyrkjebø – whose 'Se ilden lyse' had been performed during the opening and closing ceremonies at the 1994 Winter Olympics, ahead of a-ha's 'Shapes That Go Together' – had reportedly asked Pål to write a song for her. This wasn't an unusual request from a singer who was more renowned for her versatile singing voice than her songwriting, and prolific writers such as Bjørn Eidsvåg had previously penned songs for the popular singer, who'd enjoyed a string of chart-topping albums in Norway. The only problem was Kyrkjebø reportedly didn't like the song and so, almost by default, 'Time and Again' became an a-ha song.

Featuring a highly emotive vocal delivery from Morten, it was certainly one of the album's standout moments, but Pål agreed it was a song that never quite reached its full potential. Indeed, it's a slightly pedestrian take of the track that made it onto the album, and it's disappointing that the extended, more adventurous Clive Langer and Alan Winstanley-produced version, featuring piano, additional vocals and a more prominent string arrangement, didn't get the nod.

DID ANYONE APPROACH YOU?

Written by Pål Waaktaar-Savoy
Produced by Tore Johansson
Chart position: 67 (Germany)

With its combination of military beats, bleeps and almost-synthetic guitar sounds, 'Did Anyone Approach You?' ensured something of a sonic detour, with Morten's spoken word vocals adding a further experimental twist to proceedings. As a demo version of the track reveals, the song had originally utilised a 'funky drummer' approach to its rhythmic backbone, but Pål ultimately favoured Tore Johansson's

idea for a marching beat. (The co-founder of Tambourine Studios in his native Sweden, Johansson was a multi-instrumentalist who had made a name for himself as the producer of the Cardigans, scoring big hits such as 'Lovefool', 'My Favourite Game' and 'Erase/Rewind'.)

Although the song was slightly let down by some repetition in the lyrics, its memorable chorus made it a cert for single release, and it duly appeared in shops in September 2002. Once again, an array of mixes were commissioned, but the single made virtually no impact chart-wise.

The accompanying Lauren Savoy-helmed video, featuring a mixture of onstage and offstage footage of the band, was filmed on the opening day of the *Lifelines* tour at the Ullevaal Stadion [Stadium] in Oslo on 8 June 2002.

AFTERNOON HIGH
Written by Pål Waaktaar-Savoy
Produced by Clive Langer and Alan Winstanley

Featuring a jaunty, 'Marrakesh Express'-influenced motif that, oddly, recalled the Cardigans' 'Hey! Get Out of My Way', this light and breezy number found Pål with something of a spring in his step, using cheering memories ('The sunlight hits the corner of your eye / As it bounces off the morning sky / A summer in the seventies fly by') to fend off seemingly dark thoughts ('Steals the words that filled you up with doubt / Open up and let them all fall out'). But while there was much to admire about some of the creative word play on offer ('Incidental memories collide / Sentimental reveries abide'), there was a lack of consistency in the lyrics, and one wonders what Morten thought about singing lines such as 'Honey smooths the wrinkles from your bed / Gone the indentations of your head'. However, such idiosyncrasies may well have appealed to the production duo of Clive Langer and Alan Winstanley, who were renowned for their work with Madness in the first half of the 80s, as well as classic hits such as 'Reward' (The Teardrop Explodes) and 'Come On Eileen' (Dexys Midnight Runners). In addition, they had worked with numerous other acts, including Aztec Camera, Blur, David Bowie, China Crisis, Lloyd Cole, Elvis Costello, Morrissey and They Might Be Giants. As Langer told *Financial Times*' Michael Hann in 2017, they were particular about the type of act they would work with: 'We turned down things that went on to be number one,' he said. 'We turned down Madonna's 'Like a Virgin'. Didn't like it. I always thought I had integrity and my own taste. That English pop thing is what I am.'

By simply raising the tempo and adding a new drum part, Langer and Winstanley significantly improved the quirky song from its slightly sluggish origins – as evidenced by the New York demo – adding some much-welcome perkiness in the process.

ORANGES ON APPLETREES
Words written by Magne Furuholmen
Music written by Magne Furuholmen and Morten Harket
Produced by Clive Langer and Alan Winstanley
Additional production by Stephen Hague

One of the band's most experimental and divisive tracks, 'Oranges on Appletrees' represented a somewhat flawed attempt at contemporary psychedelia. On the plus side, Magne's lyrics were delightfully playful and quirky, featuring further meditations on modern living ('People come and people go / I can hear their laughter through their door / But no one's keeping score') and a series of offbeat couplets ('Birds that mate with bumblebees / Endless possibilities') to engage the listener, but the song was let down by a somewhat erratic arrangement. With its veritable melting pot of whimsical harmonies, bombastic orchestrations (recalling John Miles' proggy disco hit 'Music'), unnecessary key changes and a clumsily executed middle eight, this was a production in urgent need of streamlining.

On the *Lifelines* tour, the song was given something of a makeover, with Per Lindvall's steady beat adding a more satisfying pace, as well as some much-needed uniformity, while the addition of flute-like sounds (which, presumably, conformed to Morten's 'bohemian hippy' vision for the track) and some more prominent guitar completed the transformation. The lyrics, too, were given a tweak here and there, while some lines were simply cut (for example, 'multigender wannabes').

A LITTLE BIT
Written by Pål Waaktaar-Savoy
Produced by Ian Caple

Following three largely uptempo numbers, the pace of the album was slowed once more with this inoffensive mellotron-flavoured filler, which utilised a plaintive strum that recalled U2's 'One'.

While Pål was probably not referring to 'A Little Bit' when he later criticised the album for being 'middle of the road', this was certainly one of his more pedestrian numbers. That said, the lyrics are compelling – if a little repetitive – with the narrator appearing to reach out to someone whose relationship had ended, advising them that time would heal their wounds ('The road is long / And it will take a little work to get it back / To mend the cracks / To bridge the gap'), as well as reassuring them that they would eventually find love again ('Anyone you meet / Maybe down the street / Anyone could be that one').

LESS THAN PURE
Written by Pål Waaktaar-Savoy
Produced by Ian Caple

Featuring the bass-playing talents of Jørun Bøgeberg, this was a darker, more experimental piece that seemingly offered something of an insight into its writer's artistic disillusionment. On the surface, it's a fanciful slice of escapist drama ('We're gonna go downtown / I hear this great new place has opened up'), but there's something more cerebral and sinister lurking within the song's folk-tinged grooves, with the narrator seemingly plagued with malaise ('I'm really not sure about the choice we're making / The toll it's taking) and lethargy ('And our heads are getting wearier / And our hearts are less than pure'). Indeed, there was some speculation that the 'new place' at the heart of the song was Savoy, Pål's welcome retreat from the band politics of a-ha.

TURN THE LIGHTS DOWN
Written by Magne Furuholmen and Morten Harket
Produced by Martin Landquist and Stephen Hague

Another divisive number, Morten had originally sung 'Turn the Lights Down', but its lyrical structure and overtly romantic vibe seemed to indicate an opening for a female vocalist. It was evident from the *Minor Earth Major Sky* tour just how strong the onstage rapport was between Morten and Anneli Drecker – who had duetted to great effect on tracks such as 'I Wish I Cared' – and it seemed only logical that the pair should attempt to translate some of this chemistry to the recording studio. 'Turn the Lights Down' appeared to be the perfect fit for the pair, but Morten – who had described some of the album's productions as 'shipwrecks' – was once again unhappy with the end result, labelling the song a 'soppy ballad'.

The band did, in fact, try out a version with Clive Langer and Alan Winstanley behind the boards, along with guitarist Geir Sundstøl – who'd previously worked with Morten on the *Vogts Villa* album – and it's arguable that this was the superior take, which places Drecker's lilting vocals higher in the mix. 'Clive always felt this song had a real country vibe to it, and pushed in that direction,' said Magne. 'I think, particularly, Anneli's voice on the middle eight is a nice moment on this version.'[13]

'It is a soppy ballad, but a lovely soppy ballad,' responded Anneli to Morten's criticism. 'I love the fact that Morten has these opinions, it shows how much involved he is in the productions. I can see what he means; his vocals are more present on the Langer and Winstanley version, which is also more edgy and dramatic. But, on the album version, there is a million-bucks piano part with simple notes played – I think by Mags on the verses – which makes the whole song so much more melancholic.'

CANNOT HIDE
Words written by Morten Harket and Ole Sverre Olsen
Music written by Morten Harket and Martin Landquist
Produced by Martin Landquist

Partly on account of the number of producers involved, and partly down to the individualistic contributions of its writers, there was certainly a lack of cohesion on *Lifelines* – on both a personal and sonic level – which inevitably led to an eclectic mix of tracks. With its dynamic electro-pop aesthetic and French spoken word element in the coda, it's arguable that 'Cannot Hide' was the album's most self-indulgent production. (Magne's children can also be heard towards the very end of the recording.) However, as a demo of the track reveals, the song had seemingly been conceived as a rock track – complete with poodle-rock guitar – before its Daft Punk-esque makeover.

In terms of the lyrics, they range from the slightly seductive ('You don't know me, girl / I'm faceless in the crowd / The things I could show you, girl') to the somewhat baffling ('I feel your cat's eyes on me / Phosphor in the night'), while Magne's French rap saw him reeling off some seemingly random nonsense about stamps, postcards and phonecards, which even had French-speaking natives scratching their heads! 'I just tried this idea,' added Magne, 'and for some weird reason, Morten liked it!'

ONE IN A MILLION (Demo)
Written by Magne Furuholmen

WHITE CANVAS
Written by Magne Furuholmen
Produced by Martin Landquist

> *Life is a great big canvas, and you should throw all the paint on it you can.*
> *– Danny Kaye*

'White Canvas' is one of those songs in the a-ha back catalogue that often gets overlooked. The band never performed it in concert, and other songs from the album – such as 'Lifelines' and 'Forever Not Yours' – drew the bulk of the plaudits for being quintessential examples of their work. It's a shame, because it's arguable that 'White Canvas' is one of both Magne's and a-ha's most finely crafted songs.

It's evident from the opening bars that there's a strong John Lennon influence threading through this beautifully arranged track, while the lyrics convey a life message that could so easily have come from the former Beatle and one-time student of the Liverpool College of Art. In essence, the message is one of being both spontaneous ('Let's make the road up as we go along / Just as we planned') and audacious ('All that is needed is one leap of faith / Everything else will fall into place'), while the general vibe of the song is encapsulated in the self-explanatory couplet, 'Your life is a canvas / The colours are you'.

As one of the demos on the album remaster reveals, the song had originally been titled 'One in a Million'. While some of the lyrics survived a conceptual overhaul from the author, others were wisely culled (for example, 'One in a million / Two of a kind / Three is a point where I draw the line').

DRAGONFLY
Written by Magne Furuholmen
Produced by Clive Langer and Alan Winstanley

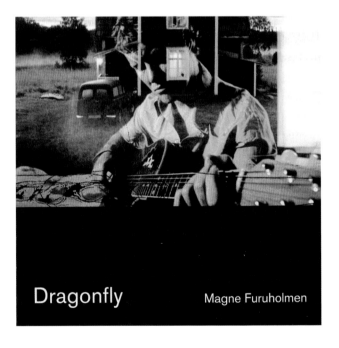

Prior to its harpsichord-flavoured makeover for *Lifelines*, 'Dragonfly' had originally been written by Magne for the soundtrack of Marius Holst's *Øyenstikker* movie, which had been released in September 2001. Shot in just 18 days, the low-budget film was based on a short story by Holst's friend, the award-winning Norwegian writer Ingvar Ambjørnsen. Holst felt the original story title, *Natt til mørk morgen* [From Night Till Dark Morning], was too dark and went with *Øyenstikker* instead. 'The dragonfly is a beautiful insect,' he explained to the BBC, 'but it's also a predator, which lives in still and muddy waters. In Ibsen's work, the smell of the swamp is an image of the past left behind and secrets buried. So, in Norwegian, the title is both beautiful and frightening.'

The dark psychological drama concerns a couple named Eddie (played by Kim Bodnia, who later starred in both *The Bridge* and *Killing Eve*) and Maria (Maria Bonnevie), who leave their troubled pasts behind them and make a new life for themselves in the idyllic Swedish countryside. But a chance encounter between Eddie and an old friend named Kullman (chillingly portrayed by Mikael Persbrandt) leads to a series of disturbing events, as the recently released prisoner attempts to coerce his former partner in crime into carrying out a revenge mission with him.

The reviews were largely positive, both in Norway and the UK, where it was released in 2003. In his four-star review for the BBC, Tom Dawson favourably compared the film with Roman Polanski's *Knife in the Water* before concluding: 'Evocatively shot in just three weeks, and apparently heavily improvised by the cast, the conviction of all the performances commands the attention, with Persbrandt's subtly unsettling presence particularly noteworthy.'

To coincide with *Øyenstikker*'s release, an EP was issued by Warner Music. It included 'Dragonfly' – which marked Magne's official debut as a solo artist – as well as the Marius Holst-helmed video, plus incidental music which had been composed for the film with Kjetil Bjerkestrand. The additional tracks comprised stark, piano-based pieces (see 'Sleep, Maria') alongside abstract vignettes that utilised more unusual instrumentation – glass armonica and idiophone – to authenticate the film's simmering tensions (see 'And Now We Are Here' and the rather unsettling 'Moths'). According to Magne, he had originally turned Holst down due to his various other commitments, but changed his mind after seeing a rough cut of the film.

Described by Magne as 'lo-fi folk', the original version of 'Dragonfly' reveals a more threadbare approach to the tender song, along with a suitably crude vocal from its writer. He'd considered getting either Kim Bodnia or Maria Bonnevie to sing the song but was reportedly talked out of it by Holst. 'Working with a great vocalist like Morten gives you a certain fear of heights,' said Magne, 'but I think the unsteadiness of my voice is sympathetic to the fragile atmosphere of the movie. It was the first and only take of the song, intended as a guide vocal really. And it was recorded at seven in the morning, but it had a strange quality to it that has survived all the way to the record.'[14]

In his review for *Dagbladet*, Anders Grønnenberg wrote: 'The bittersweet "Dragonfly" is as brittle as it is sweet. Magne Furuholmen's slightly awkward way of singing suits the low-key, acoustic sound of the song. The bassline, the melody construction and the presentation resemble both U2 and a-ha. The rest of the album is a more typical movie score . . . The soundscape creates a distinct atmosphere, and it works well in the intended context.'

The original recording was also used as a template for the a-ha demo, with Morten simply emulating Magne's vocals, but some lyrical tweaks were made prior to the *Lifelines* revamp (couplets such as 'I will never raise my voice / I will keep this tender poise' were cut).

During the *Lifelines* tour, a more acoustic version of the track was performed, with Magne on lead vocal duties.

SOLACE
Written by Magne Furuholmen
Produced by Ian Caple

With its sumptuous string arrangement and gentle electronic pulse, 'Solace' provided a satisfying audio bookend to a decidedly disjointed album. However, there were many positives to take from this veritable learning curve, and tracks such as 'Lifelines' and 'White Canvas' provided clear evidence that Magne had raised his songwriting game. 'Solace', too, exemplified his burgeoning abilities as a lyric writer. On the surface, the words are relatively downbeat ('Some sign of forgiveness / Some form of relief / Is all that she asks for'), but there's also a positivity to the song which isn't immediately apparent, and the overall message appears to be that of living for the moment, rather than wallowing in the past ('You're wasting the moment / Biding your time / No one got ahead / Standing in line').

A demo of the track reveals a work in progress, with a hymnal intro and some folky guitar giving the song a different vibe – something of a companion piece to Magne's original demo of 'Dragonfly' – but it's the album version that's the keeper. A longer, Tore Johansson-produced version of the song, which featured the percussion talents of Rasmus Kihlberg – a former session drummer at Johansson's Tambourine Studios – was seriously considered for inclusion on the album, but this particular take was far too cluttered, with the acoustic guitar part proving to be particularly distracting. 'Tore is one of the most eccentric and interesting producers we've worked with,' said Magne. 'He definitely adds a flavour of his own. This version went back and forth awhile, [with] attempts to marry TJ's electronic approach with the organic overdubs.'[15]

DIFFERENCES (Demo)
Written by Magne Furuholmen

When they were invited to perform at the Nobel Peace Prize Concert on 11 December 2001, a-ha sensed an opportunity to debut some of the new material they had been working on since June that year. However, the band were prevented from previewing a track from their upcoming new album, and so a compromise was reached in the form of 'Differences', a track which – in demo form – would eventually appear on both the 'Forever Not Yours' CD single and the Japanese version of *Lifelines*. (A new version of the track was later included on Magne's third solo album, *White Xmas Lies*, released in 2019.)

The title itself could, of course, have served as a succinct summary of the band members' creative relationships, but the earnest though melodically underwhelming track actually marked a rare foray into the world of politics. Magne had been inspired by a pre-September 11 TV documentary titled *Beneath the Veil* – which offered a harrowing female viewpoint of the brutal regime of the Taliban in war-torn Afghanistan – and penned this clarion call for action ('Raise your voice / Give us hope / Make us whole').

'"Differences" was written as a kind of ode to hopelessness and a scream for help – a silent scream for help to be specific,' recalled Magne in 2019. '. . . I wrote it as a response to this hopeless feeling that the world run by men is bound to just screw up around every turn and that, as long as women are treated this way, as long as more women are not in power, we're just gonna keep screwing ourselves over. I'm not a Christian or a particularly religious man, but I am someone who is affected by what goes on around me, and I wrote that song almost as a kind of prayer.'[16]

Accompanied by NRK's Norwegian Radio Orchestra, the band performed both 'Differences' and 'Hunting High and Low' during the annual event at the Oslo Spektrum, which was hosted by Meryl Streep and Liam Neeson. Other performers on the night included Anastacia, Natalie Imbruglia, Wyclef Jean and Paul McCartney. During the finale, all the performers congregated for a McCartney-led version of the Beatles' 'Let It Be', though Morten's voice was disappointingly underused.

THE BREAKERS (Album Out-take)
Written by Pål Waaktaar-Savoy

Prior to its repurposing on Savoy's eponymous fifth album – with Ours' Jimmy Gnecco on lead vocals – 'The Breakers' had also been considered for inclusion on *Lifelines*. With its generally reflective vibe ('I can still recall the time / Sitting in the sand / And watch the breakers as they roll upon the shore'), it may have provided the band with an alternative album-closer, in place of Magne's 'Solace'. Pål thought it was a 'classic', but his bandmates seemingly didn't agree, and it was ultimately overlooked in favour of inferior cuts such as 'Cannot Hide' and 'A Little Bit'.

What's interesting from playing both the versions back to back is that they're virtually identical, both lyrically and musically, with just the lead vocals and

Pål's guitar overdubs differentiating the original from the, arguably, superior Savoy take. With the benefit of hindsight, it's perhaps fair to say it's Gnecco's impassioned vocal delivery that wins through in this instance.

SOLE SURVIVOR (Album Out-take)
Written by Pål Waaktaar-Savoy

Although Morten was reportedly impressed with both 'Did Anyone Approach You?' and 'Time and Again', he was certainly less enamoured with some of the other songs Pål came up with for the album, boldly claiming that 'they don't have a chorus that goes anywhere'. He also added: 'I didn't want to get involved in tough discussions about songs I already knew had no place on the record, but I wound up singing them, to show that I was right. I know what I expect from Pål, and what he's able to do. But it's up to him to deliver. He turned in eight to ten numbers for the album with elements I would have been proud to do, but those weren't realised.'[17]

It's difficult to envisage what sort of reception the album would have received if the band had played it less safe and included tracks such as 'The Breakers' and this charming, well-produced oddity. But, with hindsight, such songs were, arguably, more suited to Savoy's grittier rock palette. Certainly, Pål's penchant for harmonic US rock comes across on 'Sole Survivor' – as well as a quirky, Doors-esque middle eight – but there's a resigned tone about the lyrics on this plaintive number that seems to suggest its writer was feeling that his role within a-ha was becoming increasingly marginalised ('I'm the sole survivor / Standing here alone / No one here beside me / And whether I care or not / That's not the point').

TO SHOW IT IS TO BLOW IT (Demo)
Written by Pål Waaktaar-Savoy

Morten's claim that Pål had arrived at the recording sessions for *Lifelines* with his 'Savoy hat still half-on' was partly backed up by this interesting period demo, which is notable for its audible backing vocal from Lauren Savoy. An acoustic guitar number in the vein of, say, 'Mary Ellen Makes the Moment Count', 'To Show It Is to Blow It' further hinted at the Americana-infused direction that would inform 2004's *Savoy*, but it also found Pål in something of a pensive mood, reflecting on some troubles closer to home. As he later revealed, this was a difficult period which would culminate in the deaths of Lauren's mother and her older sister, Deborah, two people whom the couple were very close to. Indeed, Pål confirmed that the song was written as Deborah's illness took a downward turn.

The title itself was perhaps an indication of its writer's desire to keep his emotions in check, while other lyrics outlined the desperation of watching a loved one fade away ('Tell the holy roller not to come on over / Thinking it'll be worth his while / Tell them natural healers, doctors and drug dealers / Running out of things to try').

CHAPTER NINETEEN

ANALOGUE

On the last two albums, the internal struggles have almost been the focus of our musical direction. Now I feel we've made a much clearer, more cohesive album, where we're ready to bring the band to a new place together.
– Magne Furuholmen, *Analogue* tour programme, 2005

Released: November 2005
Chart position: 24 (UK), 1 (Norway), 6 (Germany)

In view of the fact that creative tensions within the band had, arguably, reached their zenith during the making of *Lifelines*, it was perhaps unsurprising that it would take the best part of four years for their next studio album to appear. 'There have been many times we thought of splitting again, including around [the time of] *Lifelines*,' Magne revealed to Channel 4. 'Bands are like marriages – you have ups and downs. I wanted us to go into group therapy but in the end we just battled with our many issues in our normal intense and Scandinavian way.'

The band were still able to function amiably as a live unit, however, and the second half of 2002 saw them performing over 40 shows across Europe and also Brazil, where their popularity continued to endure. The concert line-up once again included Anneli Drecker on vocals, Christer Karlsson on keyboards and the Lindvall brothers, Per and Sven, on drums and bass, respectively.

'One thing that stays with me from all those tours is that they were always aiming for a good gig,' said Sven. 'We could play in the middle of the night in Moscow at some oligarch's wife's birthday party. The audience were so drunk that they hardly noticed that we were on stage. Still, we all tried to do a good gig and do the songs justice. That's big in my book.'

I asked Anneli if there were any particular songs she enjoyed singing during the back-to-back tours. 'I loved the acoustic break with songs like "Early Morning" and "Stay on These Roads" during the *Minor Earth Major Sky* tour the most,' she replied. 'It was also a great honour to be asked to sing "Dark Is the Night" during the Brazilian leg of the *Lifelines* tour. Singing the duet "Crying in the Rain" with Morten certainly

brings back great memories and was always a highlight for me during the shows. Standing next to Pål during "Velvet" and singing that lovely tune composed by Lauren on the choruses was nerve-racking, but wonderful.'

An excellent document of the *Lifelines* tour was released the following year: a live album, titled *How Can I Sleep with Your Voice in My Head* – sourced from the lyrics of 'The Swing of Things' – which included selected recordings from the band's shows in England, France, Germany, the Netherlands and Switzerland, plus (on the two-disc edition) a Lauren Savoy-shot documentary, which included backstage and onstage footage of the band and their entourage.

The album cover featured a striking black and white shot of a seal, which had been captured in a Danish aquarium by Oslo-born photographer Per Maning. This was a-ha's first live album, and it was preceded by a single that featured an edited version of 'The Sun Always Shines on TV'. However, neither the single nor the album were released in the UK. It was a decision that had reportedly been made by both a-ha and their management – mainly on account of their frustrations with *Lifelines* being so poorly promoted in such a key market – and the death knell was soon sounded for the band's 20-year association with the Warner Brothers label. 'As good as they were, I think that we were just too much hassle and we had too much history,' reflected Magne, 'plus we were signed to America and nobody felt a real commitment, nobody felt like it was their project. There was just too much [baggage]. We were really unhappy towards the beginning of the nineties . . . I guess we were just at odds with the record company because, I guess, they looked at the success as something positive and we looked at it like something we wanted to leave behind, so we were on a crash course with that. We were drinking beer and growing beards and long hair and hanging out in this whole kind of American Midwest, and doing different kinds of stuff which is what we were into at the time!'[1]

Having fulfilled their contractual obligation with the live album, a-ha signed a new three-album deal with the Universal label in 2004, but the recording of a new album – via the label's Polydor Records offshoot – couldn't commence until Magne, Morten and Pål had finished working on their respective side projects. In addition to performing a handful of shows with a-ha in 2003 and 2004, Pål had committed to the recording of a fifth Savoy album, while Magne – who was on something of a songwriting roll – was finally accorded the opportunity to release his debut solo album, *Past Perfect Future Tense*. The autumn of 2004 also saw the release of Jan Omdahl's revealing book, *The Swing of Things: Twenty Years with a-ha*, containing frank but fascinating new interviews with the band, plus a 12-track CD, which included a selection of very early demos. (The book was published by Press, a company which had been set up by Morten's brother, Håkon.) There was also a brand new compilation album, *The Singles 1984–2004*, released in November 2004, which rounded up most of the band's singles to date. (When it was released in the UK the following year, the retrospective was renamed *The Definitive Singles Collection* 1984–2004, and featured a slightly different tracklisting.)

CONSTANT STATE OF CHANGE

There were other one-off projects, too, so work on a-ha's eighth studio album couldn't start with earnest until February 2005. 'Each album brings a new set of things to deal with,' said Magne, 'and because of the long break between albums – and the fact that each of us has done a lot of individual projects – there was a different kind of group dynamic when we got back together. We're not so much a collaborative group these days, more three individuals working under a common umbrella and a common vision of what the band is, was and could be.'[2]

Although the official a-ha website reported that the band had spent a nice week together at Pål's New York apartment, the album was recorded in various studios. 'There was a long period of time when Pål and I practically lived together in the recording studio,' said Magne. 'Now, we make our music individually in our own studios and then present it to the other members of the group. At first, this new way of working was difficult, but now it works perfectly well, and permits each of us to have autonomy and self-confidence in our work.'[3]

In terms of the songwriting credits, there were virtually no collaborations between the bands' members. Once again, Morten brought in songs that he'd worked on with other writers and musicians, an arrangement that bore uncanny similarities to the situation of Depeche Mode's frontman, Dave Gahan, who started contributing co-written material on the synth-rock outfit's 11th studio album, *Playing the Angel*, which was released around the same time as *Analogue*.

Although the band were now writing individually, the resulting album proved to be a surprisingly more focused and cohesive product than its two predecessors. Magne partly attributed the album's coherence of sound to the mixing skills of Mark Ellis (aka Flood). His extensive CV included clients such as Nick Cave, Depeche Mode, New Order, Nine Inch Nails, PJ Harvey, Smashing Pumpkins and U2.

The band had also made a conscious decision to curtail the number of studio producers involved – something which had had a detrimental effect on their previous release – and the sessions were largely helmed by one person. The producer in question was Martin Terefe. He'd co-produced Magne's debut solo album, but his experience was extensive. The Stockholm-born songwriter and multi-instrumentalist had previously worked with a number of native and international acts, including Annika (who'd tasted fame as a member of the novelty act Rednex), Ron Sexsmith, Shéa Seger and KT Tunstall. He was also well known to the Lindvall brothers, who had both played on Sara Isaksson's Terefe-produced *Red Eden* album. (*Analogue* also featured the keyboard skills of Terefe's go-to musician, Claes Björklund, who had played on many of these acts' recordings.)

However, although Pål declared in the band's *Analogue* tour programme that the album was the 'most effortless and least painstaking' one to make, he later reflected that the sessions were fraught with more infighting: 'The same thing happened on this album as on *Lifelines*,' he said. 'I didn't feel I had enough confidence and support from the producer, which was unfortunate since I'm a big fan of his work. But I don't blame him or any of the other producers. It's a hopeless task to stay focused on the music when you're always being fed with internal political fights that go back twenty years.'[4]

The title of the album reportedly came from Morten. 'It is a reference to the quality of the sound of the similar instruments of the 70s and 80s,' he said. 'Today, machines offer perhaps more possibilities but none produce the warmth and the texture of the analogue sound. This is why many musicians still use the instruments of this time.'[5]

In addition to creating a brand new band logo, Martin Kvamme was commissioned to produce the album's leafy artwork. 'Pål suggested we use Martin,' said Magne. 'He is one of the finest graphic designers in Norway, and has done a lot of great stuff – he's an absolute pleasure to work with.'[6] Kvamme had produced the artwork for Savoy's eponymous album the previous year, while other clients included Espen Lind, Magnet, the National Bank and Popium.

PUT OUT YOUR MOURNFUL TONES

Analogue was completed in the summer of 2005 and eventually released in November that year. Prior to this, five of the songs – 'Analogue', 'Celice', 'Cosy Prisons', 'Holy Ground' and 'Keeper of the Flame' – were debuted during a huge free show in Oslo's Frognerparken [Frogner Park] on 27 August. 'It was an emotional day,' Magne later told Channel 4. '. . . After the show, we were talking to the Culture Minister and he said it was the biggest gathering of Norwegians in the country's history. That amazed us.' The event was followed by a sell-out show at the Irving Plaza in Manhattan on 12 September, the band's first US concert since October 1986. (The band also performed at the Live 8 concert in Berlin on 2 July, but sound problems resulted in their set being cut short.)

Both *Analogue* and its lead-off single, 'Celice', topped the charts in Norway, and there was plenty of praise for the album in the band's home country. Writing for *Puls*, Arild Rønsen declared it was a 'great pop record', citing it as one of the best albums of their career, while *VG*'s Espen A. Hansen concluded that it was 'packed with great songs'. Elsewhere, *Dagbladet*'s Sigrid Hvidsten wrote: 'For the first time in a long time, a-ha now appears as a band, not just a survivor of the 80s.'

In the UK, a huge promotional push – from both the band and their enthusiastic new record label – resulted in 'Analogue (All I Want)' becoming the band's first Top 10 single since 1988's 'Stay on These Roads', and there were largely positive reviews for the album, too. '*Analogue* is a mature collection of songs,' wrote the BBC's Lucy Davies. 'They're at their best at their darkest: the title track is the standout with its steady guitar-piano riff breaking out into uplifting choruses.' In their four-star review, *Uncut* magazine wrote: 'With rich new depths creeping into Morten Harket's spine-tingling falsetto, their perennially underrated emo-pop has never sounded better', while *Q* magazine singled out 'Celice', 'Cosy Prisons' and

'The Summers of Our Youth' for being 'accomplished, moving slabs of loneliness, evidence that the creative fires have been rekindled.'

The positive reviews, particularly in the UK, coincided with something of a reappraisal of a-ha's musical career, which culminated in the band's receiving an Inspiration Award from *Q* magazine in October 2006, in recognition of their widespread influence in the world of pop music. (Previous recipients of the prestigious award included Blondie, the Kinks, John Lydon, Patti Smith and U2.) 'That was a great feeling,' said Pål. 'To have such good response in the country where it all started for us, and to hear kind words coming from critics and colleagues, really gave us a boost.'[7]

In terms of the band's contemporaries, one of their most high-profile admirers was Coldplay. The band's frontman, Chris Martin, regularly sang their praises, while their bassist and drummer even ended up playing on Magne's *Past Perfect Future Tense* album. 'Coldplay have played an active part in causing a reappraisal of the band,' said Magne. 'Chris Martin is one of a generation of musicians who grew up loving a-ha; not for the image, but for the music.'[8]

Elsewhere, Keane, who had just released their successful debut album, *Hopes and Fears* – which included classic singles such as 'Somewhere Only We Know' and 'Everybody's Changing' – were another band indebted to the Norwegian trio. Indeed, on the superior follow-up, *Under the Iron Sea*, tracks such as 'Atlantic' boasted lyrics that seemingly bore Pål's signature ('I don't wanna be old and sleep alone / An empty house is not a home / I don't wanna be old and feel afraid'). (The Sussex band, who were once described by the *NME* as '*Kid A*-era Radiohead covering a-ha', actually met Magne and Morten prior to their appearance at the Quart Festival in Kristiansand in July 2004.)

However, despite the band's obvious rise in popularity, *Analogue* somehow sold fewer copies than its two predecessors, despite containing some of the best material they'd recorded since their comeback.

CELICE
Words written by Magne Furuholmen
Music written by Martin Terefe
Produced by Martin Terefe with a-ha
Chart position: 1 (Norway), 21 (Germany)

During the band's much-publicised Frognerparken show, the record-breaking Oslo crowd – said to be in excess of 120,000 people – were treated to a set that mixed familiar classics with deep cuts, plus brand new material. 'We have old songs that we have barely played live before,' Pål told *VG* in the lead-up to the show. 'It has provided extra inspiration.' Morten added: 'There will be a lot of new songs on Saturday. It is about finding a balance. One must, after all, have some respect for the expectations people arrive with.' It was certainly an event the band didn't take lightly, and *VG* also reported they had rented the Oslo Spektrum – at a considerable cost – for two days to practise their new set. On the day, a-ha gave a live debut to five new songs, which included the stunning opener, 'Celice', which

had been premiered on Norwegian radio several days prior to the event. With its striking falsetto and two-pronged guitar attack, this was one of the band's most dynamic and exciting songs since their reformation, though atypical of the album's generally reflective vibe.

The first of two co-writes with Martin Terefe, 'Celice' had initially been inspired, lyrically, by Dan Brown's second novel in the Robert Langdon series, *The Da Vinci Code*. 'I read the book quite early on before it became a big seller,' explained Magne. 'Like everyone, I was intrigued by the beginning of the book as it promises so much, but I was particularly intrigued by the character of Silas and the idea of applying this instrument of self-torture, of self-restraint, this Cilice, this belt you'd use as a self-disciplinary tool. I thought that would be an interesting image to utilise in a love lyric to describe a particular kind of relationship.' He added: 'I think we've all found ourselves in relationships, where you feel you're subjecting yourself to a hell of a lot of pain. However, I wouldn't be without those painful moments in my life as I know for a fact that they are the ones that have taught me the most.'[9]

A celluloid version of *The Da Vinci Code* – starring Tom Hanks and Audrey Tautou – was in development during this period, but 'Celice' was not included on the soundtrack of the film, which began showing in theatres in May 2006. 'I showed the song to the movie people,' Magne said during an interview for MSN and NTL World. 'They liked it, but not enough to pay. Cheapskates.'

'Celice' was released throughout Europe in October 2005, but not in the UK as the album's title track had been earmarked as the first single in the new year. Across the various vinyl and CD formats there was a somewhat unnecessary profusion of remixes by Boris Dlugosch, Paul van Dyk and Thomas Schumacher, plus a live version of the track, culled from the Frognerparken show. (An unreleased remix, by Hubert Mauracher, was eventually included on the *Time and Again* compilation in 2016.)

The promotional video was filmed in Berlin and directed by Joern Heitmann, who was well known for his work with the German electro-rock band Rammstein. The video, which incorporated heat-seeking visual effects, combined performance footage with shots of the band in a mocked-up brothel, caused something of a stir following its debut in September 2005. Magne, however, was quick to defend the clip and its sexual content: 'I do not think at all that "Celice" is a shocking video – the only thing that might shock is that it comes from a-ha. For me, "Celice" is like the evil twin of "Take On Me". It is very similar in that you are moving in and out of reality and illusion . . . "Take On Me" is a very positive video with a happy ending and "Celice" is more a story of loneliness and heartache, a long quest for passion, intimacy, closeness and love, but in a negative sense. So it's about prostitution, sex and drug abuse, it's about people who have lost their direction and about people looking for happiness, excitement and thrills.'[10]

DON'T DO ME ANY FAVOURS
Written by Magne Furuholmen
Produced by Martin Terefe with a-ha

By the time of *Analogue*'s release, it had become increasingly obvious that Magne and Pål's creative relationship had soured, and the days of the pair bouncing ideas off one another were fast becoming a distant memory. 'We write and record differently to before and now it's each man to his own,' said Magne, 'and on a couple of occasions the song is even finished before anyone else gets to hear it. And that's fine with me. It's not how I originally saw it, but it's something I've learned to live with and accept.'[11]

One song that certainly didn't include any input from Pål was 'Don't Do Me Any Favours', which had originally been conceived as a poem and then posted on Magne's website in 2005. Boasting some excellent drum work from Per Lindvall, this guitar-driven track maintained the album's early sprightly tempo, but its sardonic title and acerbic lyrics found Magne in a somewhat provocative mood ('I do not want to see myself / As someone that you saved / I'd rather be an adversary / Than to be your slave'). There were rumours that the track was about his and Pål's strained songwriting relationship ('You offer your assistance / But you won't accept my help'), but there was also speculation that it may have been a parting shot at their former paymasters at Warner Brothers, and lines such as 'Every friendly gesture / Turns my stomach inside out' were perhaps a reflection of some of the sycophancy the band had endured over the years. Either way, it made for uncomfortable reading and, unsurprisingly, the track was never performed live in concert by a-ha. (Magne did play it during some solo shows, though.)

The lyrical conjecture was seemingly dismissed by Magne, however, who told the band's official website: 'A lot of people have taken "Don't Do Me Any Favours" really personally, but hey, relax guys, ever heard of poetic licence?!'

COSY PRISONS
Written by Magne Furuholmen
Produced by Martin Terefe with a-ha
Additional production by George Tanderø
Radio mix produced by Martin Terefe, Magne Furuholmen and George Tanderø
Additional production by Martyn Phillips
Chart position: 39 (UK)

Magne's thematic and thought-provoking 'Cosy Prisons' offered clear proof of Coldplay's musical DNA, as well as a fascinating – and still relevant – poetic snapshot of a proliferating culture of shopping addicts and health food obsessives. 'I know a lot of people who are afraid to take risks; in love, in life, in most everything,' Magne explained, 'and I firmly believe you can worry so much about dying, that in the end you haven't really lived. I also know people so obsessed with health that they get sick from it. I am sure many with me feel desperation when they see through the bullshit that we try so hard to believe in; the belief that everything can be fixed or improved on, that by reading the correct how-to guides or thinking the right thoughts, that conforming to the right ideals you can somehow ease the underlying knowledge that we are all fundamentally alone and here for a short time.'[12]

Reportedly a favourite track of Morten's at the time, 'Cosy Prisons' incorporated Grandaddy-style electronics, as well as the vocal talents of Graham Nash, a former member of the Hollies and a perennial presence in the Anglo-American folk rock supergroup Crosby, Stills & Nash. Following a two-hour-plus show by the trimmed-down line-up of Crosby & Nash at Oslo's Rockefeller Hall on 9 February 2005, Morten met Nash backstage, and the 'Marrakesh Express' writer was invited to make a guest appearance on the *Analogue* album. 'We did a duet-harmony session with Graham Nash in my house in Oslo, which was a great night,' said Morten. 'I'm totally open to work with anyone where it makes sense – by saying that, I mean I wouldn't want to work with anyone for the sake of being seen with that person.'[13]

'Cosy Prisons' was also selected for single release, but a slightly improved version of the track was put together in a London recording studio in February 2006, with the aid of Martyn Phillips and Dave Bascombe. A former engineer at John Ratcliff's Rendezvous Studios, Martyn had gone on to work with acts such as the Beloved, Erasure, Jesus Jones and Kon Kan, but he'd also worked on the soundtrack album for *The Living Daylights* in 1987. 'I was doing Fairlight programming with John Barry and the Pretenders on "Where Has Everybody Gone?", whilst they [a-ha] recorded the theme,' he said. 'I also bumped into the band at a Dutch TV show when I was performing a track with Londonbeat that I had produced.'

As for 'Cosy Prisons', Martyn said: 'The track was fairly advanced when Mags came, and we spent a little while refining it. I recall it being a pre-mix session. I think we may have laid down some of the keyboard parts, such as the arpeggiated one before the third verse. I think Mags recorded his vocal harmony. I'm not sure about the strings – I think I would have made them more stereo than they ended up. Then we were likely tidying up parts and sounds with basic processing. Some of the final mix sounds as if I set it up here in ProTools to make the process easier. I remember sweetening the acoustic guitar.'

The final mix was created by fellow industry veteran Dave Bascombe, whose impressive CV includes the likes of Depeche Mode, Peter Gabriel, Lightning Seeds, Tears for Fears and the Triffids.

Some extra mixes of the track were commissioned, in addition to the accomplished demo of the song (featuring Magne's emotive vocals) but, in an era when physical single formats were fast becoming a thing of the past, these particular versions were only available digitally, due to the cancelled release of a CD single in Germany. However, the single was a minor hit in the UK and the 'Aural Float' remix did, eventually, find its way onto the *Time and Again* retrospective in 2016.

The promotional video was directed by Paul Gore, who had previously worked with New Order, Placebo, Snow Patrol and Amy Winehouse. The clip was filmed at London's Abbey Mills Pumping Station, a historic Victorian building which was also used as a location for Coldplay's 'Lovers in Japan' video in 2009.

MINOR KEY SONATA (ANALOGUE)
Written by Pål Waaktaar-Savoy
Produced by Martin Terefe with a-ha

ANALOGUE
Words written by Pål Waaktaar-Savoy and Martin Sandberg
Music written by Pål Waaktaar-Savoy, Max Martin and Magne Furuholmen
Produced by Max Martin and Michael Ilbert with a-ha
Chart position: 10 (UK), 10 (Norway), 33 (Germany)

The creation of the title track of a-ha's eighth studio album was something of a throwback to the band's early years and their method of fashioning hit singles from pre-existing material. Pål's lyric recycling ingenuity had previously paid off on big hits such as 'The Sun Always Shines on TV', and his copying and pasting skills would be called on once again for 'Analogue'.

According to Pål, the band felt they didn't have a standout single from the album, but there was one particular song – 'Minor Key Sonata (Analogue)' – that had commercial possibilities, despite a sluggish chorus and a somewhat quirky set of lyrics which, essentially, lamented the rapid onset of a digital recording age ('Come back my analogue / I hardly knew ya / The high end sloping off / A thing of beauty'). But, with its memorably simplistic piano motif and grungy guitar work, there was still plenty of potential in the song. The problem was, an album deadline was approaching and the band were fast running out of time. Pål discussed the predicament with Michael Ilbert, a vastly experienced Swedish producer and technician who'd mixed several of Savoy's songs. Ilbert's suggestion was to enlist the services of his compatriot, Max Martin (real name: Karl Martin Sandberg), whom he'd worked with on several projects, such as Celine Dion's *One Heart* album (2003). Among Martin's other high-profile clients were Ace of Base, Backstreet Boys, *NSYNC and Britney Spears, and huge hits such as 'I Want It That Way' and 'Baby, One More Time' had earned him a reputation as being one of the most respected and dependable hitmakers around. (In recent years he has enjoyed a string of No. 1 hits in the US with acts such as Katy Perry, Taylor Swift and Justin Timberlake.)

The collaboration with Max Martin proved to be a stroke of genius, and the commercial 'All I Want' chorus ensured the track was perfect single fodder. (Some of the original lyrics were included in the album booklet, presumably to explain the origins of the 'Analogue' title.) 'He did a terrific job cleaning the song up and giving it direction,' said Pål. 'He cut it to the bone and added some great things to it . . . It was finished in two or three days, which made the preceding seven months seem completely crazy by comparison!'[14]

In the UK, the newly titled 'Analogue (All I Want)' was released as the album's first single in January 2006, and the band were ecstatic when it gave them their first Top 10 hit in 18 years. 'Having a Top 10 with "Analogue" in the UK was a kick,' said Pål, 'and it made me realise that it's a big part of a-ha's make-up to get our songs on the radio . . . it's where we started.'[15]

The single's UK chart peak was emulated in Norway, but surprisingly it was only a minor hit in Germany. (Several remixes of the song were also available for digital download in that territory.)

The black and white video, filmed at Littlebrook Power Station in Dartford, was directed by Howard Greenhalgh who, following his work on 1993's 'Angel' clip, had worked with the likes of Iron Maiden, Keane, George Michael, Muse, OMD, Pet Shop Boys and Suede.

BIRTHRIGHT
Words written by Magne Furuholmen
Music written by Magne Furuholmen and Martin Terefe
Produced by Martin Terefe with a-ha

Typical of the melancholy and reflective material that Magne was writing at the time, this beautiful piano-based ballad was both a highlight of the album and one of the finest tracks of the band's career. It's suitably underlain with a light electronic fizz and a gentle strum, but it's Morten's spine-tingling vocal delivery that takes the track to a stratospheric level, evoking the ethereal qualities of singers such as Art Garfunkel. 'It's a varied album with a lot of different influences,' said Magne, 'but the real thread of the album is its melodic emphasis. Morten has an amazing voice that we sometimes forget about as we're so close to it. He always blows me away. Morten has a very defining voice and whenever you do something with him, it immediately seems to sound a lot more like a-ha than when you do it on your own. We couldn't have done this album twenty years ago, and you can't keep writing about puppy love when you're past forty.'[16]

Prior to *Analogue*'s release, 'Birthright' was issued as a promotional single in Norway, but it was rarely performed in concert. (The audience at a show at London's Shepherds Bush Empire in February 2006 were, however, treated to an acoustic rendition of the track.)

HOLY GROUND
Words written by Morten Harket, Nick Whitecross and Ole Sverre Olsen
Music written by Morten Harket
Produced by Martin Terefe with a-ha
Additional production by Kjetil Bjerkestrand

For *Analogue*, Morten brought in two songs – 'Holy Ground' and 'Make It Soon' that he'd worked on with other writers but, as he revealed to Polydor Records' Sorcha MacDonald, it was an arrangement that felt unnatural to him. 'I don't feel those songs really belong there,' he said. 'Me as a songwriter has never really been part of the songwriting team, although I wrote "Stay on These Roads" upon invitation from Mags who had the chords and I sang the chorus to him, and then we developed the song from there. So it can happen, but there's no culture for it yet. So what is natural for me is to get involved with the songs that Pål writes, or

Mags writes, or the two of them together.' (One other song of Morten's, 'Slanted Floor', was used on his next solo album, *Letter from Egypt*.)

Although *Analogue* largely encompassed all-new material, 'Holy Ground' actually dated back to the late 90s, and a clip of Morten singing an early version of the spiritual track was included in the documentary *Morten Harket: Min Jul* [My Christmas], which was broadcast on Norway's TV 2 channel in December 1999. Originally written by Morten with Ole Sverre Olsen, the song was given something of a songwriting polish by Nick Whitecross, a founding member of Kissing the Pink, who'd enjoyed a Top 20 hit with the Colin Thurston-produced 'Last Film' in 1983. The former London School of Economics graduate was well connected to Martin Terefe, having written material for the likes of Annika, Sara Isaksson and Shéa Seger.

Disappointingly, 'Holy Ground' didn't include either Magne or Pål on the recording, and it's arguable that the track should have been saved for Morten's next solo project, but with both Terefe and the dependable Kjetil Bjerkestrand at the helm, it became a veritable sonic fit for the album.

During the *Analogue* tour, the song was a near-permanent fixture of the set lists, and the live arrangement included Pål's playing of an Omnichord.

OVER THE TREETOPS
Written by Pål Waaktaar-Savoy
Produced by Martin Terefe with a-ha

The first of two songs to feature the rhythm section pairing of Jørun Bøgeberg and Frode Unneland, the dreamy, acoustic guitar-driven 'Over the Treetops' can perhaps be viewed, lyrically at least, as something of a forerunner to the pastoral 'Foot of the Mountain', with the narrator yearning for a quieter, idyllic setting, far from the bustling avenues of a sprawling metropolis ('Hey, beautiful farm on the top of the hill / Whenever I pass by / I'm thinking I will / Find someone like you / Goodbye avenue').

While the Woodstock vibe of the song was reinforced by the harmonies of Graham Nash and a sumptuous string arrangement by David Davidson, the subtle use of electronics and the distorted guitar in the finale added a lo-fi, indie folk twist.

Perhaps because the song was largely sung in falsetto by Morten, the song was never performed in concert until it was dusted off for the recent *MTV Unplugged* shows. The new country-flavoured arrangement, with Pål on 12-string guitar and Lars Horntveth on pedal steel, saw Morten singing in a deeper, more comfortable register.

HALFWAY THROUGH THE TOUR
Written by Pål Waaktaar-Savoy
Produced by Martin Terefe with a-ha

An ambitious two-part song with considerably contrasting styles, this seven-minute-plus epic has certainly divided opinion since its release. Underscored by the album's signature electronic whir, the first part features some delightfully frantic piano playing from Christer Karlsson, which is backed up by a suitably bombastic string arrangement and some lovely West Coast harmonies. The lyrics, meanwhile, offer differing views of life on the road, revealing not only the adrenaline rush of being on stage ('But when the crowd engage / And brings you to a place / You will know / Everyone can be a part of') but also the monotony of travelling and the concomitant feelings of homesickness ('Halfway through the tour / We'll be somewhere else tomorrow / And you know I can't wish for more / Than walking out the door / And make for home tomorrow').

While the first part of the song saw Pål offering a playful snapshot of the euphoria of touring, the Angelo Badalamenti-inspired ambient section was moodier and significantly less pacy, presumably designed to encapsulate the feeling of a post-tour comedown. This was clearly intelligent songwriting, but the cooling coda left many fans and critics confused. Its momentum-stalling position in the middle of the album didn't help, either, and it's arguable that the track may have worked better towards the end of the album.

A FINE BLUE LINE
Written by Magne Furuholmen
Produced by Martin Terefe with a-ha

A typically melodic and reflective ballad from Magne, 'A Fine Blue Line' features not just ruminations on the passing of time ('Time marches on ahead / One day we'll see it') but also a heartfelt capture of the band's early years ('Take a look and see / What's become of me / Remember how it used to be / People that we'd meet / Were falling at your feet'). In addition, there seems to be a reference to the time when he and Pål used to look through each other's notebooks ('We read each other's books / We gave each other looks / Like we couldn't trust ourselves / And we knew it'), while it's possible that the title itself was a reflection of the unquivering bond that existed between them. 'I tried to write things that are very direct and emotional, like Pål used to do in the beginning,' said Magne. 'I think that's what suits us best, this honest side, natural, open, being unashamed to say anything.'[17]

In terms of its chord progression it was perhaps, on paper, the simplest song on the album, but the arrangement, featuring some luscious strings and a Massive Attack-like percussive intro, ensured it wasn't lacking in sonic adventure. (Like 'Holy Ground', the track featured the drumming skills of Alex Toff, who would later play on Martin Halla's *Winter Days* album and, more recently, Rick Parfitt's posthumous *Over and Out* release.)

In 2007, the track – retitled 'The Fine Blue Line' – was recorded in Nashville by the Norwegian country singer Arne Benoni and included on his album *I'm Coming Home*, which also included songs previously popularised by Ozzy Osbourne, the Pointer Sisters and Lionel Richie, plus three duets with 'Rose Garden' singer Lynn Anderson.

KEEPER OF THE FLAME
Written by Pål Waaktaar-Savoy
Produced by Martin Terefe with a-ha

On this delightfully nostalgic track – which saw Pål once again channelling his inner McCartney – listeners were taken on a sentimental trip back to the halcyon days of his Manglerud milieu, blissfully capturing memories of a well-spent youth at his Havreveien home, where he frequently cranked up the volume of his parents' Tandberg turntable after school ('Give it up for rock 'n' roll / Give it up for rock / Give it up for how it made you feel / Give it up for vinyl days / Kicking back from school'). It's the summer of 1977, and the adolescent daydreamer is 'laying in the grass' and hatching plans 'too grand to entertain', in a country where international success was but a fanciful dream. 'Four more years and I'm outta here,' sings Morten, who in 1981 was on the cusp of linking up with Magne and Pål, and subsequently changing the Norwegian music scene for good.

During the *Analogue* tour, the song became a regular fixture of their sets, with Pål on piano and Magne on guitar. (During some shows – for instance, the Brighton Centre on 10 December 2005 – the song was properly introduced by Pål, who wasn't normally known for his onstage banter.)

MAKE IT SOON
Written by Ole Sverre Olsen and Morten Harket
Produced by Martin Terefe with a-ha

During the recording of *Analogue*, the band's new co-producer, Martin Terefe, proved to be hugely influential, not just as a songwriter and musician but also as a key exponent in the development of the band's sound, which now boasted a uniformity and identity that had, arguably, been missing since 1993's *Memorial*

Beach. However, the band were still keen to exhibit their more experimental side, and tracks such as the epic 'Halfway Through the Tour' ensured they could never be accused of being predictable: 'On this album, Martin would say, "oh that's so a-ha, that's such an a-ha moment",' said Magne, 'and we always resist that to a certain degree, because we don't want to be caricatures of anything.'[18]

Something of a gnarly filler, 'Make It Soon' starts off as a somewhat dissonant slice of folktronica before erupting into a Radiohead-like cacophony of distorted guitars and unsettling backing vocals (which were provided by Terefe). This was, arguably, more an exercise in self-indulgence than experimentation, and something of a misstep on an otherwise solid album.

WHITE DWARF
Written by Pål Waaktaar-Savoy
Produced by Martin Terefe with a-ha

This beautiful, astral ballad served as a reminder of Pål's ability to embrace something more unusual and esoteric – in this case, a burnt-out star – and craft a song around it. The vividness of the opening lines immediately sets the scene ('There's a big, black picture / And it's hanging on your wall / With stars and all the planets/ The Milky Way and all'), while the eloquent description of the star itself, as it transitions to a white dwarf, is both captivating and heartbreaking ('In a constant state of pain / You radiate away / Your last remaining heat / Your atmosphere has blown away'). However, while Pål was pleased with the lyrics, he intimated that he wasn't entirely happy with the final version, claiming it was more akin to a demo recording. It's arguable that the lead-in with the acoustic guitar sounds slightly clumsy, but this only adds to the track's charm, while the attendant spectral sound effects and wistful backing vocals make for a suitably otherworldly listen.

THE SUMMERS OF OUR YOUTH
Written by Magne Furuholmen
Produced by Martin Terefe with a-ha
Additional production by George Tanderø

Ending the album on a suitably sombre and reflective note was this stunning piano-based ballad which, arguably, represented Magne at the peak of his songwriting powers – so much so that it almost feels like a swansong at times ('There's nothing you can say / To make me change my mind').

A demo recording reveals the song had originally been sung by its writer, but it was the highly effective vocal pairing of Morten and Magne which would grace the finished recording, with the contrasting crystalline and brittle tones perfectly complementing the emotional content. It's Magne's vocals that are utilised on the verses, which play out like a movie in the songwriter's head, allowing him to rewind back to his adolescence ('Just let the plot unwind / As we look back and see / Our yesterday's entwine / The beauty and the truth / The summers of our youth'), while a more philosophical counterbalance is provided in the Morten-sung choruses, which pose a number of existential questions ('What you gonna do when lights go out? / What you gonna think it's all about? / What you gonna do when time is up?').

Had the album been sequenced a bit more thoughtfully, 'The Summers of Our Youth' would have followed on perfectly from the similarly nostalgic 'Keeper of the Flame', while it would have been an even nicer touch if Pål had been given a verse to sing. This was actually addressed via the band's official website at the time: 'There's no rules – whatever works, you know,' responded Pål. 'We all three enjoy singing, but Morten's the singer. If the song needs some croaking, Mags and myself are ready to burn, dude!'

Although the song was never performed by a-ha in concert, it was played by Magne during some of his solo shows.

CASE CLOSED ON SILVER SHORE (B-side)
Written by Pål Waaktaar-Savoy
Produced by Martin Terefe with a-ha

Tucked away on the B-side of 'Analogue (All I Want)' was this cinematic gem, which continued in the vein of cuts such as 'I've Been Losing You', 'Early Morning' and Sycamore Leaves', all centred around a murder of some description. In the latest instalment, Inspector Waaktaar places himself firmly in front of the yellow and black crime scene tape, revealing a number of tantalising clues to his audience ('Here's a stain on the ottoman / Here's a slug in the plaster wall / Here's a glass with a fingerprint . . . / Here's a room showing signs of struggle / Here's a tear in the victim's shirt'), but while there are plenty of pointers, the listener can only speculate as to who committed the deadly deed ('I wouldn't put it past the neighbour / I wouldn't put it past the maid / I wouldn't put it past the boyfriend / He'd do it in a jealous rage').

The musical backdrop – which includes swathes of electronics, grungy guitar and ghostly choral sounds – is suitably eerie and enigmatic. In addition, there's an array of effects, which include some heavy breathing and some 'lock and load' sounds, and it all adds up to being one of the band's most interesting productions of the period, and it's hard to comprehend how it was overlooked in favour of cuts such as 'Make It Soon'.

#9 DREAM (Non-Album Track)
Written by John Lennon
Produced by a-ha

'#9 Dream' had originally been included on John Lennon's *Walls and Bridges* album in 1974 and subsequently released as the follow-up to the single 'Whatever Gets You Thru the Night' (which featured Elton John on keyboards and vocals). Although the melody had largely been derived from the string arrangement of Harry Nilsson's version of Jimmy Cliff's 'Many Rivers to Cross' (which Lennon had produced), the words – notably, 'Ah, böwakawa poussé, poussé' – had come to the former Beatle in a dream. 'He woke up and wrote down those words along with the melody,' recalled his former girlfriend, May Pang, who also provided the breathy backing vocals on the track. 'He had no idea what it meant, but he thought it sounded beautiful. John arranged the strings in such a way that the song really does sound like a dream. It was the last song written for the album, and went through a couple of title changes: "So Long Ago" and "Walls And Bridges".'[19]

A-ha's version of the classic track – which *Uncut* magazine, in 2015, declared as Lennon's 24th best song – was recorded for the compilation album *Make Some Noise: The Amnesty International Campaign to Save Darfur*, which was eventually released in June 2007. The double CD included versions of John Lennon songs by artists such as the Cure, Jakob Dylan, the Flaming Lips, Green Day and Snow Patrol, although some numbers were covered twice. For the US market, where the compilation was given the title of *Instant Karma*, there were some notable changes to the tracklisting: A-ha's interpretation of '#9 Dream' was dropped in favour of R.E.M.'s rockier take, while Duran Duran's version of 'Instant Karma' was jettisoned in favour of U2's.

During the tail end of the *Analogue* tour in 2007, the band performed '#9 Dream' a handful of times. The arrangement of the song was faithful to the original, although Morten chose to sing the song's title during the chorus, utilising a melody which, perhaps purposely, had shades of George Harrison's 'My Sweet Lord'.

PART SIX

DARKSPACE – THE SOLO YEARS
2000–2008

CHAPTER TWENTY

HALF OF THE TIME

With this band, we don't need a boss, because we're all pulling in the same direction.
– Pål Waaktaar-Savoy, 2001

SAVOY – REASONS TO STAY INDOORS (2001 Album)
Produced by Pål Waaktaar-Savoy and Lauren Waaktaar-Savoy
Chart position: 8 (Norway)

Keen to sustain the momentum after the success of *Mountains of Time*, Savoy wasted no time in commencing work on the follow-up, which would once again see Pål and Lauren sharing songwriting and production duties. Pål told a-ha's official website: 'We started out doing seven songs that were left over from *Mountains of Time*, finished those up, and that gave us a big boost! They sounded good, we felt really good about it, but then, as time went by, it was like, "Oh, we'll have to have this new song there, and this one as well", and in the end it [was] all new songs.'

Still fully committed to a-ha in both a recording and performing capacity, the fact that Pål was still able to churn out songs for both acts with such regularity was an impressive feat, but there was some speculation in the media that he was squirrelling his best songs for Savoy. When reviewing their fourth album, *Dagsavisen* quipped: '*Reasons to Stay Indoors* is an album that defines the personality of Savoy more than ever before, even when the title song is so anchored in a-ha tradition than one can't help but wonder if Pål Waaktaar saves a few possible a-ha hits for his own band.'

DRIVING INTO NEW YORK CITY

What's definite about *Reasons to Stay Indoors* is that its roots are firmly planted in New York, while the couple's new-found domestic bliss also crept into some of the songs. The lyrics for 'Against the Sun' included lines about impending parenthood ('We have thought about you / Before you could be seen / Just a little heartbeat / Going bleep bleep on a screen'), while 'Once upon a Year' simply expressed the joy of their son's arrival ('Once upon a year / We had a boy / Our boy'). Elsewhere, 'Five Million Years' – a future promotional single – found Pål in a philosophical mood: 'Hundred million years ago / The dinosaurs that walked the earth were so slow / Hundred million years ahead / Luchie puts her sleepy son to bed.'

The album was largely recorded at Pål and Lauren's new (larger) apartment in New York, with drummer Frode Unneland occasionally flying over to join them. The couple's new neighbours included actor Claire Danes and the Smashing Pumpkins' frontman. 'Billy Corgan is even more shy than me,' joked Pål to *VG*. 'He doesn't even dare to greet me in the hall!'

With the arrival of Augie, they'd also had to amend their recording routine, reducing studio session time somewhat considerably. 'After we had Augie, we were with him when he was awake and got right back to work when he fell asleep,' said Pål, who added: 'I learnt to focus differently, and would usually do as much in four hours as I did in fourteen.'[1]

Somewhat inevitably, the album would end up drawing some comparisons with *Double Fantasy*, the final album by two of Manhattan's most famous residents, John Lennon and Yoko Ono, which had featured family-oriented songs such as 'Beautiful Boy (Darling Boy).' 'Lauren took it more to heart than me,' said Pål. 'She probably felt the comparison was more about blaming Yoko for separating the Beatles, and that she would be the reason for separating a-ha. I couldn't see that link at all, because Yoko is such a cool and original woman.'[2]

WE HONE OUR TRADE

Sonically, the new album didn't stray too far from the previous long-player's template, though it did employ a greater use of strings this time around, particularly on the title track. There was, however, a change of bass-playing personnel with the arrival of Jørun Bøgeberg, who'd played on several of a-ha's albums and various side projects. 'Pål is very focused on getting down the details that he has in his head,' he said, 'and at the same time he opens up for inputs and personal colouring from my own mind and my spontaneous way of playing. But if it tends to move far away from where he is likely to take the track, I would never fight for any of my ideas that are different from his. That's a hired soldier's first rule, to please the owner of the song or the producer.'

There was another a-ha connection, too, in the form of Anneli Drecker, whose vocals can be heard on the quirky synth-pop number 'Fearlist'. 'I remember a sunny day in their studio at their house in Oslo,' she said. 'I don't remember if it was planned or if it was spontaneous now – we used to hang out a lot in that period. Lauren was a good coach and producer. She knew what she wanted and how to get it from me.' Featuring off-the-wall lyrical couplets such as 'It's so itchy that you have to itch / It doesn't matter if it bleeds', it wasn't one of Savoy's greatest lyrical moments, but its inclusion was indicative of the band's willingness to experiment. Far better was the more conventional 'Paramount', which recalled the mid-90s indie pop of acts such as Garbage and Lush.

QUALITY PRODUCT

The album was preceded in September 2001 by the promotional single 'If You Won't Come to the Party', and it featured some lovely vocal interplay between the band. 'Frode has the most amazing voice,' Lauren told a-ha's official website. 'He can go so high!' Pål added: 'I think we are getting to know our voices by now. I'm singing lower now, Lauren is in the middle and Frode's at the top!'

The album arrived in early October and, once again, early copies included an additional EP of exclusive songs. Reviews were generally favourable, although the consensus among critics was that the band had played it too safe. '*Reasons to Stay Indoors* is undoubtedly a quality product,' wrote *Dagbladet*'s Sven Ove Bakke, 'and opens with two staggering pieces of classical pop of the Goffin/King and Bacharach type . . . but then the excitement levels out. Although the songs work in isolation, the whole becomes one-dimensional and undynamic.' Elsewhere, *Adresseavisen* wrote: 'Pål Waaktaar-Savoy has a phenomenal instinct and basic understanding of good pop music. When he plays on his own without the friction of a-ha, the result is easy-going and charming pop music which sounds contemporary.'

Certainly, tracks such as 'I Wouldn't Change a Thing' occupied familiar *Rubber Soul*-like territory, but there were plenty of standouts. These included the epic title track, the brooding 'Face' and 'Half of the Time', which saw Pål ruminating on his well-documented shyness ('Half of the time / I see no reason / To say much').

While the album didn't quite meet expectations, it was certainly a worthy addition to Savoy's increasingly impressive body of work. However, the release was slightly overshadowed by the events of September 11. 'We heard a bang,' recalled Pål. 'I thought it was the garbage truck that took its usual round around the block. But when we looked, the World Trade Center was on fire.' While the panic-stricken Lauren looked after the couple's son, Pål tried to remain calm and headed out for some provisions, as well as some gas masks. 'We tried to put a mask on Augie, but of course it didn't work, and he refused to wear it. The next thought was to leave town, but it was impossible. Everything was just chaos.'[3]

There was a happy postscript, however, when Frode Unneland later accepted a Spellemann award on the band's behalf for Best Pop Group.

A reissue by Apollon Records was scheduled for release in 2017, but Pål said the band's involvement with the label has ended.

SAVOY – SAVOY (2004 Album)
Produced by Savoy and Frode Jacobsen
Chart position: 7 (Norway)

There would be a wait of almost three years for the next Savoy album, as Pål was fully committed to a-ha and the recording and subsequent promotion of 2002's *Lifelines*. Tensions had been fraught during the recording of a-ha's seventh studio album, and the band who had once aspired to be like the Beatles were now slowly morphing into a version of the global phenomenon that had imploded at the tail end of the 60s. (*Lifelines* itself has often been referred to as a-ha's  own version of the Fab Four's self-titled *White Album*). As a candid John Lennon interview from 1969 attests, the similarities between the two bands were uncanny: 'The problem is that in the old days, when we needed an album, Paul and I got together and produced enough songs for it. Nowadays there's three of us writing prolifically and trying to fit it all onto one album.' He later added: 'We've always said we've had fights. It's no news that we argue. I'm more interested in my songs.

Paul's more interested in his, and George is more interested in his. That's always been. This is why I've started with the Plastic Ono and working with Yoko . . . to have more outlet. There isn't enough outlet for me in the Beatles. The Ono Band is my escape valve.'[4]

Pål's own 'safety valve' was Savoy, and the prolific songwriter was certainly grateful to return to a more receptive and amiable set-up after the internecine strife of *Lifelines*. 'Things were extremely uncomfortable at that time,' he confirmed. 'So it was probably a matter of wanting to be in a band in which everything was free and friendly, where everybody wished the best for one another. It was a natural reaction, a yin/yang thing.'[5]

ORGANIC

Savoy's fifth album – co-produced by Frode Jacobsen, a member of the rock band, Madrugada – would employ a more organic and back-to-basics approach, with noticeably less programming and a return to the melancholic intonations of *Lackluster Me*. 'I can't sit and browse menus, I'm not a computer type,' said Pål. 'I'm looking for things that speak in a direct way. Old equipment sounds different, it has more soul. And I like the challenges that lie in its limitations.'[6] The album also included guests such as Robert Burås (Madrugada), Jimmy Gnecco and the boys' choir Sølvguttene [the Silver Boys].

Such was the wealth of material available during this period that the band briefly considered releasing a double album, before opting for a standard 12-track set. One particular song that had been earmarked for *Lifelines*, but ultimately rejected, was 'The Breakers', which now featured a lead vocal from Pål's friend Jimmy Gnecco, the frontman of the rock band Ours, who by this stage had two albums under their belt. Album out-takes included 'A Break in the Clouds' – which had originally formed part of a-ha's 'There's a Reason for It' – and 'We're the Same Way', but these were later reworked for other projects.

Also included on the new opus was the stunning 'Whalebone', a song which had been written for Erik Poppe's Amanda Award-winning film *Hawaii, Oslo*. It also served a dual purpose as the album's first promotional single release in August 2004. The track was also notable in that it recycled, to great effect, the 'O weeping night / O grieving sky' lyric from a-ha's 'Locust', one of the *Memorial Beach* standouts. '"Whalebone" is classic Pål Waaktaar-Savoy,' wrote *VG*'s Espen A. Hansen. 'A warm, drowsy and beautiful pop song created for lazy summer evenings.'

Like the band's previous album, *Savoy* was not short of New York references, from the wonderful laid-back vibe of 'Girl One', with its South Street Seaport setting and Byrds-like guitar, through to the gorgeous snow-covered 'Watertowers', which harked back to the *White Album* stylings of *Lackluster Me*.

SOMBRE

By the time of the album's release, the city of New York was still coming to terms with the events of September 11, and there's certainly a pervading sense of despair on the album. This is evident on more politically imbued tracks such as the school ground drama of 'Shooting Spree', a Lennon-inspired narrative about a gunman who 'Kills everyone that gets in the line of him and his gun / Then shoots himself when he's done'. And then there was the brooding, funereal closer, 'Isotope', which saw the band ruminating over environmental affairs against a soundscape of guitars, electronics and backwards effects – permeated throughout with some chilling death bells.

Elsewhere, creative frustrations were vented on 'Is My Confidence Reeling?' Against a musical backdrop that evoked John Lennon circa 1970, Pål ventured, 'What's the point of writing songs that no one hears? / Little waves of sound falling on deaf ears.' However, as Pål later confirmed, the lyrics had hidden depths: 'The song is not just about me complaining because people don't listen to my songs,' he said. 'That was a very sad time for Lauren. She had two sisters, now she has only one. Her sister Debbie was ill for a year and a half and died at that time. This has also flowed into this song, including in the middle eight. I felt I had to say something about it, but at the same time it was something I was very reluctant to do . . . Another song on the record is called "Cyna". That was Debbie's middle name. We wrote the song for her and played it to her in the hospital.'[7]

The Woodstock playfulness of 'Bovine' ('You have to be gifted / To get me out of bed') did ease some of the underlying dolefulness, but Savoy's 'brown' album was a largely sombre affair.

REBIRTH

To signify what the band felt was a rebirth, the album was simply titled *Savoy* and released at the end of August 2004 on their own *Eleventeen* label, with a distribution deal in place with Universal Music's Sonet imprint. With the recording of a-ha's next album six months away, there was a clear window in which to give the album a good promotional push, and the band scheduled an extensive Norwegian tour – featuring Furia's Maya Vik on bass duties – throughout September and October. 'We have taken the promotion of the previous albums too lightly,' Pål told *Dagbladet*. 'This time we are going to do more to break through. We owe it to this album.'

Unfortunately, *Savoy* lacked a big radio hit and the album had slumped to No. 27 by its second week. Some people speculated there was a knock-on effect from the band's disastrous appearance at the annual Øyafestivalen [Øya Festival] on 13 August – a performance which was blighted by technical difficulties. The reviews for the album were mixed, too. *Panorama*'s Paul A. Nordal awarded the 'smooth and varied' *Savoy* a generous 5/6. '"Whalebone" is perhaps the platinum's most immediate highlight,' he wrote, 'but there is no reason not to highlight more of the same calibre: The opening track, "Empty of Feeling", is one of them, the gorgeous closing track, "Isotope", is another.' Elsewhere, *Dagsavisen*'s Erik Wiggo Larsen described *Savoy* as 'Melodious and catchy guitar-based pop', while Stein Eastbø's verdict for *VG* was 'consistently good, but not sensational'. At the other end of the spectrum, however, *Puls* writer Anders Finslo clearly had an axe to grind during his incendiary review, which included some rather uncomplimentary remarks about Lauren. 'We are talking about a band with two Spellemann prizes sitting on the mantelpiece,' he complained, 'and a member who is referred to as Norway's undisputed "pop king".'

The band also had to endure the disappointment of poor ticket sales on certain tour dates, and *Dagsavisen* sensationally reported that only 19 people had pre-booked tickets for a show in Kristiansand, while they also claimed that only 50 people had seen the band perform in Stavanger. However, some of the fans in attendance during this tour reported that the performances were among the best of Savoy's career to date, and there were several glowing reviews in the media, too. Other positives to take from this period included another Spellemann nomination (for Best Pop Group).

SAVOY – SAVOY SONGBOOK VOL. 1 (2007 Album)

Produced by Michael Ilbert and Savoy
Chart position: 7 (Norway)

Once his promotional duties with Savoy had concluded in 2004, Pål's musical pendulum swung back to a-ha, with the recording of *Analogue* scheduled for February 2005. With Pål committed to a-ha, Savoy effectively went into hibernation before re-emerging with the *Savoy Songbook* album in 2007.

Aside from working on a brace of tracks for *Analogue*, Frode Unneland worked on projects such as *The Miniature Mile* – the follow-up to Popium's 2004 album,

Camp – during the interim, while Lauren contributed to Anneli Drecker's second solo album, *Frolic*, in 2005, a vocal part on 'The Monkey Trap'. 'I originally sang the harmony myself,' said Anneli, 'but I thought it would be better to have Lauren's voice blending in with mine, so that the message in the lyrics would come out more. If two people say that "the monkey trap is dangerous", then it is a statement – if one person says it, it is more an assumption. Also, that song and those lyrics are inspired by the movie *Mulholland Drive*, and it was Lauren who told me to go and see it, so I had her in my mind while composing and programming the song. I think our voices blend perfectly together on this song.' The track, which *Dagbladet*'s Øyvind Rønning declared as one of the highlights of the album, also included a highly effective Blancmange sample. 'Well spotted!' said Anneli. 'I was a huge fan of Blancmange since 81! My original demo version was without that sample, but I needed a groove and sampled "Don't Tell Me" for fun. It was meant to be a remix but my label wanted the version with the sample in it for the album. So now I share 50/50 royalties with Blancmange on that track, which I really do not mind at all! They contacted me on Myspace – this was before Facebook – and said they loved the song! One of the best days in my whole career – it was like getting an email from Santa Claus!'

In addition to his work with a-ha, Pål also found time to add a vocal to Furia's 'Goodbye Sweet Sorrow', a fine track – lifted from their 2006 album, *Piece of Paradise* – which included lyrics that could so easily have adorned one of the pages of his many notebooks ('The times that I fall down / You're always there to catch me / Suffering in silence / Defenceless and fragile').

BIGGER AUDIENCE

Savoy's next project was a career retrospective, featuring an album of seven rerecordings and three new tracks, plus a second disc of previously released band favourites. This wasn't a particularly novel concept as pop history shows that many acts have rerecorded their own material in the past. For example,

Kraftwerk's 1991 album, *The Mix*, featured new versions of some of their best work (effectively serving as a 'greatest hits'), while in 2004, Brian Wilson rerecorded abandoned tracks that dated back to the Beach Boys' legendary *Smile* sessions in the late 60s. Even a-ha have rerecorded their own songs, the best examples being their ersatz take on 'The Living Daylights', and, much further down the line, an acoustic rendition of 'Take On Me'. (In recent years, acts such as Blondie, Kate Bush, Squeeze and the Wonder Stuff have all tinkered with their back catalogue, with varying degrees of success.)

As Pål explained, the opportunity to revisit their back catalogue and freshen up some of the songs was difficult to resist: 'We feel that we have a really good back catalogue, which deserves a bigger audience. The previous albums have been released in Norway and in some other countries. When we decided to make a collection of Savoy songs for a wider release, we wanted to record them again to make it sound fresh . . . I have always envied Woody Allen who gets to do his films two times; once to see how everything looks, and another time that is the final version. That's the way it should be done!'[8]

Boasting a bigger recording budget than they were accustomed to, the *Savoy Songbook* album was co-produced by Michael Ilbert – who had also worked on *Analogue* – during a highly productive two-week period at LoHo Studios in New York, and many of the tracks were cut live. 'Our previous recordings have been more of a piecemeal,' said Pål. 'We recorded some parts, and added other instruments little by little. This time we were all sitting in a ring in the studio recording the songs live. Eighty per cent of the sound on the songs will be from one take, and the rest is overdubs. This gives the recording session another dynamic.'[9]

According to Pål, the band recorded 18 songs and chose the ones that worked the best for the album. Lauren, however, had to be convinced about the inclusion of 'Lackluster Me' and pushed for more uptempo material to be included: 'That's how it's always been with Pål,' she said. 'He writes ballads, and then others have to convince him to increase the tempo. That's what happened with a lot of the a-ha songs as well.'[10]

CORRECTION FLUID

Of the new tracks presented, 'Karma Boomerang' impressed the most, and it was released as a promotional single in April 2007. The track was once again inspired by New York – in this case, the Grey Dog coffee house in Carmine Street, a few blocks away from the couple's home. 'They have a jar for tips with the writing "Karma Boomerang",' explained Pål. 'I guess the idea is that it gives you good karma to put some money in it, that what you give comes back in return to you. I thought that deserved a song.'[11] With its sleek harmonies and infectious chorus, the catchy pop song was redolent of the band's *Mountains of Time* period. *VG*'s Thomas Talseth was also impressed: 'The married couple's project may not always have received fair treatment, but one thing is certain, "Karma Boomerang" is better than most of the material that a-ha have included on their last few albums. The song is remarkably nice and safe, but also irresistibly ingratiating.'

With regard to the rerecordings, it's questionable whether there were significant improvements to the original tracks, and it's arguable that a single-disc compilation may have served as a better introduction to the band. This view was partly shared by *VG*'s Morten Ståle Nilsen when the album was released in Norway in August 2007. 'CD 2, which probably should have been the first disc of this collection, still shows that their best moments are both stronger and more varied than one might think at first.' Elsewhere, *Dagsavisen*'s Bernt Erik Pedersen wrote: 'In little moments, this collection shows Pål Waaktaar-Savoy's greatness as a songwriter . . . But too often he disappears into a grey fog of whining indie rock.' *Aftenposten*'s Cecilie Asker described the rerecordings as 'pop with correction fluid', and added: 'Savoy are more concerned about correcting old mistakes than risking potential new ones'.

According to Pål, there are no immediate plans to release a second volume.

DREAM TICKET

In May 2008, the three members of a-ha came together to showcase their side projects at some unique shows in both Oslo and London. A dream ticket for a-ha fans, Magne, Morten and Pål each performed individual sets before converging as a-ha for a brief set that included a taste of their next album. 'I remember thinking that this is my last show ever, now I can quit,' said Frode Unneland years later. 'But that was only for a short moment. I remember being quite nervous but I think it turned out to be a very good show.'

Both Morten and Magne had released new albums that month – *Letter from Egypt* and *A Dot of Black in the Blue of Your Bliss*, respectively – while the Genepool label had picked up Savoy's album for UK release that month. According to Morten, this interesting marketing idea came from one of his bandmates. 'It was Magne who threw the idea into the lap of our promoter in England,' he said. 'He immediately got such a good response that Magne had to say, "Hold on, the others don't know about it yet, they probably don't want to!"'[12]

CHAPTER TWENTY-ONE

KRYPTONITE

Like Pål, Magne managed to maintain a high musical profile throughout the first decade of the new millennium, and a veritable explosion of creativity – described by him as a 'dam that broke' – resulted in both a huge stockpile of poems and his first bona fide solo albums. This was of course concurrent to a-ha's recording, touring and promotional commitments, plus various other music-related projects.

There was also the occasional art commission which – true to his high profile and his increasing reputation in that field – attracted headlines, both nationally and internationally. In 2000, Posten Norge (the Norwegian postal service) invited Magne to create a stamp to tie in with Valentinsdagen [Valentine's Day] the following February. Having collected stamps 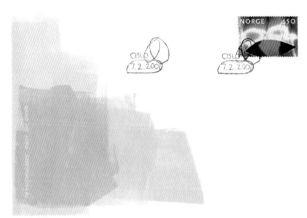 during his youth, Magne was grateful for the opportunity and threw himself into the project, unconventionally – and painstakingly – creating his miniature designs in 1:1 scale using tweezers. The following year, Magne attracted headlines for all the wrong reasons. Following the commission of a Christmas tree decoration outside Oslo's main railway station, Magne controversially used banknotes and coins from his 14,000 kroner fee to adorn the tree. 'It shows a new quality that we don't usually associate with money,' he told a-ha's official website. 'It can have an aesthetic beauty.' Unsurprisingly, the tree was soon after stripped by thieves, and Magne was accused of self-indulgence.

In addition to further exhibition work, new songs were written, some of which he said weren't really suited to a-ha. 'It wasn't until a-ha got back together in 2000 that I rediscovered my childhood passion for making three or four-minute pop songs,' he said. 'But I started to realise I wasn't being completely fulfilled in the group and suddenly this material began coming out of me that I felt didn't belong in an a-ha situation. Initially, I wrote them as a-ha songs but then I realised it wasn't about that – it was a more personal journey and I recorded them as a solo project.'[1]

MAGNE F – PAST PERFECT FUTURE TENSE (2004 Album)
Produced by Magne F and Martin Terefe
Chart position: 14 (Norway)

It feels a bit silly to say this, but I recorded this album feeling that it is this decade's
most important record. It is, at least, the best material that I have ever created.
– Magne Furuholmen, *VG*, 2004

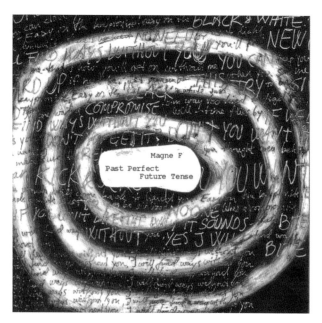

The title of Magne's debut solo album was, ostensibly, a summary of a-ha's career up until that point, juxtaposing the glamour of their early successes and the tensions of more recent years. (The keyboardist had even suggested it as a title for their 2003 live album, though the idea was reportedly rejected by Pål.) As both the quality and prolificacy of his recent songwriting output had suggested, Magne had hit something of a purple patch and, given that a-ha were now out of contract – for the time being at least – it seemed only logical that he would exploit a gap in his busy schedule and record a long-overdue solo album.

Magne had of course already provided lead vocals for the 'Dragonfly' single – as well as a-ha's 'The Way We Talk' and 'The Summers of Our Youth' – but for a musician who wasn't famed for his vocal abilities, a whole album featuring his distinctly fragile and weathered voice was uncharted territory. 'I sing out of pure necessity, just to convey my lyrics,' he said. 'If I am going to publish a solo record, first I must dare to show who I really am . . . I have to sing with the voice I have. I'm no Morten Harket – vocally, he is a nuclear weapon next to my firecracker – so the most important thing is to show it as it is.'[2]

The album was co-produced by Martin Terefe and recorded at the Swedish musician's Kensaltown recording studio in London, which had opened in January 2004. Although Magne played many of the instruments, some of the songs were enriched by strings, while other guest players included trumpeter Nils Petter Molvær, Travis guitarist Andy Dunlop, drummer (and web designer) Frode Lamøy and Mercury Music Prize nominee Ed Harcourt.

Perhaps more significantly, the album also featured Coldplay's rhythm section of Guy Berryman (bass) and Will Champion (drums) on a handful of tracks. 'We met when both our bands were on the road,' explained Magne. 'Chris Martin had been waxing lyrical about a-ha in the music press and there's a lot of respect between our bands. I played Guy the demos of my solo album and he became involved and brought Will with him. They have something special with what they do in Coldplay and you recognise it when they get going.'[3]

Magne's vocals – pitched somewhere between Chris Martin and the Flaming Lips' Wayne Coyne – proved to be the ideal conduit for a dazzling array of introspective lyrics that were among his best to date, offering a revealing portrait of a musician hitting middle age. But while the songs daringly revealed some of their writer's vulnerabilities, Magne's quirky sense of humour was still prevalent throughout, ranging from acerbic put-downs on 'Kryptonite' ('No one likes a compromise / If you don't like the way it sounds / Well, bite me') to almost Monty Python-like couplets on 'All the Time' ('And everything you've learned is shit / You don't know what to do with it').

The musical influences, meanwhile, were seemingly numerous, with the chilling lo-fi folk of 'Little Angels' immediately calling to mind Radiohead. Elsewhere, 'You Don't Have to Change' could easily have been penned by Neil Finn, while 'All the Time' subtly recalled the melodic artistry of Burt Bacharach. '2cu Shine' bore a Prince-like title and splashes of U2-esque guitar, while the John Lennon influence on 'No One Gets Me but U' was a tad more obvious, evoking the Beatles musician's cathartic Plastic Ono Band period, while daringly name-checking his childhood heroes in the process ('Every dreamer needs a doer to get things done / Every Paul needs a Yoko to be a John'). Other standouts included 'Kryptonite', with its rustic electronica and strong chorus, the luxuriant ballad 'Envelop Me', which wouldn't have sounded out of place on Ed Harcourt's *Here Be Monsters* album, and the R.E.M.-like title track itself, whose lyrics may well have been an acknowledgement of strained relationships within the band ('There was a road we could have gone down / To avoid our recent disasters / I remember so well what you said to me / We are who we were always going to be'). 'Past Perfect Future Tense' – which had been performed at the Vinterspillene [Winter Games] festival in Lillehammer earlier in the year – was also released as a single, accompanied by a promotional video that was directed by Magne. 'Kryptonite' was also released as a single in the UK, ahead of the album's March 2005 release there.

PAIN IS GREY

Perhaps fearing that his surname of Furuholmen was a mouthful for the average buyer, the album was simply credited to Magne F, while the release on his own Passionfruit label further emphasised a low-key approach. The reviews of the album were mixed, particularly in the Norwegian media, with many outlets rightly praising the songs but rather unfairly criticising the vocals. 'Furuholmen can write gorgeous songs,' wrote *VG*'s Espen A. Hansen. 'He demonstrates that fully on *Past Perfect Future Tense*. On the other hand, he has a voice that, basically, only a mother could truly love. Still, it works in an odd way.' Thomas Olsen's miserly 2/6 review for *Panorama* was considerably more blunt, however: 'Furuholmen has emphasised in several interviews that he sings with the voice he has. Yes, but sometimes silence *is* actually golden.' In his review for *Dagbladet*, Sven Ove Bakke had a contrary view, stating: 'One of Magne Furuholmen's great strengths is that he doesn't really sing that well,' while *Adresseavisen*'s reviewer praised Magne for his 'thought-provoking and well written lyrics that rise above the obvious and clichéd.' In the UK, the album reviews were mainly positive, however, and it was eloquently described by *The Scotsman* as 'lush, epic, folk-tinged rock.'

The Norwegian release of the album in September 2004 coincided with a new

art exhibition, *Payne's Gray*, which launched at the Henie Onstad Art Centre. With its melancholy title a play on words ('pain is grey'), the exhibition saw Magne deliberately utilising a drab colour palette. 'All the good reviews I have received have focused on being a good colourist,' he told *Adresseavisen*, 'which is why I have now moved in the opposite direction. If I do what is expected of me, I put myself in an artistic checkmate. I always have to operate beyond my expectations.'

The exhibition included William S. Burroughs-style cut-ups of various lyrics and poetry, rearranged to add a unique perspective to each print. A 264-page book, featuring artwork, poetry and photography, was also published to coincide with the exhibition, which later travelled to London's Paul Stolper Gallery and the Edinburgh Printmakers studio. Both the album and exhibition were heavily promoted by Magne, and there were a number of tour dates. Magne's live band included Rune Lamøy (bass) and Frode Lamøy (drums), plus guitarist Dan Sunhordvik, who would appear on Magne's next album.

MAGNE F – A DOT OF BLACK IN THE BLUE OF YOUR BLISS (2008 Album)
Produced by Various
Chart position: N/A

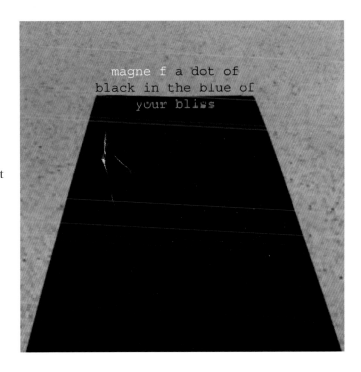

By the spring of 2005, a-ha had started work on the *Analogue* album, a project that would see Magne maintaining his solid songwriting form. Its subsequent release and accompanying tour would ensure that a follow-up to the well-received *Past Perfect Future Tense* set wouldn't appear for another three years, but the self-confessed workaholic still managed to work on several other projects during this busy period.

In addition to further exhibitions and commissions, Magne contributed to the recording of 'Indian Ocean', Cat Stevens' first pop record since 1978's *Back to Earth* album. Following his conversion to the Muslim faith in December 1977, the writer of classics such as 'Matthew and Son', 'The First Cut Is the Deepest' and 'Wild World' had changed his name to Yusuf Islam, sold his guitars and shunned the music world for many years, but a gradual return to the limelight culminated in the writing of a brand new single in aid of children orphaned in the wake of the

Boxing Day tsunami in 2004. 'Like everyone else, I was so shaken by the enormity of this human tragedy, and the song just came without effort,' said Islam. 'It is my contribution towards helping to rebuild the broken spirits of the victims of the disaster.'[4]

The assembled band included Magne, Ed Harcourt, Travis drummer Neil Primrose and Ged Lynch, a former member of Black Grape and the Icicle Works. 'I've been a huge fan of Cat Stevens from before,' Magne told a-ha's official website. 'Hearing new material coming out of Yusuf's mouth was kind of mind-blowing.'

The project was also dear to his heart since a-ha's former saxophonist Sigurd Køhn and his son had died during the tsunami. Further to the January 2005 recording session, Magne also donated a piece from the *Payne's Gray* exhibition to a Red Cross auction – *Kunst for flomofrene* [Art for the Flood Victims] – at the Henie Onstad Art Centre. 'Little Angels' was also dedicated to Køhn at a benefit show that month, while a-ha dedicated 'I Call Your Name' to their former bandmate during their Frognerparken show in the summer.

THE LONGEST NIGHT

At the end of 2005, the trumpeter Nils Petter Molvær released his highly acclaimed album *er*, which included a piano part from Magne on 'Only These Things Count'. Molvær and Magne had previously been commissioned to perform an experimental, multifaceted piece – featuring loops and electronics from Raymond C. Pellicer – during the Vinterspillene festival in February 2004. The pair later provided original music for a highly rated four-part NRK documentary, *På jakt etter paradiset* [In Search of Paradise] – broadcast in 2008 – about the Norwegian explorer Thor Heyerdahl, who had famously led the Kon-Tiki expedition in 1947, sailing by raft from Peru to the Tuamotu Islands in Polynesia.

Magne also played keyboards on *Banquise*, the second album by the French musician Cyril Paulus. Released in 2006, the Martin Terefe-produced album also included guest players Ed Harcourt and Neil Primrose.

Later in the year, Magne and Terefe also produced the debut album by the Oslo-based band Harrys Gym. According to a report in *Dagbladet* in February 2007, the songs had been recorded at Terefe's Kensaltown studios during an 'intense three months', but the recordings were eventually abandoned after the band grew tired of life in London. The band's singer, Anne Lise Frøkedal – whose sister, Linn, would later perform with Savoy in 2018 – told NRK P3: 'I think all of us were pleased with the finished album, but the problem was, it took an incredibly long time to get anything released. So we decided to go home.' The band eventually recorded a self-produced and self-titled album, featuring largely all-new material, at their own studio in Oslo, releasing it to high acclaim in October 2008. Frøkedal added: 'We are much more satisfied with this album than the one we did over there.'

Magne was also one of the contributors – along with Martin Terefe associates such as Ron Sexsmith – to the soundtrack of the award-winning 2007 movie *The Longest Night in Shanghai*, which was described in some quarters as China's answer to the Sofia Coppola classic *Lost in Translation*. The film centres around a Chinese taxi driver and a Japanese make-up artist who have been thrown together by fate. The soundtrack, titled *Travel with Music*, included the short instrumentals 'Guy Romance' and 'Bass Theme', written by Magne, Martin Terefe and Guy Berryman.

Perhaps more significantly, the following year also saw the debut of Magne's new experimental combo, Apparatjik, a name that was ostensibly derived from the Russian word *apparatchik* (meaning 'bureaucrat'), although a more verbose explanation would arrive later. The fledgling band included not only Terefe and Berryman but also Jonas Bjerre from the Danish rock band Mew, whom Magne was a fan of.

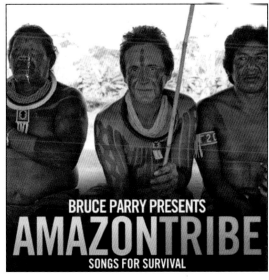

The supergroup had originally come together to provide the theme – titled 'Ferreting' – for the BBC documentary series *Amazon*. 'It was actually the idea of a mutual friend of ours, Martin Terefe, who's a producer,' Berryman told Coldplay's official website. 'We wrote and recorded that song in a very small studio in Copenhagen in about three hours, so we were quite surprised to see it being received so well.' The track was also issued as a promotional single, while the tie-in soundtrack album, *Songs for Survival*, included other exclusive songs by various acts – many of which were in collaboration with indigenous musicians – including Johnny Borrell (Razorlight), Hot Chip, Yusuf Islam, Skin (Skunk Anansie), KT Tunstall, will.i.am and Mike Oldfield, whose daughter, Molly, produced the album with Martin Terefe. All profits from the release were donated to Survival International, a charity that campaigns for the rights of indigenous peoples. 'I hope the album is going to raise awareness about the beautiful people and tribes of this earth who have been lost without us even knowing,' wrote Yusuf Islam in the album's liner notes. 'It's a matter of making people aware and that is what we are all joining in to do.'

RISE TO THE CHALLENGE

By the time of *Amazon*'s broadcast on the BBC in October 2008, Magne's second solo album had been in UK shops for almost six months, licensed to the same label – Genepool – that had released Savoy's *Songbook* retrospective the same month (May). The album had been recorded at Lou Mazuc on the French Riviera the previous summer, while some of the songs were performed during the third annual *Punktfestivalen* in Kristiansand at the end of August 2007. Magne's live band at that time included Jonny Sjo (bass) and Karl Oluf Wennerberg (drums).

As for the album's personnel, Sjo and Wennerberg were joined by bassist Guy Berryman and guitarist Dan Sundhordvik, who'd previously worked with singer Venke Knutson. (Knutson later competed with – among others – Morten's daughter Tomine for the chance to represent Norway at the Eurovision Song Contest in Bærum in 2010.) Production was simply credited to 'the people who made the record', which included the string arranger, Bernt Moen, and the technicians, George Tanderø and Jon Marius Aareskjold.

While Martin Terefe was ostensibly not involved with the recording of the album itself, his influence could certainly be felt on tracks such as 'Running Out of Reasons', a folky, Nick Drake-sounding track which included some subtle sonar-like effects, reminiscent of the production on the *Analogue* album. Like other tracks on the album, the riff was repurposed for a-ha's next album (see 'Riding the Crest'), while the song itself was later covered by Tini Flaat Mykland.

Significantly, Terefe also had a hand in the writing of 'The Longest Night', a title that was likely sourced from the film *The Longest Night in Shanghai*, whose soundtrack both he and Magne had contributed to. One of the standout cuts on the album, the bright melody and verses were later utilised in a highly effective remodelling of 2009's 'Foot of the Mountain'.

One other track to get the 'green' treatment was 'Come Back', whose keyboard refrain was later recycled for 'The Bandstand'. The song itself, whose melody recalled the gnarly Britpop tones of 'Slide Away' by Oasis, was also notable for its gritty lyrics ('Come down off your pedestal / Come down off your high horse / Come get some dirt under your fingernails').

While it's arguable that the songs didn't quite match the quality of its predecessor, this was in many ways a far more satisfying collection, with the increased use of synths adding some welcome texture throughout. The musicianship, too, had improved, while the vocals were noticeably less fragile and tentative, with some of the new songs – particularly the U2-esque 'Too Far, Too Fast' – benefitting from a more confident and upfront delivery. Other standout tracks included the John Lennon-channelling ballad 'Time and Place', which one critic likened to Coldplay, and the title track itself, which included gently pulsating synths and some typically compelling lyrics ('The brown grassy hills of your wall to wall / The fake ancient war chest beats in the hall / The prophetic words in the library all speak of isolation')

QUICK TO CRITICISE

Although the alliteratively titled *A Dot of Black in the Blue of Your Bliss* received a commercial release in May 2008, it had actually been released as a slimmed-down six-track mini-album at the beginning of the year, with Magne creating some unique artwork to go with each of the signed limited edition copies. (The artwork was divided up from a giant piece that the musician had put together in Oslo City Hall's west tower on 22 January.) The album was then made available for download via his Myspace site, a medium he'd previously used to upload some of the album's demos.

In April, another unique six-track version of the album was released, with 'Come Back' being replaced by 'Watch This Space'. Perhaps taking inspiration from Prince, who had controversially given away copies of his then-current album, *Planet Earth*, with copies of the *Mail on Sunday* newspaper the previous year, the special CD was cover-mounted to copies of the Norwegian fashion magazine *Elle*.

As for the album reviews, to a certain extent these mirrored those of Magne's previous release, with some critics once again deciding to focus on the vocal aspect of the product. 'He writes songs that could easily fit in with the rest of the a-ha repertoire,' wrote *Bergensavisen*'s Bjørn Tore Brøske. '. . . However, the somewhat weak vocals lessen the overall quality of an otherwise very nice, organic and melodious album.' The view was echoed by *Dagsavisen*'s writer in their 4/6 review: 'He can write songs, but he can't sing. His voice is weak and unimpressive, and so many of these recordings sound like demos . . . But, in spite of it all, the songs are pretty good.' Elsewhere, *Dagbladet*'s Øyvind Rønning was keen to make yet another Coldplay comparison, despite the fact that the 'Yellow' hitmakers had actually been heavily influenced by a-ha: 'It sounds like Magne is coming out of a rehearsal with Coldplay – especially on "Running Out of Reasons" – but in no way can he match Chris Martin's vocal splendour.'

As part of a unique triple bill that also included Morten and Savoy, the album was promoted by Magne and his band during shows at both the Rockefeller in Oslo and London's Royal Albert Hall. The mini-tour was also preceded by a series of warm-up shows – using the 'Fagmen' pseudonym – at the Palace Grill in Oslo. 'This is almost like the times before a-ha started,' said Magne. 'I think this has given me heart palpitations – this is almost more risky than when we played for 200,000 in Rio!'

CHAPTER TWENTY-TWO
SHOOTING STAR

With the wheels of the a-ha machine in full motion during the first half of the decade, it was virtually impossible for Morten to commit to the recording of a new solo album. As the singer would explain, running two projects concurrently was not an option, and a-ha ultimately took priority: 'I find myself in a very difficult situation, because I am so ready to carry on with what I'm doing – it's all I want, basically,' he reflected. 'But then, all of a sudden, I sit there also with some very promising and interesting signals from the band – from Pål and Magne – and I find myself in a tight spot, where I either become the one who blocks a new round with a-ha because I choose to do my own stuff, or I put my own stuff aside, which is eventually what I did.'[1]

But while Morten felt he had to park his solo album ambitions, he did find the time to work on several (low-key) projects. In December 2000, EMI released a Salvation Army charity album in Norway titled *Perleporten* [Pearly Gates], which had been produced by Jørn Christensen, who'd previously worked with the likes of CC Cowboys, Cirkus Modern, deLillos, De Press and Roxette. The project – which also included Bel Canto, Bjørn Eidsvåg and DumDum Boys' Prepple Houmb – saw Morten duetting with Velvet Belly's Spellemann award-winning singer Anne Marie Almedal on 'Han er min sang og min glede' [He Is My Song and My Joy], a gorgeous stripped-back version of a country standard that had previously been recorded by Elvis Presley and ABBA's Anni-Frid Lyngstad.

In November 2001, Sølvguttene released *Sølvguttene synger julen inn* [The Silver Boys Sing Christmas], which included Morten's sumptuous interpretation of 'Mitt hjerte alltid vanker' [My Heart Always Wanders], a traditional Scandinavian Christmas hymn that dates back to the 18th century. (Morten had previously performed the song on Norwegian TV in December 1987.)

At the other end of the musical spectrum, the Pakistani Sufi rock outfit Junoon released a compilation album, *Daur-e-Junoon*, in March 2002, which included a studio version of 'Piya (Ocean of Love)', a song Morten had performed with the band during a show in Oslo in September 2001.

Morten also performed on a similarly Eastern-flavoured track by Earth Affair in 2004. Co-written with Håvard Rem, 'Gildas Prayer' appeared on both a promotional single and an album titled *Chapter One*. Described as a 'a groove mixture of jazz, hip-hop and ambient influences from around the globe', the album was masterminded by Gulli Briem, a drummer and founding member of the Icelandic jazz-funk band Mezzoforte, who had enjoyed a Top 20 hit in the UK with 'Garden Party' in 1983.

MORTEN HARKET – LETTER FROM EGYPT (2008 Album)

Produced by Kjetil Bjerkestrand
Co-produced by Morten Harket
Chart position: 1 (Norway), 33 (Germany)

The recording and subsequent promotion of a-ha's *Analogue* album had kept both Morten and his bandmates busy between 2005 and 2006. The band wouldn't start recording their next album until 2008, so there was a convenient break in the schedule to record the long-awaited English-language follow-up to *Wild Seed.*

Produced by long-standing musical associate Kjetil Bjerkestrand, *Letter from Egypt* included a number of musicians who were well known to Morten, including Dance with a Stranger guitarist Frode Alnæs, D'Sound bassist Jonny Sjo and a-ha drummer Per Lindvall.

The new album mainly comprised songs Morten had co-written with Ole Sverre Olsen. 'The album is mirroring things that have happened now,' he said, 'but also stuff from back then, and I am sitting on a lot of material that I haven't released. There's a lot more songs than what this album is representing; it's just 12 songs, and it's not enough!'[2]

As for the title of both the song and the album, Morten explained: 'This song was written in Egypt, and it comes in a shape of a letter. In a sense, it's a letter to ourselves.' He added: 'The songs on the album are essentially interrelated to each other, so you'll find other aspects of what is in the lyrics of "Letter from Egypt" in other songs.'[3]

While most of the songs had been composed by Morten and Ole Sverre Olsen, the album's lead-off single, 'Movies' – released in November 2007 – was a cover version of 'My Woman' by the Norwegian band Locomotives, who had disbanded in 2001. Morten had been a long-time admirer of the song, following a serendipitous meeting with the band in 1994. The original track, which later appeared on Locomotives' 1999 album, *Albert*, was almost demo-like, with its minimal use of vocal and guitar and metronomic percussion, but its infectious chorus – which was given a slightly quirky lyrical tweak – seemed purpose-built for Morten, and its selection for single release was certainly justified. Along

with the title track of his new album, the song was performed at the Nobel Peace Prize Concert in December 2007, while a snippet of the single was also featured in a Sony Ericsson mobile phone advert, which was also broadcast around that time.

The next single to be released, in April 2008, was 'Darkspace' – subtitled 'You're with Me' – which featured another strong chorus and a memorable riff. ('All of You Concerned', a bonus track on the single, had originally been written during the *Wild Seed* era, but the melody was adapted for *Vogts Villa*'s 'Jeg kjenner ingen fremtid'.) With regard to the lyrics, Morten explained: 'This "dark space" is a place inside yourself, when you are by yourself, and you take with you whatever it is you take with you, and you close everything else out, because that thing that's with you is so important.'[4]

A NAME IS A NAME

Another promotional single, released in June, saw a more familiar name on the publishing credits. 'We'll Never Speak Again' had previously appeared on 1997's *Hotel Oslo* soundtrack album – which had been written and recorded by Magne and Kjetil Bjerkestrand – and later cut during sessions for a-ha's comeback album, *Minor Earth Major Sky*. Morten's repurposed version of the song, featuring Magne instead of Anneli Drecker on backing vocals, was one of the album's standout cuts. (Magne was also credited with inspiring the 'Marley' chant on the title track.) 'I am impressed by the high pitch he chose to sing in, I must say,' said Anneli. 'He could have made it easier for himself but that is not what Morten is about. To me, it is just a different version, neither better nor worse. But it is never boring to listen to Morten singing.'

Other highlights included 'Send Me an Angel', a more electronic-based track that was perhaps better suited to a-ha, while the more abstract 'There Are Many Ways to Die' included some captivating imagery in its ghostly verses ('I hear the sound of water / Boats are drifting by / I've been waiting here for centuries'). Elsewhere, the album's title track was beautifully enriched by the choral voices of Sølvguttene, whom Morten and Savoy had previously collaborated with.

One track became the theme song for *A Name Is a Name*, Sigurjón Einarsson's movie about Macedonia, which was described as 'a film about a nation held hostage because of its name'. The Icelandic film-maker was a long-time friend of Morten's, and the pair had previously worked together on the East Timor

documentary *Sometimes I Must Speak Out Strongly*. (The 2009 film also included 'Jewels up High' by Gulli Briem – another of Morten's previous collaborators – and this track later appeared on the second Earth Affair album, *Liberté*, released in 2014.)

One track that, arguably, didn't fit was 'Shooting Star', and this throwaway number was replaced with 'Slanted Floor' on the German edition of the album.

RETURN TO SENDER

While *Letter from Egypt* provided Morten with two Top 5 hit singles in Norway, the media in his homeland weren't particularly receptive to the album and its largely mid-tempo range. Indeed, *VG*'s Stein Østbø criticised the album for its 'mid-paced monotony' before concluding: 'Morten Harket can sing the phone directory and make it seem both melodic and lyrically exciting. There is a security in it, and that is the keyword with this record – safe.' Østbø's criticism of the album was also mirrored by *Panorama*'s Dagfinn Bergesen, who amusingly headed up his 2/6 review with 'Return to Sender'. 'Most of the songs are uninteresting and seem to lack spirit and empathy,' he wrote. '. . . *Letter from Egypt* is an unexciting and highly ordinary release from an artist who deserves better.' Elsewhere, *Adresseavisen*'s Ole Jacob Hoel wrote: 'Things never take off . . . Most of it becomes a bit like refined 90s adult pop; craftsmanship according to the book.'

In terms of both its critical and commercial impact, the album didn't quite hit the heights of its predecessor, but it did provide the singer with a second chart-topper in Norway. Plans to promote the album internationally were cancelled, though, as a-ha were due to start recording their ninth studio album in the autumn.

WALLS OF SEPARATION

Morten also lent his vocal talents to the ambitious *Songs Across Walls of Separation* project, which had been curated by *Poetenes Evangelium* producer Erik Hillestad. Three years in the making, the project entailed the unusual process of sourcing vocal parts from various musicians across the globe, and then building an original composition around each of the recordings. The new melodies were painstakingly created by Hillestad's studio band – comprising Anders Engen, Audun Erlien and Knut Reiersrud – before being given something of a Westernised twist, which involved bringing in singers such as Sarah Jane Morris (who had initially enjoyed some success in the 80s with the Communards) and Tom Russell. Morten's contribution to this 'virtual' album of cross-cultural duets was 'Garden of Love / Kar Sa Myon', a collaboration with the Asian singers Rukhsana Murtaza and Abdul Rashid Farash.

The September 2008 release of the album tied in with a peace concert

at Vågen harbour in Stavanger, with Morten performing a 12-song set on a bill that included actors, singers, children's choirs and amateur theatre groups, the aim of which was to raise awareness about child refugees, as well as highlighting the need to break down the walls separating the rich from the poor.

PART SEVEN
THE LAST HURRAH
2009-2010

CHAPTER TWENTY-THREE
FOOT OF THE MOUNTAIN

Making and finishing the album is a pain in the neck. But the initial moments, when you have something and it turns into something – when you're writing – there is an energy among the three of us that only happens when [we] are together. That energy is still infectious.
– Magne Furuholmen, *The Guardian*, 2009

Released: June 2009
Chart position: 5 (UK), 1 (Norway), 1 (Germany)

Despite the fact that *Analogue* had deservedly earned a-ha some of their best reviews in years – not to mention a first visit to the Top 10 of the UK singles chart in 18 years with the title track – it was reported in the Norwegian media that it was the band's poorest-selling album to date. Although it's arguable that the album lacked uptempo tracks, there was no doubting the quality of the product – nor the efforts of both the band and their new record label in promoting it – so it came as something of a surprise that *Analogue* had underperformed in key territories such as Germany and the UK. The buck, ostensibly, stopped with the band's manager, and *VG* reported in April 2006 that a-ha had parted company with Brian Lane. When Pål spoke to them the following year, it was apparent that the guitarist didn't miss him: 'Morten, Magne and myself like to do our own things in addition to a-ha,' he said, 'but Brian Lane regarded side projects as a threat – that they were actually a sabotage for the whole of a-ha – while we ourselves didn't see it as a problem at all. Quite the contrary, we feel that it strengthens the band.'

Lane's position, following an operational shake-up, was filled by Harald Wiik, a former musician who had scored a Norwegian Top 5 hit in 1990 with the Celtic rock-flavoured 'Brave Young Boy', as one half of Money Talks (which included his brother Sverre). (The duo's track 'In a Trance' had been included on the soundtrack for *The Karate Kid, Part III* the previous year.) Wiik had also released a single on EMI in 1982 – as Brødrene Wiik – with his brothers, Sverre and Øystein, which included keyboards from Robert Alan Morley, who worked as a technician at Tore Aarnes' Octocon Studio in the mid-80s. Aside from working on recordings by the likes of Y Me and Kjersti Grov, Morley was also privy to some of a-ha's early demos. 'The first time I heard "The Sun Always Shines on TV" and "Take On Me", I knew they had a hit song,' he said. 'I later met Morten in another studio in Oslo called Ambience Studios. I used to work there for a while. I worked a lot with his daughter Tomine on several recordings – mostly dubbing of cartoons and movies, but on some songs as well – so I really know Tomine much better than her father! I also know Harald Wiik very well. We used to play a lot together in the studio, and I also worked with Harald in a studio before he became the manager for a-ha.'

HARALD WIIK

Can you tell me a bit about your musical background?
I come from a classical musical family background where everyone played and had lessons from an early age. Inspired by my older brother Sverre, I ditched piano and got seriously into playing the drums around the age of 10 and have played in various bands ever since. We always had big ambitions, and the success of a-ha was the direct reason for Sverre and me deciding to move to Los Angeles with Money Talks and getting signed by Curb/MCA. We never quite made it, but the six years we spent in Los Angeles were a great experience and I still feel those years are the foundation for all I do today. I am also very thankful for working with our manager at the time, Paul Palmer, and our producers Kim Bullard

and David J. Holman. Tremendous, knowledgeable lads helping us avoid getting lost In Hollywood!

How well did you know Magne, Morten and Pål before they shot to fame in the mid-80s?
I didn't know any of them, but I followed their every move in 1985 – from both a musician's and a Norwegian's perspective. I can still remember exactly where I was and how it felt when 'Take On Me' went to No. 1 in the USA – I was a huge fan!

Do you have any favourite albums or tracks?
My favourite albums are the first two, and my favourite track is 'Hunting High and Low' with the live strings.

How did you end up managing the band?
I worked with Pål and Savoy from 1999, and he was the only one I knew, even though I had briefly met Magne and Morten. Up until then I had tried all sorts of things in the music business with varying degrees of success. I had tried my luck as an artist and writer, produced records, worked as an A&R at Sony Music Norway, as well as doing some booking and management. In 2002 I got really fed up with the music business and started law school. That went really well until Pål called in 2005 to ask me to help him look at some a-ha agreements. During the fall of 2005 I started working for a-ha Network alongside the law studies, and in February 2006 I was asked to take over from Brian Lane as their manager. The law studies suffered – even though I finally got my degree – but I finally felt like I had found my place in the record business, and the rest has been a dream come true and a hell of a ride!

A PUSH IN THE RIGHT DIRECTION

Although the band played a few shows in the summer of 2007, most of the *Analogue* tour dates had been completed by the end of November 2006. In May 2007, Pål told *VG* that the band had started work on the next a-ha album, but the project had to be put on hold as each member focused on their individual projects. Pål was the first out of the blocks with the *Savoy Songbook* album that summer and was reportedly so keen to carry on working on the follow-up to *Analogue* that Lauren and Frode were entrusted with starting preliminary work on the next Savoy record without him.

Unfortunately, Magne and Morten were unable to join Pål since they were too busy with their own projects, and the band's impatient guitarist was left to vent his frustrations during an interview on the Norwegian TV channel TVTromsø. 'The trouble with us, is that we're never in sync,' he said. 'Right now, I'm eager to get going on the new album. I'm telling everybody that the new album is coming out next year and that it's going to be great. But the other two are, of course, just starting to get into their solo projects again and want to prioritise those for the time being.'

By the time the band had come together in May 2008 for a mini-tour, there was audial confirmation that work on the next record had resumed. During these unique shows, in which each member of the band played a selection of tracks from their various projects, two brand new a-ha songs were debuted in the finale, and the sound of the infectiously catchy 'Riding the Crest' seemed to indicate a return to the band's synth-pop roots. 'There's something really interesting in the clinical kind of cold sound of a synthetic soundscape,' said Magne. 'I find the grandeur of the songwriting – and the almost operatic approach of Morten's singing – much more appealing to me as a listener in that setting.'[1]

There was certainly a concerted effort to recapture some of the magic of their early recordings but, as Magne later explained, this related more to the band's original methods of building songs up from scratch, rather than simply dusting off the old Korgs, DX7s and LinnDrums:  'By kind of sacrificing the naive sequencing and that very precise arrangement through synthesisers – and little multi-layered motifs and riffs – and moving more towards a rock and orchestral sound, the magic got a bit lost for me,' he said. 'I wanted to reclaim some of that territory . . . Not to try and pick up from where *Stay on These Roads* stopped, not to forget about the mid-career stuff, but to see what would happen if we [brought] that into the mix now. I would have gone even further had I been alone in deciding, but we ended up where we are as a kind of compromise, with everyone kind of doing their bit to reach that result.'[2]

A return to the old way of working was also reflected in both the number of songs on the album (10) and the actual songwriting credits. These largely bore Pål's name, but there were also several co-writes with Magne. 'The outset was quite exciting,' said Magne. 'It showed me, proved to me, over the course of three or four songs – the first five songs of the album, basically – that we can still do interesting stuff together when we co-write, and we can still add something to each other's creative process.'[3]

Morten consciously chose not to contribute material but, as Magne explained, his contribution to the album was not to be underestimated. 'It's very much a three-person effort on every level,' he said, 'and any attempt to write the story differently always kind of bugs me. People do tend to look at it very superficially and then define roles very clearly, based on personality or based on what they think they know, and sometimes we do feel very annoyed . . . It reminds us of the annoying feeling of our early career, of having to point out that we are musicians making music and not just pop stars waving from balconies!'[4] In a separate interview, Morten stated that he always had the final say when it came to the material choices: 'What Pål and Magne present is never a finished song . . . If I can't do anything with the lyrics, I refuse to sing it. Otherwise, I would be a bad singer. Only when I can identify with a song does it have a chance to become good.'[5]

Magne had wanted to title the new album *Digital* – in direct contrast to the more organic *Analogue* – and this more electronic direction was employed during a productive period in the autumn of 2008 at both Water Music in Hoboken (New Jersey) and Beat 360 Studios on Ninth Avenue (New York). 'We spent five weeks in Hoboken recording the first rough version of the album,' said Pål. 'I came with tons of instruments. New [toys] every morning, like old synthesisers and string machines, Omnichord, stylophone, Moog, mellotron, guitars of every shape and size.'[6]

As Pål later revealed, applying a 'Sydenham' mindset in the modern environs of his New York neighbourhood wasn't easy: 'To make a more technology-based album was easier said than done,' he said. 'It's a long time since we've made an album this way, and things have changed somewhat since! Back then, we did all our own programming, often just firing off tones on a synthesiser that you would play for your dear life as the track went down!' He added: 'With the new album, it took some time to get used to current working methods.'[7]

Helming the initial sessions in the US was Beat 360 owner Mark Saunders, a highly experienced studio engineer and producer who had worked with the likes of the Cure, Erasure, Ian McCulloch and Tricky.

MARK SAUNDERS

How did you end up working on Foot of the Mountain?
I think a-ha reached me through my management. They had already started the album with someone else – a friend of mine, Danton Supple, if I remember correctly. I seem to remember asking him what they were like to work with.

Were you a fan of theirs?
I was a big fan of 'Take On Me' – I mean, who couldn't be, it's got one of the all-time greatest pop riffs known to man in it! Living in the US for 21 years, I think I'd forgotten about how many other good songs they'd written – I don't think they got a lot of airplay in the US. I'm a huge pop fan, though, especially of finely crafted synth-pop and a-ha excel in that. Plus, Morten's voice is pretty amazing. I went to see a-ha playing in New York and, a couple of minutes into 'Take On Me', I remembered the ridiculously high note that was yet to come and wondered how Morten would get up to it – but he nailed it beautifully.

Brian Eno once said that sometimes the best thing a producer can do is stay away and make the tea, but other producers of course favour a more hands-on approach. What's your approach?
I like being hands on, especially when it comes to drum programming and synth action. Maybe you should ask Morten this question, though, because at a party at Pål's house a while after the album was finished, he told me I had loads of great ideas but needed a producer to rein them in! I felt this was a bit unfair because he wasn't around a lot of the time when I was working with Magne or Pål. It's true, there were a lot of ideas floating around in the studio, but most of the time I seemed to be working with either Pål or Magne and not much time with both of them in the room at the same time. This was a bit tricky as they had pretty different views about what direction the material should go in. Magne wanted it to stay in a more synth-pop vein while Pål seemed to want to push it into a more organic, indie guitar direction. In the end, the album seemed to end up as a pretty great blend of both Magne's and Pal's influences, but at the time it seemed that quite often we'd switch gears from being in a synth mode to a guitar mode – or vice versa – before we got to finish an idea. In hindsight, I probably should have been tougher in keeping Magne and Pål in the same room more often.

Overall, though, what were Magne, Morten and Pål like to work with?
I have to say that all three of the band are really good guys – very well
rounded, polite and respectful people. And it was great to see a band that

have been together
that long look in great
shape, are healthy
and really enjoying
their lives. One part of
the process I really
enjoyed once was to
record Morten, Pål
and Magne standing
around one mic
singing background
harmonies. They
sounded fabulous
and they seemed to work incredibly well together, too.

One other thing about working with Pål: He would have these great
chord sequences for songs but occasionally would throw an odd one in – a
real spanner in the works! Technically it would work, but pop sensibility
wise, it wouldn't. They would be very un-a-ha-like and he would take a bit
of persuading to drop them for the sake of the band's reputation! There are
certainly none on the final album, thankfully!

What else can you remember about the making of the album?
I felt like a lot of material was already programmed and recorded before
we started at Water Music. That was my first time in that studio and I really
liked it. I know Pål wanted to use a proper old vintage board, but it felt a
bit sacrilegious to me to be in a huge studio with a beautiful big old Neve
[mixing desk] when we were mostly using two channels of it to monitor
the outputs of the Mac running Logic Pro on it! I don't think we used more
than two or three channels at a time for recording guitars, piano or vocals.
The assistant on the session ended up recording vocals in a separate room
because of time restraints, while the rest of us continued working on the
tracks.

One evening, Water Music owner Rob Grenoble took us all out sailing
on the Hudson River on his pretty large yacht when a photographer came
to do a photo shoot for the band. We were out at sunset, and the sun going
down with Manhattan in the background was spectacular.

YOU'RE IN CONTROL NOW

Some of the recordings from these initial sessions were retained, but other tracks
– notably, 'Foot of the Mountain' – were ultimately reworked after the album's
production resumed in January 2009. 'The energy of the city may have had an
effect on the music,' said Morten, 'but we didn't complete [the album] in New
York. We had to go back to Norway just to let things cool off a little and then pick it
up. And we did – we nailed it.'[8]

In terms of the production, there were certainly echoes of *Minor Earth Major
Sky*, in that the album was started in New York and then completed in Europe.
'Things sort of disintegrated a little,' said Magne. 'We brought in Steve Osborne in
the UK and we did some recording at Real World, Peter Gabriel's fantastic studios
down in Bath. The album is essentially split in two. I continued working with
Steve Osborne in the UK and Pål worked pretty much over the phone with Roland
Spremberg in Hamburg. I tried to adhere to the kind of electronic ideas that we
started with, and Pål was going more into a kind of American sound – something
I was trying to get away from. I wanted something more British, I always felt that
this was our return to our British roots, as it were.'[9] (Steve Osborne, whose clients
included the likes of Doves, Happy Mondays, Placebo, New Order and U2, also
mixed the album.)

Guest musicians included drummer (and childhood fan) Karl Oluf Wennerberg,
whose credits included recordings by Bel Canto, Maria Mena and Lene Marlin,
whose chart-topping debut single, 'Unforgivable Sinner', was reportedly the
fastest-selling in Norwegian history. He'd also played on Magne's album *A Dot of
Black in the Blue of Your Bliss*, and has since established himself as an integral part
of a-ha's studio and live set-up.

Magne's vision for a back-to-basics album – with a limit on the number
of outside influences – soon dissipated once other musicians, such as Erik
Ljunggren, were brought in to help with programming, while the addition of
strings on some of the tracks meant that further compromises were made.
However, the resulting album largely adhered to the original brief of creating a
more synth-based product.

NORDIC TIMBRE

The album cover, featuring the iconic spike-shaped mountain of Kyrkja in
Southern Norway, was designed by Martin Kvamme, who had also produced
the *Savoy Songbook* and *Letter from Egypt* artwork. 'The band felt that their
Norwegian background was something that hadn't been explored enough, at least
when it came to album artwork,' wrote Kvamme on Facebook. '. . . The album title
helped us quite a lot. I knew that this was somehow a poetic quote and that they
were not necessarily talking about a mountain, but we wanted something majestic

a-ha

foot of the mountain

the stunning new album

epic ★★★★ the times
a fine specimen ★★★★ independent on sunday
unmistakable pop brilliance **evening standard**
a great return ★★★★ news of the world
a-ha's dark fires still smoulder ★★★ Q

and simple . . . I also wanted it to be quite abstract, so that it appears more like a symbol, rather than an illustration of one specific place.'

Overall, the album didn't attract the same critical response as its predecessor, but many of the UK's reviewers were impressed with the band's new musical direction. In his review for *The Quietus*, Iain Moffat wrote: 'Almost quarter of a century on, they continue to intrigue and inspire in a fashion that many of their ostensible successors could never begin to dream of, and *Foot of the Mountain* very much finds them continuing to play to their strengths.' Elsewhere, *The Times*' Pete Paphides said: 'A-ha's excellent ninth album heralds a partial return to the keyboard-prodding simplicity of their early records – refracted, as ever, through Morten Harket's sad Nordic timbre.' Writing for the BBC, Tom Hocknell declared that the album was 'a welcome return to the electronica of their early hits and a glorious reminder of their soaring melodies.'

Across the North Sea, however, Norwegian reviewers weren't so keen. Bernt Erik Pedersen's write-up of the album for *Dagsavisen* was perhaps the most uncomplimentary: 'A-ha, in an interesting parallel with Depeche Mode's latest album [*Sounds of the Universe*], have advised that they have returned to their roots and discovered the old synth sounds again. It sounds exciting but, unfortunately, these are the synth sounds of Falco, [Baltimora's] "Tarzan Boy" and other kitschy Europop . . . Not the cool, experimental and intelligent synth-pop that a-ha produced in the mid-80s. "Take On Me" was the sound of futuristic technology. "What There Is", on this album, is the sound of an Alphaville B-side.' Writing for

VG, Thomas Talseth felt the album was too clinical and concluded that something was missing: '"Sunny Mystery" is the song that best describes the album as a whole: It has several beautiful melody lines, the sound is stylish and clean. Something is smouldering in there, but something is preventing its potential from being realised.'

While the reception for *Foot of the Mountain* was mixed, it certainly outperformed its predecessor in terms of its sales. Aside from topping the charts in Germany, it also gave the band their first Top 10 album in the UK for over 20 years. This was no mean feat, especially considering that the music industry was still in the relatively early throes of digital downloading and increasingly influential social media marketing.

Later in the year, as part of an art portfolio project of Magne's, a unique purple vinyl 12-inch was pressed, which accompanied the first 500 prints from his new *Alpha-Beta* series. (Pål has a print with the letter P in his Oslo home.) Titled 'Word Symphony', the record included bizarre, avant-garde sound collages, featuring discordant cut-ups of vocals from the *Foot of the Mountain* album.

THE BANDSTAND

Words written by Pål Waaktaar-Savoy
Music written by Magne Furuholmen and Pål Waaktaar-Savoy
Produced by Mark Saunders

Perhaps more than any other track, 'The Bandstand' perfectly encapsulated the album's retrograde aesthetic. Its crisp synth motif instantly evoked the sound of the band during their imperial phase, while the lyrics offered both a nostalgic and romantic snapshot of a musician on the cusp of stardom ('Cold and windblown on the old bandstand / You and I walking hand in hand / A neon glow shining down on us'). The setting in this instance was New York, and the song found Pål reminiscing about an early stateside trip. 'Songs are like a photo album,' he said, 'they can really send you back. And this one reminds me of arriving at Port Authority with $35 in my pocket, sporting really high, yellow – almost see-through – synthesiser hair, wearing a tiger shirt and a brown suit, looking like an alien!'[10] (Coincidentally, one of the first US TV shows the band appeared on, in September 1985, was *American Bandstand*.)

'The Bandstand' was the first of five co-writes with Magne, and the intermittent synth riff that characterised the song was sourced from the keyboardist's track 'Come Back'. 'Pål has always been very good at taking something that I've written and pairing it with something he's written,' he said. 'Some of the thrill for me, on a songwriting level, was to revisit that old way of doing things because we have been writing very separately over the last ten years. A song like "The Bandstand", for instance, is a classic example for me of going into the room and remembering how it was all those years ago and getting reignited by the possibilities that were there.'[11]

In concert, a more dynamic arrangement of the song was played. The intro was slightly elongated and the guitars were cranked up, while audiences were treated to the sight of Morten playing electronic drums in the final third.

RIDING THE CREST
Words written by Pål Waaktaar-Savoy
Music written by Magne Furuholmen and Pål Waaktaar-Savoy
Produced by Steve Osborne, Erik Ljunggren and a-ha
Pre-production by Mark Saunders

The album's paciest track, 'Riding the Crest' had initially been inspired by what Pål termed the 'electro-blues' of Arcade Fire's second studio album, *Neon Bible*, an album which Lauren claimed the songwriter had played to death upon its release in 2007. 'I was just in Arizona,' she told Norway's *Elle* magazine in September that year, 'and my husband had to listen to the album over and over throughout the entire seven-hour drive. The result was that we got lost!' It's evident that the song's propulsive drive was inspired by cuts such as 'The Well and the Lighthouse', but the catchy keyboard motif that opened 'Riding the Crest' was actually sourced from Magne's 'Running Out of Reasons'.

In terms of the somewhat hedonistic lyrics, there is little ambiguity in the song, and lines such as 'Truly wasted at a rave / Riding the crest / Of a high and beautiful wave' leave little to the imagination, while lyrics such as 'Some sugar to make the pill go down' are less Mary Poppins and more pill poppings. It wasn't the first time Pål had included 'pills' in his lyrics, however, and in August 2007, *Aftenposten*'s Espen A. Eik had ventured whether the couplet, 'You take your crystal pill / You get an instant thrill' in 'Karma Boomerang' was Savoy's 'Lucy in the Sky' moment. 'Well, you can choose,' replied Pål. 'It's either about heavy drugs. Or it could be a reference to the pills Lauren is taking against her lactose intolerance.'

'Riding the Crest' was debuted during the band's mini-tour in 2008, but the lyrics were later given a polish.

WHAT THERE IS

Words written by Pål Waaktaar-Savoy
Music written by Magne Furuholmen and Pål Waaktaar-Savoy
Produced by Steve Osborne, Erik Ljunggren and a-ha
Pre-production by Mark Saunders

Pål's idea to utilise the recurring motif that appeared in Magne's soundtrack for 1994's *Ti kniver i hjertet* suggested he had been paying far more attention to his bandmates' solo work than had been intimated in the media, and it also confirmed his position in the band as its most innovative recycler. 'I had written those words for another song,' he said, 'but they fitted so well here, and we were under a deadline.'

As it turned out, the crisp, electronic treatment of this memorable riff turned out to be an inspired move, which was beautifully embellished by Kjetil Bjerkestrand's string arrangement. Pål's lyrics, meanwhile, were a curious juxtaposition of near-Biblical phrasing ('It's what it is / It's what it was / It's what will be here / After us') and more modern, existentialist thinking ('There is a gentle breeze / Playing in your hair / Come take a bow / While you're still all there').

FOOT OF THE MOUNTAIN

Words written by Magne Furuholmen and Pål Waaktaar-Savoy
Music written by Magne Furuholmen, Pål Waaktaar-Savoy and Martin Terefe
Original version produced by Mark Saunders
Album version produced by Roland Spremberg
Chart position: 66 (UK), 8 (Norway), 3 (Germany)

The title track from *Foot of the Mountain* marked, perhaps, the only time in a-ha's career they were encouraged by someone outside of the band – in this instance, Harald Wiik – to fuse two different songs together. Pål, however, claims this version of the song wasn't sanctioned by him. 'I never gave permission for anyone to carve out pieces of my song and insert it somewhere else, nor present it to the record company,' he said. 'I never understood how they would expect me to be excited by this song, considering the circumstances and with Magne's verse lyrics saying less than flattering things about me.'

I asked Magne to offer his version of events. 'There was a different version of "Foot of the Mountain" which we had worked on together, with a completely different verse. I quite liked this version, too. Meanwhile, I had recorded a version for a-ha of one of the songs I had from my solo project, titled "The Longest Night". The problem was that during this entire album, we had gotten into a very "careful" place in our way of relating to each other, avoiding conflict totally. And even though we kind of helped each other out on our respective songs, we did so without truly engaging with each other, and completely without putting our hearts and souls into it. As a result, we had no creative friction and, perhaps for this reason, no single in sight.

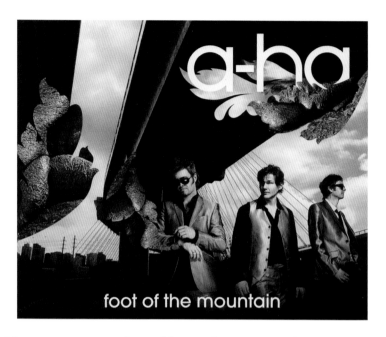

'Harald, our manager, saw the problem and, recognising that we were not going to fix it, he took it upon himself to do it. With the help of Erik Ljunggren, who was also part of the recording process, he sliced up two songs – one from Pål and one from me – and turned it into a demo for the "Foot of the Mountain" version you know today. This was quite shocking, process-wise, but when I heard it I thought it sounded surprisingly good. In any case, this was how Pål and I used to write together back in the 80s; we often joined two songs written separately together. For example, on "Manhattan Skyline", where I wrote the ballady 6/4 parts and Pål wrote the rockier symphonic parts.

'In his frustration, Harald showed the new "Foot of the Mountain" to the record company without telling us, and they absolutely loved it and wanted it as a single. Now we had a dilemma. Pål went ballistic. At first, I found his reaction kind of understandable, to be honest, but at the same time it was really destructive, as we were actually very close to being dropped from the label at that point.

'Morten and I decided instead to work on the track with producer Steve Osborne, to make the best possible version of it, and in the process we found something we really believed in. The next day, an email from Pål arrived, where he withdrew his part of the song. This was the straw that broke the camel's back for me. Morten and I communicated that if Pål did this, then it was the ultimate proof of the band spirit being dead, and that we would consider going on as a-ha without him. Within an hour or so, Pål changed his mind. He did sanction it, otherwise we neither could or would have released it.'

As Pål recalled prior to the release of the album, the original idea of the song was to contrast the environs of a bustling city with a more idyllic setting: 'I live in New York, and to kind of refrain from going crazy, since I'm from Norway, we started going out to Woodstock in the weekends and there's an artist community there. There's a guy who couldn't stand modern life anymore, and he bought himself a hundred acres and created an artist community because he felt modern life was too fast. But this was in 1910 – you can imagine what he would feel like now! So that kind of inspired me to write something, because I love living in New York, but I always wonder would I love it even more living in the open, by the foot of the mountain.'[12]

It's arguable that the original take, produced by Mark Saunders, included lyrics that more accurately captured the essence of the song ('Twelfth Street looks alright / In the dawning light / Everybody's on their way to work / But we could live by the foot of the mountain'), while the sounds of street chit-chat, footsteps and sirens provided a welcome ambient touch. But it was a track that didn't quite fit the aesthetic of the album.

'I remember thinking, when I heard the final version, that it was a genius move,' said Mark Saunders. 'I really like the final version a lot – a very uplifting version. I worked on a completely different version at Water Music that was more groove-based. I felt I wasn't given the chance to bring it to fruition, but it wasn't as good as the final version. Pål asked me, after the album was released, about using my version as a remix but I would have needed Morten to resing some vocal notes to make it work properly, so it never happened.'

The original version of the song, however, was eventually released on the deluxe edition of *Cast in Steel*, which surprised Mark. 'I would have finished it off better,' he said. 'Now I have software that I didn't have back then that would have let me mould the vocal melody to the track seamlessly. This version just makes Morten sound like he's a crap singer, which he's obviously not! I'm really surprised the band let this go out. Now I'm hearing it again, I would have loved to finish it properly. I would have added acoustic guitars, I think, and made the drums a lot more interesting – these drums were just kind of a template to work with.'

While Pål was clearly incensed by the new production, which yielded a confusing set of lyrics, Harald's idea proved to be something of a creative masterstroke. With its bright piano motif, which saw the band out-Keaning Keane, the single rewarded a-ha with their highest chart placing in Germany since 'Take On Me'. (As a reflection of its popularity, it was also selected to be the official theme for the 12th IAAF World Championships in Athletics, and the band performed it at the opening ceremony in Berlin.)

Bolstered by a striking Olaf Heine-directed video, which perfectly complemented the vibe of the song, the single premiered on Norwegian radio in April 2009, reportedly just hours after it was completed. 'This is the right way of doing it in 2009,' Harald told *Dagsavisen*. 'There was demand for a new a-ha single from radio stations all over Europe. That's why we decided to distribute it immediately.' (As a result of ever-changing consumer demands, the single was a download-only release, except in Germany where a two-track CD, which included a radio edit, was issued.)

The song was also parodied in 2009 by the Norwegian comedy duo Bye and Rønning, who amusingly integrated parts of both 'Take On Me' and 'The Sun Always Shines on TV'.

Pål's original verse melody and some of the lyrics were later recycled on 'Beautiful Burnout', which marked the debut release by Waaktaar and Zoe, in 2016.

REAL MEANING
Words written by Pål Waaktaar-Savoy
Music written by Magne Furuholmen and Pål Waaktaar-Savoy
Produced by Steve Osborne, Erik Ljunggren and a-ha
Pre-production by Mark Saunders

In his review of the album for the BBC, Tom Hocknell was keen to note its underlying melancholia, writing: 'The sad heart at many of a-ha's songs is often overlooked, and here "Real Meaning" unfolds with a plaintive piano motif and brilliantly dispenses with a chorus; it's heartbreaking.' The dreamy song was described by the band's official website as a 'happy accident', reporting that Pål had spontaneously started writing it after being greeted by his answering machine while calling home from Russia. 'As a joke, I started singing away and this song fell out,' he said. 'I meant every word, though.'[13]

The song was beautifully sung by Morten in a more hushed style, drawing out the fragility and insecurity of the lyrics ('Don't fix you / And leave me for some other guy / And I sure will / Miss us when we're done').

SHADOWSIDE

Written by Pål Waaktaar-Savoy
Produced by Roland Spremberg
Single version produced by Martin Terefe and Roland Spremberg
Chart position: 22 (Germany)

The second of two new songs that were debuted during the band's mini-tour in 2008, 'Shadowside' had, according to Pål, originally been written for one of Norwegian production duo Stargate's recording artists, but the project had fallen through. But their loss was certainly a-ha's gain, as the desperately bleak track saw its writer traversing the *skyggeside* – the dark side – of his soul, candidly revealing there was a facet to his personality that had the potential to eat away at a relationship ('The shadowside you say I have / Is making everything go bad / You say I don't care enough / For all the things that I have got').

From its Joy Division-like title through to the towering gloominess of the chorus ('If you're letting go of me again / In the shadowside I'll end'), this represented a fresh songwriting peak for Pål, while its devastating final key change was an album highlight. 'There is a vocal range of five different keys,' said Pål, 'and few other vocalists would be able to pull that off. When I'm writing specifically for a-ha, I know what I have to work with vocally, who I can trust will achieve it.'[14]

Pål described the finished product as being uniquely Nordic, while *The Times*' chief rock critic, Pete Paphides, eloquently labelled it as a 'masterpiece of pop desolation'.

An alternative version of the track, co-produced by Martin Terefe, was selected for single release, and a promotional video was filmed at the Tresor nightclub in Berlin. (It was directed by Uwe Flade, whose previous clients included the likes of Depeche Mode, Franz Ferdinand and Rammstein.) Although the single became a minor hit in Germany, the new edit was far too heavy-handed, with some of the lyrics being cut during the transition from verse to chorus. This was a song that

291

needed space, and by tightening up the arrangement, it arguably lost some of its magic. 'Those type of edits rarely do the song any favours,' agreed Pål.

In 2012, the song was covered by bilingual singer Caurie de Cristal (aka Sonia Dersion) and included on her album *Celebration with Roses.*

NOTHING IS KEEPING YOU HERE
Written by Pål Waaktaar-Savoy
Produced by Roland Spremberg
Chart position: 65 (Germany)   ·

While the gloomy introspection of 'Shadowside' had represented a new melancholic peak for the band, in some respects the track was eclipsed by 'Nothing Is Keeping You Here'. One of the first songs to be written for the album, it was reportedly part-inspired by folk singer Nick Drake, who in 1974 had died from an overdose of the prescribed antidepressant amitriptyline. There has been a great deal of speculation as to whether the overdose was deliberate, and the media response to the singer's death is ostensibly referred to in the original demo of the song ('The absence of a note / 'Twas all the papers wrote'), while the lyric 'From the world, detached / Unto a girl you latched / It never got too far' appears to be a

reference to Drake's former girlfriend, Sophia Ryde.

Since the singer's untimely death, there has been an upsurge in interest in his back catalogue, and his recordings have influenced a plethora of artists – including Badly Drawn Boy, Belle and Sebastian, the Cure, Stephen Duffy and Norway's Kings of Convenience –

and it's probable that the couplet, 'You knew your day to shine / Would come without you here', was a reference to this posthumous upturn. The opening line, meanwhile, appears to have been sourced from Savoy's 'Best Western Beauty', which begins: 'I'm watching the light changing over the hills'.

The slower tempo utilised in the demo certainly complemented the largely downbeat lyrics, but the finished version benefitted hugely from a brighter, more uptempo delivery, accentuating both its wistful and melodic qualities. 'This is an unashamedly passionate album,' said Magne. 'It's uptempo but not exactly upbeat. Upbeat means happier, and I don't think this is the case.' Pål added: 'It's a happy/sad kind of thing. You can change how a song comes across to the listener, as we've done many times in the past, by giving a song the opposite arrangement to what you'd expect.'[15]

The song was selected for single release, although contemporary, more trance-like mixes of the track – by Steve Osborne and Roland Spremberg – were commissioned. Osborne's version, however, didn't include the intro, which has often been compared to the Harry Nilsson classic 'Everybody's Talkin'.

The promotional video, filmed at a derelict power station in Berlin, was directed by Uwe Flade.

MOTHER NATURE GOES TO HEAVEN
Written by Pål Waaktaar-Savoy
Produced by Roland Spremberg
Pre-production by Mark Saunders

Given Morten's strong interest in nature and environmental issues, it was perhaps no surprise that, in the build-up to the release of *Foot of the Mountain*, many fans speculated that 'Mother Nature Goes to Heaven' had been penned by the singer, while some interviewers were seemingly under the same illusion. To Morten's credit, he gave a typically considered response to a German journalist asking him about the track and the 'state of the world': **'Of course, it's naive to say that we are saving the world now,'** he replied. 'Each individual must be aware of the extent to which his behaviour disturbs the balance of nature. We need to reflect on what makes life valuable, and to develop a vigilance toward those processes that lay the foundations. If the human being wants to continue to call himself human, he has to take responsibility for his own actions. Otherwise, we would only be machines that are looking for a permanent stimulant.'[16]

In his album review for *AllMusic*, Jon O'Brien described it as 'a wishy-washy and meandering attempt to highlight the plight of the environment, which suggests the band is much better at tackling more personal themes than heavy-handed issues'. The line 'And there will be no sadder day / When all the birds have flown away' certainly delivered a devastating blow, but like many of Pål's songs, there was a more emotional layer below its earthy surface. The song had reportedly been written in the wake of his mother-in-law's death and lyrics such as 'Things you could do asleep / In a not too distant past / Are trying your patience harder now' were perhaps indicative of seeing someone slowly succumb to illness.

With its emotive vocal and dense instrumentation, it's arguable that the original, more intense demo – with Per Hillestad on the drum stool – packed a greater emotional punch, but the finished version, evocative of *Ultra*-era Depeche Mode, benefitted from some mournful harmonies and synth embellishments.

The song wasn't performed during the *Foot of the Mountain* shows, but it was dusted off during the *Cast in Steel* tour several years later.

SUNNY MYSTERY
Written by Magne Furuholmen
Produced by Steve Osborne, Erik Ljunggren and a-ha
Pre-production by Mark Saunders

> *We are asleep. Our life is a dream. But we wake up sometimes, just enough to know that we are dreaming.*
> – Ludwig Wittgenstein

Considering Magne's towering songwriting presence on the preceding two albums, it came as something of a surprise that only one song on *Foot of the Mountain* was solely credited to him. Against a New Order-esque backdrop, this sprightly late addition to the album glides along in an almost trance-like manner, with the narrator hinting at some horror he is attempting to erase from his conscience ('You can sail the seven seas / You can climb the highest mountain / To try dissolve these memories'). But, in true Kafka-like tradition, we never quite get to the bottom of the drama ('Because no one knows for sure / The outcome of this sunny mystery'). Adding to its lyrical appeal was a highly quotable transcendental couplet ('Life is the dream that you wake up to / Dreams are the life from which you wake').

'It was inspired by the name of my sister's two cats, called Sunny and Mystery,' said Magne. 'Her family and mine were on holiday together, and I was talking to the kids about how anything can be an inspiration for writing and, as a way of proving it, I wrote a song with the name of these cats as a title.'

START THE SIMULATOR
Written by Pål Waaktaar-Savoy
Produced by Mark Saunders and Roland Spremberg

True to the band's synth-pop influences, this beautiful, galactic requiem has shades of Orchestral Manoeuvres in the Dark – not just in its complex waltz-time structure and choral sounds, but also its unusual lyrics, which cleverly integrated

NASA space mission jargon ('Switch to Omni Bravo / B Bus undervolt', etc). During OMD's imperial phase in the early 80s, the erudite synth-pop act were recording songs about telephone boxes ('Red Frame/White Light'), aeroplanes ('Enola Gay', 'The Messerschmitt Twins'), oil refineries ('Stanlow') and long-redundant forms of communication ('Telegraph'), and it's arguable that 'Start the Simulator' wouldn't have sounded out of place on an album like *Architecture and Morality*. (Years later, OMD recorded 'Our System' for 2013's *English Electric* album, which incorporated sounds from a Voyager space mission.)

'The basic idea,' said Pål, 'was to make a song using only technical terms and phrases, and still make it very emotional and personal – there is such poetry in the old Apollo manuals.'[17] It's evident that Pål's source for much of the lyrical content was the transcripts of the ill-fated Apollo 13 mission in 1970, and much of the dialogue was also included in Ron Howard's Academy award-winning dramatisation in 1995. (Pål had also worn one of the spacesuits from the movie in the video for 'Minor Earth Major Sky' earlier in the decade.)

According to Pål, recording the track wasn't straightforward. 'It was quite a hard song to record as it changes both time signatures and keys as it goes along,' he said. 'What sounded so simple on the piano got very quickly complicated when it was translated to a full arrangement. I think we got there in the end, though!'[18] But despite the track reaching its technical 'splashdown' and the band, arguably, delivering one of their most beautiful songs, 'Start the Simulator' received something of a critical mauling upon its release. Writing for *musicOMH*, Christopher Monk described it as 'an unspeakably naff extended spaceflight metaphor', while *Consequence of Sound*'s writer, Alex Young, unfavourably compared it to Radiohead: 'It feels like the whole group gave up and let Thom Yorke finish the album off past "Nothing Is Keeping You Here" . . . "Start the Simulator" plays out like an *In Rainbows* B-side.'

Pål later declared that the track was his favourite on the album. 'At the core, "Start the Simulator" is almost like a big Spector-type torch song,' he said. 'I was pretty happy with the writing on that one and the middle eight is more "out there" than I usually do.'

He was, however, unhappy with the version that ended up on the album. 'Somehow, in the mastering or in the pressing, the track was reduced to a lopsided, mono version of itself,' he said. This was rectified in 2015 when the superior 'Stereophonic Mix' – referred to by Pål as the 'real version' – was included on the two-disc version of *Cast in Steel*, which presented the song in all its widescreen glory.

MANMADE LAKE (Unreleased Album Out-take)
Written by Pål Waaktaar-Savoy

Although only 10 tracks
were included on *Foot of
the Mountain*, the band
did work on other songs
during this period. One
known out-take was
'Manmade Lake', which
was so close to making
it onto the album that
a proof of the cover,
featuring the track in
the running order, was
published on Stian
Andersen's website.
(The band's official
photographer, Andersen
later published a portfolio
of his work, which

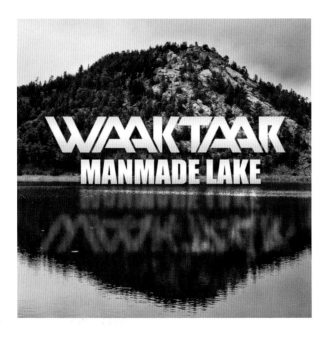

included an introduction by Magne.) With its 'Constellations in the sky / Ursa
major and satellites' lyric, it would have led perfectly into 'Start the Simulator', but
the track didn't make it to the album mastering stage, and 'Sunny Mystery' was
included in its place. 'Morten and Magne voted it out,' said Pål.

In February 2014, Pål surprised fans with a free download of a new version of
the track, released under the name of Waaktaar, and later made the stem files
available for fans to download and remix in a contest. 'It's been a favourite of mine
for a while,' he said of the distorted oddity. 'It was written around the overdriven
guitar riff in the outro and I've been looking for a way to present it. The voice is run
through a guitar amp which I thought strengthened the mood and related to the
words, particularly in the second verse. Sort of like a ground-to-air type voice.'[19]
With regard to the lyrics, Pål said more recently: 'I had an idea of these two friends
having a tender moment, connecting deeply with nature and the universe and all,
except that they're intoxicated and out on a fake lake.'[20]

The original Waaktaar version was certainly charming, with a lo-fi production
that recalled both *Monster*-era R.E.M. and Grandaddy (whose singer, Jason Lytle,
was a confirmed fan of a-ha's), but the final version – released by Savoy in 2018 –
benefitted from a more natural, less distorted approach.

A QUESTION OF LUST (BBC Session)
Written by Martin L. Gore

During promotion in the UK of both *Foot of the Mountain* and its title track, the band undertook a wealth of promotion which would culminate in a-ha's highest placing in the album charts for several years. Aside from several TV interviews, the band also did plenty of radio work, including a session at London's Maida Vale Studios for Dermot O'Leary's show on Radio 2. Mixing familiar classics with newer material, such as 'Riding the Crest' and 'Foot of the Mountain', the band also surprised listeners with a version of Depeche Mode's affecting ballad 'A Question of Lust', the second single to be lifted from the Basildon outfit's *Black Celebration* album in 1986.

The members of a-ha had never hidden their admiration for the band, and their influence was certainly evident on their latest opus, so this was an inspired choice, even if the run-through of the track was a bit pedestrian by their standards, omitting both the middle eight and the counter vocal in the second verse. The band did, however, score extra points for picking a more unusual single; at the time it was only the second of Depeche Mode's singles to feature Martin Gore on lead vocals, while it also marked the band's lowest chart placing in the UK (No. 28) since their debut single, 'Dreaming of Me', stalled at No. 57 in 1981.

Interestingly, 'A Question of Lust' had also been covered by Norway's Poor Rich Ones, who had previously reworked 'Hunting High and Low'.

CHAPTER TWENTY-FOUR
ENDING ON A HIGH NOTE

There is a lot involved in making a good racing team work well, and at some point you have to think there has to be more to life than just racing.
– Magne Furuholmen, *Daily Express*, 2010

Back in June 2009, the BBC published a largely positive review of *Foot of the Mountain*, stating that the predominant use of electronics on the album had brought the band full circle, before signing off with the somewhat prophetic 'it is difficult to see where they go from here'. At this point, there was no indication that the trio, who'd reformed in 1998, were about to announce their disbandment. Despite a few negative reviews, the reaction to the album had largely been positive, and there'd been some healthy sales to match – not just in Norway but also in key territories such as Germany and the UK. During promotional interviews, Magne had even intimated there were plans for a new album, so it came as something of a shock when the split announcement arrived on 15 October 2009, just 12 days before the band were about to set off on the German leg of the *Foot of the Mountain* tour. 'We've literally lived the ultimate boy's adventure tale, through a longer, more rewarding career than anyone could hope for,' read the statement. 'Doing this now will give us a chance to get more involved in other meaningful aspects of life, be it humanitarian work, politics, or whatever else – and of course through new constellations in the field of art and music. We are retiring as a band, not as individuals. Change is always difficult and it is easy to get set in one's ways. Now it is time to move on.'

It transpired that the decision had been driven by Magne, while Morten, perhaps sensing an opportunity to fully focus on his solo career, was seemingly keen to play ball: 'All things do eventually come to an end,' he said. 'We can look back at a fantastic 25-year career, and we're now experiencing success once again. We're riding on a really good wave. Getting the opportunity to end things while you're on top of your game is a privilege. We've been at it for 25 years with a lot of highlights, where the artistic life, working as an artist, has been the most important thing. Because that's what we set out to do when we left for London in 1983.'[1]

However, as Pål revealed during a German TV documentary, the decision wasn't unanimous: 'If there was an opponent, it was probably me, because I was sort of halfway into the next album and writing for that. So I kind of advocated doing one more album. But having said that, I am kind of excited. There's lots of other stuff we can do, and that's exciting.'

Another musician who was disappointed was drummer Karl Oluf Wennerberg, who had not long joined the band: 'As a fan myself, I think it's sad that they're ending the band,' he said. 'But they're saying that it would be difficult to record another album, that it would be hard to achieve . . . I think it's a brave decision to put an end to it.'[2]

ARRHYTHMIA

While Pål was obviously disappointed by the decision, in hindsight it was perhaps partly driven by Magne's health issues. During an interview in September 2009, the keyboardist had opened up about his struggles with atrial fibrillation, a condition that causes an irregular heart rate. (Other high-profile sufferers include Billie Jean King, Barry Manilow and Gene Simmons.) A patron of the AF Association, Magne had first encountered symptoms of the condition in the 80s, but he wasn't properly diagnosed until a scary incident in the late 90s, following a drive home from a record company meeting. 'Suddenly, I had a strange feeling of drifting away,' he recalled, 'a bit like I was falling asleep, although I wasn't tired. My head lolled forward and then I jerked awake again in shock. I pulled over immediately and realised my heart was racing. Luckily, I was only doing 30 miles per hour so there was no accident. But it was frightening.'[3]

Although the medication flecainide would control the symptoms of his heart irregularities, he was still prone to mild attacks. 'For the past six months, while promoting the new album, I've had an attack almost every night,' he said. 'I pop a pill and normally it goes away after a few hours. Usually, I'll just read or do some work.'[4]

A life-changing medical procedure at Haukeland Hospital in 2012 would ultimately free Magne of the symptoms, but at the time the diagnosis had taken a huge toll on his life, both personally and professionally. 'Morten and Pål have been great about it – they don't treat me differently,' he added. 'They understand we can't argue too much over songs, because it could end up with me having an attack later.'[5]

BRING THESE PROCEEDINGS TO A CLOSE

A-ha's decision to break up made headlines around the world and dumbfounded the majority of their considerable following. But the fans could at least console themselves with the fact that the band were bowing out at the top of their game, and the announcement that there would be final tour meant their tenure would be extended by another year. It would prove to be one of the band's busiest years since they'd broken through in the mid-80s, and a special one at that.

Beginning in Argentina on 4 March 2010, the appropriately named *Ending on a High Note* tour would stretch to over 70 international shows, culminating in a final performance at the Oslo Spektrum exactly nine months later. In September, at the Døgnvill Festival in Tromsø, the band were joined on stage by Anneli Drecker, who fondly remembered the occasion: 'It was fantastic being on stage with the guys again after so many years and, even more so, in my own hometown. I sang on "Crying in the Rain", and it was raining I recall. Also, on a personal level, it was good having closure after the 1987 experience, from being the intimidated 17-year-old girl standing in the far back during their concert to being the mature mother of three, standing next to Morten on stage. It felt like the circle had closed.'

Aside from the farewell shows, there was an updated edition of Jan Omdahl's book, a farewell single, a two-disc compilation album – which collected all of the band's singles and selected deep cuts – plus special editions of the band's first two albums. Overseen by Bill Inglot – who had notably remastered the Monkees' excellent back catalogue – the two-disc versions of *Hunting High and Low* and *Scoundrel Days* included a wealth of bonus material. 'Everything has been lovingly mastered from the original tapes,' said Pål. 'On top of that, we've added all the demos which, for my money, were sometimes better than what we ended up with.'[6] (The band also performed both albums in their entirety at special shows at the Oslo Konserthus and London's Royal Albert Hall in October 2010.)

Morten found the time to add his vocals to 'Den stilleste timen' [The Quietest Hour], a charity single that had been penned by Ole Paus – Norway's own Bob Dylan – in the wake of the Haiti earthquake in January 2010. Morten also performed 'O bli hos meg' (an emotional Norwegian-language version of 'Abide with Me') at the

subsequent charity concert, although the recording wasn't included on the *Dugnad for Haiti* [Aid for Haiti] album.

Elsewhere, the release of *Yohan: Barnevandrer* in March 2010 marked Morten's return to the big screen. The big-budget family film – which also starred Kris Kristofferson – saw Morten reunited with Grete Salomonsen, the director of *Kamilla og tyven* and its sequel.

BUTTERFLY, BUTTERFLY (THE LAST HURRAH)

Written by Pål Waaktaar-Savoy
Produced by Martin Terefe
Chart position: 98 (UK), 13 (Norway), 22 (Germany)

With its aching melancholia and glossy synth-pop aesthetic, 'Butterfly, Butterfly (The Last Hurrah)' initially sounded like a hold-off from the *Foot of the Mountain* sessions, but the recording of the band's bittersweet swansong had, according to Pål, stemmed from a request from Warner Brothers to record a brand new song for their career-encompassing *25* compilation, and the reflective lyrics certainly confirm its freshness.

While the guitarist admitted he'd have preferred to have recorded one last album, the chance to record one last song was gleefully taken up. Additionally, it also gave him an opportunity to immortalise some of his feelings about the break-up ('These stained glass wings could only take you so far') and his impending freedom from the media spotlight ('Tomorrow / You don't have to say what you're thinking / You don't have to mean what you say'), as well as a pointed reference to some of the band's working methods ('Overthinking every little thing').

Heartbreakingly melancholic, yet upbeat at the same time, the song captured the essence of the band's sound, and it perfectly rounded off their extraordinary career. 'I think this is one of the best songs Pål has written in a long time,' said Magne during NRK's 'P3 Morgen' radio show, 'and an appropriate ending in my view.'

Mixed in May 2010 and released to Norwegian radio the following month, the song attracted some good reviews from the national press. *VG*'s Stein Østbø awarded it 5 out of 6, calling it 'a swansong that grows and grows with each new listen', while *Dagbladet*'s Eirik Kydland declared that it was 'classic a-ha'.

The song was released as a digital download in Norway in July, and during the same month, the band filmed a video at the foot of a flyover in Shoreham-by-Sea, overlooking the English seaside town's airport. Fittingly, the band recruited an old friend to helm the clip, as Magne explained: 'We decided to use Steve Barron for the video, reaching back to close the circle. The first time we worked with Steve was for "Take On Me", and the last time was on "Butterfly, Butterfly (The Last Hurrah)". It was also a reminder of how things change. The first time was a huge budget; this time it was a guy with a small camera set-up. The tools had become minimal! A reminder that times in the music business had changed and how little a-ha had changed.'[7]

The video cleverly integrated footage from some of the band's Barron-directed videos to give it a real nostalgic feel, while stop-motion techniques were used for the symbolic butterfly animation sequences. 'It was really nice to work with a-ha again,' said Barron, 'especially as I had not made a music video for such a long time . . . We shot under a flyover near Brighton that had three roads leading off in different directions, and I asked Morten, Pål and Mags to embrace, get close, almost uncomfortable and then silently say goodbye. It was certainly very powerful on the day. It seemed to sum up how much they had been through together and still stayed as one.'[8] It's certainly a moving clip, and Barron's use of both the song's metaphors in the visual effects and the close-ups of the band – their weathered faces looking desperately sad – makes for a decidedly wistful watch.

A two-track CD single released in Germany and the UK included an edit of the track, as well as an alternative version. Steve Osborne's production of the song boasted a more leaden, indie rock sound, as well as some alternative lyrics ('There will come a time in the morning / You will find a way to begin'). Like the attendant *25* retrospective, the sleeve included the band's horrendous – and ill-advised – chunky new logo. 'I also hated this bubble writing,' said Pål. 'My thumb went down, but I was overruled.'[9]

The song was also performed during the band's farewell shows, but a straight version of the track was replaced by a more emotive acoustic rendering.

SAY HELLO, WAVE GOODBYE (BBC Session)
Written by Marc Almond and David Ball

During promotion for the *25* compilation in September 2010, the band completed another BBC session at Maida Vale Studios, this time for Ken Bruce's show on Radio 2. Aside from an acoustic run-through of 'Butterfly, Butterfly (The Last

Hurrah)', which had been released as a single in the UK that month, the band also taped a version of Soft Cell's classic torch song 'Say Hello, Wave Goodbye', which had previously been covered by artists such as David Gray.

The band were known admirers of the synth-pop act – whose cover of 'Tainted Love' had dominated the airwaves during Magne and Pål's first trip to the UK as a duo in 1981 – and the combination of Dave Ball's adventurous electronics and Marc Almond's introspective, and often provocative, lyrics would prove to be pivotal in the shaping of a-ha's sound.

'Say Hello, Wave Goodbye' had originally been released in January 1982 and followed its predecessor, 'Bedsitter' – another track that Pål was particularly fond of – into the upper reaches of the singles chart. The song concerned a mismatched couple ('You in a cocktail skirt / And me in a suit'), whose stormy affair had ended in somewhat theatrical style ('Standing in the door of the Pink Flamingo / Crying in the rain'). As Almond told *Mojo* magazine, the song was heavily influenced by his time in Soho, the bohemian epicentre of London's red-light district. 'That was Brewer Street in the rain,' he explained, 'outside the Pink Piano bar where the drag artists used to sing, with the neon light from the Raymond Revue Bar reflected on the wet streets. It was what [debut album] *Non-Stop Erotic Cabaret* was about, what Soft Cell was about, what I was about.'

Sonically, a-ha's version of the track was faithful to the original, though it disappointingly omitted its dramatic spoken word section ('We've been involved for quite a while now / And to keep you secret, it has been hell'). Almond was certainly happy with the interpretation, though: 'I loved a-ha's version of "Say Hello, Wave Goodbye",' he enthused. 'It was fantastic, because I'm a big fan of a-ha. Morten Harket has a great voice and they're a great band. Also, being partly Norwegian myself, I'm very fond of them.'[10]

BOWLING GREEN (Live Recording)
Written by Terry Slater and Jacqueline Ertel

A smooth, pastoral trip into the peaceful sunshine of the bluegrass belt, where the Ohio river meets the wide old Mississippi, where the corn stands tall and the barns are brown, where the postman sings and the milk comes by horse and cart in large, silver urns, and where the fields meet the noontide sky in a haze of soft, warm indigo. I have never been to Kentucky. I have only heard the Everly Brothers sing.
– Andy Wickham, *The Everly Brothers Sing*, 1967

During the second encore of the final date of the *Ending on a High Note* tour, the band brought out their custom-made acoustic guitars for a rendition of the

Everly Brothers' final Billboard hit, 'Bowling Green', which they dedicated to their former manager Terry Slater, who was in the audience that night. The somewhat overproduced 1967 single, which features some pleasing Beach Boys-like vocals, but rather unnecessary woodwind adornments, had been penned by Slater, who was the harmony duo's bass player during this period, though it is invariably co-credited to Phil Everly's first wife, Jacqueline Ertel. (Song sheets from the period indicate Phil Everly as the co-writer, which seems more logical as the track had reportedly stemmed from a guitar riff he'd played to Slater.) The track has been covered several times over the years – notably by Glen Campbell in a string-heavy arrangement – but originally appeared, along with other material by Slater, on the album, *The Everly Brothers Sing*, which interestingly featured some rather poetic liner notes from Andy Wickham, the man who would, 16 years later, sign a-ha to the Warner Brothers label.

Due largely to some technical problems experienced on the night, both 'Bowling Green' and 'The Bandstand' didn't appear on 2011's commemorative live album, DVD and Blu-ray. It's a shame, because it was clear that some thought had gone into the acoustic arrangement of 'Bowling Green', which included the whistling parts from the Everlys' original demo.

On the day of the band's final show, a statement by Magne – on behalf of the band – was posted on the band's official website: 'This is the end for us,' it partly read, 'and we will not know what a future together could have brought. But we do know what the past has held; it was pretty amazing to be a part of it. From the start as childhood friends, to the peak of our career, and all the points in between, a-ha has coloured our lives in ways we don't even seem to comprehend ourselves. This is as far as the road took us – but, hey, we came a fair distance by any standard!'

The final show at the Oslo Spektrum provided a fitting finale for the band, who were bowing out on their terms and literally 'ending on a high note' as the final bars of their signature song reverberated around the famous arena. But was it really the end? 'We fell together, we fell apart,' said Pål at the time. 'Who knows? There's no forever thing.'[11]

PART EIGHT

A BREAK IN THE CLOUDS – THE SOLO YEARS
2009–2014

CHAPTER TWENTY-FIVE

SCARED OF HEIGHTS

I will not try to save the world, open an orphanage in Africa and write a children's book.
– Morten Harket, *Gala*, 2010

Although a-ha had drawn a firm line under their 25-year recording career in December 2010, they did reform just eight months later, albeit in somewhat exceptional circumstances. In the wake of the terrorist atrocities in both Oslo and the island of Utøya in July 2011, the band performed a beautiful Kjetil Bjerkestrand-arranged version of 'Stay on These Roads' during the memorial ceremony at the Oslo Spektrum the following month.

By this time, the band's members had moved on to other projects: Pål formed the short-lived Weathervane with Jimmy Gnecco, while Magne, in addition to his art projects, worked on new music with his supergroup, Apparatjik. Meanwhile, Morten had started recording the follow-up to *Letter from Egypt*, following a post-Christmas breather. 'There was a great period of relaxation in January and February, but in March I was at it again,' he told *VG*. 'I couldn't wait any longer . . . It was time to start planning. The machinery was still warm, the system was up and running. So I didn't want to wait until I became slow and lazy.'

MORTEN HARKET – OUT OF MY HANDS (2012 Album)
Produced by Various
Chart position: 37 (UK), 1
(Norway), 3 (Germany)

In the final stages of the second phase of their career, a-ha had not only consolidated their return to the synth-pop of their early years with cover versions of 'A Question of Lust' and 'Say Hello, Wave Goodbye', 2009's *Foot of the Mountain* also saw them return to the 10-track template they'd employed on their first three albums.

It was a sound and format that suited the band and, to the surprise of many people, Morten utilised this set-up for his next solo album, not only retaining the services of part of the team that had made *Foot of the Mountain* – which included drummer Karl Oluf Wennerberg, keyboardist Erik Ljunggren and producer Steve Osborne – but also including an exclusive Pet Shop Boys track. (The revered synth-pop duo, who had previously penned songs for the likes of Lisa Minnelli, Dusty Springfield and Tina Turner, later included their version of 'Listening' on their 'Memory of the Future' single in December 2012.)

On two other tracks, Morten teamed up with Joakim Berg and Martin Sköld from the band Kent, who were popular in both Norway and their homeland of Sweden. The threesome co-wrote 'Lightning', while Morten came up with an English-language version of Kent's 2002 hit 'Kärleken väntar' [Love Is Waiting], which had originally featured on their fifth album, *Vapen & Ammunition*. '"Burn Money Burn" is unavoidably a political song,' Morten explained to *Dagbladet*. 'It's first and foremost about values, but there's also a direct criticism of the money system we live by which, quite frankly, I feel is extremely dangerous, because there are only certain values in life that can be measured in money.'

TAKE IT OUT OF MY HANDS

One of the album's most memorable tracks was 'Scared of Heights', which was selected for single release in both the UK and Germany. The original track by Espen Lind, which had largely been built around a charming ukulele strum, topped the charts in Norway in 2008 and formed part of his fifth album, *Army of One*. According to Morten, Harald Wiik had initially suggested covering the Lind song, but it was Magne who had encouraged him to cover Norwegian hits. 'Magne came up with the idea that I should pick out good Norwegian songs and take them abroad,' he told *VG*. 'I liked that thought, and it's something that I will pursue on my next solo albums as well. Not just to be kind, but because these songs will be relevant and more than good enough in markets where they haven't been released before.'

Aside from his collaborations with Kent, there was another Swedish connection, too, with the new album marking the debut of Morten's songwriting alliance with the prolific songwriter, musician and producer Peter Kvint. (As well as working with the likes of Natasha Bedingfield and Britney Spears, Kvint had also produced Andreas Johnson's ubiquitous hit 'Glorious').

Elsewhere, *Fame Academy* winner David Sneddon co-wrote 'Keep the Sun Away' with James Bauer-Mein, his songwriting partner in the Nexus (they had previously worked with, among others, Hurts on their debut album, *Happiness*), while steadfast collaborator Ole Sverre Olsen was credited with co-writing four tracks, including future single 'I'm the One'. '[That] song is about finding out who you are and that it's okay to make mistakes in life,' Morten later explained to the German magazine *Jolie*. 'A human is a complex being and has to make compromises when interacting with other people, but only if you are honest with yourself and take conscious decisions.'

Previous collaborator Håvard Rem was involved, almost by default, contributing 'When I Reached the Moon', which dated back to the *Wild Seed* era. One other track, 'Undecided', which appeared on the digital version of the album, was provided by the writing/production team of Snowdrop, who included Girl Happy's Tor Einar Krogtoft-Jensen (who'd also played on Magne's 'Dragonfly' single) and Christian Engebretsen, plus Hågen Rørmark, a close friend of Pål's who'd previously played harmonica on Savoy's 'Is My Confidence Reeling?' (Girl Happy also opened for a-ha during their free show in Frognerparken in 2005.)

For the front cover of the album, Morten was photographed by the Nevada-born Just Loomis, who had published a book of his a-ha photographs – which included a foreword by Magne – the previous year. 'He photographed us with a-ha for the first cover we did – *Hunting High and Low* – so there's a lot of history there,' Morten told the German talk show host Stefan Raab. 'I met up with him in Los Angeles last year and we went for a shoot. And we ended up in the water – well, I did anyway!'

LIKE A FLASHBACK

A promotional single, 'Lightning', was released to Norwegian radio in February 2012, but reviews were mixed. *Aftenposten* certainly weren't impressed: 'With a title like this, one might expect some rumble and noise, but there is a surprising lack of energy here.' The review was indicative of the reception the album was about to receive from the Norwegian media, with *Dagbladet*'s assessment perhaps the most damning: 'Unfortunately, *Out of My Hands* turns out to be a lazy and unsubstantial addition to Harket's five-album solo discography,' wrote Sven Ove Bakke. 'Catchy at times, but unimaginative, and strikingly predictable.' Elsewhere, *Adresseavisen*'s Veronika Søum wrote: 'Warmth and sincerity are in short supply on *Out of My Hands* . . . Harket's sensitive vocals are almost drowned out by the synth arrangements. Certainly, the arrangements are good and the production is flawless, but that's exactly what makes it all so boring.' Writing for *Drammens Tidende*, Jon Vidar Bergan concluded that '*Out of My Hands* is an unexciting album with a number of mediocre songs, and Harket disappoints by including new versions of two fairly recent hits. As usual, his vocal performance is very good, but he should try a different approach on his next album if he wants to distance himself from a-ha.'

However, despite the largely negative reception, the album provided Morten with another chart-topper in his homeland, and it even crept into the Top 40 of the UK charts. The reviews were slightly more favourable in the UK, but Morten was unable to avoid some of the criticisms he'd received in Norway. Writing for *MusicOMH*, Laurence Green declared: 'The album's chief sin is the programmed, safe predictability of it all; almost as if a record label exec has built a robotic replica of Harket in their office, programmed it to pump out songs, flicked the switch and stood back to await the results.' In his review for the BBC, Nick Levine described Morten as a 'maestro of melancholy', but declared: 'Harket's clearly operating within his comfort zone, which sometimes leads to blandness; even his impeccable vocal performances can't save the glib platitudes of "I'm the One" or [the banal chorus of] "Lightning".'

But while some of the criticisms were justified, this was a surprisingly cohesive work – especially given the vast number of songwriters, musicians and producers that were involved in its making – and a perfectly serviceable synth-pop album that made full use of Morten's impressive vocal range. 'Scared of Heights' and 'Burn Money Burn' were certainly standout cuts, but there was plenty to enjoy elsewhere. 'Listening', featuring one of the Pet Shop Boys' signature symphonic arrangements and a typically deft lyric from Neil Tennant ('I know your tastes in food and wine / But never really what's on your mind') was another clear highlight. Elsewhere, 'I'm the One', despite its slightly pedestrian chorus, could have fitted in seamlessly on *Foot of the Mountain*, 'Keep the Sun Away', the album's most electronic track, included a playful Daft Punk-like twist with its robotic vocals – a sequel of sorts to a-ha's 'Cannot Hide' – and there were some wonderful Ultravox-like flourishes on the spiritual title track.

KNIGHTHOOD

Following on from a European tour in April and May 2012, Morten performed some shows in both Oslo and South America, where he'd remained popular since his time in a-ha. (Morten's familiar-looking live band included drummer Karl Oluf Wennerberg, keyboardist Erik Ljunggren and guitarist Dan Sunhordvik.)

In August, Morten received a Green Music Award for his long-standing commitment to electromobility, renewable energies and the protection of the rainforest, but there was a far more prestigious honour to come. In November that year, he received a knighthood from the King of Norway, Harald V. During a special ceremony at the Gamle Logen concert hall in Oslo, the three members of a-ha were each awarded the Order of St. Olav, a 'reward for distinguished services rendered to Norway and mankind', and a recognition of the band's outstanding musical contribution. 'When Pål, Magne and myself set a course for England, we had great plans,' he said during his speech, 'but we didn't imagine that, 30 years later, we would be here at Gamle Logen to be appointed knights!'

The knighthood rounded off a successful year in which he'd re-established himself as a solo artist, while his voice-over skills in *Lille speil på veggen der*, a Norwegian language version of *Mirror, Mirror* (a family fantasy movie based on the story of Snow White), added a further string to his bow. (Premiering in March 2012, the movie also featured the voice-over skills of Morten's daughter Tomine.)

When it came to promoting the album's final single ('I'm the One'), however, Morten was seemingly keen to move swiftly on to his next project. 'At the moment, my heart is not in it,' he told the German magazine *Focus*. '*Out of My Hands* is like an old wife – I don't want to meet her, because I'm in love with what's happening now. This is my dilemma.' Morten had already started work on his next album.

MORTEN HARKET – BROTHER (2014 Album)

The process of recording this album is the best I've ever experienced . . . When the material really hits you, when the songs have a distinctive character, that's when I'm reminded why I got into music in the first place.
– Morten Harket, *VG*, 2014

Produced by Peter Kvint and Morten Harket
Chart position: 56 (UK), 1 (Norway), 11 (Germany)

By the end of 2012, Morten had begun working with Peter Kvint on the follow-up to *Out of My Hands*, which was scheduled for release in October the following year. 'We have built up this trust between us and have a really good collaboration going,' Kvint told *Musikkpraksis* magazine. 'There are creative sparks flying constantly and we always end up with something when we sit down to write.'

The recording sessions would see Morten abandoning the synth-pop approach of the previous album, aiming instead for a more organic sound. 'I didn't like the a-ha machinery on *Out of My Hands*,' he told *VG*. 'The a-ha backstory was still present in my system, but I was impatient and didn't want to wait before starting again. This is a much more peaceful project, without all that noise. Don't get me wrong, I'm very happy with *Out of My Hands* and everything that happened afterwards, but now I don't have those connections anymore. There's an open sky before me and I feel completely free. This definitely feels like a new start.'

Work on the new album at Kvint's studio in Södermalm, near Stockholm, followed successful songwriting sojourns to both Kristiansand in Norway and Ilha Grande (a beautiful island off the coast of Rio de Janeiro), with most songs credited to Morten, Peter Kvint and Ole Sverre Olsen. Musicians included drummer Per Lindvall, pianist Jesper Nordenström and cellist Björn Risberg.

There was one notable distraction from the sessions, with Morten performing 'Wind of Change', with the Scorpions in Athens during a series of acoustic shows in mid-September 2013. Morten's version of the worldwide hit was included on the popular German band's *MTV Unplugged – Live in Athens* album, which was released in November that year. (The performance was also captured on a DVD and Blu-ray release.)

I SEE A NEW BEGINNING

By the end of 2013, Morten was ensconced in a 19-date tour of Germany, performing five tracks a night during the popular *Night of the Proms* concerts. Morten debuted 'There Is a Place', which was released as a download single in November, and 'Did I Leave You Behind?', which was eventually left off the album. 'We decided not to include it on the album because we felt that it stood out a bit from the rest of the material,' explained Peter Kvint during a Facebook Q&A. 'It sounded a bit different from the rest of the songs. However, it's fully produced and mixed and will be released later in some form; probably as a single.'

'There Is a Place' was a beautiful piano-based ballad, and a clear indicator that Morten had reverted to the more organic soundscapes that had informed his earlier solo outings. 'I can't really say that we tried to simulate any previous record of Morten's, or any other album,' claimed Kvint. 'Somewhere halfway through the process I remember Morten saying that he had the same feeling about these songs that he had for the songs on *Wild Seed*. That album was also written in a rush of inspiration and quite quickly. Which was also the case with *Brother*.'

The first song the pair composed for the new album was the extraordinary title track, which was inspired by Maajid Nawaz's highly rated memoir, *Radical:*

My Journey Out of Islamist Extremism. 'We were listening to Radiohead the day we wrote it,' recalled Kvint on Facebook. 'We were in a boathouse by the sea in Kristiansand, where we had two great writing sessions for the album . . . The theme of the song is two brothers who have chosen different paths and how to define the relationship between them. Morten wanted to write about Christianity and Islam and the tension between the two, but it's also about humanity and how we can't live without each other.'

Impeccably produced, with a double-tracked vocal that beautifully blended Morten's baritone and falsetto, 'Brother' was premiered at the Spellemann awards ceremony in January 2014 and released as a single shortly afterwards. The memorable video, featuring Morten submerged in water, was directed by his friend, the film-maker Harald Zwart, whose credits included the 2010 remake of *The Karate Kid* and the promotional videos for the 'Velvet' and 'Forever Not Yours' singles.

WORDS CAN TAKE US MANY PLACES

Boasting a simple sleeve design, the *Brother* album was released in April 2014 and gave Morten his fourth chart-topper in Norway. It also enjoyed a six-month residency in the album charts on the back of some largely positive reviews. 'The title track's longing melancholy, naked sensitivity and timeless reflection on the term identity sets the standard,' gushed *Aftenposten's* Svein Andersen, while *Drammens Tidende's* Jon Vidar Bergan praised it for its 'elegant, well-crafted and catchy pop'. *Dagbladet* were slightly harder to please, though: '*Brother* starts

well,' wrote Torgrim Øyre, 'but gradually fades away in a stream of identical semi-ballads that do not take him to places he has not been before.'

In the UK, *Brother* was Ken Bruce's Album of the Week on BBC Radio 2, but the reviews were also mixed. Writing for *The Upcoming*, Keira Trethowan declared it was 'fabulously produced' before concluding: 'If you are looking for an album that's soulful yet fiery, simple yet effective with plenty of variety, then *Brother* is one for you'. But *Classic Pop* were less enthusiastic in their two-star review: 'Although Harket's musings on identity, individuality and even death clearly mean much to him,' wrote Mark Frith, 'this is an album that should have delivered much more to the listener.'

It's arguable that *Brother* rarely strayed outside of its safe, MOR comfort zone, but it was a fine addition to Morten's catalogue of solo work, with the title track ranking as one of his greatest songs. Other highlights included 'Heaven Cast', which recalled the melodic songwriting artistry of Neil Finn, and 'Whispering Heart', which boasted a soaring chorus that Pål would have been proud of, while the meditative closer, 'First Man to the Grave', was a sumptuous slice of Nordic melancholia.

Morten was certainly pleased with the album, although he admitted he wasn't completely happy with the production of 'Safe with Me', a song that sonically stood out due to its programmed drums. 'That's a very primal song, basic and simple, but also very distinct. So we had to remove all the extra fluff and crap,' he confided to *Musikkpraksis*. 'But that's also one of the songs I like the most on the album. That one, "There Is a Place" and "Brother". Those songs have the clearest identities.'

A third single release, 'Do You Remember Me?', coincided with the start of a tour in support of the album, which included several festival dates in the summer. Morten's backing band included Lars Danielsson (bass), Christer Karlsson (keyboards), Vicky Singh (guitar) and Per Lindvall (drums).

Towards the end of the tour, Morten announced to Norway's Radio 102 that he'd begun working with Peter Kvint on new material, but plans for a new solo venture would eventually be derailed.

CHAPTER TWENTY-SIX
COME TOGETHER

Is Apparatjik something revolutionary? Is this the new synthesis of art, music,
science, and technology? Or are these guys sitting around in some humdrum office,
trying out random stimulants to entertain their overactive brains?
– Autumn Andel, *QRO* magazine, 2010

Following the release of 'Ferreting' in October 2008, it initially appeared that the
formation of Apparatjik was just a one-off collaboration between Magne, Guy
Berryman, Martin Terefe and Jonas Bjerre, created with the specific purpose of
penning a theme for Bruce Parry's BAFTA award-winning *Amazon* documentary
series and its accompanying soundtrack. After all, all four members of the
so-called supergroup were busy with their day jobs, particularly Berryman,
the bassist for Coldplay, who had released their fourth album, *Viva la Vida*
or Death and All His Friends, in June that year. (Ending in March 2010, the
subsequent world tour would see the hugely popular band playing over 170
shows.) Additionally, Magne had started working on a-ha's *Foot of the Mountain*
album, while Jonas Bjerre had completed the recording of a fifth album by the
Danish progressive rock band Mew. Meanwhile, Martin Terefe had resumed his
production duties, working on projects such as Howie Day's third studio album,
Sound the Alarm.

As it would transpire, however, the recording of 'Ferreting' was just the start of
an eventful journey for the curiously named art-rock combo. 'About four months
later, we met for an ill-fated skiing trip, damn near killing Jonas and putting the
rest of us to shame,' explained Magne. 'This turned into an impromptu recording
session, the likes of which none of us has ever experienced.'[1]

The band were accurately described as 'a collective fusing interest in science
and culture, tangential in nature, with cross-field collaborators in the worlds of
music, art, fashion and the scientific community'. Magne was, of course, already
well established as the band's veritable *multikunstner*, and his performance with
Nils Petter Molvær at the Vinterspillene festival in 2004 – which also included
a group of ice sculptors sharing the stage – would point towards Apparatjik's
somewhat unconventional musical odyssey.

Jonas Bjerre was no stranger to the world of arts either. The artwork for Mew's 1997
debut album, *A Triumph for Man*, for instance, included some of his drawings,
but the keen artist would soon take an interest in other aspects of the cult band's
presentation, too, including stage projections during their live shows. 'It's
something I started doing pretty early on,' he explained. 'I saw a few other bands,

and they always kind of ripped off old material, or used old movies or something like that, and I thought it would be more fun to do something that was really connected to our band. I was working in post-production and animation at the time, so I started fiddling with it. I think I did it partly because I didn't really feel at ease with my role as a frontman of the band. So I thought, if I could do this, it compensates a bit for me just staring at my shoes the whole show.'[2]

In tandem with his career with Mew, Bjerre's strong interest in cinema would also lead to scoring the music for the Finnish movie *Game Over* (2005), as well as short films such as *He Who Stayed Behind* and *Pandasyndromet* (both 2008). His post-production credits – which typically involved compositing and special effects – included the film *Tango Cabaret* (2001), while his animation skills were utilised in the video for the Biosphere mix of the Blacksmoke Organisation's 2008 single 'Danger Global Warming'.

Elsewhere, Guy Berryman's outside activities included photography, which he'd studied at the Bartlett School of Architecture in London. Some of his work appeared in the booklet for Coldplay's *Viva la Vida* album and, later, a-ha's *Foot of the Mountain*.

MYSTERIOUS STORYTELLING

In terms of the band's musical DNA, Magne's influences were already well documented, but a fondness for Radiohead would certainly manifest itself on Apparatjik's debut album, not just on cuts such as 'Arrow and Bow', 'Datascroller' and 'Electric Eye', but also the artwork itself. Additionally, Berryman was a big Pink Floyd fan, while Terefe lists Deep Purple, Kraftwerk and Steely Dan as bands he listened to while growing up in Stockholm. (It's highly probable that Apparatjik borrowed the title of 'Josie' from Steely Dan's Billboard hit of the same name.)

As for Bjerre's influences, these were varied, too. Although a penchant for alternative rock acts such as Dinosaur Jr., My Bloody Valentine, Nirvana, Pixies and Sonic Youth would ultimately lead to the formation of Mew in his late teens, a keen interest in film scores and 80s music – which had been instilled in him from a young age – would also prove pivotal to the shaping of the fledgling band's sound. The first record he bought was 'The Love Cats' (the Cure), but his parents also exposed him to acts such as Kate Bush, Eurythmics, Jean-Michel Jarre and, significantly, Duran Duran. Years later, he would guest on the Birmingham band's *Paper Gods* album, contributing vocals and guitar to 'Change the Skyline'.

A-ha, too, had an impact on the Frederiksberg-born youngster. 'I was absolutely crazy about "Take On Me" when it was released,' he confirmed. 'I wasn't very old then, but I became hooked on them because a-ha had a drama in their music that not many others had.'[3]

APPARATJIK – WE ARE HERE (2010 Album)

If you were expecting Apparatjik to sound like 'Viva La Vida' meets 'Take On Me',
then you are going to be sorely disappointed.
– Sean Michaels, *The Guardian*, 2009

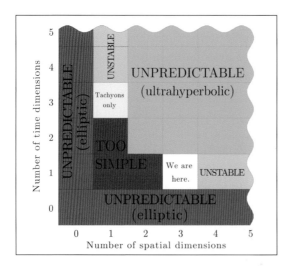

Produced by Apparatjik
Chart position: N/A

Although it had been completed during the winter of 2008–2009, Apparatjik's debut album wouldn't appear in shops until February 2010, delayed by the imminent release of new a-ha and Mew albums. However, the band used their social media presence to propel an interesting pre-release campaign in the interim, which included previews of songs such as 'Snow Crystals', plus assorted multimedia that was accessible via digital Easter eggs. (The band's official website was launched in September 2009.) During the fun and creative, though somewhat pretentious campaign, members from the band's broad fan base were invited to become their friends via Myspace – men were referred to as tachyons while women were amusingly labelled apparat-chicks. It later transpired that the ringleader of much of this cyber tomfoolery was Magne, who later wrote on his Myspace site: 'The intellectuals among you have already found this out; for the foreseeable future I mean to dedicate my weird and wily contributions to weblife to a most inspiring communal congregation of comrades . . . I'm of course more than happy for you to follow me, should you have the inclination.'

Joining the band on this journey were honorary apparatjiks Karl Oluf Wennerberg and Erik Ljunggren – referred to, simply, as Karl A and Erik A – and a single was eventually released in November 2009, following both the launch of Magne's latest art exhibition, Alpha Beta, and the shock announcement that a-ha were to split after a farewell tour the following year.

Featuring a composite of shoegazing guitar work and Kraftwerk-like electronics, the futuristic six-minute epic 'Electric Eye' set out the band's music stall, with some of the lyrics – for example, 'I could be a soldier / I could be a humanoid / I could be an ion' – neatly tying in with one of the band's bizarre bulletins (courtesy of their 'EyeOn Committee'), which outlined in verbose detail a parallel universe which cast 'the apparatjik' as genetically engineered super soldiers designed by the military. 'Only a select few human scientists really understood the science behind Ionian technology,' read part of the convoluted text, 'and after a number of years, bio-mechanical technology developed by the Ions was introduced to humans – this included bionic limbs, electric eye, everlasting organs, brain boosters and endless others.'

SUPERSONIC SOUND

In terms of Apparatjik's sound, the cinematic indie rock of Mew would certainly filter into the quartet's electronic-tinged musical make-up – with Bjerre taking lead vocals on many of the tracks – but each member of the band brought something different to the table. No ideas were rejected, no matter how outlandish, and the end result was a highly experimental, yet surprisingly coherent album which perhaps required repeated listens to fully appreciate. Certainly the somewhat chaotic opener, 'Deadbeat', with its dissonant beats and contrasting electronics, provided an early challenge, but there were more immediate and radio-friendly songs to be found on this veritably diverse and often playful collection. 'I think all four of us have in common an ear for beautiful melodies,' said Bjerre, 'and working together we get to try out some of the things that don't really fit into our other bands. It's a lot of fun!'[4]

With its lullabying melody and general Coldplay-like vibe, the Magne-fronted 'In a Quiet Corner' arguably boasted the greatest commercial appeal, but there were plenty of other standouts, too, including the hypnotic 'Snow Crystals', with its chiming rhythms and intermittent melodic bursts, and then there was 'Arrow and Bow', a more frantically paced slab of electronica, which at times sounded like Wayne Coyle fronting the Yellow Magic Orchestra.

Unsurprisingly, given both the a-ha and Coldplay connection, *We Are Here* was widely reviewed upon its release, and there was a generally enthusiastic response, particularly in the UK. 'If you're a fan of Mew's complex but melodic progscapes and a-ha's windswept, existentialist techno-pop, you'll love *We Are Here*,' wrote Paul Lester for *The Guardian*, 'which is a Mew album in all but name while also recalling the harder moments from the a-ha catalogue, when they pretend they're not Scandinavian sex-hunks but lapsed Doors and Wishbone Ash fans (true) who know how to rock out.' Writing for *musicOMH*, Max Raymond agreed that the album required repeated playing: 'It's inevitable for a debut "supergroup" record that there will be flaws, but if the listener is prepared to stick with it then some delights and unexpected treats will be in store for them. Jonas, in particular, is on terrific vocal form and it showcases how vital he is to Mew.' Elsewhere, in his glowing review for the BBC, Mike Diver wrote: 'If you didn't know who was involved, you'd assume Apparatjik was a brand new band of previous unknowns . . . It might never be much of a going concern for its members, but Apparatjik could easily attain an admirable level of recognition.'

Inevitably, though, there were some accusations of self-indulgence. 'It's a common theme among most "supergroups"; it sounds more like a few guys playing around in the home studio just for the fun of it, with relatively little investment in the final outcome,' wrote *Beats Per Minutes'* Ian Barker. Over in Norway, *Dagbladet's* Eirik Kydland was slightly more dismissive of the hobbyists' efforts: '*We Are Here* sounds like a band rehearsal, where all the members get to do as they please . . . Everyone sings, everyone plays a little guitar, everyone presses the synths a bit. Certainly fun for those involved but, as a record, this becomes too sketchy, sprawling and dull.'

THERE'S NO STAGE FRIGHT

Prior to the start of a-ha's farewell tour in Argentina in March 2010, Apparatjik released a digital version of *We Are Here* on 1 February, the same day they made their live debut during the 11th annual CTM festival in Berlin. The band's performance took place inside a specially constructed cube – labelled the Apparatjik Light Space Modulator – which had been inspired by a contraption invented by the Hungarian artist and Bauhaus professor László Moholy-Nagy. Various graphics and animations were projected onto the cube, creating a

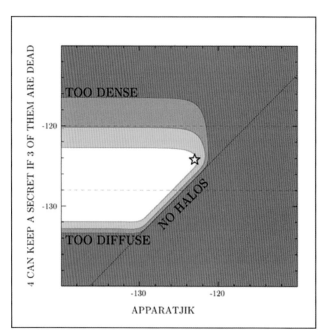

veritable visual feast for the audience and the perfect accompaniment to the band's electronic experiments. Although the band members were holed up inside the cube, their shadows were often visible, meaning the audience could see them – replete with bizarre headwear – playing their instruments or just simply dancing.

Although the title of the non-album single, '4 Can Keep a Secret if 3 of Them Are Dead', was arguably more compelling than the song itself, its download-only release in May certainly kept the momentum going as the band prepared to issue physical formats of *We Are Here* – via the band's Metamerge Un Ltd label – in the summer. Formats included a special Bolshevik Box – which was launched at the band's second live show at Hugo Opdal's *Go with the Fl*ø art festival in June – and a two-disc edition, which included a DVD that collected various music videos and random clips of the band. Elsewhere, an iTunes release also included extra tracks such as 'One Less Thing to Worry About', which utilised the melody from Magne's 'Come Back'.

In September 2010, the band transported their cube to London's Hyde Park and performed at the Serpentine Pavilion. With a-ha on the verge of completing their *Ending on a High Note* tour between October and December, it would prove to be Apparatjik's final show of an eventful year.

APPARATJIK – SQUARE PEG IN A ROUND HOLE (2012 Album)
Produced by Apparatjik
Chart position: N/A

Magne was ostensibly a free agent following a-ha's split in December 2010 and was keen to reactivate Apparatjik. However, any new projects would once more have to fit in with his bandmates' busy schedules. Guy Berryman would spend much of the new year with Coldplay, not only putting the finishing touches to their new concept album, *Mylo Xyloto*, but also touring extensively in its support. Martin Terefe, too, was heavily in demand as both a musician and producer, and during this period his name would grace the credits of recordings by, among others, Beverley Knight and Mads Langer.

Having wrapped up one particular chapter of Mew with

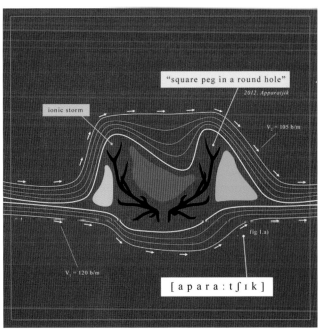

Eggs Are Funny, a career-encompassing compilation album in October 2010, Jonas Bjerre's time was limited, too, largely due to his increasing soundtrack work, which included the score for Rune Schjøtt's film *Skyskraber* [Skyscraper], released in September 2011. But, as the busy musician confirmed, there was the occasional window of opportunity for the band to get together and continue their somewhat unorthodox journey. 'It's rare that we are able to find a time when no one is on tour, or recording, or doing something else,' he said. 'So we get together in short and very intense periods.'[5]

On 25 February 2011, the band performed during the opening ceremony of the striking, newly renovated Deutsche Bank Twin Towers in Frankfurt, while the following month there was a trio of shows – inside their customary cube – at Berlin's modern art museum, the Neue Nationalgalerie [New National Gallery]. These shows were of particular significance to the band as the museum had been designed by the revered architect Mies van der Rohe, a former director at the same Bauhaus school where László Moholy-Nagy had taught. Prior to these special shows, fans were encouraged to submit their artwork to potentially be projected onto the cube. 'Apparatjik invites you to start your art career at the top and work your way down!' began the band's latest amusing bulletin. 'Normally it takes a lifetime for an artist to get into the door of a national gallery. We say get it out of the way now – and start enjoying yourself!'

The band also tested out new material such as the anti-disco track 'Combat Disco Music', which was released as a download-only single later that month. 'My thought was, why don't we take the music that we like and marry it to the music we didn't like and see what happens,' explained Magne. 'What if we take someone like the Clash and Donna Summer. Some people may like Donna Summer and I don't . . . and some people might not like the Clash, but I do. "Combat Disco Music" was something more like a conceptual thing. It had humour, it had irony; it had forcing yourself to perform music that someone else might like but you are not really a big fan of.'[6]

PRE-MIXING

There would be further one-off shows in Russia and Austria later in the year, while the year was rounded off in typically idiosyncratic style with the release of the band's sophomore record, *Square Peg in a Round Hole*, in November. As it would transpire, however, this particular version of the album was just a draft, one that was accessible via Issue A of the band's Apparatjik World magazine on a special iPad app, which also included videos, pictures and other digital paraphernalia. Shortly afterwards, fans who had actively responded to the announcement of an 'agreeneryouniverse' initiative earlier in the year were rewarded with a free download of the album. Participants were encouraged to plant trees and provide photographic evidence of their environmental endeavours.

Further consolidating their unconventional approach to releasing new music, the band announced that the iPad version was the first of 11 formats of their album. Fans were encouraged to get involved in the process of creating further drafts of the album, which would culminate in a definitive release in the new year. 'On the new album we have collaborated with other artists,' wrote the band, 'and now we want to invite our fans and other musicians to contribute by commenting, voting for ideas or taking raw elements from the album and work with, embellish and submit back to us.'

Stem files were made available for remixing – or 'pre-mixing' – and contributors whose work ended up on the final version on the album were rewarded with a credit in the CD's booklet. (Draft 7 was simply a high-quality FLAC version of the original mix, produced in collaboration with the Queens Award-winning loudspeaker company Bowers & Wilkins and their online community, Society of Sound.)

THE CIRCUIT HAS A SWITCH

The definitive version of *Square Peg in a Round Hole* was released on 21 February 2012. The distinctly more electronic album marked a significant progression from their debut, with the band adding more contemporary and urban flavours.

On 'Do It Myself' and the excellent opener, 'Timepolice', the band were joined by Auto Goon, aka N*E*R*D vocalist Pharrell Williams, who would later score huge hits with the likes of 'Happy', 'Blurred Lines' and 'Get Lucky'. 'Apparatjik works in cells around the world as an open platform for collaborations,' explained Guy Berryman. 'After working with Pharrell in Miami, Martin

[Terefe] came home with a demo of a fantastic song titled "Do It Myself" which they had written together, and we just said, "Hey, let's just add some bits and use this as an Apparatjik song!" I love the fact that a musical collective can be this unpredictable.'[7]

On their latest adventurous outing, the band's more erratic side was represented by experimental pieces such as the dissonant industrial ephemera of 'Pakt', while their quirky humour was prevalent on cuts such as the goofily titled '(Don't Eat the Whole) Banana' and 'Combat Disco Music', which utilised a number of memorable Frankie Goes to Hollywood-aping hoo-has! Other standout tracks included 'Tell the Babes', which included a killer chorus from Bjerre and some driving bass work from Berryman, and 'Gzmo', which recalled the rhythmic prowess of acts like the Creatures' (see 'Fury Eyes'). One thing that rankled with some critics was the increased use of vocoder, but it proved to be highly effective on tracks such as the Magne-fronted 'Control Park' and 'Cervux Sequential', whose chorus melody recalled latter-day Duran Duran.

SPACE-AGED

The album reviews weren't so widespread this time around, but they were certainly mixed. 'Apparatjik make curious, space-aged electro-pop, with plenty of heavily effected vocals and disco beats. The production is sickly sweet, and the rhythms are incessant and infectious,' began Nicholas Watmough in his review for *The 405*. He was, however, highly critical of the lyrical content and concluded: 'Sadly, this is a fairly throwaway collection of sugar-hyped little pop songs.' Elsewhere, in his miserly one-star review for *musicOMH*, Andy Jex clearly wasn't impressed with the production. 'Vocoder vocals on *every* track become wearing even if you are Kanye West,' he complained. 'Such treatment buries any vestige of a tune and gives the impression of dayglo mid-80s synth-pop pastiche with nary a nod to irony, shoulder pads or poodle perms. The unrelenting reliance on vocal effects soon tires and sounds lumpen, dated and uninspired.' Other reviews, however, were more generous. 'The best part is that, unlike most supergroups, Apparatjik actually sound like a decent band,' wrote *DIY*'s Alex Yau. '. . . Not that it'll happen anytime soon, but should their main projects ever fall through, Apparatjik should be the perfect safety net for each member to fall back on.' In her review for *contactmusic.com*, Chantelle Pattemore felt the band's unorthodox approach was holding them back: 'They seldom conduct interviews, they perform on stage in a box masked from view, and their apparent fascination with the futuristic spans throughout their website and promotional material as well as the music itself. It is, perhaps, this less conventional approach that has hindered their music being appreciated on a greater scale which is a shame as their work is both hugely enjoyable and meritorious in terms of experimentation.'

AUDIOVISUAL

In April 2012, the band announced plans for another live show, which would see them literally thinking outside of the box – stepping outside the comfort zone of their Light Space Modulator. 'After all the recent cube controversy, Apparatjik has decided to do the most radical thing ever,' began the band's latest bulletin. 'Something so new, so daring, so never before been seen, so not imagined, nor indeed realised: a full-length concert stage performance, with music . . . and visuals. And – hold on to your hatnicks – Apparatjik will perform facing the audience!'

The scene of the band's latest – and largest – concert to date was the main stage at one of Europe's largest festivals, Roskilde, in Denmark. Other performers throughout the weekend included Björk, the Cure, First Aid Kit, Alison Krauss, Mew, Bruce Springsteen and Jack White, and the opportunity for Apparatjik to present their music to a broad audience on the opening day was gratefully snapped up. 'The Orange Stage at Roskilde is an iconic arena for everyone who's into music,' Magne told *Aftenposten*. 'We see this as an opportunity to further expand on our format. The music has always been a natural part of Apparatjik, but has until now been integrated in an audiovisual language and hasn't been allowed to play the leading role. This time it will get a more natural main focus.'

In true Apparatjik style, however, the music often played second fiddle to the visual element of their often surreal performance, which saw them playing the first part of the set attired in hilarious bodybuilder outfits – designed by the Danish Moonspoon Saloon label – and masks of the member of the band who was deemed to have the lowest profile. 'We came out wearing masks of Martin Terefe, because no one knew him,' explained Magne. 'Everybody wanted to interview me, Guy and Jonas. So we said, "Okay, we are going to walk around in Martin Terefe masks because we want to make him famous". We are trying to take every situation and to make some fun out of it, to turn it upside down rather than being angry.'[8]

Also joining in on the onstage shenanigans were DJ Aretïve – who completed a 20-minute set in tandem with a bizarre alien fashion parade – and guest Canadian vocalist Lowell (aka Elizabeth Boland), who would later release a mini-album, titled *If You Can, Solve This Jumble*, in conjunction with Apparatjik in October 2012. Also sharing the stage was an antlered motorcycle, named Rudolph the Chrome Nosed Reindeer, which had been designed by the band and displayed at the Dunkers culture centre in Helsingborg, Sweden. All in all, a typical day at the office for Apparatjik. There was, predictably, a mixed reception in the media, but the band were praised for their ambitious production, which ultimately resulted in a financial loss.

There were other live appearances in 2012, too, including a performance in September at the opening of the Astrup Fearnley Museum of Modern Art in its new location at Tjuvholmen's waterfront, overlooking the Oslofjord. In December, the band – replete with their shiny Moods of Norway-designed suits and antlered helmets – performed with Sølvguttene at Oslo's Museum of Contemporary Art. The starting point for the unique concert – wackily titled the Apparatjik Xmess Extravaganza: Santa Bells Bob – was the exhibition *I Wish This Was a Song: Music in Contemporary Art*, which interpreted the movements of visitors to the museum and turned them into song. The words from English Christmas songs were also fed through a random word generator and sung, vocoder style, as part of the quirky piece, titled 'Everybody Is a Composer'.

Earlier in the year, Magne also made a special appearance – along with Harrys Gym singer Anne Lise Frøkedal – during Robyn Hitchcock's set at the third annual *Go with the Flø* festival in June. Opening the event was an intriguing piece that Magne had put together using sounds from both a shipyard and a farm, which was blasted through an enormous horn-shaped loudspeaker, appropriately named Desibel [Decibels]. 'People can expect a really powerful sound,' Magne told Ålesund's daily newspaper, *Sunnmørsposten*, prior to the fanfare. 'The bass frequency is capable of physically moving a cow. We will of course try to spread the sound carefully, but the sound collage is meant to give the audience both a mental and physical experience.' He jokingly added: 'I think this will be a radio hit on P3 this summer!'

THE VOICE – NORGES BESTE STEMME

By the time of the release of *Square Peg in a Round Hole* in February 2012, Magne was several weeks into a relatively lengthy stint as a mentor on the inaugural Norwegian version of the popular talent show *The Voice*. (Filming for the blind auditions had begun the previous December.) As he later told the gathered throng at the a-ha fan convention in Oslo in October 2014, he initially had reservations about the show, but he was eventually persuaded to take part by his eldest son, Thomas Vincent, who was then part of the production crew.

'I went in with the attitude that I was going to meet young artists that I was excited about from a music point of view and hopefully work with them later on,' he said. One such artist was Martin Halla, the eventual winner of the competition who had seemingly applied to be on the show on a whim. 'I sat in my sofa at home, watching TV, when a commercial announced a new talent show called *The Voice*,' he recalled. 'I thought to myself, "Why not?", and I applied.'[9]

To capitalise on the success, winning mentor Magne oversaw the recording of Halla's *Release Me* EP, which included versions of songs that had appeared on the show – including 'Hurt' (Nine Inch Nails) and 'Take It with Me' (Tom Waits) – plus a new version of 'Dragonfly'.

WINTER DAYS

Following the Top 10 success of the EP, Halla began working on his debut album, *Winter Days*, which was largely recorded at Kensaltown Studios, with Magne and Martin Terefe in a hands-on role, producing, playing various instruments and co-writing many of the songs. Halla brought in some accomplished songs of his

own, such as the title track, but he was also paired up with a number of experienced songwriters during the album's making, including Nick Whitecross – who'd previously co-written a-ha's 'Holy Ground' – and Glen Scott, a multi-instrumentalist who had previously worked on Terefe-produced recordings by the likes of Beverley Knight, James Morrison, Ron Sexsmith and Leona Naess. Paul Herman's CV was extensive, too, with the former Faithless guitarist having co-penned

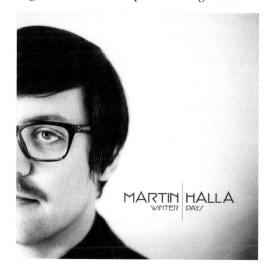

hits such as 'Thank You' (Dido) and 'I Bruise Easily' (Natasha Bedingfield). 'It has been an exciting process,' said Halla. 'I've never written songs with others before, so it was a little alien. But, eventually, a new landscape opened up.'[10]

Other contributors included 'Suddenly I See' hitmaker KT Tunstall and Apparatjik collaborator Lowell, plus Marte Eberson, who was then a member of an expanded line-up of Highasakite. A cover version of the Academy Award-winning song 'Falling Slowly' was also included in the strong 12-track set. The song had originally been included in the Dublin-based movie *Once* and was penned by its lead actors, Glen Hansard and Markéta Irglová.

Other contributing musicians included drummers Neil Conti – a former member of Prefab Sprout – and Alex Toff, who had played on the aforementioned 'Holy Ground'. David Davidson was employed to oversee the string arrangements, while guest vocalists included Tini Flaat Mykland – a fellow contestant on *The Voice* – and Karoline Wallace, a friend of Halla's who had attended the same Bergen music school as him, the Grieg Academy.

Following its release in March 2013, *Winter Days* achieved a Top 5 placing, despite some mixed reviews. The general consensus was that the songs were well crafted and beautifully sung, but some critics were disappointed that Halla wasn't more involved in the songwriting process. 'Obviously it is not tempting for a newcomer to refuse a firm, helping hand from a pop legend, but on this record, Halla is best when he is in control,' wrote *Dagbladet*'s Rannveig Falkenberg-Arell. 'Of course, there is no guarantee that the rest of his songwriting would have maintained the same level, but it would have been exciting to at least have had the opportunity to hear what might have come out of a record that was not just partially, but completely Halla's.'

Following the release of *Winter Days*, Halla co-wrote a song for Tini Flaat Mykland's 2014 debut album, *Undo My Heart*, but he kept a relatively low profile, later admitting he felt uncomfortable as a solo artist. Although a follow-up to his debut was mooted, his output largely comprised the odd single – for example, 'Losing My Mind' and 'You Are Loved' – and collaborations with other artists, including Maria Arredondo and Jack Taylor. He also wrote material for other acts – such as Donkeyboy – and even took part in another singing contest, competing with artists such as Øystein Wiik – Harald's brother – during the fourth season of *Stjernekamp* [Battle of the Stars], an ongoing series which aims to find the ultimate entertainer. (Øystein Wiik had previously been heavily involved in the musical version of Jostein Gaarder's *Sophie's World*, whose official soundtrack also included Morten.)

More recently, Halla has formed a new trio – named LÖV – with Highasakite outcasts Marte Eberson and Øystein Skar. The band are currently being managed by Harald Wiik.

UNDO MY HEART

Tini Flaat Mykland, who had been singing and dancing from a very early age, had previously competed in the Norwegian version of *Pop Idol* – whose guest judges included Anneli Drecker – in 2004. Eight years later, Tini took part in the inaugural season of *The Voice*, under Magne's mentorship. I asked her how much she knew about a-ha then. 'I knew a lot of their songs, but very little about the band and their amazing history in general,' she said, 'but my parents did!'

As for Tini's own musical influences, these are varied. 'I've been – and am – inspired by a lot of different artists, from jazz and soul to instrumental new age and classical music,' she said. 'As a vocal nerd, I search for the sound and the way it makes me feel. For me, that is a more interesting field to explore.'

Although the Kristiansand-born singer would be eliminated during the battle phase of *Voice*, Magne's unwavering support for his new protégés meant she wouldn't become a fast-forgotten footnote in the show's history. Such was his level of commitment that he admirably turned down the opportunity to appear on season two of the show, focusing instead on developing the careers of his acts. Martin Halla, the winner of the show, understandably received his immediate attention, but Magne was also keen to work with the Kristiansand-born singer. 'She was a bit secretive to begin with,' said Magne. 'She wasn't really the kind of singer that tries to impress you. She just does her thing, and that's really what I love about her. It just took a little time to realise the strength of her emotive powers as a singer.'[11]

'His support has meant the world,' said Tini in 2014. 'It's given me so many opportunities to grow and develop as an artist, and his wisdom has always been there to guide me. He's someone I turn to for tips and inspiration, and he always has some good advice for me.'[12] Those initial opportunities included an appearance on Martin Halla's *Winter Days* album and a duet with veteran pop singer Engelbert Humperdinck. Released in March 2014, the Martin Terefe-produced album – titled *Engelbert Calling* – included duets with the likes of Elton John, Lulu, Willie Nelson, Cliff Richard and Smokey Robinson. Tini's contribution to the star-studded double set was a version of the Shirley Bassey hit 'Kiss Me, Honey Honey, Kiss Me', the vocal of which had been produced by Magne at his Passionfruit studio in Oslo. 'I actually didn't meet Mr Humperdinck myself,' confirmed Tini. 'I recorded the duet in Norway with him in my ears. I do have it on my bucket list to meet this legend, though.'

At the turn of the year, Tini also released a vinyl-only EP, which included songs that would eventually appear on her debut album, plus 'The Ladies' Gentleman's Club', which had been penned by Canadian singer Lowell. The special picture disc – featuring Magne's distinctive artwork – was sold exclusively via the luxury waterfront hotel the Thief, the name of which had been derived from the Tjuvholmen area of Oslo it was located in, one rich in a fascinating history of smuggling and piracy. The previous year, the swanky hotel had opened a special Furuholmen-designed Apparatjik suite, one of many rooms that had been adorned with valuable artwork by the likes of Sir Peter Blake and Kjell Nupen. 'We have created a small corner of the Apparatjik World,' said Magne in the press release. 'We wanted to design a room that would make whoever stays here smile and shake their heads at the same time.'

Credited, simply, to 'Tini', *Undo My Heart* was released in October 2014. Like *Winter Days*, it was largely recorded at Kensaltown Studios, with Magne and Martin Terefe at the helm. Returning musicians included drummer Neil Conti and the multi-instrumentalist Glen Scott, while David Davidson was on hand once again to arrange the string parts. Additional musicians included Danish drummer Kristoffer Sonne, a current member of James Blunt's live band.

Both Magne and Terefe contributed songs to the album, which included a new version of 'Running Out of Reasons'. Returning songwriters included Espen Gulbrandsen, KT Tunstall and Nick Whitecross, but there were some new names on the credits as well, including Cass Lowe, who had previously co-written songs with Alison Moyet for her highly acclaimed 2013 album, *The Minutes*. Additionally, the stable of experienced writers included Sarah Dawn Finer – a former Eurovision Song Contest entrant who shares a birthday with Morten – and Jack McManus, whose CV boasted clients such as Boyzone, 2010 *X-Factor* winner Matt Cardle and the Wanted. Tini also chipped in with three co-writes on a diverse collection of songs. 'I was really happy to work with so many great songwriters, musicians and artists in the making of *Undo My Heart*,' she said. 'I loved being a part of a bigger team where we all had the spot to shine in the best way we knew. I was all new to songwriting, so for me it was important to work with people that knew what they were doing.'

In conjunction with Magne's artist development company, Vox Watch Music, the album was manufactured and distributed by Coop, one of Norway's largest supermarket chains.

Tini also bagged support slots during shows in Norway by both Morten – who was then promoting the *Brother* album – and James Blunt, whose *Moon Landing* album had been partly produced by Martin Terefe. In a further promotional coup, the album was innovatively played during flights on the country's low-cost airline, Norwegian, and there was even an album-launching performance by the singer on the Oslo–Bergen flight. 'I felt high!' said Tini. 'It was so cool to do something other than what's expected, and to see all the surprised faces of the passengers on board was a moment for the memory book.'

Sadly, however, the singer's music career itself didn't quite take off. She received some favourable notices following a showcase in London, but the album was not a big hit. Tini was grateful for the experience, however. 'I have a lot of memories of that time,' she said, 'but one of the best things about it all is the people I got to know and work with, and the beautiful moments we shared together in music. I feel so humbled and grateful for this adventure. I really love the album and I am very proud of it.'

At the time, the album received mixed reviews in Norway. Writing for Kristiansand's local newspaper, *Fædrelandsvennen*, Rune Slyngstad favourably compared Tini with the likes of Carole King, Norah Jones and Carly Simon, but felt she didn't take enough risks, vocally. He also felt the album was frontloaded with its best tracks – namely, 'You Can't Have It Both Ways', 'Send My Star' and the title track – which were all released as singles. *Dagsavisen*'s Espen Hågensen Rusdal concluded that the way in which it was marketed and distributed rendered it a 'product more than an artistic work', while Juliann Larsen's 2/6 review for *Gaffa* was more brutal: 'The album borders on the irritating,' she wrote, 'with a few parts just good enough to get on the radio. It seems like a project without purpose and meaning – unless, of course, the goal was to be profiled in an aircraft magazine.'

Since the release of *Undo My Heart*, the singer – who attained a degree in retail management in 2012 – has worked on new material but has ostensibly prioritised a career in fashion and design. 'I think life appears in chapters, but music is a constant in my life,' she said. 'I will always have music, just in different scales. I am a person who is driven by the force of solutions, and I love working with different projects and using different personal skills. So, through music, fashion, design and hosting events, I collect valuable experiences that, who knows, one day I will turn into another album.'

Tini did, however, secure a job as a-ha's backing vocalist for the first six shows of the European leg of the *Cast in Steel* tour in 2016. (Anneli Drecker took over for the rest of the tour.) 'I was really amazed to see how extremely big they are outside Norway,' she said, 'and the fans are just amazing. They really made me feel welcome in every city, which I had no expectations of. I remember Morten whispered to me on stage in Moscow, "Look down there, you have fans!" I turned around just before leaving the stage and saw a crowd with a big poster saying, "Welcome Tini!" That really touched me!'

More recently, Tini contributed backing vocals to Magne's *White Xmas Lies* album. 'It's been seven years since we started working together,' said Tini, 'and what impressed me then, as much as now, is the way he brings out the potential in me. He always makes me feel comfortable, but he also has that constructive eye that challenges me to stretch beyond my own expectations.'

MAJORS AND MINORS

Although, ostensibly, Martin Halla and Tini Flaat Mykland had been the artists that had – commercially speaking at least – gained the most from their time on *The Voice*, there were other acts that benefitted, too. Monika Blomeid, who had defeated Tini following a duet of 'Nothing Compares 2U' in the battle phase, had been tipped to win the competition but eventually lost out to Martin Halla.

The Gjerdrum-born singer, who had to be talked into entering the competition, had gained valuable experience while living in the UK, graduating from the LIPA (Liverpool Institute for Performing Arts) in 2010. Singing credits included backing vocals on 'History of Modern (Part One)' by OMD, whose frontman, Andy McCluskey, was a 'companion' of the LIPA. Having performed an original song, 'London Bound', during the semi-finals of the competition, she later signed a deal with Universal, releasing singles such as 'Ghost' (2012) and 'Marilyn' (2014) under the name of Monika May, which she had also used during her time in the UK.

Marius Beck, too, made it to the business end of the competition and released a single, titled 'Back with Me', via iTunes in October 2012. The following year, Magne and Martin Terefe produced a download-only five-track EP – titled *Majors & Minors* – at Kensaltown Studios, which included wholly original material. Around this time, Beck also co-wrote and played on 'All We Ever Had Is Gone' for Tini Flaat Mykland's debut album.

'The common denominator for all of them is that they stood out for their artistic integrity when I heard them and, subsequently, when I worked with them,' Magne said during 2014's a-ha fan convention. 'But what I like about working with these artists is it gives me a kind of little time machine to go back to a moment when I was in the studio for the first time, without any baggage and just a lot of passion for making music . . . It's exciting to be in the studio, to write, to record, and they're all extremely talented.'

MAGNE FURUHOLMEN – BEATLES (2014 Album)

My own musical journey really started with listening to the Beatles while growing up, and it is such a thrill to be allowed to work with this iconic material and to be a part of presenting this great story on film.
– Magne Furuholmen, 2013

Right from the outset of a-ha's international breakthrough in 1985, Magne had cited the Beatles as a key musical influence, even claiming his band had modelled themselves on the Liverpudlian hitmakers, who had been just as popular in Norway as the rest of the world, racking up an impressive 21 No. 1 hits there. So the chance to score some original music for a movie adaptation of his friend Lars Saabye Christensen's bestselling book, *Beatles*, was difficult to resist. First published in Norway in 1984, the coming-of-age novel centred around a group of teenaged Fab Four obsessives growing up in Oslo in the 60s and 70s, and it later spawned two sequels: *Bly* (Lead) and *Bisettelsen* [The Funeral].

His strong interest in the band had also filtered into his art career, with exhibitions such as *Norwegian Wood* (2013), whose woodcut designs had been derived from some of their song titles and lyrics. 'It's been so long since I did

331

woodcuts, so I felt it was time,' Magne told *Dagbladet*. 'Then this *Beatles* movie popped up, and that kind of triggered this whole exhibition. It's not a coincidence that I used the Beatles as a theme, but there are a few coincidences that have led to this exhibition being what it is.' (There was a follow-up exhibition in 2014, too, named *Norwegian Remix*, which included oil paintings instead of woodcuts.)

Although Magne's involvement in the film project was officially announced in April 2013, the film had been in development for several years. Along with the film's producer, Jørgen Storm Rosenberg, the directors – Joachim Rønning and Espen Sandberg – had acquired the movie rights from Christensen in 2009. 'It's a book we grew up with,' said Rønning. 'For us it's like the first movie about the first youth generation that didn't automatically do the same jobs as their fathers and mothers. It's the first rebellion, especially in Europe and Scandinavia.'[13]

Work on *Beatles* didn't begin in earnest until the completion of the Rønning/Sandberg-helmed, Oscar-nominated *Kon-Tiki* movie, which was released to universal acclaim in 2012. At the top of the movie makers' list of priorities was securing the rights to include some of the Beatles' songs in the movie. 'The process is looking very positive,' Sandberg told *Dagsavisen*. 'We just have to have faith that Paul McCartney will say yes.'

Magne actually wrote a letter to Paul McCartney in support of the project, later telling *Dagbladet*: 'I wrote that, without the Beatles there wouldn't have been a-ha, and emphasised the importance of using original song material. Pål, Morten and I were like the boys in the novel. Because of the Beatles, we dared to have big dreams.'

Following months of negotiations – and an undisclosed sum of money changing hands – the film-makers eventually received the clearance to use songs such as 'Let It Be', 'Paperback Writer', 'Sgt. Pepper's Lonely Hearts Club Band' and 'She Loves You' in the movie. Other songs included in the film – but not on the soundtrack – included 'Bread and Butter' (the Newbeats), 'Suzanne' (Leonard Cohen) and 'Up on the Roof' (the Drifters).

Despite the major soundtrack coup, however, both Rønning and Sandberg were forced to abandon the project following an approach to direct the fifth instalment of Walt Disney's *Pirates of the Caribbean* series, which was understandably difficult to turn down. (Interestingly, the resulting movie included a cameo from Paul McCartney.) Victims of their own success with the seafaring *Kon-Tiki* movie, the in-demand duo promptly hired Danish director Peter Flinth to helm the movie – which began shooting in the summer of 2013 – and oversaw its completion as executive producers.

Upon its release in August 2014, the film received mixed reviews, with many critics feeling the adaptation of Christensen's culturally significant book had been largely unsuccessful. 'The film is unlikely to receive the same classic status as the novel,' wrote Jorunn Egeland for *Side 2*. 'One of the things that made the novel a classic is that it captured the era and adolescence in a brilliant way. There are countless books on youthful friendship and love, but Christensen's book differs from the crowd. And right here lies one of the film's problems: It does not stand out enough.' Elsewhere, in Kjersti Nipen's review for *Aftenposten*, the disappointed reviewer felt the essence of the book had disappeared: '*Beatles* is a bittersweet and nostalgic upbeat story, but it's not just that. The novel has a darker undertone of cynicism and disillusionment, but on film many of the barbs are smoothed out.'

However, other reviewers, including *VG*'s Jon Selås, congratulated the film-makers for the casting and the excellent chemistry between the young actors. *Kinomagasinet*'s John Berge also praised the 'feel good' movie for its authenticity and was particularly impressed by the visual effects and costumes. '*Beatles* is a well made, very well executed portrayal of a bygone era,' he concluded.

BEATLES FOR SALE

One thing many of the critics did agree on was the quality of the score, but Magne confirmed during 2014's a-ha fan convention that he was slightly disappointed with the end result. 'I wanted to make a much more radical score than what ended up [in the movie],' he said. 'There was a kind of a struggle, a fight between me and the director – who came in a little bit late in the process – to make him understand what I was trying to do. So, to my mind, the last version that I heard was a compromise where they had used my music in a way that I wasn't a hundred per cent satisfied with.' Magne did, however, indicate he was happy with the actual album. 'The album is different,' he said, 'because I made the album afterwards; a little bit more like I wanted the movie to sound . . . I said, "This is what you should use" and, of course, they didn't listen.'

Overseeing the production of the film's score was Magne's former Timbersound partner, Kjetil Bjerkestrand, and many of the parts were laid down at Abbey Road Studios, using old microphones and tape reels to give the music added period authenticity.

Most of the string arrangements were supervised by David Davidson, who had reportedly flown in from Nashville. 'David Davidson has a PhD in Beatles strings and is a fantastic guy,' Magne told *Dagbladet*. 'He has done string arrangements for a-ha in the past, so I know him well.' Other tracks, such as 'Kim's Triumph' and 'Will She or Won't She', featured the talents of the London Philharmonic Orchestra, while more familiar names on the album credits included Karl Oluf Wennerberg (drums), Dan Sundhordvik (guitar) and Johnny Sjo (bass).

Although the resulting soundtrack album was a largely instrumental work, it did include some vocal tracks, including Magne's fragile but affecting interpretation of 'Yesterday', the much-covered classic which Morten himself had performed in concert in 2001. 'We initially tried to use the original Beatles version,' Magne told *Dagbladet*, 'but that particular scene screams for something less perfect, and I thought it could be worth a try. It was of course necessary to do a completely different version, as I could never get close to the original one, but the idea was that it needed a certain roughness to match the scene's atmosphere.'

Fronting the album was Apparatjik's charismatic version of John Lennon's 'Come Together', recorded in collaboration with both Icona Pop – who'd scored a worldwide hit with the memorable 'I Love It' – and the Swedish electropop duo's compatriot and collaborator, Erik Hassle. Magne also supervised the recordings by the Spellemann-nominated band Hvitmalt Gjerde, whose members would also appear in the movie as the fictional band, the Snowflakes. Several of the Bergen band's original songs featured in the movie, including 'Et kyss til' [One More Kiss], a nifty, Monkees-esque slice of garage pop that was in keeping with Magne's ambition for an authentic 60s sound. Elsewhere, 'Sukker og salt (Sugar and Salt)' – credited to the Rosenberg Allstars – featured some impressive harmonica playing from Magne and a lead vocal from actor Louis Williams, who was cast as lead character and narrator Kim Karlsen in the movie.

The *Beatles* soundtrack was released, digitally, in September 2014, shortly after the film's release in Norway. It was eventually issued as a CD and limited edition vinyl LP two years later, when it was released in Japan – under the new title of *Yesterday* – by the film soundtrack specialists Cinema-kan.

CHAPTER TWENTY-SEVEN

WEATHERVANE

Following a-ha's farewell shows in December 2010, Pål was approached at an aftershow party by film-maker Morten Tyldum, who had been looking for a song for his new movie, *Hodejegerne* [Headhunters], which was based on Jo Nesbø's bestselling thriller. At the time, Pål had almost finished writing a song that detailed a scenario in which he had been left at home for a week while his wife holidayed in London ('So you're going for a week to sort out your head / So you left me here to keep things going'). 'When I read the script, it felt like a good fit,' Pål told *VG Nett*. 'There are a lot of undercurrents in the movie that could work well with the song. It looks like a really great film.'

The end result was the 'Weathervane' single in June 2011, recorded in collaboration with Jimmy Gnecco, who was well known to Pål, not only through his support slot for a-ha the previous year but also as a lead vocalist on Savoy's version of 'The Breakers' in 2004. 'I met Pål in 1996 through a mutual friend named Greg Calvert [Savoy's original bassist],' he recalled in 2016. 'We talked for a bit about doing something together and then started to do things here and there. I always loved a-ha and then Pål's band, Savoy – I wanted to be the singer.'[1]

'This chance to front a new project again was just too good to let go,' Pål told *VG Nett*. 'I like the way this has evolved. Weathervane hasn't been put together on a whim – we have known each other for a long time and Jimmy has just the right vocal range that my songs need to reach their full potential.'

Accompanied by a video that was filmed in Woodstock and directed by Lauren Savoy, the song didn't stray too far from the synth-pop of Foot of the Mountain and its attendant swansong, 'Butterfly, Butterfly (The Last Hurrah)'. Beginning with some lovely Elton John-esque piano flourishes and featuring a typically soaring chorus, the song would have been perfect for a-ha. Its melancholic properties were certainly appreciated by *VG*'s Morten Ståle Nilsen, who wrote: 'The beat is fierily electronic, the piano plays along resignedly, the tone is grandiosely sad . . . Everything is as it should be in Waaktaar's anxious universe.'

During interviews to promote the single, Pål hinted that the Weathervane project could potentially stretch to an album, and there was talk of releasing more singles prior to a potential album release at the end of the year. 'I always have a bunch of things lying around and I may end up using the songs intended for a-ha in Weathervane,' he said. 'We have already tested out some stuff in the studio.'[2]

Having performed the track with the band during the Amanda Awards in August, there was also talk of Frode Unneland joining Weathervane on a permanent basis, but the project ultimately wound up.

The band's only officially released song was eventually repurposed for Savoy's 2018 album, *See the Beauty in Your Drab Hometown*. The updated version employs a slower tempo and strips away the piano that characterised the original track, while the new lead vocal is imbued with distortion. 'We're using an old microphone that used to be a telephone on the song, so it sounds like it's recorded a hundred years ago,' explained Pål. 'Frode is doing his best sort of Band harmonies on the pre-chorus, where he's being Richard Manuel and Rick Danko at the same time!'

GOOD GOODBYES

The next few years would see Pål stockpiling songs for Savoy and other artists, including Jimmy Gnecco's daughter, Zoë. In 2012, Pål and Lauren helped out their studio engineer Eliot Leigh – who was using the pseudonym, Infuze – on a dubstep recording titled 'Far Away', supplying lyrics and a guide vocal melody. Pål also produced a song – later released by Savoy as 'Bump' – for *Scent of a Woman*, a short film that Lauren had directed in 2013. Pål also appeared on Hågen Rørmark's album *Alt eller ingenting* [All or Nothing], performing drums on 'Ensom leter' [Solitary Searcher]. Rørmark had met Pål via chance following the terrorist attacks in September 2001 and later played harmonica on Savoy's 'Is My Confidence Reeling?', as well as playing acoustic guitar during their mini-tour in 2008.

One other significant project during this period was Linnea Dale's 2014 album, *Good Goodbyes*, which Pål had a big hand in. 'I loved her voice from the first moment,' he told *VG*. 'It doesn't matter what kind of microphone or filters you use, it's all there from the get-go. She has her own knack for melodies, and an unusual way of using words. It flows beautifully.' He added: 'This is the first time I've done something like this, and I liked it.'

Dale was a former finalist on season five of the Norwegian version of *Pop Idol* in 2007 and – following some tuition from guest mentor Morten, who also performed 'Movies' on the night – sang a version of 'Velvet' during an a-ha-themed live show. However, the performance was criticised by the judges, who couldn't look past the fact that the singer had forgotten to insert her in-ear monitors. Although she was eliminated from the contest after the round, the then-16-year-old singer was grateful for the experience, telling *VG*: 'It has been fantastic to be part of this, and to get as far as I have done.' Following a two-year break, she guested on Donkeyboy's 2009 debut album, *Caught in a Life* – which included the Norwegian chart-topper 'Ambitions' – and later performed with them as a-ha's support act on the *Foot of the Mountain* tour.

She eventually released her debut solo album, *Lemoyne Street*, in 2012, before teaming up with Pål. Three songs were co-written and produced by him at his

Brooklyn studio, namely 'Better without You', 'Sweet Life' and the outstanding 'With Eyes Closed', which shares the same percussive lift as Kate Bush's 'Running Up That Hill'. 'It was fabulous,' Dale told NRK P1. 'I have enormous respect for him as a songwriter, so it was great to go over there. We started out with a pre-production session here in Oslo where we tested out some ideas, and then I flew over to New York and spent a week there a while later.'

Another album track, 'High Hopes', was selected as a potential entry for the Eurovision Song Contest in Denmark in 2014, but despite a strong showing in the final of the Melodi Grand Prix at the Oslo Spektrum, Carl Espen's power ballad 'Silent Storm' eventually emerged as the winner. 'High Hopes' was also singled out for praise by Stein Østbø in his album review for *VG*,

but he was seemingly not that impressed with the rest of the album: 'Not even Pål Waaktaar-Savoy can bring magic to the anonymity that characterises large parts of the record,' he concluded. However, the reviews elsewhere were more generous. 'There is a lot of elegant and stylish pop music here,' wrote *Adresseavisen*'s Vegard Enlid. '. . . Both in voice and looks, she has the potential to become a Norwegian Lana Del Rey.' *Dagsavisen*'s Espen Hågensen Rusdal also praised Dale for the 'dark quality' of her vocals and 'High Hopes' for its 'tight production and grand chorus'.

PART NINE

THIS IS OUR HOME
2015–2019

CHAPTER TWENTY-EIGHT

CAST IN STEEL

*A-ha will never return after 4 December 2010. There will be no more album
releases or concerts.*
– Magne Furuholmen, *Dagbladet*, 2009

Released: September 2015
Chart position: 8 (UK), 2 (Norway), 4 (Germany)

When a-ha made their official announcement to reform, following weeks of
teasers and speculation – and four years to the day since their curtain call at
the Oslo Spektrum on 4 December 2010 – they weren't the first act to make
such a spectacular career U turn, and they certainly won't be the last. Indeed,
throughout the history of popular music, there have been numerous instances
where artists and bands have reneged on their bold – and often premature –
decisions to either retire from touring or break up altogether.

At the peak of his career in the early 80s, Gary Numan announced his retirement
from touring in 1981, but following a series of spectacular farewell shows at
Wembley Arena in April that year, the synth-pop pioneer was back on the road

less than 18 months later. In 1984, when a drug-addled Status Quo embarked on a huge tour – which included a seven-night residency at the Hammersmith Apollo – it was meant to mark the end of the road for the veteran rockers and the start of a solo career for their frontman, Francis Rossi. But following their so-called final show at the Milton Keynes Bowl in July 1984, they opened Live Aid almost a year later, before touring extensively with a new line-up during the ensuing years. And then there was the Eagles, who reformed for some live shows in 1994, following their acrimonious split in 1980. For the resulting live album, they humorously titled it *Hell Freezes Over* after a much-used quote from the US rock band's co-vocalist and drummer Don Henley, which referred to the likelihood of them ever reforming.

'I believed – and hoped – that a-ha was a finished chapter,' Magne told Dagbladet, 'but you're allowed to change your mind. I said it was over, but I was wrong.'

I THINK I WILL TRAVEL TO RIO

A-ha's well-publicised reunion was precipitated by an invitation to perform at the *Rock in Rio* festival in September 2015. With the Brazilian city forming the scene of, arguably, the band's greatest live triumph in 1991, it was an invitation that was difficult to resist. 'It did feel like something that was impossible to say no to,' said Magne. 'It was almost like, "Okay they're throwing a birthday party for you, are you gonna come?"'[1]

At this stage, the band's reunion was seemingly restricted to just one concert, which would neatly tie in with the 30th anniversary of both the festival and the band's international breakthrough. 'We haven't made any additional plans beyond Rio,' Magne told NRK, 'and it was difficult enough to rally the troops for this concert. In a moment of bravado, we agreed to do this, and then we'll see if it leads to something more. The plan now is just to appear at *Rock in Rio* once more to celebrate the festival and ourselves.'

Just three months later, however, during a press conference in Berlin in March 2015, tentative details of a brand new studio album – titled *Cast in Steel* – and tour were announced. The media reaction to the news was mixed, and one particular Norwegian journalist was seemingly incensed by a-ha's return, which they confirmed was only for a set period: 'They have signed a "two-year contract", which emphasises that a-ha is no longer a band, but a business enterprise,' wrote *VG*'s Thomas Talseth 'I would like to remind you that, in 2009, Furuholmen claimed to *VG* that there was a greater chance of ABBA being reunited than a-ha getting together again. And that's one reason why we remember ABBA as a pure, unblemished and unique success story.'

The reactions from the band's fans were also mixed, particularly from those who had travelled from far afield to witness the band's final shows in Oslo. 'I do not understand why people are so hard on us that we're back,' responded Morten. 'When we broke up, that was for real. The separation was necessary for us . . . In my view, the break has done us good. We all believed in the separation, and our comeback is just as real.'[2]

IN TRANSIT

Before a-ha's initial announcement in December 2014, a reunion hadn't seemed likely. Morten had re-established himself as a solo artist, gaining favourable reviews – and commensurate sales – for his *Brother* album. Magne, meanwhile, had busied himself composing the score for the *Beatles* film, as well as contributing to recordings by Marius Beck, Tini Flaat Mykland and Martin Halla, all acts he had mentored during Norway's version of the hit reality TV show *The Voice* in 2012. He'd also co-written 'Breathe' for the Backstreet Boys and released a second album of intergalactic highbrow pop with Apparatjik. As recently as October 2014, the multitalented ensemble had performed two shows – in conjunction with the Norwegian Radio Orchestra – at the Fosnavåg Konserthus, which had opened its doors that month. This was all of course in addition to his dual career as a visual artist, and a compendium of his works, titled *In Transit*, was published in 2013. There were other commissions, too, including cover designs for both Steve Barron's memoir, *Egg n Chips & Billie Jean: A Trip Through the 80s*, and ophthalmologist Jon Ståle Ritland's unusual poetry collection, *I bane rundt en gul ball* [Orbiting the Yellow Ball], which is centred around the world of tennis.

Despite his slightly flippant remark at the Berlin press conference that he'd been 'super busy and released one song' ('Manmade Lake'), Pål had actually worked on a number of projects during the band's hiatus, and was also grateful for the opportunity to spend some quality time with his son. During a period which he likened to having a day job, he collaborated with Jimmy Gnecco on 'Weathervane' and contributed to albums by Linnea Dale and Hågen Rørmark. As he told *Dagbladet* in 2015, there were other projects in the pipeline, too: 'Me and Lauren have a new Savoy album almost ready,' he said, 'while my own solo album is all finished. I have also written and produced an album with Jimmy Gnecco's daughter, Zoë, which I'm hoping will be released later this year.'

It also transpired that Pål had worked with Morten on a number of new songs during the summer of 2012, with the singer cherry-picking his favourite tracks – a process the guitarist likened to the band's time in Nærsnes in 1982. 'That was actually the best part of this record for me,' said Pål. 'We did it all without anyone knowing, without deadlines and all that stuff. It was, in a way, like a return to the London years, and we had no obligations.'[3]

There were some initial discussions about releasing the material as a duo, but the project was eventually put on ice. Morten forged ahead with his solo career and the songs would lay dormant, before eventually resurfacing on Waaktaar & Zoe's *World of Trouble* album and *Cast in Steel* itself.

As Pål later revealed, Magne had been made aware of the potential duo project: 'I think Harald [Wiik] told Magne that we were working on something, and at first he thought it was a sort of side project,' he said. 'However, during the summer, we discovered that the songs we recorded were too a-ha-like to not be a-ha. Magne had to make a decision, and I think that pretty much knocked him off balance. After all, it was he who felt the greatest urge to end a-ha.'[4]

As Morten later revealed, he didn't view these secret sessions as the start of an a-ha project. 'I certainly felt free from that way of thinking,' he said. '. . . Songs are songs, and if Pål has a few songs up his sleeve and wants me to sing them and see what happens, to people outside that would be an a-ha happening, so to speak, but to us it wasn't. It wasn't about that, it was freed from that. So it could just be he and I coming together on a song, looking at something.'

It's hard to imagine what sort of reaction would have greeted a Harket/Waaktaar album – particularly among a-ha's fandom – but, eventually, the likelihood of such a project soon evaporated once Magne decided he wanted to be involved. 'The other two wanted to do it,' he said, 'and I had to decide: Do I block it, let them do it without me, or make a fool of myself, with my statements about this being the end.'[5]

EACH ON OUR OWN

As was the way with a-ha in the new millennium, the process of recording a new album was blighted by band politics. Gone was the back-to-basics approach employed so successfully on *Foot of the Mountain*, which largely saw Pål restored as the band's primary lyric writer. In its place was the more democratic template that fans had been accustomed to since *Minor Earth Minor Sky*.

Returning musicians included drummers Karl Oluf Wennerberg and Per Lindvall, but there were also some new faces. These included boyhood fan Even Ormestad, the bassist with experimental jazz combo Jaga Jazzist, who would later become a permanent fixture in a-ha's live set-up. 'I've been standing in front of the mirror and playing bass to a-ha songs since before I was a teenager,' he said prior to the ensuing tour, 'so I should be well-prepared!'[6]

True to form, Pål had a stockpile of songs to choose from, as did Morten, who had resumed his songwriting partnership with Peter Kvint, following the successful *Brother* album. As for Magne, while he was relatively late to the party, he relished the challenge of integrating some new songs. 'I was surprised how natural it felt for me to be writing lyrics with Morten in mind,' he said. 'I mean, when I write for my own voice, there are big areas that overlap, but there are certain things that I know he will react to or won't like, but I didn't feel like it was an imposition. I didn't feel like I was trying to make my own album and then would be crushed if he didn't like it. It was more a case of me trying to look for something that would work . . . I was just really surprised that I'd missed it. I missed thinking about a-ha.'

COME BACK, MY ANALOGUE

Almost like a flashback to the *Lifelines* era, much of the work on *Cast in Steel* was done independently of each other, and with a number of different producers on board. Pål's idea to revisit the band's old method of working, with just one producer – in this case, Alan Tarney – overseeing the whole album was later rejected. 'I just always felt that he really understood our thing, you know,' he explained during the Berlin press conference. 'We did a show at the Albert Hall and I invited him for that. He sat next to my parents and said, "I'm the one they used to quarrel with in the 80s!" He knows us before we were us. So it's kinda cool to go back to him. You can set back the time and make it a little more naive again. It's all about just the song, how that chorus hits and how Morten sounds in it. He's got a lot of knowledge about music. He's just got that no-nonsense feel that I like and respect a lot. So it's been great to be in contact with him again, and I hope he can be a part of this album.'

According to Morten, 10 demos were sent to Tarney, but in the end only three of his productions made it to the finished album. 'It was exciting how the edited pieces gradually came back to us,' said Morten in the lead-up to the album's release. 'That was undoubtedly Alan Tarney! He has a very different approach to music than we do.'[7]

Pål later confirmed that neither Morten nor Magne was interested in meeting up with the veteran producer, with the latter making the point clear during the March press conference: 'Pål is the one who's been working with Alan,' he said. 'We've worked in very different ways, which is not something that's new to us. We have made quite a few albums like this, where we are based in different places, working on our own material, but with a-ha as the overriding factor . . . To a certain degree, it's the type of album we can make at this point. For all the romance of harking back to the beginnings, I think part of the reality is that we live very different and separate lives. But a-ha is a legacy that we have together; it's a common fate.'

As for the album's musical orientation, this was something else that couldn't be agreed on. 'The three of us are never in sync regarding the direction of a new album,' said Morten. 'Sometimes one wants it more retro, the other less; one wants more guitar, the other more synths.'[8]

WE'VE MADE IT TO THE END

Another challenge facing the band, given the vast pool of material at their disposal, was deciding on a final tracklisting for the album. 'The songwriting is always the easiest part,' said Morten. 'The hard part is trying to agree on which songs that will end up on the album. That is always an enormous challenge. Personally, I'm surprised by how strong the new album has turned out to be. It's not inferior to our earlier albums.'[9]

Since they'd not used an A&R man since the *Minor Earth Major Sky* album, the band were entrusted with coming up with the final selection themselves – a process Pål described as 'total chaos' during an interview with *VG*. 'How are we supposed to agree on things, when all three of us have different things that we care about?' he said. 'It ends up being so much noise, and it saps so much energy that I'm like, "Okay, next album!" I feel like I need another ten years before I can listen to this album again.'

During the press conference, Tom Bromley – who would also ghostwrite Morten's 2016 memoir, *My Take on Me* – quoted the opening lines of 'Open Face' before his interview with the band, but the track didn't make the final cut, and the version that Pål recorded with Zoë Gnecco was eventually released instead. Other songs under consideration during this period included 'Did I Leave You Behind?' – which had been earmarked for Morten's *Brother* album – plus 'Digital River', 'Hold Me' and 'Karma King', which, at the time of writing, remain unreleased. One of Magne's out-takes, 'The End of the Affair', was included on the deluxe version of the album, but there was another song, titled 'Flags in the Air', which he claims was rejected outright. It was later recorded as a duet with his son, Filip Clements. (As a birth announcement from the period reveals, the name Clements had originally been given to Magne. 'My father wanted this name for me,' he confirmed, 'but my mother said no.')

TRIUMPHANT RETURN

With all the challenges presented to the band during its making, it was perhaps surprising that *Cast in Steel* turned out as well as it did. During a month which also included the release of new albums by their contemporaries Duran Duran and New Order, *Cast in Steel* dropped in September 2015, housed in a dichromatic sleeve that featured a relatively new Just Loomis shot of the band as well as the reinstatement of the original a-ha logo, missing since 1993's *Memorial Beach*. Sadly, the opportunity to include a broader selection of out-takes on the deluxe two-disc version of the album was squandered, and alternative versions of tracks from *Foot of the Mountain* were somehow deemed to be of more interest to the purchaser.

Despite the marketing pitfalls, however, there was a generally good response to a-ha's comeback album, particularly in the UK, and most critics agreed that the opus added to – rather than blemished – their legacy. '*Cast in Steel* is a triumphant return,' wrote Chris Gerard for *PopMatters*. 'It's wonderful to hear one of the most underrated bands of the last three decades back with such a powerful musical statement.' Alan Morrison's review for *The Herald* was similarly enthusiastic: 'If they continued to write dreamy pop classics like the title track and "She's Humming a Tune", I'm sure no one would complain if a-ha went on forever.' In his review for *Classic Pop* magazine, Wyndham Wallace queried the release of 'Under the Makeup' as the first single, but concluded: 'On the evidence here, a-ha are best when they choose not to try too hard. Honestly, they should break up more often.'

In Norway, however, the media weren't quite as receptive to the comeback album, and there was a sense that the band had a target on their backs following their decision to return. The band's slight dip in popularity was also reflected in the chart placing for the album, which was held off the top spot by the Weeknd's second album, *Beauty Behind the Madness* (a title that perhaps belonged more to a-ha than the Canadian R&B star!). *VG*'s Stein Østbø claimed that *Cast in Steel* continued in the vein of *Foot of the Mountain* but wasn't a classic album. 'As a whole, the record suffers from an almost provocative lack of tempo change,' he wrote. Elsewhere, *Dagbladet*'s Torgrim Øyre also agreed about its supposed one-dimensional pace, labelling the collection a 'sedate trot'. 'It's hard to muster great enthusiasm for this comeback,' he concluded. *Adresseavisen*'s reviewer, meanwhile, felt the album lacked substance: 'It balances on a knife edge between the luxuriously beautiful and the luxuriously insubstantial,' wrote Vegard Enlid. '. . . The record is more a tribute to the 80s than the more contemporary Coldplay-esque adult pop they have delivered in the 2000s.' Despite the mixed reviews, a-ha received their first Spellemann nomination in several years, and the ensuing tour was both a commercial and critical success.

Fans were also spoilt with a number of reissues in 2015, which included expanded editions of *Stay on These Roads*, *East of the Sun, West of the Moon* and *Memorial Beach*, as well as a mouth-watering super deluxe edition of *Hunting High and Low*, which stretched to five discs.

In short, it was great to have them back.

CAST IN STEEL
Written by Pål Waaktaar-Savoy
Produced by Erik Ljunggren and Pål Waaktaar-Savoy

Additional vocal production by Peter Kvint and Morten Harket
Something of a composite of the terms 'cast iron' and 'set in stone', the emotive title track of a-ha's 10th studio album was not, as some people suggested, a reflection of the band's immovability; furthermore, couplets such as 'I'll never get over what we said / It lingers in my head' were not indicative of Pål's state of mind in the wake a-ha's 2010 split, which the band's biggest cheerleader had been opposed to. Instead, this was a comfortingly nostalgic and heartfelt snapshot of a more innocent time in someone's life ('We made a pact / Eye to eye / Cross your heart / And hope to die'), with its vivid, cinematic opening ('Meet me at the turnaround / Stop your car and look around') and signature melancholic stamp revealing what fans had missed during the band's enforced hiatus.

The sentiments of the mid-paced song are beautifully enriched by a lush, but not overpowering, string arrangement, while its melodic bass work and subtle flourishes of electronics make for an engaging opening listen, and it's difficult to fathom why this was overlooked as the opening single in favour of 'Under the Makeup'. However, a black and white lyric video was created for the song, serving as a tantalising foretaste of the album, while a new, glossier mix by Steve Osborne, featuring a more dramatic intro and swathes of extra keyboard parts, was later released as a download-only single. (Both versions of the song were played during the *Cast in Steel* tour.)

UNDER THE MAKEUP
Written by Pål Waaktaar-Savoy
Produced by Erik Ljunggren and Pål Waaktaar-Savoy
Vocal production by Peter Kvint and Morten Harket

According to Pål, the writing of this sophisticated ballad marked a rare occasion where the lyrics were written first, and it concerns a relationship that has ostensibly weathered over time ('Meanwhile our hearts turn to stone / Shaped by wind / Boulders slowly moulded over time') and seemingly on the cusp of ending ('If you wanted out / Didn't I let you go / . . . Tenderness escapes so easily').

Like the album's title track, it had originally been recorded by Pål and Zoë Gnecco, and the original lyrics of the track – as performed by them during Savoy's sole live show in 2018 – confirm that it was written with a female singer in mind ('You wanna see me under the makeup / Let all the worry vanish away / You wanna hold me / Like it's the last time'). Pål felt that Morten's interpretation, which was written in a different key, gave the song more of a romantic vibe, and his bandmate later praised his efforts: '[It's] definitely one of the songs I knew Morten had a very strong feeling about as a symbol of the strengths of Pål's writing,' said Magne. 'I like it when Pål is not afraid to be passionate and declare that his heart is on the sleeve. I push for that, and these are the songs which touch me.'[10]

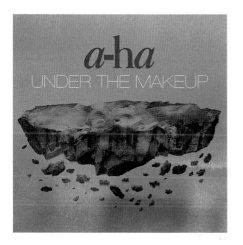 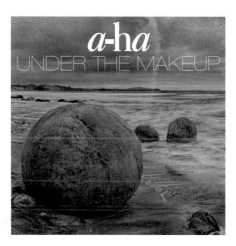

Befitting of its strong emotional content, the ballad was enhanced by a suitably grandiose string arrangement, which arrived courtesy of Even Ormestad's Jaga Jazzist bandmate, Lars Horntveth, who co-ordinated the session via Skype. According to Horntveth, the arrangement had been inspired by James Bond soundtrack composer David Arnold's work on Björk's 1993 hit, 'Play Dead'.

With its stark, piano-led intro and bombastic string arrangement – which is brought more to the fore in the Cenzo Townshend mix – 'Under the Makeup' was a brave choice for a comeback single, but *Adresseavisen*'s Vegard Enlid thought it was well-judged: 'The song sticks in your head right at the first line and melody change,' he said. 'It only takes eight seconds to realise that this is a really good choice as a single.' Other reviews in the band's homeland were positive, too. *VG*'s Stein Østbø labelled it 'archetypal a-ha' and 'impossible to dislike'. However, he felt the string arrangement was over the top: 'This song doesn't need strings to underscore the drama of the lyrics and melody, this song needs a more sparse arrangement around Morten Harket's voice'. Elsewhere, *Dagbladet*'s Torgrim Øyre wrote: 'Thanks to Harket's trademark vocals and Pål Waaktaar-Savoy's very distinct melodic signature, it's hard for a-ha to do much wrong as long as they stick to their basic formula.' However, not every reviewer was as complimentary. Dagsavisen's

Espen Hågensen Rusdal declared that the strings couldn't hide the song's weaknesses, and concluded: 'A-ha is now more reminiscent of a vanity project than a pop group with good ideas.'

'Under the Makeup' officially premiered on Norwegian radio in July 2015, but there was some controversy over its cover as the crumbling rock design had already been used by Victor Chissano on his single 'I'm a Renegade'. The situation was downplayed by the band's management, however, and another stock image – featuring Koekohe Beach's Moeraki Boulders – appeared in its place soon after.

A lyric video utilising the Koekohe imagery was also streamed, but an official video – featuring *Forbrydelsen* [aka *The Killing*] actress Sofie Gråbøl – was also commissioned for the John O'Mahoney mix of the track, which toned down the radio version's windswept histrionics.

During the ensuing tour, the band performed a more moving, stripped-back version of the song, highlighting both the candour and vulnerability in the lyrics.

THE WAKE
Music written by Morten Harket and Peter Kvint
Words written by Morten Harket and Ole Sverre Olsen
Produced by Peter Kvint and Morten Harket

Marking Peter Kvint's debut on an a-ha album was this deceptively light, mid-paced number, which the band opened with on some of the early shows on the *Cast in Steel* tour.

With its majestic chorus, pulsating synth-bass work and shards of Peter Hook-esque guitar, 'The Wake' not only maintained the album's early form but also served as a reminder of Ole Sverre Olsen's lyrical prowess. Both the funereal title and lyrics ('Baby, this is a wake / None of us will escape / Who we are') are certainly

consistent with other co-writes such as 'First Man to the Grave' and 'There Are Many Ways to Die', which feature curious meditations on mortality, while there's also an air of mystery about the track ('Stung by normality / Wronged by your family / Conventions aside') that's almost Waaktaar-like in its scope.

It's a highly subjective piece, but it's possible that Olsen was drawing once again from his 1998 book *Den døde mannen*, which concerns a man ruminating on his drug-addled life, in addition to coming to terms with his posthumous existence.

FOREST FIRE
Music written by Magne Furuholmen, Morten Harket, Martin Terefe and Peter Kvint
Words written by Magne Furuholmen
Produced by Steve Osborne, Magne Furuholmen and Erik Ljunggren
Vocal production by Peter Kvint and Morten Harket

Deviating quite dramatically from the album's early mid-tempo pace was this unashamedly commercial crowd pleaser, though something of a retrogression to the Europop of tracks such as 'I Won't Forget Her'. However, while 'Forest Fire' was full of dazzling keyboard work and swathes of fire metaphors that almost bordered on parody ('We are flames in the forest fire / Rising from within / That's where we begin / And we fuel desire'), there was no denying this was the album's catchiest and most immediate track. It's arguable that the vocals were pitched too high, but this was rectified during live performances, with Magne's backing vocals providing a welcome counterpoint.

Unsurprisingly, it was selected for promotional single release, while an alternative mix by Steve Osborne was also accessible via the internet.

OBJECTS IN THE MIRROR
Written by Magne Furuholmen
Produced by Steve Osborne, Magne Furuholmen and Erik Ljunggren
Vocal production by Peter Kvint and Morten Harket

Despite the fact it (almost) shared its title with a 20-year-old Meat Loaf ballad, the name of this mid-paced track actually stemmed from a poetry collection of Magne's titled *Birthrightis*, and it found its writer in a sentimental mood, revisiting some of the ground that had been covered on prior nostalgic cuts such as 'The Summers of Our Youth'. In 'Objects in the Mirror', Magne takes listeners on an engaging trip down life's highway, reflecting on a past that continues to catch up with him ('You've come so far / In your comfortable car / Now objects in the rear-view mirror / Seem closer than they are'). But rather than simply delivering a meditation on fame, the thinly veiled protagonist acknowledges the steering influence of his family ('When the world was at your feet / Love would make your life complete / No one makes it on their own'), as well as reflecting on the good times along the way in the Pet Shop Boys-esque middle eight ('Come on now / It's not so bad / Thinking back on the fun we had').

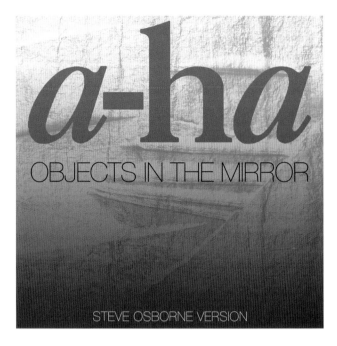

Driven both by the band's potent new rhythm section and an elegant string arrangement by David Davidson, 'Objects in the Mirror' also featured a typically pristine vocal from Morten, whose falsetto work in the final third really accentuates the song's emotive pull. With the subtle perforation of guitar and keyboards also adding some welcome layers, the end result was one of the album's highlights.

The track was also selected for release as the final single to be culled from the album in 2016 and a Steve Osborne mix – which included an earlier fade – was available for download. Meanwhile, the sentiments of the song were beautifully interpreted in the accompanying video by Magne's Apparatjik bandmate Jonas Bjerre. The memorable semi-animated promo clip interspersed ground and aerial shots of Manglerud, along with various photos of Magne, Morten and Pål in their formative years, images that were also used as backdrops on the *Cast in Steel* tour.

DOOR AJAR
Written by Pål Waaktaar-Savoy
Produced by Pål Waaktaar-Savoy and Alan Tarney
Pre-production and guidance by John O'Mahoney

One thing a-ha could rarely be accused of was predictability, and this oddly titled curveball certainly confirmed that the band were still capable of producing experimental and thought-provoking music. 'Our songs already have far too many chords to be played in dance clubs,' said Pål. 'We also want to do unpredictable things. The most interesting ideas always come to you unexpectedly. The older you get, the harder it is to surprise yourself.'[11]

Playing out like a modern-day companion piece to the Kafta-esque narrative of 'Scoundrel Days', 'Door Ajar' finds its protagonist in a similarly dreamlike state, hallucinating as his body crashes against the bedding ('I hit my head on the pillow hard / I heard a noise from the boulevard / And it made me go down / I left the door to my room ajar / Felt the rumble of the streetcar'). But from the 'pillows of ashes', a towering chorus arises, which is almost 'Waterloo Sunset'-like in its melodic execution, but Joy Division-esque in its lyrical expression ('Feelings forsaken / Faded and scattered / Would you come running / If you could hear me'). The 'Door Ajar' refrain, meanwhile, has shades of 'The Blue Sky' in its deft simplicity.

With such an evocation to their heyday, who better to oversee the recording than one of the band's original producers, Alan Tarney? 'Many producers of today place great emphasis on the beat,' said Pål, 'because this increases the chance to be played on the radio. Alan focuses on the melodies.'[12] The melody of the song – which includes a potent 'do-do-do' earworm – certainly cuts through the complex tapestry of gently fizzing electronic sounds, processed guitar parts and synthetic vocals, and the end result is a truly compelling piece that perhaps requires repeated listens to fully appreciate.

LIVING AT THE END OF THE WORLD
Music written by Morten Harket and Peter Kvint
Words written by Morten Harket and Ole Sverre Olsen
Produced by Peter Kvint and Morten Harket

Another highlight of the album was this fine electro-ballad, which displayed further evidence of Morten's growing maturity as a songwriter. Its lyrics – co-written by Ole Sverre Olsen – ostensibly deal with impending mortality ('Sometimes it leaves me with fear / Never saw the horizon this near'), but its passionate chorus and underlying spirituality ('See, there is something I know / We are not whom we're told') offsets any gloomy overtones. Crisply produced, Morten's satin-smooth vocals drift beautifully over a warm bed of shimmering synths, perfectly complemented by Matthias Bylund's understated string arrangement.

MYTHOMANIA
Written by Magne Furuholmen
Produced by Magne Furuholmen and Erik Ljunggren
Vocal production by Peter Kvint and Morten Harket

'This song is about twisting truth and spinning a yarn of subtle little lies which ultimately leads to a lonely place,' explained Magne. 'I used the word mythomania as a country or place, kind of like Transylvania. It was interesting to look at a mythomaniac as someone who physically moved into an imaginary castle in an imaginary place. In other words, someone who has left a common understanding of things, as well as any trace of communal reality behind, in pursuit of the most comfortable or personally desirable version of events or history.'

As becoming of a song with such biting lyrics, the soundtrack is suitably icy, with analogue synths combining with thick, ridged basslines to produce a track redolent of *Sounds of the Universe*-era Depeche Mode, with a soupçon of OMD-esque choral flourishes thrown into the mix. It's a little slow and pedestrian by the band's standards, however, and a more dynamic production may have taken it to another level.

SHE'S HUMMING A TUNE
Written by Pål Waaktaar-Savoy
Produced by Pål Waaktaar-Savoy and Erik Ljunggren
Pre-production and guidance by John O'Mahoney

Unsurprisingly, given that it's cut from the same musical cloth as the title track of *Scoundrel Days*, the origins of 'She's Humming a Tune' can be traced back to the band's early years in Sydenham, and its vintage is nicely emphasised by a bookend of vinyl crackles. But it was never actually recorded at John Ratcliff's Rendezvous Studios. Instead, it existed in handwritten format – another song immortalised in one of Pål's many notebooks, which brimmed with ideas, sketches and hopes for the future ('Oh I'd like to go to England / And make a million pounds', began one entry from December 1981). But these notebooks were left behind as a-ha's career went into overdrive in the wake of the phenomenal success of 'Take On Me', with an indignant Ratcliff taking temporary ownership of this veritable treasure trove as Terry Slater took full managerial control of the band.

Sadly, it would take the intervention of two passionate fans – as well as a substantial sum of money – to reunite Pål with his lost notebooks over a quarter of a century later (in June 2011). By this point, some of the pages were missing, having mysteriously found their way onto auction sites such as eBay, something Ratcliff denied doing. The former Rendezvous Studios owner was accused in some quarters of holding the notebooks to ransom, but he countered that the monies received were recompense for his work with the band, which he always felt was devalued.

Although Pål and John Ratcliff eventually benefitted from what *Aftenposten* described as a 'rescue operation', there were other beneficiaries, too. The Rockheim Museum in Trondheim gratefully took possession of the studio's Brenell Mini-8 multitrack recorder and included it in one of their excellent displays, while the retrieval of various tape reels meant the band's fans were finally able to listen to professionally mixed demos of tracks – which had previously been leaked onto the internet – via 2015's super deluxe edition of *Hunting High and Low*. And then there was 'She's Humming a Tune', which Pål had ostensibly forgotten about. 'When I got the books back, I saw the text and remembered, "That one, yes, that was cool", he said. 'Then I thought it would be cool to record this particular one now.'[13]

Based on some of the lyrics, it's perhaps safe to assume that the song was penned in the early throes of Pål's relationship with Lauren, with lines such as 'Decisions are weighing / Ever so hard on her mind / And I don't suppose she knows / Everything that's bound to happen' hinting at some early uncertainty (and insecurity). Pål also said the original version of the song was sourced for the middle eight of 'Take On Me', which would date the song to 1983.

Although the song was played during the *Cast in Steel* tour, the track wasn't included on the vinyl version of the album.

SHADOW ENDEAVORS
Written by Pål Waaktaar-Savoy
Produced by Pål Waaktaar-Savoy and Alan Tarney
Pre-production and guidance by John O'Mahoney

A song of contrasting styles, 'Shadow Endeavors' – spelt the American way – represented another throwback to the band's past, with Pål cleverly repurposing a disused verse from an early version of 'Scoundrel Days' ('Oh it only ever happens to me once / Doesn't come again / I think somebody lost me here / Afraid and lonely / A long time ago') and affixing it to a disparate section. With its glistening electronic intro, the audaciously experimental piece instantly draws listeners into its EDM-style void, with Morten's smooth but slightly offbeat falsetto providing the focal point, unfurling classic Waaktaar vignettes such as: 'Why say a thing to another living soul / Let us pay no mind / To a world that seems unkind'. By contrast, the coda deadens the meandering pace, tying a wistful bow around its melancholic wrapping.

As with 'Door Ajar' (and, later, 'Goodbye Thompson'), Pål was assisted in the programming by his go-to studio engineer, Eliot Leigh, plus Kurt Uenala, a Swiss musician who had previously worked with Depeche Mode – in both a technical and songwriting capacity – on their underrated *Delta Machine* album.

GIVING UP THE GHOST
Written by Magne Furuholmen
Produced by Magne Furuholmen and Erik Ljunggren
Vocal production by Peter Kvint and Morten Harket

With its devilishly sinister dark wave tones, 'Giving Up the Ghost' rounded off a largely successful triptych of compositions from Magne, fully justifying his decision to clamber aboard the a-ha ship at the 11th hour. Underpinned by a muscular rhythm and punctuated throughout with some incisive guitar work – à la Martin Gore – and gloriously dramatic orchestral swells, this was another standout production.

Given its spectral title, the lyrics are suitably chilling ('You sever all my heads / You place them on your bed'), while occasionally evoking the deathly poetry of Jim Morrison ('On a coal-black sea, the sky's on fire / Failed attempts at a funeral pyre / Deep as dreams of dark desire / The flames are growing ever higher').

Like 'She's Humming a Tune', the track was annoyingly omitted from the vinyl version of the album.

GOODBYE THOMPSON
Written by Pål Waaktaar-Savoy
Produced by Pål Waaktaar-Savoy and Alan Tarney
Pre-production and guidance by John O'Mahoney

It has been well over a quarter of a century since Pål was enraptured by the city of New York, and its wondrous allure has crept into many of his songs over the years, including 'Daylight's Wasting', 'Face', 'Foot of the Mountain', 'Karma Boomerang' and 'Man in the Park'. Much of the inspiration was derived within the radius of his home in Lower Manhattan, and a stroll one day through Thompson Street – whose previous residents included Scandinavian favourite Frank Zappa – spawned the title of another Waaktaar classic.

Spotting a sign that read 'Goodbye Thompson' in the window of a shop that was on the verge of closing, the ever-industrious Pål seized upon its melancholic possibilities, envisioning a store owner who has put his heart and soul into running a business, only for his dreams to be quashed ('I tape the sign to the door / Here we pinned all our dreams / Now the store is no more / . . . See my head hanging low / All my energies spent').

Boasting a deceptively simple soundtrack that occasionally calls to mind Radiohead – and embellished by some desperately mournful harmonies in the chorus – this was pretty bleak songwriting, but somehow symptomatic of an age in which many new businesses fail to thrive. 'What comes after what was / That was once strangely new / What awaits up ahead, I wish I knew,' sings Morten, whose understated vocal perfectly conveys the store owner's uncertain future.

The drums on the track were provided by Joe Mardin – the son of revered producer Arif Mardin – whose expansive CV boasts legendary clients such as the Bee Gees, George Benson and Chaka Khan.

THE END OF THE AFFAIR (Album Out-take)
Written by Magne Furuholmen
Produced by Erik Ljunggren and Magne Furuholmen
Vocal production by Peter Kvint and Morten Harket

During an interview with *Adresseavisen* in July 2010, Magne revealed some of his favourite books, which included Fyodor Dostoevsky's *The Idiot* and Cormac McCarthy's *The Road*. Another favourite was Graham Greene's *The End of the Affair*, which provided the inspiration for this tender ballad. With its glacial folk aesthetic and gently sparkling keyboard work, this was considerably different in tone to other songs written during the period, and it arguably wouldn't have sounded out of place on one of Timbersound's soundtracks. The lyrics, which are a little trite in places ('And it seems we no longer care / Absence makes the heart grow fonder'), loosely mirror some of the emotions stemming from Greene's bestseller, which is based around the turbulent fall-out from a wartime affair.

One of the lines from Greene's book, 'I've caught belief like a disease,' was also adapted for Magne's 'Mythomania'. 'Every book I read I mark every word or line that triggers something in me,' Magne once wrote on one of his Myspace blogs, 'and when I finish the book I write them all down in my notebook filed under "lines from literature", so I know where they came from. A book that doesn't give me lines is not a good book . . . in my book.'

DIGITAL RIVER (Unreleased Album Out-take)
Written by Pål Waaktaar-Savoy

'Digital River' was introduced as a new song during the second half of the band's performances on the recent *Hunting High and Low* tour, but this sprightly number – evocative of mid-period Depeche Mode – had been taped during sessions for *Cast in Steel*. Pål said it would have made a great single but, for one reason or another, it never made the final cut. It's certainly an intriguing number, with its author offering something of a sardonic viewpoint on internet gaming culture ('Down a digital river we will flow / Climb a virtual mountain, don't you know / Enter mythical places, clicks away / What a wonderful way to spend a day') and the stupefying effects of digital communication ('You send a line, I send you mine / Auto spell / Back we go, to and fro / Brain carousel'). Pål simply described it as 'ponderings on a virtual world competing with the real one'.

CHAPTER TWENTY-NINE
MTV UNPLUGGED – SUMMER SOLSTICE

Released: October 2017
Chart position: 6 (UK), 14 (Norway), 3 (Germany)

Having re-established themselves as both a recording act and touring band, a-ha were keen to keep the momentum going, and in mid-December 2016 they officially announced they would be releasing a new live acoustic album, which would include a mixture of old and new songs being selected from a series of intimate shows. 'After such a long time, a-ha have now become a band that simply continues from project to project,' said Magne. 'This turned out to be a very healthy approach for the three of us, because going acoustic also had the taste of a new project.'[1]

While such a project had been discussed many times, the announcement was something of a surprise as the band had, ostensibly, moved on to other ventures following the conclusion of the *Cast in Steel* tour. Pål had signed a new recording deal with Drabant Music, debuting 'Beautiful Burnout' – the first single to be lifted from *World of Trouble*, his upcoming album with Zoë Gnecco – in September 2016, and plans were also in place to release a brand new Savoy album. However, a-ha had already come out of retirement once and, although their return was originally touted as a two-year project, fans were well used to expecting the unexpected.

Of course, many of a-ha's contemporaries from the 80s have dabbled with the acoustic format over the years. Spandau Ballet used their *Once More* album as a springboard for their 2009 comeback; Erasure reinterpreted many of their well-known songs for their 2006 acoustic album, *Union Street*, while Nik Kershaw utilised the format to great effect on his 2010 album, *No Frills*. In a concert setting, the likes of Midge Ure, China Crisis (see the *Acoustically Yours* album) and Howard Jones (see *Live Acoustic America*) have all enjoyed some success by employing a more stripped-back approach. And then there are the rock veterans Status Quo, whose brace of *Aquostic* albums and shows reinvigorated and extended the band's career.

Throughout their live career, the band had performed pared-down versions of many of their songs in concert (for example, 'Birthright', 'Lifelines', 'Stay on These Roads', 'Velvet' and 'The Weight of the Wind'), but until this point had resisted offers to perform an entire set of acoustic songs.

I WANT MY MTV

Initially billed as 'An Acoustic Evening with a-ha', the project was subsequently given the MTV branding. From a historical viewpoint at least, this made perfect commercial sense. While they'd never performed an *MTV Unplugged* set during the programme's heyday, a-ha's initial flurry of success in the US was largely down to the exposure the MTV network gave their iconic video for 'Take On Me', eventually propelling it to the top of the Billboard charts. (The band also won several awards at the MTV Video Music Awards in September 1986.)

The *MTV Unplugged* shows that came to prominence in the early 1990s featured an array of both established and contemporary acts. Rock and pop luminaries such as Eric Clapton, Paul McCartney, Bruce Springsteen and Rod Stewart certainly benefitted from the wider exposure of their back catalogues, racking up some bestselling (and sometimes award-winning) albums along the way. At the height of their popularity in 1993, Nirvana recorded an acoustic set in New York that, arguably, resulted in one of their finest albums.

From 2000 onwards, the show's popularity tailed off, however, and the specials have been somewhat more sporadic, but performances by acts such as Miley Cyrus, Florence & the Machine and Shawn Mendes have boosted the show's profile in recent years.

MODERN JAZZ

While the electronic technology of the 1980s characterised much of the band's early recordings, tracks such as 'And You Tell Me' and 'Hunting High and Low' hinted at a more acoustic foundation to their songwriting. 'We don't use much technology at all when we write the songs,' confirmed Pål. '[So] the idea of an entirely acoustic show makes total sense. Playing all these songs now in their acoustic versions is like returning to their origins.'[2]

Magne agreed that the project represented something of a return to the band's roots. 'We started as a band back before a-ha, writing and recording on acoustic instruments,' he told Jo Nesbø during a press conference in September 2017. 'And then, when we moved to England and formed a-ha, we discovered a whole music scene that had moved on to electronica, and we were a part of that first wave. And we started incorporating that and that kind of defined our sound. But all along, we've added acoustic instruments on almost all the songs. So it's not really something new in that regard.'

Tapping into their progressive rock past was the highly experienced producer and multi-instrumentalist Lars Horntveth, who had already worked with the band on string arrangements for *Cast in Steel*. A former Spellemann award winner, Horntveth had gained a good reputation as a producer, helming albums for artists such as Susanne Sundfør (including 2010's *The Brothel*, the first of four Norwegian chart-toppers). In addition to his work with Norwegian rock band the National Bank, Horntveth has recorded several albums with experimental jazz outfit Jaga Jazzist.

For the *Summer Solstice* project, Horntveth assembled a band that included a-ha's settled rhythm section of Even Ormestad (bass) and Karl Oluf Wennerberg (drums), plus pianist Morten Qvenild, a member of the National Bank who had also worked with Jaga Jazzist and Susanne Sundfør. Completing the line-up was a string section comprising Madeleine Ossum, Emilie Lidsheim and Tove Margrethe Erikstad.

In the end, the choice of producer proved to be pivotal, as Morten explained: 'Lars is a stubborn guy, he's a strong character himself. And we really need somebody who has greater balls than brains, who is strong and one-track-minded enough to stand up for what he thinks is right. And he was commissioned by us to attack the songs freely – no directions given by us – because we needed to strip every song. We needed to reset everything, so that we could kind of rediscover the songs . . . Lars attacked it so that we had something to respond to . . . and respond we did. We hated what he did, and that was great, because we needed to react; we needed to have something to respond to.'

Horntveth's recollection of the experience mirrored that of Morten's: 'Working with the three of them has been enjoyable and fun, but very frustrating,' he said. 'I have been utterly pissed off at times, and so have they. After all, they're not used to a stubborn bastard like me interfering like this – but it's been very healthy. Deep down I think they like it, even if they have hated me at times!'[3]

Horntveth spent several months working on prospective arrangements for the show's concerts but, due to his touring commitments with Jaga Jazzist, the number of shows was whittled down from four to two. However, while the scheduling problem was rectified reasonably easily, choosing a venue for the brace of shows wasn't so straightforward. 'I wanted to build up a whole TV studio near London, but the band didn't want that,' Harald Wiik told *Aftenposten*. 'They wanted to go to the Amazon or the Brazilian city of Belém, but that proved to be too difficult. Then Magne figured we could do something "Norwegian", inside a stave church, but that would be too small – although Morten suggested we solve the problem by simply using the mannequins from the "Sun Always Shines on TV" video as our audience!'

Eventually, the band settled with Giske, a remote island in the Sunnmøre district of Møre og Romsdal in Western Norway. Following some preliminary sessions, the band resumed rehearsals at the island's state-of-the-art studio, Ocean Sound Recordings (a facility that the Scottish band Travis used to record their 2013 album, *Where You Stand*), while the nearby Øygardshallen venue would provide the setting for the actual shows on 22 and 23 June 2017.

'This was probably the most down to earth project that we've done, in front of probably the smallest audience we've ever played for,' Magne told BBC Radio Manchester. 'But it's not just a case of taking the songs back to how they were originally written – more often than not they're written on a piano or an acoustic guitar – but it's also about trying to take them in a different direction. We're 11 people on stage for this project and for the upcoming tour. You have instruments that belong to different eras; you have things from centuries ago that Mozart wrote music for, and basically what you do is go into a situation where the dogma is only acoustic instruments miked up, that's all there is.'

PUSH AND PULL

The subsequent live album was released on 6 October – the 31st anniversary of the release of *Scoundrel Days* – in an array of different formats, including a hits-heavy single CD, an unexpurgated double CD, a DVD, Blu-ray and a special fanbox, which included various paraphernalia. (Interestingly, the cover design was similar to Michael Patrick Kelly's *iD Live* album, which was also released that month.)

As a celebration of both their musical heritage and their considerable back catalogue, it certainly impressed, although two of the band's albums – *East of the Sun, West of the Moon* and *Cast in Steel* – were sadly bypassed. There were surprises aplenty, however, including a considerably slower and heartfelt rendition of 'Take On Me' and a stunning version of Bridges' 'The Vacant', but the inclusion of two previously unreleased songs – 'This Is Our Home' and 'A Break in the Clouds' – ensured that the shows weren't just a simple retread of the band's past.

What was also impressive, aside from the high level of musicianship on offer, was some of the adventurous – and often sonically challenging – new arrangements. As was well documented, there was some real push and pull with the project's producer, but it's evident that Lars Horntveth occasionally got his own way. 'This Alone Is Love', for example, was ingeniously arranged with a jazz-like time signature, with the rarely played track featuring some infectious harpsichord.

True to the spirit of the original *MTV Unplugged* shows, the band introduced a number of musical guests during the two performances – a mixture of influential artists and younger, more contemporary performers. Introduced by Magne as 'An American with Swedish genes', Lissie is a Rock Island-born singer who, in addition to working with the likes of Robbie Williams and Snow Patrol, has released four solo albums to date. No stranger to performing cover versions – for example, Fleetwood Mac's 'Go Your Own Way' – Lissie certainly impresses on a duet of 'I've Been Losing You'.

Ingrid Helene Håvik, who traded vocals with Morten on an epic version of 'The Sun Always Shines on TV', was a more local talent, based in the nearby town of Ålesund. A regular user of the recording facilities of Ocean Sound Recordings, Håvik has released one album as a solo artist, but she is better known as a member of the Spellemann award-winning indie rock band Highasakite. Their *Silent Treatment* album reached No. 1 in Norway and spent an impressive 120 weeks in the charts.

Elsewhere, Echo & the Bunnymen's Ian McCulloch joined the band for a laid-back run-through of 'Scoundrel Days' and a version of the mid-80s classic 'The Killing Moon', while Alison Moyet performed a fine version of 'Summer Moved On', with the key being slightly lowered to accommodate the former Yazoo singer's husky tones.

Other highlights include Magne's classic 'Lifelines', which was rearranged so that the spine-tingling 'one chance' lyric was pleasingly introduced into the song earlier than in its studio counterpart; 'Over the Treetops', another rarely played song, included some lovely harmony vocals and 12-string guitar playing, while 'Living a Boy's Adventure Tale' included a stunning vocal from Morten. It was evident, however, that some tracks worked better than others (the versions of 'Analogue' and 'Foot of the Mountain', for example, seemed a little leaden), but overall it was a crowd-pleasing set.

In his review of the single-disc edition for *Classic Pop* magazine, Steve Harnell praised Morten for his 'pristine falsetto' before concluding: 'This is an immaculate collection of subtle songcraft that's gained a whole new lease of life in this setting'. Other reviews weren't so gushing, however. 'There is no doubting the musicianship of the trio but some of the drama of the original recordings is lost here,' wrote *The Irish Times*' Lisa Allen. 'Nevertheless, this collection will please devoted fans.' In the Norwegian media, *VG*'s Morten Ståle Nilsen agreed that some of the arrangements lacked the drama of the studio recordings, singling out the likes of 'Summer Moved On' and 'Forever Not Yours', before adding: '"Hunting High and Low" and "The Living Daylights" naturally lend themselves to new, string-dominated arrangements, but "Take On Me" loses its infantile bounce in what is the concert's most brave and/or daring interpretation. The song survives, but it will surely split people and fans.' Integrating a review of the DVD, Nilsen also felt the show lacked warmth and camaraderie: 'The three tolerate each other and safeguard the dignity of the songs . . . and Pål almost sprints off the stage when it's over.'

Nilsen's onstage criticism contrasted sharply with the band members' feelings in the lead-up to the show, however. 'This current process has given us an incredible team spirit,' said Magne, 'and a creative exchange that we haven't had in many years.'[4] Morten was also in agreement with his bandmate, declaring: 'Suddenly we're a band again. Suddenly we understand why we're together, and we're in agreement like never before.'[5]

The close bond that was formed during this period inevitably led to questions about a prospective new a-ha album. Typically, Pål was the most optimistic about such a project: 'When we recorded our last few albums, we were sometimes working pretty isolated from each other. We should do this again – sitting and recording in the same room together for a couple of weeks or months and see what comes out as a result. We may argue about a lot of things, but we are also a band that has very close ties.'[6]

While Lars Horntveth's production methods had inadvertently brought a-ha closer together, thought of a new album would have to be put on hold as the band prepared for an arena tour in support of *Summer Solstice*. Performing in the cosy environs of Øygardshallen in Giske was one thing, but how would the shows' intimacy translate to arenas such as the Oslo Spektrum and London's O2? 'It's not really about the number of people,' responded Magne during the Berlin press conference, 'it's what you make happen in that room, making that moment glow . . . It will be strange to go from a 300-audience to a 10,000-audience or whatever, but we are used to that format, too. The challenge for us is that we have to make sure we don't slip into trying to change the musical content out of panic, thinking there's 10,000 [who] are gonna get bored shitless if we continue this way. We have to stick with the plan.' Stick to the plan they did, and the tour at the beginning of 2018 was both a success and a springboard for another chapter in their extraordinary career.

THIS IS OUR HOME (Live Recording)
Written by Magne Furuholmen
Produced by Lars Horntveth

Opening the brace of Giske shows was this beautiful piano-based ballad, whose refrain of 'This is our home / This is where we belong' seemed to perfectly encapsulate the spirit of the occasion, as well as perhaps signposting a more certain future for the mercurial Norwegians. Both the lyrics and the chord progression are simple, but its familiar, melancholic allure is both comforting and immediate, harking back to the sensitive songcraft of classic Furuholmen cuts such as 'Birthright', 'Lifelines' and 'White Canvas'. Complementing this gorgeous opener are some soothing string parts and gentle harpsichord flourishes, with the piece slowly building to full band involvement.

The track was also played during some of the earlier shows on the *Electric Summer* tour in 2018 but was eventually replaced by 'Sycamore Leaves'.

A BREAK IN THE CLOUDS (Live Recording)
Written by Pål Waaktaar-Savoy
Produced by Lars Horntveth

Also making its debut during the Giske shows was this country-flavoured number of Pål's, featuring a pleasing composite of harpsichord, pedal steel guitar and strings. Featuring lyrics such as 'A momentary setback' and 'A temporary shutdown', it would have been easy to equate the track with the band's split, but a section of the song had originally formed part of an early version of 'There's a Reason for It' (2002). It was later picked up during sessions for Savoy's eponymous fifth album, but ultimately dropped as the trio eventually ruled out the idea of releasing a double set. Grasping the opportunity to introduce a new song into the unplugged set, the prolific songwriter delved into his stockpile of unreleased songs. 'I was looking for something that would work acoustically and fit Morten's voice,' he said.

Though less immediate than 'This Is Our Home', its lyrical threads are certainly more intricate, with some familiar Waaktaar introspection ('Like before / I'm hiding more than I show') and affection ('I do appreciate you being there for me / I can't make it any other way') on offer.

SOX OF THE FOX (Live Recording)
Written by Pål Waaktaar-Savoy
Produced by Lars Horntveth

One of the standout moments from the acoustic shows was 'Sox of the Fox'. Previously known as 'The Vacant', the song originally appeared on Bridges' debut album, *Fakkeltog*. Morten, who has regularly professed his love for the album, tells the 300-strong audience in Giske that he'd been 'pestering' his bandmates to do the song for over 30 years, and the new version – which faithfully mirrors the original arrangement – provides one of the set's thrilling moments. 'None of the musicians we played with had heard the song before,' recalled Magne during Bridges' press conference at the Rockheim Museum in August 2018. 'The first thing they said was, "Oh, this is really heroic music". I think our distinctive character, which we have always believed in, was present already at that time.'

'When they played it at the second show in Oslo [in 2018], I was sitting together with our old producer, Svein Erichsen,' recalled Bridges' bassist Viggo Bondi, 'and he sang out loud the entire song when a-ha played it. People around us looked at him, and I think they were thinking, "Who is this old guy signing the Bridges song?!" It is a fantastic song. A part of the history is that Morten visited me at home after he heard us playing it and other songs at Morten's and my high school in Asker in December 1979. Actually, he was quite shy, and in a clumsy way he indicated that he wanted to join the band – but we were not interested. All this came back to me when I heard a-ha playing the song.'

THE KILLING MOON (Live Recording)
Written by Will Sergeant, Ian McCulloch, Les Pattinson and Pete de Freitas
Produced by Lars Horntveth

Prior to the introduction of Echo & the Bunnymen's Ian McCulloch to the stage, Magne tells the audience how much of an impact the enigmatic Liverpudlian band had had on a-ha, citing their second album, *Heaven Up Here*, as a key influence. 'We modernised our sound because of these guys,' he said. Oozing typical onstage charisma, McCulloch and the band run through a laid-back version of 'Scoundrel Days', its sombre tones a perfect fit for a singer whose own musical influences include the likes of the Doors, the Velvet Underground and Scott Walker. But it's the version of the Bunnymen's signature song, 'The Killing Moon', that carries the greater emotional resonance, with Morten and McCulloch trading verses and choruses to great effect.

The song was originally released as a single in January 1984, hitting the Top 10 in the UK. Writing for *Smash Hits*, Heaven 17's Martin Ware wrote: 'My first reaction was, "Yet another Doors rip-off", but after listening to it all the way through, it's better than The Doors. I can't profess to ever having been a Bunnymen fan, but this could go some way to changing that.'

The review of the parent album *Ocean Rain* was considerably more pronounced, however, and a self-aggrandising press advertisement labelled it as 'The Greatest Album Ever Made'. While the band's fourth album didn't quite live up to its billing, there's certainly a case for 'The Killing Moon' being one of the greatest songs of that decade.

'One of the great things about the song is that it still surprises me when I sing it live,' McCulloch said in 2017. 'I think it took me 25 years to realise that, not only was it about predestiny, it was about everything. You can slice that lyric up wherever you like, but it's as profound as 'To be or not to be . . .'. It's almost like a soliloquy delivered by a priest. That song is actually the answer to the big question. It's got real power.'[7]

TAKE ON ME (2017 Version)
Written by Pål Waaktaar-Savoy, Magne Furuholmen and Morten Harket
Produced by Martin Terefe

Ever since its worldwide success, the popularity of 'Take On Me' and its era-defining video has endured, but for a while the band enjoyed something of a love/hate relationship with the song. Indeed, by the time of the *Memorial Beach* tour in the 90s, the band had dropped it from the set list, as if to suggest it had become something of a millstone around their necks. But, as Magne reflected to Channel 4 years later, they had long been reconciled with the song: 'Every milestone becomes a millstone. We had a kind of psychosis over that song and we kind of became obsessed with proving it wasn't our defining moment. Of course, the truth is that it *was* our defining moment and it was futile to worry about it. The psychosis is over now. We're at peace with our history.'

Indeed, rather than biting the hand that feeds, the band have continued to sanction the song's use in TV commercials (for example, Volkswagen in 2013) and countless TV series (*Family Guy*, *The Simpsons*, *The Leftovers*, etc) and movie soundtracks (*Grosse Point Blank*, *Deadpool 2*, *A Dog's Purpose*, etc). The song has also been covered numerous times over the years. A1 took their perfunctory cover of the song to the top of both the UK and Norwegian charts in 2000, while acts as diverse as Tori Amos, Metallica, Reel Big Fish, Trevor Horn and Weezer have all put their own spin on the iconic track, in both a live and a studio capacity. In addition, part of the track was successfully interpolated in Pitbull's 2013 hit 'Feel the Moment' (featuring Christina Aguilera), while an innovative tropical house makeover of the track in 2015 – which audaciously stripped away the song's

distinctive riff – was deemed worthy of a performance with its remixer, Kygo, during the Nobel Peace Prize Concert that year. 'It's always fun to hear new versions,' Magne told *Dagbladet*. 'It's pretty ballsy of him – he has made quite a different version.'

On the island of Giske, the band seemingly took back ownership of the song that had had such an enormous cultural impact, presenting it in a fresh, ballad-like style. 'It went from being an uptempo synthesiser-driven pop song to a much more melancholic, yearning ballad in this slowed-down arrangement,' said Magne. 'It shows with much more clarity how the song, at its core, is not some stand-alone upbeat track, but belongs squarely inside our catalogue alongside more thoughtful, darker songs like "Scoundrel Days", etc.'[8]

Morten also agreed that the new treatment of the iconic track drew on its melancholic foundations: 'There are other aspects to this song that you don't immediately recognise,' he told Channel 4. 'It's a bouncy, sort of happy-go-lucky type of song with a kind of a melancholic streak to it. But the way we've done it now makes it more of a psalm-like, spiritual song.'

The band tried out acoustic arrangements with both Lars Horntveth and Martin Terefe before deciding to go with the latter. 'He came up with ideas for "Take On Me" that we ended up preferring to Lars' more complex production ideas,' said Morten. 'They were both good in different ways – we just ended up going with the simplest version.'

A studio version, utilising a slightly quicker tempo, was also released as a download-only single in December 2017, accompanied by a special lyric video which included images of Giske. This followed an acoustic performance of the track by the trio – with Martin Terefe on pump organ – during a BBC 'Children in Need' show at Wembley's SSE Arena in October.

During the following year, the band also promoted an orchestral treatment of the song for the *80s Symphonic* compilation, which included other period classics such as 'The Killing Moon' (Echo & the Bunnymen), 'Smalltown Boy' (Bronski Beat) and 'Vienna' (Ultravox).

The popularity of 'Take On Me' shows no sign of abating in the modern age. In 2019, both the song and video were the subject of a brand new three-part documentary, featuring new interviews with the band, as well as Bunty Bailey (who was reunited with Morten at the Savoy Café video location in Wandsworth), Michael Patterson, Alan Tarney, Andrew Wickham and more. To tie in with the original single's 35th anniversary, the band also issued a special limited edition blue vinyl single, which duly climbed to the top of the UK Physical Singles chart.

Such is its commercial power, the song even has its own official social media pages, accentuating Morten's view that it enjoys a parallel career to the band's. 'It's a much-loved track,' said Magne. 'One of the things you never know is what is going to define your career. You certainly don't expect it to happen on your first single. As a young band you're always pushing the next album, the next single. You're excited about the new things. Thirty-five years down the line, even we have to tip our caps and say, you've really been a tireless soldier on our behalf.'[9]

PART TEN

THE LIGHT WE LOST – THE SOLO YEARS
2015-2019

CHAPTER THIRTY
SUNLIT BYWAYS

With his a-ha commitments completed (for the time being at least), Pål was able to turn his attention to the completion of albums by Savoy and his collaboration with Zoë Gnecco, which had been officially announced in the spring of 2016.

WAAKTAAR & ZOE – WORLD OF TROUBLE (2017 Album)
Produced by Pål Waaktaar-Savoy
Additional production by Eliot Leigh
Chart position: N/A

'The collaboration started when a-ha did its big goodbye tour in 2010,' said Pål during a Facebook Q&A. 'I thought I would make a batch of songs that I could present for other artists to sing. I wrote about 13, 14 songs and asked Jimmy Gnecco if his daughter Zoë would be interested in singing a guide vocal on the demos. During the previous tour he had played me a snippet of her singing from his phone and I thought she had an absolute killer voice. The second I heard her voice on the tracks, I felt she owned them.'

Zoë was in her mid-teens when she started recording with Pål and had to fit in sessions around her schoolwork. She did, however, have plenty of singing experience under her belt. 'I started singing in a band when I was 11,' she said, 'but from the time I was 2 or 3 my mum has embarrassing videos of me singing to the Monkees in the mirror, and since then I haven't looked back. I started playing live around the age of 11 and music has always been my passion. From then on, up to working with Pål, I travelled in my summer breaks from school up and down the East Coast a bit, playing shows with a music school which just continued to solidify my love for music.'

While Zoë was familiar with a-ha's work, citing 'Take On Me' as the first song she loaded onto her first-ever iPod, she said that Queen were one of the greatest influences in her life: 'One of my first-ever CDs was a Queen *Greatest Hits* album,' she said, 'and when I was in elementary school and the other girls my age were listening to Britney Spears, I was blasting "Fat Bottomed Girls" on my Walkman and singing "Somebody to Love" at the talent show. But Freddie's devotion to being unapologetically himself – while also having the voice of a God – was something, from a young age, I clung to and aspired for.'

ALWAYS MIXING OLD WITH NEW

While Pål played most of the instruments on the album, a few musicians were drafted in to perform on some of the tracks, including drummers Karl Oluf Wennerberg and Joe Mardin. On the excellent 'Open Face' – a synth-pop track which had also been considered for inclusion on Cast in Steel – the keyboards were played by Depeche Mode collaborator Kurt Uenala.

From the pool of songs the New York-based duo recorded, some would eventually be reworked on Cast in Steel, while the roots of some of the other tracks were in the band's past. The origins of 'They to Me and I to Them' could be traced back to the early days of a-ha when titles like 'She's Humming a Tune', 'We're Looking for the Whales' and 'Touchy!' formed part of a provisional list of debut album contenders (Pål said the verses were completely rewritten). Some of the lyrics to 'Beautiful Burnout', meanwhile, stemmed from the original Mark Saunders-produced version of 'Foot of the Mountain'.

Elsewhere, 'Winter Wants Me Empty' was a cover of Savoy's 'Unsound', with some lyrical tweaks, while the more politically charged album closer, 'The Sequoia Has Fallen', had originally been inspired by a trip to the Redwood National Park in California during Pål's honeymoon.

While on paper World of Trouble sounded like a collection of out-takes, it was actually an impressively cohesive album, with several standout tracks. There was a lovely 1960s feel to 'Beautiful Burnout', with its gorgeous strings and easy-going West Coast vibe, while the ethereal second single, 'Tearful Girl,' demonstrated the versatility of Zoë's voice. As Pål remarked to the BBC, he was certainly impressed with her vocals: 'From the very first session I really just loved her voice and that super rich mid-range. She was also very good at just zoning into the mood of the song, which I'm super sensitive to. I could see for every take we did, she would get closer and closer to where she needed to be. For me that was such a kick as a songwriter, because a lot of the times you have to make that up in the arrangement.'

Other highlights included 'They to Me and I to Them', which showcased Pål's considerable guitar-playing skills, while there was some captivating imagery in the lyrics ('Monochrome-like pictures / Adorn the entrance hall / Floor-to-ceiling walnut shelves / Embrace the wall'). Elsewhere, 'Mammoth' was as epic as its title suggested and featured another of Pål's signature soaring choruses, complete with some lovely harmonies and lyrics that may well have been referencing some of Magne's well-publicised artistic endeavours ('Saw your face right there in the paper / . . . You had done something or another / The first in its field / The world's biggest whatsit / Or some big deal').

While Zoë found it surreal to be working with a musician she'd admired from a young age, the process of recording the album was seemingly painless: 'When I started working with Pål, I was much younger – about 14/15 years old – and something that I won't ever forget was how patient he was. It was a truly incredible environment for me to grow from and grow up in, as he was so incredibly supportive and nurturing, while also pushing me to sing and approach things in ways I never had prior. I was never nervous working with him as I always felt so comfortable. We would sit in the studio, and I vividly remember him singing bits and pieces of songs to me on guitar and working with me through them. I was elated to be there witnessing it, let alone being able to sing myself. It all felt like a movie or a dream, and definitely a point in my life I will never forget.'

I asked Zoë if she had any favourite tracks from the sessions. 'That is tough!' she replied. 'I think one of my top favourites is "Open Face". I will never forget recording that song and the instantaneous love and connection I had to it. "Laundromat" was one of the first we ever recorded so that is also close to my heart . . . but they all mean something special to me in a different way.'

PARALLEL

Due to a-ha's reformation, the release of *World of Trouble* – the front cover of which featured a photo of Zoë taken in New York's Mott Street – wouldn't appear in shops until February 2017, but the singer wasn't frustrated by the delay. 'I am a firm believer that everything happens for a reason,' she said. 'I remember being genuinely so excited for a-ha, but there was also a sort of surreal feeling, as both instances were happening in somewhat parallel. Specifically, though, hearing

Morten sing songs I also had the pleasure of recording was really a wild moment, as I remember singing along to him as a little kid.'

Sadly, the Steve Osborne-mixed album slipped by virtually unnoticed as attentions switched to a-ha's next project, while the reviews in the Norwegian media were mixed, too. Writing for Gaffa, Ann-Sofi S. Emilsen singled out 'Ancient Arches' and 'Laundromat' for praise, but accused Pål of lacking innovation. 'For Waaktaar, this project reveals that he is idle when it comes to new ideas,' she concluded. In his review for *Dagsavisen*, Bernt Erik Pedersen agreed it lacked ambition: 'It is so anonymous that one has to constantly remind oneself that it is actually one of Norwegian pop's foremost songwriters of all time in action,' he wrote. However, *Vårt Land*'s Olav Solvang noted that Zoë's vocals fitted 'perfectly with Waaktaar's quirky, and at times demanding, songs,' while the writer Arild Rønsen also gave the album a 'thumbs up,' praising Pål for the quality of the songs and its 'traditional, yet modern' sound.

Live dates weren't possible because of Pål's a-ha commitments, but Zoë did make a star turn during Savoy's show at Parkteatret – a converted Oslo cinema the following year, performing 'Beautiful Burnout', 'Under the Makeup' and 'World of Trouble', as well as replicating Simone Larsen's backing vocals on 'Velvet'. 'That night was truly incredible,' said Zoë. 'It was my first-ever time in Norway, and the crowd was unlike anything I'd ever experienced in my life thus far. The amount of love, support and energy in the room is something I won't ever forget.'

Since the show, Zoë has kept a relatively low profile, but she is keen to forge ahead with her highly promising music career. 'I am still singing,' she said. 'I'm writing a lot right now and teaching myself how to do some recording/production on my own. I have also been working on some collaborations. If the opportunity arose to work again with Pål in the future, I wouldn't hesitate, so who knows?!'

SAVOY – SEE THE BEAUTY IN YOUR DRAB HOMETOWN (2018 Album)
Produced by Pål Waaktaar-Savoy and Lauren Savoy
Additional production by Eliot Leigh
Chart position: 7 (Norway)

With the release of the career-invigorating *MTV Unplugged – Summer Solstice* album, a-ha's stock had, arguably, not been as high since their mid-00s heyday. Pål himself was particularly busy in 2017, and a flurry of activity was precipitated, in part, by the departure of his son, Augie, who had enrolled at a Los Angeles college. 'We were football parents for 15 years,' he told *Dagbladet*. 'It was full speed all the way – now a void has emerged.' Aside from contributing 'A Break in the Clouds' to the widely acclaimed acoustic project, the musician also released the impressive *World of Trouble* album in collaboration with Zoë Gnecco. He was also the subject of the Norwegian-language book Tårer fra en stein [Tears from a Stone], by Ørjan Nilsson that attracted some very favourable reviews. It was also announced that Pål had mixed the second album by Bridges, which had been languishing in the vaults since 1981.

In January 2017, Pål revealed that a new Savoy album had been mastered. It was pencilled in for release in September that year, but ultimately delayed

due to the October release of *MTV Unplugged – Summer Solstice*. However, with a small window available before a-ha commenced their acoustic tour, it could finally be released in January 2018.

BATTLE OF THE BANDS

Boasting a title that L.S. Lowry would have been proud of, *See the Beauty in Your Drab Hometown* was Savoy's first album release in over a decade. Commitments to a-ha and other projects delayed the release of new material and, bizarrely, such was the length of their hiatus that another Brooklyn-based electronic rock band named Savoy sprang up in their place. 'I couldn't believe it,' Pål told *Dagbladet*. 'We take a little break, and these guys show up!' Though the couple were clearly disappointed, Lauren Savoy was able to make light of the situation: 'We should have arranged a Battle of the Bands at a local bar and settled the case there!'

Since the release of *Savoy Songbook Vol. 1*, drummer Frode Unneland also busied himself with a number of projects, releasing albums with acts such as Evig Din For Alltid, the Thank Yous and West Side Tennis Club, whose debut opus included a song written by Lauren, titled 'In the Waters Glow' (the track also features her distinctive vocals).

Lauren herself later resumed her career as a film-maker, releasing the acclaimed 12-minute short film *Scent of a Woman* in 2013. In recent years she has continued to develop ideas for both film and television, including a series centred around the controversial radio evangelist Aimee Semple McPherson.

DARK DANCE

According to Pål, the title of the album – which was sourced from the lyrics for 'January Thaw' – wasn't about Manglerud, the satellite town where he'd spent his formative years. 'It's more about the grass always being greener on the other side,' he told Dagbladet. 'The point is that you have to be actively looking for beauty. It's easy to dismiss it – and sometimes you don't even have the chance to go somewhere else.'

However, it's safe to assume the oldest song on the album – 'Falls Park' – was written in Manglerud. Thanks to the retrieval of his old notebooks in 2011, Pål was able to revisit forgotten songs such as 'She's Humming a Tune' and 'They to Me and I to Them'. Written in his mid-teens, 'Falls Park' was a song that predated the Bridges era, and it later formed part of a hindmost list of potential a-ha songs, but it was never demoed. With its irresistible Merseybeat melody, soothing accordion sounds and light, bossa nova backing, this was a clear album highlight, perforated with some charmingly nostalgic vignettes ('I watch from afar / Lunch bag and tea in a jar / Whistling leaves and distant cars / Falls Park / I watch from afar').

Also included on the album were updated versions of 'Manmade Lake' and 'Weathervane', tracks that were written during a great period of uncertainty following a-ha's retirement-that-never-was in 2010, while the anthemic 'We're the Same Way' had originally been taped during sessions for Savoy's eponymous fifth album.

Elsewhere, the ephemeral 'Bump' had originally been written by Lauren for inclusion in the aforementioned *Scent of a Woman*, which was shortlisted for several awards, winning Best Short at the Broad Humor Film Festival in 2013. Described as 'a short film about love, sex and lactose intolerance', it featured Ryan Eggold – who currently stars as Dr Max Goodwin in the TV series *New Amsterdam* – among its small cast. The album's lightest and most throwaway number, it featured some catchy Beach Boys-esque harmonies.

Perhaps the biggest surprise on this album – given the patchwork look about the tracklisting – was just how fresh and contemporary it sounded. The strong use of modular synths certainly marked this out as a Savoy album unlike any other, with some tracks continuing in the vein of some of a-ha's more recent synth-pop experiments (see 'Door Ajar' and 'Shadow Endeavors'). The album opener – and first single – 'Night Watch' (featuring guest drummer Karl Oluf Wennerberg), certainly set the tone. With its simple 'Just let it go' refrain, combined with some airy keyboard atmospherics and U2-like guitar work, it was a deceptively conventional listen at first, but a playful midsection of squelchy synths created a welcome diversion. 'The breakdown part in "Night Watch" is one of my favourite bits on the album,' wrote Lauren on Facebook, 'and I want to go further with it. I'd love a whole album filled with unusual riffs like that!' Pål added: 'A lot of time I feel we get tunesmithy where melody is the king and everything else has to follow, so on this album we wanted to let things be more random so we didn't fill up all the space. For example, on "Night Watch" we had three melodies which could work and I started with the groove first.'

The album's second single, 'January Thaw', was another of the couple's hybrid tracks (see also 'Whalebone') and included the chorus from a 'catchy punk song' of Lauren's called 'Edie', while the wonderfully titled 'Shy Teens Suffering Silently' combined cold synth sounds – à la Gary Numan – with mid-period Beatles pop sensibilities. Meanwhile, the cathartic Goth rock of 'A Month of Sundays' – which was steeped in the doom-laden tradition of post-punk luminaries such as the Cure, Echo & the Bunnymen and Joy Division – saw Pål continuing to experiment with his monstrous Moog synth. 'While Pål has a dark dimension as a composer, he is also good at making dance music,' Lauren told Dagbladet. 'I call it "dark dance", which I think is something new for us. Just like the album title, we're mixing ugliness with beauty, darkness with light.'

'Sunlit Byways' was perhaps the catchiest track on the album, and its radiant chorus and gorgeous backing vocals certainly hit the spot. 'It puts me in a good mood when I listen to that song,' said Lauren. While Pål's distorted vocals let the track down slightly, it's a lovely pop song that resonates with both warmth and optimism ('When we walk through sunlit byways / Grab my hand when things go sideways / As they sometimes will').

Overall this was both a confident and adventurous collection, and the music press largely agreed. In the UK, Classic Pop's Wyndham Wallace wrote: 'This quiet comeback is worthy of its weighty title. Part of the appeal derives, perhaps surprisingly, from Waaktaar, whose gloomy but reassuring voice echoes both Brian Eno's and Stephen "Magnetic Fields" Merritt's.' Over in Norway, VG's Tor Martin Bøe decided the album was 'undoubtedly one of the most consistent set of songs the married couple has delivered since their debut', while Arild Rønsen, the former editor of Puls magazine, neatly summarised the album's melodic appeal: '*See the Beauty in Your Drab Hometown* is one of those albums that sneaks up on you, and it gets better and better with every listen.'

Although there were some initial plans to do some summer shows, the band ended up performing just once (in Oslo) in support of the album. The live band included Linn Frøkedal (keyboards) and Chris Holm (bass), players who'd been recommended by Sondre Lerche, a musician and friend of Lauren and Pål's.

CHAPTER THIRTY-ONE
THE SEASON TO BE MELANCHOLY

It was in May 2018 – during a Facebook Q&A to mark 10 years since the release of *A Dot of Black in the Blue of Your Bliss* – that Magne announced a Christmas album was in development. True to his Christian upbringing, Morten had previously performed at Christmas concerts and recorded hymns such as 'Mitt hjerte alltid vanker', while Pål had released the mischievous 'Xmas Time (Blows My Mind)' in 1997 ('Water gun for Tommy / Power tools for Ma / Everybody's waiting / What to get for Sandy / Daddy gets a tie / Everybody's happy . . . for a while'). Now it was Magne's turn.

Of course, much had happened during that decade, not least the sensational news in 2014 that a-ha had reformed after their much-publicised split in 2010. However, while a third solo album would prove to be elusive, there was certainly no shortage of interesting music, as his *Beatles* soundtrack and work with Apparatjik would attest.

In addition to balancing his dual career as a musician and visual artist, Magne also branched out into other areas during this period. In May 2015, and in partnership with the entrepreneur Simen Staalnacke, he launched S&M Feelgood Factory, a company which specialises in non-alcoholic beverages. Spotting a gap in the market during a period of abstinence from alcohol, the pair started experimenting with natural ingredients in a makeshift lab, and the colourful concoctions were distributed to their friends as Christmas gifts. 'All of a sudden, friends started asking for more,' said Magne. 'A friend of a friend was given our "Holy Moly" to drink and loved it, and he approached us about maybe making it available in some bars in Oslo.'[1]

A HEROINE FOR OUR TIME
While there's been no sign of a follow-up to Apparatjik's *Square Peg in a Round Hole* album, the multitalented ensemble have continued to function, making one-off appearances at special events such as 2016's Festspillene i Bergen [Bergen International Festival], which Magne also chaired until 2019. The band's Day of the Dead performance there served as a tribute to the mid-1800s Mexican freak show performer Julia Pastrana, who suffered from hypertrichosis, a genetic condition that causes abnormal hair growth, earning her cruel monikers such as 'the apewoman'. She tragically died, aged just 26, following complications arising from childbirth.

During the performance, which was brought to life by a visual narrative from a design combo known as Void, the band were joined by both Karl Oluf Wennerberg and Even Ormestad, as well as the Spanish singer Concha Buika, whose 2015 album, *Vivir sin miedo* [Live without Fear], had been co-produced by Martin Terefe. (Buika later released a version of Apparatjik's 'Deadbeat' as a single.)

A few years later, in September 2018, there was a special Apparatjik exhibition at the Pumphuset gallery in Sweden to mark 10 years since the release of their debut single, 'Ferreting', an event which also showcased the work of the American artist Foxito. During an appearance at the MDF Festival in Poland the same month, the band also premiered A Heroine for Our Time, a piece of music that served as a preview of Magne's proposed opera about Julia Pastrana, an ongoing project which had first been mooted in 2013. The piece, conducted by Rune Bergmann, was performed in collaboration with both Concha Buika and the Szczecin Philharmonic Symphony Orchestra.

LOOKING THROUGH A GLASS ONION

In addition to his musical endeavours – which include a guest appearance on Janove Ottesen's 2017 album, *Artisten & Marlene* – there has also been further visual arts work. In 2015, Edinburgh's Dovecot Gallery hosted the *Peeling a Glass Onion* exhibition, whose centrepiece was an incredible tapestry that had been based on one of Magne's *Norwegian Wood* exhibition designs, titled 'Glass Onion'.

Other collaborative exhibitions included *Marginalia* (2016), which saw Magne teaming up with *Beatles* author Lars Saabye Christensen, and *Texture* (2016), the result of 18 months of work with Queen Sonja of Norway, who had been studying printmaking for a number of years. 'Her energy and her experience as a visual artist and printmaker

allow me to relate to her as an artistic colleague, and not just a queen,' said Magne. 'It takes courage to do this in her position. She does not have to expose her art to public scrutiny, and could have just kept doing it as a hobby. The fact that she chooses to hold exhibitions and carry out projects time and again only testifies to her genuine passion and fearless stubbornness, which in my eyes are essential characteristics for an artist.'[2]

More recently, in June 2019, Magne's *Ignis* exhibition opened at the Telemarksgalleriet in Notodden, featuring an array of cylindrical ceramic sculptures named after cities, which were then arranged randomly on a giant chessboard. 'I have, like everyone else, been following [chess grandmaster] Magnus Carlsen,' Magne told Varden. 'That's made him become a part of my works, except on this chessboard it's impossible to understand the rules and who has the upper hand. After all, chess is a game where the pieces fight for positioning, conquest and domination. I have given the pieces city names, and the sculptures have been influenced by my own personal associations with those cities.'

MAGNE FURUHOLMEN – WHITE XMAS LIES (2019 Album)

This is a classic pop record, the best song collection I've ever written.
– Magne Furuholmen, VG, 2019

Produced by Magne Furuholmen and Bjarne Stensli
Chart position: N/A

During the summer of 2018, Magne began writing the songs that would form the basis of his third studio album, *White Xmas Lies*. 'I had the title track which I had written many years ago,' he said in 2019, 'and I had never finished the lyrics for it – I just had the title and a few odd lines. I started last year thinking I would record and release it for last Christmas, so I spoke to my manager about it, and he said, "Well you aren't leaving a lot of time for preparation for anyone to release it".'[3]

According to Magne, the trigger for the concept behind his third solo album was a stroll down Fifth Avenue in New York where, in the display window of a luxury store, he came across some Christmas trees that had been sprayed with artificial snow, while Rolex watches dangled opulently from the branches. 'I am ashamed to be part of a Christmas which these days seems to be mostly about buying more and more shit that no one needs or even really wants . . . a tacky, superficial celebration in stark contrast to the original Christmas message of hope, charity, and compassion,'[4] the musician later lamented.

Magne's reaction was to conceptualise a dark and melancholic wintry album, something that would not only reflect his views on an increasingly commercialised festive period and the proliferating loss of its key values, but one that would also serve as an antidote to a saccharine array of what he would term in the title cut as 'cheesy songs'. His manager liked the concept but persuaded him to hold off its release for another year. However, by the time the recording sessions had begun in earnest at the end of 2018, the songwriter had amassed enough songs for two albums, with some tracks straying from the original concept. He briefly considered releasing two different records before opting for a one-stop double set.

SEASONS TO BE UNCHEERFUL

The concept of a Christmas-themed album isn't a new one, of course, and, from time immemorial, a wide-ranging number of acts have jumped on the festive bandwagon, from classic acts such as the Beach Boys, James Brown, the Carpenters, Johnny Cash and Elvis Presley, through to more current acts such as Michael Bublé, John Legend, Kylie Minogue and Robbie Williams.

In terms of a-ha's synth-pop contemporaries, there are two acts of note who have produced material close to what Magne was trying to achieve with his latest project. In 2009, the Pet Shop Boys released their imaginatively titled *Christmas* EP, which included 'It Doesn't Often Snow at Christmas' ('Christmas is not all it's cracked up to be / Families fighting around a plastic tree / Nothing on the TV that you'd want to see / . . . The Christmas message was long ago lost / Now it's all about shopping and how much things cost'). And then there was Erasure, who released the *Snow Globe* album in 2013, featuring covers of traditional songs alongside original material of a more wistful nature. 'Everything about Christmas has been written already,' keyboardist Vince Clarke told *Billboard*. 'We thought it would be more interesting to look into the darker side of the season. For a lot of people, Christmas is not a happy time.'

It's Clarke's sentiments that are echoed in the press release for *White Xmas Lies*. 'I am lucky to have a family around me, but for many people, Christmas is a rough time, and a harsh reminder of loss, longing, and crippling loneliness,' explained Magne. 'I wanted to try and make an album which would be meaningful also to those who fall outside our commercial Christmas frenzy, an album which looks at the more melancholic, darker sides to Christmas: broken family ties, things we sweep under the rug, resentment hidden behind fake, jocular smiles.'

HELLS BELLS

Somewhat appropriately, the album was recorded at a converted cabin in the mountains of Norefjell, a popular ski resort which had previously served as a location for some of the alpine skiing events at the Winter Olympics in 1952. The sessions included many of the musicians who had worked with a-ha during their *MTV Unplugged* and *Electric Summer* shows in 2018, including Karl Oluf Wennerberg (drums), Even Ormestad (bass), Madeleine Ossum (violin) and Emilie Lidsheim (viola). Additional musicians included cellist Ingvild Nesdal Sandnes and vocalist Tini Flaat Mykland, whom Magne had worked with during and after his sole season as a mentor on *The Voice* in 2012, and whose ethereal tones provided an album highlight in the Sting-esque 'Come Back Home'.

Another familiar face was co-producer Bjarne Stensli, a highly experienced studio technician and former drummer with Harrys Gym, a band who had recorded – and then scrapped – an album co-produced by Magne in 2006.

Like Erasure's aforementioned *Snow Globe* album, some cover versions were also included in the lengthy set, but it's fair to say that Magne's two choices were somewhat surprising. 'Hells Bells' was a track that had originally opened AC/DC's seminal seventh studio album, *Back in Black*, in 1980. The suggestion to cover the song came from Harald Wiik, who was a big fan of the Australian band. Though not a fan himself, Magne was particularly drawn to the line, 'You're only young, but you're gonna die', and accepted his manager's challenge of putting a melancholy spin on a rock anthem. 'I relished the opportunity to turn it on its head and try to see if I could bring something to the song that wasn't there before,' he said. '. . . For me, covers that sound anywhere near the original are pointless.'[5]

The other cover to receive a significant sonic makeover was the closing track, 'Father Christmas', which had originally been recorded by the Kinks during sessions for their *Misfits* album (it was released as a stand-alone single in November 1977). Set to a sprightly punk rock-like backing, the Ray Davies-penned song – which has also been covered by the likes of Bowling for Soup,

Cheap Trick, Green Day, OK Go and Smash Mouth – concerns a man dressed as Father Christmas who is accosted outside a department store by a gang of youths demanding money instead of toys ('Don't give my brother a Steve Austin outfit / Don't give my sister a cuddly toy / We don't want a jigsaw or monopoly money / We only want the real McCoy'). 'The lyrics are heart-stopping, sad and dark, and I just wanted to try my hand at that,' said Magne. 'I'm a huge Kinks fan to begin with, so it's always risky to try something like that, but I thought if I go with the lyric and try to make it the opposite of what the Kinks did and make it heartfelt and sad, then maybe it could work.'[6]

Also included on the album was an electronic treatment of 'Differences', a song that had originally been demoed by a-ha in 2001 and then performed at the Nobel Peace Prize Concert in December that year. 'I always thought the song was a lot more catchy than what we had done,' Magne told *Rolling Stone*. 'It's one of the saddest songs I've ever written, but on this album it's the brightest and catchiest piece.' With its clarion call for peace, it was also, lyrically, a perfect fit for the album ('Show the way / Lead us home / We are lost / Give us hope').

Like the two cover versions, the new version of 'Differences' featured playing and programming from Morten Qvenild, who had toured with a-ha in 2018. 'He's a really talented keyboard player and a producer and he wasn't a part of the *White Xmas Lies* project to begin with,' explained Magne. 'But I had this idea for the covers and we started looking at where I was with the record and I said I had this idea for "Hells Bells" and for "Father Christmas", and I also wanted to do a cover version of one of my songs that we did with a-ha. So I gave him the directions and I interpreted what came back to me in a way that structured it and fixated it into where it is today. But he played a crucial part in unleashing the ambition I had for those three songs. And that was the only thing he did on this record. I told him I really wanted to have this mix between *Blade Runner* and *Stranger Things*.'[7]

THIS IS NOW AMERICA

The first single to be lifted from *White Xmas Lies* was released at the end of August 2019 by Magne's new record label, Drabant Music, who had also released Savoy's latest album. Although not thematically representative of the album, the track ably demonstrated that he was still a potent songwriting force. Paraphrasing the title of David Bowie's hit collaboration with the Pat Metheny Group, the stunning 'This Is Now America' saw Magne veering into rarely visited political territory, delivering some pointed commentary on both the tenure of President Trump – whom he refers to as 'a monkey at the wheel' – and what he perceives as the dying American dream ('Shooting stars and muscle cars / Fairy lights and apple pie / Now we wonder where they are'). 'America is, in many ways, still a barometer of where the world is at,' wrote Magne on his Instagram account. 'It is still a symbol of the Western mind and of all our hopes combined . . . hopes that sadly seem to be growing faint.'

Playing out like a melodic collision between Cat Stevens and Radiohead, the track saw Magne firmly setting out his musical stall, while at the same time offering something topical and thought-provoking in the lyrical department. However, not everyone was as appreciative of his well-intentioned lament, and there followed something of a social media backlash. 'I am not a citizen of America, so I was of course aware that some Americans might find it difficult or problematic that I would comment on their situation not having lived there,' he responded. 'But then, there's also a lot of American fans who are  strongly aware that I gave them something by writing that song, that I somehow formulated how they feel. You never know. I write songs for everyone, I don't write for one group of people. I don't want to estrange anyone with my work, but at the same time I have my opinions and I'm not afraid to say what I mean.'[8]

Somewhat bizarrely, a month later Magne was asked by *Rolling Stone* to comment on a short clip shared by President Trump that, visually, appeared to utilise some of the animation techniques used in the iconic 'Take On Me' video. 'You write a song in your youth and you don't write for a particular group of people one way or another; you write it for everyone,' he responded. 'But then stuff like this happens . . . We make our music for everybody. We didn't intend to make our music part of a divisive campaign and, all things equal, would have preferred it not to have been.' Asked what he thought of the clip, Magne amusingly replied: 'Even blind pigs can find truffles.'

SUMMER FADES TO WINTER

Tying in with the start of a-ha's year-long *Hunting High and Low* tour in Dublin, *White Xmas Lies* was released in October 2019. Like *A Dot of Black in the Blue of*

Your Bliss, a limited edition version was also created, with 200 copies containing a unique piece of art (it sold out almost immediately).

The album was preceded by another single, 'The Light We Lost', that was more reflective in tone than its predecessor ('As summer fades to winter / And the ground is hard with frost / There's no point in overthinking'). The beautiful opener, 'There Goes Another Year', was also selected for single release and, like its two predecessors, was accompanied by a lyric video that was directed by the musician's son, Thomas Vincent. The track was also selected by the Norwegian Salvation Army as their official Christmas song.

Other album highlights include 'The Season to Be Melancholy', which included some typically dark humour from its writer ('Our heads are in a spin / Out comes the xmas punch / But you just take it on the chin') and the stunning title track – complete with a delightful, Wrecking Crew-esque midsection – which relayed in eloquent detail the forced jollity of Christmas ('Once every year / We gather 'round here / In hopes for the time to come / The old and the young / We sing cheesy songs / And pretend that we all belong').

Elsewhere, there was 'Dark Days, Dark Nights', which saw Magne channelling Radiohead's 'Pyramid Song' on a blissfully bleak outing ('We held the future in our hands / But let it go'), one that contrasted with the deceptively light 'A Punch-Up on Boxing Day', which featured some sprightly keyboard flourishes that harked back to a-ha's sonic origins.

While there was arguably a case for slimming down the 17-track album to a more streamlined single set, this was easily the best set of songs that Magne had written outside of a-ha, and most critics bought into his snow-capped concept. '*White Xmas Lies* provides an unexpected but overdue rejoinder to the season's forced good humour,' concluded *Classic Pop*'s Wyndham Wallace, 'a refreshing shot of realism designed to address Yuletide's normally disregarded dark side.'

Although a short tour was ruled out, the musician did perform at Kulturkirken Jakob [the Church of Jakob] in Oslo on 4 December, in conjunction with the Salvation Army who had invited their own guests to the one-off show (a limited number of tickets were also made available to fans via a lottery system). Reprising her vocal role on the album, Tini Flaat Mykland also took part. 'It's a dark and melancholic album, that doesn't decorate the truth and isn't trying to make things sound better than what they are,' she said. 'Christmas, for many people, is a difficult time and we should never forget that. I think Magne has done a fabulous job with this album.'

Throughout December 2019, Magne also released alternative mixes of the album tracks via his Instagram account.

BONUS CHAPTER
THE FUTURE

At the time of writing, a-ha were partway into a year-long tour, with the band playing their classic debut album in full, alongside a selection of hit singles and deep cuts. The tour will culminate in a brace of shows at the Oslo Spektrum on 27 and 28 November 2020.

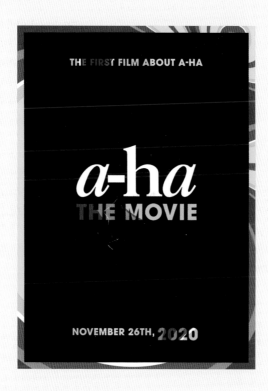

The same month will also see the premiere – at the spherical Colosseum cinema in Oslo – of *a-ha: The Movie*, a documentary that not only follows the band over a period of four years but also tells their fascinating story using exclusive new interviews. The movie is the brainchild of Thomas Robsahm, who is directing it along with the award-winning film-maker Aslaug Holm, who received international recognition for her highly personal 2015 documentary *Brødre* [Brothers], which followed the lives of her two young sons over an eight-year period.

Thomas Robsahm's own experience in the film industry is considerable. Starting off as an actor in films such as *Fem døgn i august* [Five Days in August] – which also starred his mother, Margrete – he later made his directorial debut with 1992's *Svarte pantere*, whose cast included Anneli Drecker. As a writer, producer and director, his CV is vast, and he received a prestigious Amanda Award for *S.O.S.* in 2000. In recent years he has joined the production company Oslo Pictures, producing acclaimed films such as *Håp* [Hope] and the Joachim Trier-directed *Thelma*.

According to Thomas, he's wanted to make an a-ha movie for several years. 'My first idea was to film the recording of a-ha's next album, after *Foot of the Mountain*,' he told me. 'I had met Magne at the premiere of one of my previous films in 2009, and when I presented the idea to him he was positive to the idea. The only problem was, there would not be a new album – the band were planning to go out on a high note. I remember asking him to get in touch for the comeback, but he answered that it was more likely ABBA would get back together. Now, as we all know, ABBA have gotten together at last, but a-ha got back faster. Only, they forgot to tell me. So, after *Cast in Steel* was released in 2015, I got back in touch. To my and, especially, manager Harald's surprise, they all said yes. Since then I have been trying to film them.' I asked him what he finds so appealing about the band's music. 'The combination of catchy, melancholic, dramatic songs, intriguing lyrics and Morten's amazing voice is impossible to resist,' he replied. 'I love so many songs, and you will know some of my favourites when you see the film.'

In addition to his live duties with a-ha, Morten has also been working as a mentor on the Norwegian version of *The Voice* since its fourth season and also contributed significantly to Ørjan Nilsson's insightful book *Hjemkomst – Morten Harket 1993–1998*, which was published in September 2019. In terms of new music, Morten has kept a relatively low profile outside of a-ha. In 2017 it was reported that he had begun working on new material with Peter Kvint, but in what guise these new songs will appear remains to be seen. However, in December 2019, a seasonal song – titled 'I Look to You This Time of Year' – was released, in collaboration with singer-songwriter Elvira Nikolaisen.

Buoyed by the reaction to *White Xmas Lies*, Magne is planning more live shows this year. 'Both recording and releasing this album was a really nice process,' he said. 'I am happy that, in some small way, it seems to have made Christmas more bearable for some.' He hasn't ruled out the possibility of further work with Apparatjik, either: 'We have projects lined up, but I think for me, it has to be something really radical to make sense. It was so free and unpretentious, so different and liberating for us all in the beginning. If we can regain that sense of total irreverence and devil-may-care attitude, then I am in . . . all the way.'

As for Pål, he has been helping his son True August to realise his own musical ambitions, and his self-titled debut EP arrived, digitally, in April 2019 – a second

EP is currently in development. Pål told me he has a solo double album ready to go and, despite all the tensions within the band, still remains hopeful of recording another a-ha album.

The recording of a new album has seemingly already been ruled out by Magne, however. 'I wouldn't hold my breath on that one,' he told *Billboard*. 'It feels like we've recorded enough, given enough new music to the world as we have.' He added: 'I pretty much have the same relationship with Pål and Morten as I do to my brothers. You meet occasionally. You have a bond that's there because of your shared history, you've tried to avoid scuffles and infighting and arguments . . . It's pretty much like family, for good and bad.'

'All three of them are brilliant and very strong-willed, but not necessarily in agreement,' said Harald Wiik. 'Spinal Tap had two visionaries in the band – I have three!'

ACKNOWLEDGEMENTS

I'm extremely grateful to the following for their invaluable contributions to
this book:

Dag Bøgeberg, Jørun Bøgeberg, Viggo Bondi, Pål H. Christiansen, Anneli Drecker,
Espen Farstad, Magne Furuholmen, Tonje Waaktaar Gamst, Zoë Gnecco, Erik
Hagelien, Øystein Jevanord, Matthew Letley, Sven Lindvall, Robert Alan Morley,
Tini Flaat Mykland, Martyn Phillips, Thomas Robsahm, Mark Saunders, Steve
Sidwell, Pål Waaktaar-Savoy and Harald Wiik.

My grateful thanks also go to: Junior Braz, Paul Browne, Marija Buljeta, Helene
Brygmann, Neil Cossar and all at This Day in Music Books, Suzie Dent, Richard
Evans, Eva Clerck Gange, Sissel Guttormsen, Audun Hagen, Lynsey Halliday, Tom
Korsvold, Greg Lansdowne, Patricia MacDonald, Carlos Maciá, Celice Neo, Terje
Nilsen, Ørjan Nilsson, Terje Pedersen and Tara Sparkes.

Special thanks to Sara Page and Jakob Sekse.

PHOTO CREDITS

Jørun Bøgeberg (Pages 127, 135, 139, 145, 148 and 154), Viggo Bondi (Pages 37, 56,
58 and 74), Marija Buljeta (Page 1), Henning Kramer Dahl (Pages 3, 28 and 31),
Suzie Dent (Pages 166, 175 and 264), Svein Erichsen (Page 27), Øystein Jevanord
(Pages 22 and 23), Fritz Johannessen (Pages 7 and 19), Carlos Maciá (Page
387), Martyn Phillips (Page 48), Rockheim (Page 47), Mark Saunders (Pages 279
and 282), Jakob Sekse (Pages 302, 312, 313, 362 and 363), Per Arne Skjeggestad
(Page 17) and Arne Svendsen (Page 13).

Henning Kramer Dahl's photos have been used by kind permission of
Eva Klerck Gange.

BIBLIOGRAPHY

Pål H. Christiansen, *The Scoundrel Days of Hobo Highbrow* (Forlaget Fabula, 2002).

Annelise Furuholmen Nøkleby, *Boken om a-ha: Veien til topps: Magnes mor forteller* (Filetab Support Services, 1985).

Håkon Harket and Henning Kramer Dahl, *Så blåser det på jorden* (Aventura Forlag, 1986).

Morten Harket, *My Take on Me* (Edel, 2016).

John Hay, *Masterpieces of Chinese Art* (Phaidon Press, 1974).

Marcel Leliënhof and Jonas Forsang, *Rom 13* (Forlaget Press, 2012).

Ray Manzarek, *Light My Fire: My Life with the Doors* (Century, 1998).

Tor Marcussen, *The Story So Far* (Zomba Books, 1986).

Ørjan Nilsson, *Tårer fra en stein* (Falck Forlag, 2017).

Ørjan Nilsson, *Hjemkomst* (Forlaget Press, 2019).

Jan Omdahl, *The Swing of Things: Twenty Years with a-ha* (Forlaget Press, 2004).

Jan Omdahl, *a-ha: The Swing of Things 1985–2010* (Forlaget Press, 2010).

Alf Prøysen, *Mrs Pepperpot Stories* (Red Fox, 2000).

Rob Tannenbaum and Craig Marks, *I Want My MTV: The Uncensored Story of the Music Video Revolution* (Plume, 2012).

John Taylor, *In the Pleasure Groove: Life, Death and Duran Duran* (Sphere, 2012).

ENDNOTES

CHAPTER ONE

1. Hugo Eriksen, *Backstage* (2004), magazine interview
2. Ørjan Nilsson, *Tårer fra en stein* (2017)), p. 63
3. *Smash Hits Yearbook 1988* (1987), interview
4. Official a-ha website (2006), interview
5. Jan Omdahl, *a-ha: The Swing of Things 1985–2010* (2010)), p. 22
6. Ørjan Nilsson, *Tårer fra en stein* (2017), p. 66
7. Ray Manzarek, *Light My Fire: My Life with the Doors* (1998), p. 304

CHAPTER THREE

1. *Classic Rock* magazine (2010), magazine article
2. Wyndham Wallace, *The Quietus* (2015), website article
3. Morten Harket, *My Take on Me* (2016), p. 56
4. Wyndham Wallace, *The Quietus* (2015), website article
5. Vik Bansal, *musicOMH* (2006), website article
6. Dennis Hunt, *LA Times* (1986), newspaper interview

CHAPTER FIVE

1. Phil Parsons, *Look-in* (1985), magazine interview
2. John Ratcliff, *a-ha 1983 to 1985 Episode 2* (2007), YouTube video
3. John Ratcliff, *a-ha 1983 to 1985 Episode 2* (2007), YouTube video
4. John Taylor, *In the Pleasure Groove: Life, Death and Duran Duran* (2012), p. 126
5. Tor Marcussen, *The Story So Far* (1986), p. 76
6. John Ratcliff, *a-ha 1983 to 1985 Episode 2* (2007), YouTube video
7. John Ratcliff, *a-ha 1983 to 1985 Episode 2* (2007), YouTube video
8. Jenny Valentish, *Financial Times* (2016), website article
9. John Ratcliff, *a-ha 1983 to 1985* (2007), YouTube video
10. Barbara Davies, *Daily Mirror* (2006), website article
11. Jan Omdahl, *The Swing of Things: Twenty Years with a-ha* (2004), p. 399

CHAPTER SIX

1. Phil Parsons, *Look-in* (1985), magazine interview
2. Richard Buskin, *Sound on Sound* (2011), website article
3. David Hepworth, *Smash Hits* (1980), magazine interview
4. Pat Gilbert, *Women and Captains First* (2009), album liner notes
5. Kieron Tyler, *Hunting High and Low* (2015), album liner notes
6. Pat Gilbert, *The Power of Love* (2009), album liner notes

CHAPTER SEVEN

1. Wyndham Wallace, *The Quietus* (2015), website article
2. Ben Beaumont-Thomas, *The Guardian* (2015), website article
3. Ben Beaumont-Thomas, *The Guardian* (2015), website article
4. Tor Marcussen, *The Story So Far* (1986), p. 59
5. Jan Omdahl, *The Swing of Things: Twenty Years with a-ha* (2004), p. 42
6. Morten Harket, *My Take on Me* (2016) p. 135
7. *Countdown* (1988), magazine interview

CHAPTER EIGHT

1. Robert Veiåker Johansen, *Aftenposten* (2015), website article
2. Richard Buskin, *Sound on Sound* (2011), website article
3. Lars Brandle, *The Industry Observer* (2019), website article
4. Richard Buskin, *Sound on Sound* (2011), website article
5. Richard Buskin, *Sound on Sound* (2011), website article
6. Kieron Tyler, *Hunting High and Low* (2015), album liner notes
7. Liam Allen, *BBC* (2010), website article
8. Rob Tannenbaum and Craig Marks, *I Want My MTV: The Uncensored Story of the Music Video Revolution* (2012), p. 200
9. Rob Tannenbaum and Craig Marks, *I Want My MTV: The Uncensored Story of the Music Video Revolution* (2012), p. 164
10. Rob Tannenbaum and Craig Marks, *I Want My MTV: The Uncensored Story of the Music Video Revolution* (2012), p. 200
11. Morten Harket, *My Take on Me* (2016), p. 145
12. Phil Parsons, *Look-in* (1985), magazine interview
13. Rob Tannenbaum and Craig Marks, *I Want My MTV: The Uncensored Story of the Music Video Revolution* (2012), p. 201
14. Eamon O'Neill, *Eon Music* (2019), website article
15. Jenny Valentish, *Financial Times* (2016), website article
16. Tor Marcussen, *The Story So Far* (1986), p. 59

17. Ørjan Nilsson, *Tårer fra en stein* (2017), p. 80
18. Kieron Tyler, *Time and Again: The Ultimate a-ha* (2016), album liner notes
19. Ørjan Nilsson, *Tårer fra en stein* (2017), p. 186
20. Ørjan Nilsson, *Tårer fra en stein* (2017), p. 268

CHAPTER NINE

1. Paul Lester, *Record Collector* (2009), magazine article
2. Paul Lester, *Record Collector* (2009), magazine article
3. Kieron Tyler, *Scoundrel Days* (2010), album liner notes
4. Simon Thompson, *Female First* (2006), website article
5. Jan Omdahl, *The Swing of Things: Twenty Years with a-ha* (2004), p. 80
6. *Smash Hits Yearbook 1988* (1987), magazine interview
7. Kieron Tyler, *Time and Again: The Ultimate a-ha* (2016), album liner notes
8. Morten Harket, *My Take on Me* (2016), p. 185
9. *TV Cream*, website article

CHAPTER TEN

1. George Simpson, *Daily Express* (2018), website article
2. Morten Harket, *My Take on Me* (2016), p. 214
3. Taylor, *In the Pleasure Groove: Life, Death and Duran Duran* (2012), p. 267
4. Morten Harket, *My Take on Me* (2016), p. 214
5. George Simpson, *Daily Express* (2018), website article
6. Ørjan Nilsson, *Tårer fra en stein* (2017), p. 220
7. Morten Harket, *My Take on Me* (2016), p. 215
8. Kieron Tyler, *25* (2010), album liner notes
9. Simon Thompson, *Female First* (2006), website article

CHAPTER ELEVEN

1. *The Scotsman* (2004), website article
2. Rob Tannenbaum, *Billboard* (2015), magazine interview
3. *No.1* (1987), magazine interview
4. Michael Cable, *Daily Express* (1995), Newspaper interview
5. Richard Lowe, *Smash Hits* (1988), magazine interview
6. Kieron Tyler, *Time and Again: The Ultimate a-ha* (2016), album liner notes
7. Kieron Tyler, *Time and Again: The Ultimate a-ha* (2016), album liner notes
8. Paul Lester, *Record Collector* (2009), magazine article
9. Richard Lowe, *Smash Hits* (1988), magazine interview

CHAPTER TWELVE

1. Stefano Terracina, *UNO* (1991), magazine interview
2. Richard Lowe, *Smash Hits* (1988), magazine interview
3. Ørjan Nilsson, *Tårer fra en stein* (2017), p. 203
4. Stig Myhre, *Puls* (1999), magazine interview
5. Gill Pringle, *Daily Express* (1991), newspaper interview
6. Paul Lester, *Record Collector* (2009), magazine article
7. Kieron Tyler, *East of the Sun, West of the Moon* (2015), album liner notes
8. Jan Omdahl, *The Swing of Things: Twenty Years with a-ha* (2004), p. 213
9. Morten Harket, *My Take on Me* (2016), p. 243
10. Ørjan Nilsson, *Tårer fra en stein* (2017), p. 270
11. Kieron Tyler, *East of the Sun, West of the Moon* (2015), album liner notes
12. Ørjan Nilsson, *Tårer fra en stein* (2017), p. 196
13. Kieron Tyler, *Time and Again: The Ultimate a-ha* (2016), album liner notes
14. Fiona Gibson, *Just Seventeen* (1988), magazine interview

CHAPTER THIRTEEN

1. Kieron Tyler, *Memorial Beach* (2015), album liner notes
2. Paul Lester, *Record Collector* (2009), magazine article
3. Jan Omdahl, *The Swing of Things: Twenty Years with a-ha* (2004), p. 223
4. *SoundBase Online* (2010), website article
5. Kieron Tyler, *Memorial Beach* (2015), album liner notes
6. Stein Østbø, *VG* (2005), website article
7. Warner Brothers press release (1993)
8. Ørjan Nilsson, *Tårer fra en stein* (2017), p. 273
9. Warner Brothers press release (1993)
10. Arild Rønsen, *Puls* (1993), magazine interview
11. Ørjan Nilsson, *Tårer fra en stein* (2017), p. 273
12. Arild Rønsen, *Puls* (1993), magazine interview
13. Warner Brothers press release (1993)
14. Warner Brothers press release (1993)
15. Warner Brothers press release (1993)
16. Warner Brothers press release (1993)
17. *Ending on a High Note* tour programme (2010)
18. Warner Brothers press release (1993)
19. Arild Rønsen, *Puls* (1993), magazine interview
20. Warner Brothers press release (1993)
21. Ørjan Nilsson, *Tårer fra en stein* (2017), p. 85
22. Michael Cable, *Daily Express* (1995), newspaper interview

CHAPTER FOURTEEN

1. Vik Bansal, *musicOMH* (2006), website article
2. Graham Gouldman, *And Another Thing* (2000), album liner notes
3. Ando Woltmann, *.No* magazine (2008), magazine article

CHAPTER FIFTEEN

1. Stig Myhre, *Puls* (1999), magazine interview
2. Ørjan Nilsson, *Tårer fra en stein* (2017), p. 212
3. Kieron Tyler, *Lackluster Me* (2016), album liner notes
4. Kieron Tyler, *Lackluster Me* (2016), album liner notes
5. Jan Omdahl, *a-ha: The Swing of Things 1985–2010* (2010), p. 215
6. Kieron Tyler, *Mountains of Time* (2017), album liner notes
7. Jan Omdahl, *a-ha: The Swing of Things 1985–2010* (2010), p. 237
8. Jan Omdahl, *a-ha: The Swing of Things 1985–2010* (2010), p. 213

CHAPTER SIXTEEN

1. *Lifelines* (2002), tour programme
2. Marcel Leliënhof and Jonas Forsang, *Rom 13* (2012), p. 19
3. Donna Ferguson, *The Mail on Sunday* (2018), newspaper interview
4. Bernt Erik Pedersen, *Dagsavisen* (2008), newspaper interview
5. Mette Dybwad Torstensen, *Kunst* (2012), magazine article
6. Mette Dybwad Torstensen, *Kunst* (2012), magazine article

CHAPTER SEVENTEEN

1. Jan Omdahl, *a-ha: The Swing of Things 1985–2010* (2010), p. 197
2. Kieron Tyler, *25* (2010), album liner notes
3. Paul Lester, *Record Collector* (2009), magazine article
4. Daryl Easlea, *Louder* (2016), website article
5. Daryl Easlea, *Louder* (2016), website article
6. Jan Omdahl, *a-ha: The Swing of Things 1985–2010* (2010), p. 206
7. Kieron Tyler, *Time and Again: The Ultimate a-ha* (2016), album liner notes
8. Jan Omdahl, *The Swing of Things: Twenty Years with a-ha* (2004), p. 217
9. Paul Lester, *The Guardian* (2016), website article
10. Ørjan Nilsson, *Tårer fra en stein* (2017), p. 222
11. Ørjan Nilsson, *Tårer fra en stein* (2017), p. 186
12. Jan Omdahl, *The Swing of Things: Twenty Years with a-ha* (2004), p. 296

CHAPTER EIGHTEEN

1. Paul Lester, *Record Collector* (2009), magazine article
2. Ørjan Nilsson, *Tårer fra en stein* (2017)
3. Jan Omdahl, *a-ha: The Swing of Things 1985–2010* (2010), p. 221
4. Jan Omdahl, *a-ha: The Swing of Things 1985–2010* (2010), p. 221
5. Jan Omdahl, *The Swing of Things: Twenty Years with a-ha* (2004), p. 76
6. Jason Rosam, *Rainbow Network* (2006), website article
7. Richard Evans, *This Is Not Retro* (2009), website article
8. Kieron Tyler, *Time and Again: The Ultimate a-ha* (2016), album liner notes
9. *Fifteen Questions* (2013), website article
10. Magne Furuholmen, *Lifelines* (2002), CD single liner notes
11. Kieron Tyler, *Time and Again: The Ultimate a-ha* (2016), album liner notes
12. *Indiepoprock* (2004), website article
13. Magne Furuholmen, *Lifelines* (2002), CD single liner notes
14. Official a-ha website (2001)
15. Magne Furuholmen, *Lifelines* (2002), CD single liner notes
16. Marija Buljeta, *ALTvenger* (2019), website article
17. Jan Omdahl, *The Swing of Things: Twenty Years with a-ha* (2004), p. 326

CHAPTER NINETEEN

1. Richard Evans, *Remember the Eighties* (2006), website article
2. Jason Rosam, *Rainbow Network* (2006), website article
3. *D-Side* (2006), website article
4. Jan Omdahl, *a-ha: The Swing of Things 1985–2010* (2010), p. 244
5. *D-Side* (2006), website article
6. Official a-ha website (2006)
7. Official a-ha website (2009)
8. Official a-ha website (2009)
9. Jason Rosam, *Rainbow Network* (2006), website article
10. *Hit Parade* (2005), website article
11. Richard Evans, *Remember the Eighties* (2006), website article
12. Official a-ha website (2006)
13. Official a-ha website (2006)
14. Jan Omdahl, *a-ha: The Swing of Things 1985–2010* (2010), p. 244
15. Official a-ha website (2006)
16. Jason Rosam, *Rainbow Network* (2006), website article
17. *D-Side* (2006), website article
18. Richard Evans, *Remember the Eighties* (2006), website article
19. May Pang's official website

CHAPTER TWENTY

1. Ørjan Nilsson, *Tårer fra en stein* (2017), p. 93
2. Ørjan Nilsson, *Tårer fra en stein* (2017), p. 187
3. Håkon Moslet, *Dagbladet* (2001), website article
4. Alan Smith, *New Musical Express* (1969), newspaper article
5. Jan Omdahl, *a-ha: The Swing of Things 1985–2010* (2010), p. 213
6. Bernt Erik Pedersen, *Dagsavisen* (2004), website article
7. Ørjan Nilsson, *Tårer fra en stein* (2017), p. 276
8. Official a-ha website (2007)
9. Official a-ha website (2007)
10. Espen A. Eik, *Aftenposten* (2007), website article
11. Leif Gjerstad, *Adresseavisen* (2007), website article
12. Geir Rakvaag, *Dagsavisen* (2008), website article

CHAPTER TWENTY-ONE

1. Andrew Williams, *Metro* (2005), website article
2. Stein Østbø, *VG* (2004), website article
3. Andrew Williams, *Metro* (2005), website article
4. *Mountain of Light* (2005), website press release

CHAPTER TWENTY-TWO

1. *Letter from Egypt* EPK (2008), YouTube video
2. *Letter from Egypt* EPK (2008), YouTube video
3. *Letter from Egypt* EPK (2008), YouTube video
4. *Letter from Egypt* EPK (2008), YouTube video

CHAPTER TWENTY-THREE

1. Decca Aitkenhead, *The Guardian* (2009), website article
2. Richard Evans, *This Is Not Retro* (2009), website article
3. Richard Evans, *This Is Not Retro* (2009), website article
4. Richard Evans, *This Is Not Retro* (2009), website article
5. Samir H. Köck, *Die Presse* (2009), website article
6. Jan Omdahl, *a-ha: The Swing of Things 1985–2010* (2010), p. 270
7. Official a-ha website (2009)
8. Official a-ha website (2009)
9. Richard Evans, *This Is Not Retro* (2009), website article
10. Official a-ha website (2009)
11. Richard Evans, *This Is Not Retro* (2009), website article
12. *Foot of the Mountain* EPK (2009), YouTube video
13. Official a-ha website (2009)
14. Sven Ove Bakke, *Dagbladet* (2009), website article
15. Official a-ha website (2009)
16. Samir H. Köck, *Die Presse* (2009), website article
17. Official a-ha website (2009)
18. Official a-ha website (2009)
19. Official a-ha website (2009)
20. Drabant Music press release (2018)

CHAPTER TWENTY-FOUR

1. Rolv Christian Topdahl, *Aftenposten* (2009), website article
2. Torill Frislid Gustafson, *Vennesla Tidende* (2010), website article
3. David Hurst, *Daily Mail* (2009), website article
4. David Hurst, *Daily Mail* (2009), website article
5. David Hurst, *Daily Mail* (2009), website article
6. Ben Rayner, *Toronto Star* (2010), newspaper article
7. Kieron Tyler, *Time and Again: The Ultimate a-ha* (2016), album liner notes
8. Jimmy Brown, *Promo News* (2010), website article
9. Ørjan Nilsson, *Tårer fra en stein* (2017), p. 228
10. *BANG Showbiz* (2019), website article
11. Ben Rayner, *Toronto Star* (2010), newspaper article

CHAPTER TWENTY-SIX

1. Autumn Andel, *QRO* magazine (2011), website article
2. Gregg McQueen, *The Aquarian Weekly* (2015), website article
3. Johnny Andreassen, *ABC Nyheter* (2009), website article
4. *Coldplaying* (2015), website article
5. Allyson Song River Jaynes, *Music Matters Magazine* (2017), website article
6. Anastasia Koshelko, *EQO1ST* (2012), magazine article
7. *DIY* (2012), website article
8. Anastasia Koshelko, *EQO1ST* (2012), magazine article
9. *We Love Nordic* (2013), website article
10. Øyvind Mo Larsen, *Romerikes Blad* (2013), website article
11. *Introducing Tini* (2014), YouTube video
12. Julie Lindén, *Scan Magazine* (2014), magazine article
13. Nancy Tartaglione, *Deadline* (2013), website article

CHAPTER TWENTY-SEVEN

1. *Architect of Sound* (2016), website article
2. Ørjan Nilsson, *Bergensavisen* (2011), website article

CHAPTER TWENTY-EIGHT

1. *Cast in Steel* EPK (2015), Universal Music Group video
2. Steffen Rüth, *Berner Zeitung* (2015), website article
3. Robert Veiåker Johansen, *Aftenposten* (2015), website article
4. Ørjan Nilsson, *Tårer fra en stein* (2017), p. 160
5. Jenny Valentish, *Financial Times* (2016), website article
6. Erik Munsterhjelm, *Tønsbergs Blad* (2015), website article
7. Olaf Neumann, *Mittelbayerische* (2015), website article
8. Steffen Rüth, *Berner Zeitung* (2015), website article
9. Olaf Neumann, *Mittelbayerische* (2015), website article
10. Kieron Tyler, *Time and Again: The Ultimate a-ha* (2016), album liner notes
11. Olaf Neumann, *Mittelbayerische* (2015), website article
12. Olaf Neumann, *Mittelbayerische* (2015), website article
13. Robert Veiåker Johansen, *Aftenposten* (2015), website article

CHAPTER TWENTY-NINE

1. Max Dax, *MTV Unplugged – Summer Solstice* (2017), album liner notes
2. Max Dax, *MTV Unplugged – Summer Solstice* (2017), album liner notes
3. Robert Hoftun Gjestad, *Aftenposten* (2017), website article
4. Robert Hoftun Gjestad, *Aftenposten* (2017), website article
5. Robert Hoftun Gjestad, *Aftenposten* (2017), website article
6. Max Dax, *MTV Unplugged – Summer Solstice* (2017), album liner notes
7. Rob Hughes, *Louder* (2017), website article
8. Max Dax, *MTV Unplugged – Summer Solstice* (2017), album liner notes
9. Lars Brandle, *Billboard* (2019), website article

CHAPTER THIRTY-ONE

1. *ShoppersBase* (2015), website article
2. Andreas Francisco, *Scandinavian Traveler* (2016), website article
3. Mark Millar, *XS Noize* (2019), website article
4. Drabant Music press release (2019)
5. Mark Millar, *XS Noize* (2019), website article
6. Mark Millar, *XS Noize* (2019), website article
7. Marija Buljeta, *ALTvenger* (2019), website article
8. Marija Buljeta, *ALTvenger* (2019), website article

A-HA